IN THE EYE OF THE STORM

Other Books by Max Lucado:

On the Anvil
No Wonder They Call Him the Savior
God Came Near
Six Hours One Friday
The Applause of Heaven

IN THE EYE OF THE STORM

MAX LUCADO

WORD PUBLISHING
Dallas·London·Vancouver·Melbourne

IN THE EYE OF THE STORM
A DAY IN THE LIFE OF JESUS

Unless noted otherwise, scripture quotations are from The Holy Bible,
New International Version. Copyright © 1973, 1978, 1984 Interna-
tional Bible Society. Used by permission of Zondervan Bible
Publishers. Those marked KJV are from the King James Version of the
Bible. Those marked TLB are from The Living Bible, copyright 1971 by
Tyndale House Publishers, Wheaton, Ill. Used by permission. Those
marked NEB are from the New English Bible, Copyright © the Delegates
of the Oxford University Press and the Syndics of the Cambridge
University Press, 1961, 1970. Reprinted by permission.

Library of Congress Cataloging-in-Publication Data:

Lucado, Max.
    In the eye of the storm : a day in the life of Jesus / Max Lucado.
        p. cm.
    Includes bibliographical references.
    ISBN 0–8499–0890–6
    1. Christian life—1960– 2. Consolation. 3. Jesus Christ—Person
and offices. I. Title.
    BV4501.2.L82   1991
    248.4—dc20   91–21854
                                                            CIP

6 7 8 9 BVG 11 10 9 8

Printed in the United States of America

To Robert and Elsie Forcum

> two ambassadors with a love for the church
> and a burden for the world

CONTENTS

Acknowledgments

Here's a salute to some special friends who made this book possible.

First to the folks at Word Publishing:

Kip Jordon, Byron Williamson, Ernie Owen, Joey Paul, and Roland Lundy—It's a privilege to be on the team.

Dave Moberg, Tom Williams, Susan Russell, Ed Curtis, and Michal Rutledge—Creativity unlimited!

Nancy Norris and Leslie Hughes—We know who really keeps the office working.

Stephen and Amanda Sorenson—You can cross my "t's" and dot my "i's" anytime. Thanks for the great editorial work.

And to my church family at Oak Hills:

Mary Stain—My supersecretary who corrects my mistakes, takes my calls, keeps me prompt, and saves my neck on a daily basis. Thank you so much.

Elsie Clay, Marcelle Le Gallo, and Kathleen McCleery—Our secretarial staff who help Mary so she can help me. Thanks again.

Glen Carter, Jim Toombs, John Tuller, Pat Hile, Jeff Pickens, and Rod Chisholm—Six co-workers who make my work a joy.

Karen Hill, Rod Chisholm, and Allen Dutton, Jr.— Thanks for proofreading the manuscript.

The members of Oak Hills Church—You make every Sunday a homecoming.

And to the Lucado family:

Jenna, Andrea, and Sara—three little girls who've taken my heart hostage.

And most of all, to my wife Denalyn—a decade with you has convinced me: there is a heaven, and you don't have to die to go there.

BEFORE
YOU
BEGIN . . .

CHIPPIE THE PARAKEET NEVER saw it coming. One second he was peacefully perched in his cage. The next he was sucked in, washed up, and blown over.

The problems began when Chippie's owner decided to clean Chippie's cage with a vacuum cleaner. She removed the attachment from the end of the hose and stuck it in the cage. The phone rang, and she turned to pick it up. She'd barely said "hello" when "sssopp!" Chippie got sucked in.

The bird owner gasped, put down the phone, turned off the vacuum, and opened the bag. There was Chippie—still alive, but stunned.

Since the bird was covered with dust and soot, she grabbed him and raced to the bathroom, turned on the faucet, and held Chippie under the running water. Then, realizing that Chippie was soaked and shivering, she did what any compassionate bird owner would do . . . she reached for the hair dryer and blasted the pet with hot air.

Poor Chippie never knew what hit him.

A few days after the trauma, the reporter who'd initially written about the event contacted Chippie's owner to see how the bird was recovering. "Well," she replied, "Chippie doesn't sing much anymore—he just sits and stares."

It's hard not to see why. Sucked in, washed up, and blown over . . . that's enough to steal the song from the stoutest heart.

Can you relate to Chippie? Most of us can. One minute you're seated in familiar territory with a song on your lips, then . . . The pink slip comes. The rejection letter arrives. The doctor calls. The divorce papers are delivered. The check bounces. A policeman knocks on your door.

Sssopp! You're sucked into a black cavern of doubts, doused with the cold water of reality, and stung with the hot air of empty promises.

The life that had been so calm is now so stormy. You're hailstormed by demands. Assailed by doubts. Pummeled by questions. And somewhere in the trauma, you lose your joy. Somewhere in the storm, you lose your song.

Ever found yourself in a storm of life? If so, if Chippie's story is your story, then I'm glad you picked up this book. I wrote it with you in mind. I wrote it because there is a day in the life of Christ that you need to know about.

Aside from the Crucifixion, it is the most stressful day of his life. A roaring sequence of bad news, demanding crowds, and doubting friends. Twenty-four hours in which Jesus faces the same gale-force fears that you and I face. Waves of pressure slam. Winds of anxiety blow. Clouds of darkness billow.

Yet through it all Jesus remains calm. He endures the day without losing his song. I'd like to help you see how he did it.

First we'll consider the *stress of demands*. Jesus handled twelve hours of chaos. What did he do to keep his cool? What did he know that gave him strength? If your days are bookended with deadlines and "chuck-it-all" frustrations—then you'll like this section.

The second section is entitled *Storms of Doubt*. Have you ever found yourself in a storm and wondered why Jesus doesn't pull you out? The disciples did. While Jesus went up the mountain, they went out on the sea. The storm came, their boat bounced, and they were left with a long night of fear and a long list of questions. "Jesus knows we're in a storm. Why doesn't he come?"

Sound familiar?

The final section of the book deals with a third source of anxiety—the *sting of failure*. In the twilight hours of that night we discover a sweet story of grace, Peter's attempt to walk on water. What began as a step of faith ended up as a belly flop of fear. If you've ever wondered what God does when we fail, then read this section and allow the hand that saved Peter to touch you.

Storms come. They come quickly. They pounce ferociously. If you are in one, then you know what I mean. If you're not in one today, you know as well as I—one may be in tomorrow's forecast.

My prayer is that this book will leave you better prepared. My prayer is that you will find some word, some story, some verse, or some thought that will convince you that he is very near. I pray that as you read you will be reminded that the same voice that stilled the rage on the Sea of Galilee can still the storm in your world.

Read on, friend, and be assured—he is closer than you've ever dreamed.

STRESS
OF
DEMANDS

1

FROM
CALM
TO
CHAOS

*M*AYBE YOU CAN RELATE TO the morning I just had. It's Sunday. Sundays are always busy days for me. Sundays are always early days for me. Today promised to be no exception.

With a full slate of activities planned, I got up early and drove to church. There was not much traffic at 6:00 A.M. I had the roads to myself. The orange of dawn had yet to break the nighttime spell on the summer's black sky. The twilight sparkled. Cool air wafted.

I parked outside my church office and took a minute to enjoy the quietude. I set down my books, picked up my coffee, and leaned against the car.

It was just the star-studded sky and me. Across the city, lights flickered. Shadowed trees slept. The night was calm: no noise, no hurry, no demands. That would all change within a couple of hours. Let a few thousand alarm clocks buzz and a few thousand garage doors open, and the serenity would be invaded as suburbia awakened. But at the moment, suburbia slept.

Life is like that sometimes. There are jaunts in life's journey that are as glassy as a midnight lake on a windless night. No noise. No rushing. No crises. There are measures in our music where the conductor silences the kettledrum, and only the flute is allowed to sing.

And sing she does. Under the spell of her song, dead-lines aren't as deadly. Death is distant. Dear ones are still dear and sometimes near. The eclipsing clouds of fear and debts and angry phone calls have passed. And, for a while, your world is moonlit.

Mine was. I sat on the hood of my car, sipped my coffee, and toasted the stars. They twinkled their response.

It was calm. But calm has a way of becoming chaos.

With a briefcase in one hand and a coffee cup in the other, I walked and whistled across the parking lot to the office door. To enter my office, I had to get past the sleeping dog of the twentieth century: the alarm system. I set down my briefcase and unlocked the door. I picked up my briefcase and walked in.

The code box on the wall was flashing a red light.

I'm not too electronically inclined, but I do know what a red light on an alarm system means: "Punch in the code, buddy, or get ready for the music."

I punched in the code. Nothing happened. I punched in the code again. The little red light kept blinking. I punched it in again. Time was running out. The little light snickered at me. I could hear the message being sent up and down the wires to all the neon-eyed alarm gremlins. "Man your sirens, everybody. Ol' do-do brain is entering his bank-card number again!"

I kept pushing, the clock kept ticking, the light kept flashing, and the gremlins were getting excited. "Get ready! Ten seconds and counting. Ten, nine, eight . . ."

"Oh, no," I groaned, "it's about to hit."

The siren pounced on me like a mountain lion. I thought we were under nuclear attack. Floodlights flash flooded the hallway, and red strobes turned. I kept pushing buttons, and the alarm kept blaring. You'd have thought it was a breakout at Alcatraz.

My pulse raced, my forehead moistened, and my situation was desperate. I raced down the hall to my office, pulled open the lap drawer of my desk, and found the phone number of the alarm company.

I could barely hear what the man said when he answered. When I understood what he said, I could scarcely believe he had said it.

"What do you mean, 'What's the matter?'" I exclaimed. "Can't you hear?"

"Yes, I punched in the code," I screamed. "It didn't do any good!"

The next twenty minutes were loud, demanding, confusing, and aggravating. I was speaking to technicians I couldn't see about equipment I didn't understand trying to understand words I couldn't hear.

That's when the policeman came. He tapped on the window. I opened it. "I can't get the thing to shut off!" I yelled.

"You the preacher here?" he asked.

"Yes," I yelled.

He just shook his head and walked away, probably muttering something about what they don't teach in theology courses.

Finally, for no apparent reason, the siren ceased. The lights shut off. What had been an air-raid shelter became an office again. I walked back to my desk, sat down, and sighed. *What a way to begin the day.* The morning lesson I had prepared was lying on my credenza. I picked it up and read the first line: "When calm becomes chaos."

"Appropriate," I muttered.

Ever happened to you? When was the last time your life went from calm to chaos in half a minute? ("How many examples would you like?" you ask.) When was the last time you found yourself pushing buttons that didn't respond, struggling with instructions you couldn't hear, or operating a system you didn't understand?

You enter the wrong computer code and lose eighteen months worth of ledgers in a matter of seconds. Calm volcanoes into chaos.

A message on your answering machine tells you that the report you are scheduled to give next week is due tomorrow. Good-bye sleep. Hello all-nighter. Good-bye calm. Hello chaos.

The mechanic who promised that the car would be ready today in time for the trip says, "I know I promised, but it's much worse than we thought. Your side axle disjointed, causing the U-joint to descramble the electronic ignition that is hand-assembled in Lower Tasmania and . . ."

"Grrrr."

If you've ever had your spouse call you at the office and say, "Just got a letter from the IRS. They are going to audit . . ."

If your boss has ever begun a conversation with these words: "You're a good worker, but with all this talk about a recession we have to cut back . . ."

If your teenager has ever walked in and asked, "Does our car insurance cover the other guy's car?"

Then you know that life can go from calm to chaos in a matter of moments. No warnings. No announcements. No preparation.

Little red lights blink, and you start pushing buttons. Sometimes you silence the alarm; sometimes it rips the air like a demon. The result can be peace or panic. The result can be calm or chaos.

It all depends on one factor: Do you know the code?

For me, this morning became chaos. Had I been prepared . . . had I known the code . . . had I known what to do when the warning flashed . . . calm would have triumphed.

The next few pages will usher you into a day in Jesus' life when the calm could have become chaos. It has all the elements of anxiety: bad news and a death threat, followed by swarming demands, interruptions, inept disciples, and a blazing temptation to follow the crowd. In twenty-four pressure-packed hours, Jesus was carried from the summit of celebration to the valley of frustration.

It was the second most stressful day of his life. As soon as one alarm was disarmed, another began blinking. The rulers threatened. The crowds pressed. The followers doubted. The people demanded. When you see what he endured that day, you will wonder how he kept his cool.

Somehow, though, he did. Although the people pressed and the problems monsooned, Jesus didn't blow up or bail out. In fact, he did just the opposite. He served people, thanked God, and made cool-headed decisions.

I want to help you see how he did it. I'd like to share with you a few "internal codes" that you desperately need. Equip yourself with these internal codes, punch them in when the red lights of your world start to flash, and you will be amazed at how quickly the alarms will be disarmed.

A few words of explanation:

If you are looking for external adjustments, you won't find them here. I won't say anything about dressing for success or power language or popularity schemes. You can buy many books that will help you externally, but this isn't one of them.

What you will discover in this book are attitudes . . . godly attitudes . . . a way of viewing people and problems as modeled by the Master.

If you want external alteration, look elsewhere. If you want internal development, read on. If you want to see how

God handled—and handles—hassles, then I've got some thoughts to share with you.

Let's do something. Let's take the principles modeled by Jesus into our day-to-day whirlwind of demands and decisions. Let's take a few minutes and observe God under pressure. Let's watch his face. Listen to his words. Observe his choices. And see what we can learn. Let's watch Christ in a pressure-cooker environment and try to answer this question:

What did Jesus know that allowed him to do what he did?

2

GOD
UNDER
PRESSURE

A DAY IN THE LIFE of Christ.

Call it a tapestry of turmoil, a noisy pictorial in which the golden threads of triumph entwine with the black, frazzled strings of tragedy.

Call it a symphony of emotions, a sunrise-to-sunset orchestration of extremes. One score is brassy with exuberance; the next moans with sorrow. On one page, the orchestra swells in adoration. On the next, Jesus solos the ballad of loneliness.

Whatever you call it, call it real. Call it a day in which Jesus experiences more stress than he will any other day of his life—aside from his crucifixion. Before the morning becomes evening, he has reason to weep . . . run . . . shout . . . curse . . . praise . . . doubt.

From calm to chaos. From peace to perplexity. Within moments his world is turned upside down.

In the tapestry, though, there is one thread that sparkles. In the symphony, there is one song that soars. In the story, there is one lesson that comforts. You've heard it before, but you may have forgotten it. Look closely. Listen intently. Be reminded:

Jesus knows how you feel.

If you've ever had a day in which you've been blitzkrieged by demands, if you've ever ridden the roller coaster of sorrow and celebration, if you've ever wondered if God in heaven can relate to you on earth, then read and reread about this pressure-packed day in the life of Christ.

Take heart. Jesus knows how you feel.

———————————————

He begins the morning by hearing about the death of John the Baptist: his cousin, his forerunner, his coworker, his friend.[1] The man who came closer to understanding Jesus than any other is dead.

Imagine losing the one person who knows you better than anyone else, and you will feel what Jesus is feeling. Reflect on the horror of being told that your dearest friend has just been murdered, and you will relate to Jesus' sorrow. Consider your reaction if you were told that your best friend had just been decapitated by a people-pleasing, incestuous monarch, and you'll see how the day begins for Christ. His world is beginning to turn upside down.

The emissaries brought more than news of sorrow, however; they brought a warning: "The same Herod who took John's head is interested in yours." Listen to how Luke presents the monarch's madness: "Herod said, 'I beheaded John. Who, then, is this I hear such things about?' *And he tried to see him*"[2] (emphasis mine). Something tells me that Herod wanted more than a social visit.

So, with John's life taken and his own life threatened, Jesus chooses to get away for a while. "When Jesus heard what had happened, he withdrew by boat privately to a solitary place."[3]

But before he can get away, his disciples arrive. The Gospel of Mark states that the "apostles gathered around Jesus and reported to him all they had done and taught."[4]

They return exuberant. Jesus had commissioned them to proclaim the gospel and authenticate it with miracles. "They went out and preached that people should repent. They drove out many demons and anointed many sick people with oil and healed them."[5]

Can you imagine the excitement? Can you envision the scene? A reunion of twelve friends. A reuniting of disciples with their teacher. A homecoming bubbling with testimonies:

- Peter describing a lame man he healed.
- John telling of a crowd he taught.
- Andrew recounting the deliverance of an epileptic.
- James relating to Jesus how the crowds followed him wherever he went.
- Matthew reporting the healing of a blind woman.

Remember, these disciples were ordinary men. They weren't orators, scholars, kings, or saints. They were fishermen and a tax collector, common laborers who, by God's power, had taken a nation by storm. The emotion? Exuberance. In a matter of moments, Jesus' heart goes from the pace of a funeral dirge to the triumphant march of a ticker-tape parade.

And look who follows the disciples to locate Jesus. About five thousand men plus women and children![6] Rivers of people cascade out of the hills and villages. Some scholars estimate the crowd to be as high as twenty-five thousand.[7] They swarm around Jesus, each with one desire: to meet the man who had empowered the disciples.

What had been a calm morning now buzzes with activity. "So many people were coming and going that they did not even have a chance to eat."[8]

I've had people demand my attention. I know what it's like to have a half-dozen kids wanting different things at the same time. I know the feeling of receiving one call with two other people waiting impatiently on other lines. I even know what it's like to be encircled by a dozen or so people, each making a separate request.

But twenty-five thousand? That's larger than many cities! No wonder the disciples couldn't eat. I'm surprised they could breathe!

The morning has been a jungle trail of the unexpected. First Jesus grieves over the death of a dear friend and relative. Then his life is threatened. Next he celebrates the triumphant return of his followers. Then he is nearly suffocated by a brouhaha of humanity. Bereavement . . . jeopardy . . . jubilation. . . bedlam.

Are you beginning to see why I call this the second most stressful day in the life of Christ? And it's far from over.

Jesus decides to take the disciples to a quiet place where they can rest and reflect. He shouts a command over the noise of the crowd. "Come with me by yourselves to a quiet place and get some rest."[9] The thirteen fight their way to the beach and climb into a boat.

And, for a few precious moments, the world is quiet again. The din of the crowd grows distant and the only sound is the slap of the water against the hull. Jesus' heart is weighted by sorrow and buoyed by joy. He watches his followers swapping stories of victory. Then he raises his glance and sees on the horizon Tiberias, the city constructed by John the Baptist's murderer, Herod. Joy suddenly alloyed with indignation causes his fists to clench and his eyes to moisten.

Who would question his desire to get away from the people? He just needs a few hours alone. Just a respite. Just a retreat. Time to pray. Time to ponder. Time to weep. A time without crowds or demands. A campfire wreathed with friends. An evening with those he loves. *The people can wait until tomorrow.*

The people, however, have other ideas. "The crowds learned about it and followed him."[10] It's a six-mile walk around the northeastern corner of the Sea of Galilee, so the crowd takes a hike. When Jesus got to Bethsaida, his desired retreat had become a roaring arena.

"Surprise!"

Add to the list of sorrow, peril, excitement, and bedlam the word *interruption*. Jesus' plans are interrupted. What he has in mind for his day and what the people have in mind for his day are two different agendas. What Jesus seeks and what Jesus gets are not the same.

Sound familiar?

Remember when you sought a night's rest and got a colicky baby? Remember when you sought to catch up at the office and got even further behind? Remember when you sought to use your Saturday for leisure, but ended up fixing your neighbor's sink?

Take comfort, friend. It happened to Jesus, too.

In fact, this would be a good time to pause and digest the central message of this chapter.

Jesus knows how you feel.

Ponder this and use it the next time your world goes from calm to chaos.

His pulse has raced. His eyes have grown weary. His heart has grown heavy. He has had to climb out of bed with a sore throat. He has been kept awake late and has gotten up early. He knows how you feel.

You may have trouble believing that. You probably believe that Jesus knows what it means to endure heavy-duty tragedies. You are no doubt convinced that Jesus is acquainted with sorrow and has wrestled with fear. Most people accept that. But can God relate to the hassles and headaches of my life? Of your life?

For some reason this is harder to believe.

Perhaps that's why portions of this day are recorded in all the Gospel accounts. No other event, other than the Crucifixion, is told by all four Gospel writers. Not Jesus' baptism. Not his temptation. Not even his birth. But all four writers chronicle this day. It's as if Matthew, Mark, Luke, and John knew that you would wonder if God understands. And they proclaim their response in four-part harmony:

Jesus knows how you feel.

A friend of mine was recently trying to teach his six-year-old son how to shoot a basket. The boy would take the basketball and push it as hard as he could toward the goal, but it always fell short. The father would then take the ball and toss it toward the basket, saying something like, "Just do it like this, son. It's easy."

Then the boy would try, and miss, again. My friend would then take the ball and make another basket, encouraging his son to push the ball a bit harder.

After several minutes and many misses, the boy responded to his father's encouragement by saying, "Yeah, but it's easy for you up there. You don't know how hard it is from down here."

You and I can never say that about God. Of the many messages Jesus taught us that day about stress, the first one is this: "God knows how you feel."

Read how J. B. Phillips translates Hebrews 4:15:

For we have no superhuman High Priest to whom our weaknesses are unintelligible—he himself has shared fully in all our experience of temptation, except that he never sinned.

The writer of Hebrews is adamant almost to the point of redundancy. It's as if he anticipates our objections. It's as if he knows that we will say to God what my friend's son said to him: "God, it's easy for you up there. You don't know how hard it is from down here." So he boldly proclaims Jesus' ability to understand. Look at the wording again.

He himself. Not an angel. Not an ambassador. Not an emissary, but Jesus himself.

Shared fully. Not partially. Not nearly. Not to a large degree. Entirely! Jesus shared fully.

In all our experience. Every hurt. Each ache. All the stresses and all the strains. No exceptions. No substitutes. Why? So he could sympathize with our weaknesses.

A politician dons a hardhat and enters the factory like he is one of the employees. A social worker goes to the inner city and spends the night on the streets with the homeless. A general walks into the mess hall and sits down with the soldiers like he is one of the enlisted men.

All three want to communicate the same message: "I identify with you. I can understand. I can relate." There is one problem, though. The factory employees know that the politician's hardhat will come off when the television crew is gone. The derelicts know that the social worker will be in a warm bed tomorrow night. And the soldiers are well aware that for every meal the general eats in the mess hall, he'll eat dozens in the officers' quarters.

Try as they might, these well-meaning professionals don't really understand. Their participation is partial. Jesus' participation, however, was complete. The writer of Hebrews states with double clarity that Jesus "shared *fully* in *all* our experience" (emphasis mine).

A bookstore owner in the Northwest once told me about an angry lady who stomped into his store carrying my book, *God Came Near*. She slammed the book on the counter, said a few less-than-kind things about the book, and then screamed loudly enough for everyone on the block to hear, "My God didn't have pimples!"

I know the paragraph that put the spark in her tinderbox. It reads like this:

> Jesus may have had pimples. He may have been tone-deaf. Perhaps a girl down the street had a crush on him or vice-versa. It could be that his knees were bony. One thing's for sure: He was, while completely divine, completely human.[11]

I can understand why the woman became upset. I can relate to her discomfort. We quickly fix a crack in the stained glass. We rub away any smudges on the altar. There is something *safe* about a God who never had callouses. There is something *awesome* about a God who never felt pain. There is something *majestic* about a God who never scraped his elbow.

But there is also something *cold* about a God who cannot relate to what you and I feel.

If I had a moment with that lady, I would ask her, "Jesus may not have had pimples, but don't you hope that he could have?"

Every page of the Gospels hammers home this crucial principle: God knows how you feel. From the funeral to the factory to the frustration of a demanding schedule. Jesus understands. When you tell God that you've reached your limit, he knows what you mean. When you shake your head at impossible deadlines, he shakes his, too. When your plans are interrupted by people who have other plans, he nods in empathy. He has been there. He knows how you feel.[12]

Before we resume our chronicling of this stressful day in Jesus' life, let me take you to another day—one far more recent, in a place closer to home.

February 15, 1921. New York City. The operating room of the Kane Summit Hospital. A doctor is performing an appendectomy.

In many ways the events leading to the surgery are uneventful. The patient has complained of severe abdominal pain. The diagnosis is clear: an inflamed appendix. Dr. Evan O'Neill Kane is performing the surgery. In his distinguished thirty-seven-year medical career, he has performed nearly four thousand appendectomies, so this surgery will be uneventful in all ways except two.

The first novelty of this operation? The use of local anesthesia in major surgery. Dr. Kane is a crusader against the hazards of general anesthesia. He contends that a local application is far safer. Many of his colleagues agree with him in principle, but in order for them to agree in practice, they will have to see the theory applied.

Dr. Kane searches for a volunteer, a patient who is willing to undergo surgery while under local anesthesia. A volunteer is not easily found. Many are squeamish at the thought of being awake during their own surgery. Others are fearful that the anesthesia might wear off too soon.

Eventually, however, Dr. Kane finds a candidate. On Tuesday morning, February 15, the historic operation occurs.

The patient is prepped and wheeled into the operating room. A local anesthetic is applied. As he has done thousands of times, Dr. Kane dissects the superficial tissues and locates the appendix. He skillfully excises it and concludes the surgery. During the procedure, the patient complains of only minor discomfort.

The volunteer is taken into post-op, then placed in a hospital ward. He recovers quickly and is dismissed two days later.

Dr. Kane had proven his theory. Thanks to the willingness of a brave volunteer, Kane demonstrated that local anesthesia was a viable, and even preferable, alternative.

But I said there were two facts that made the surgery unique. I've told you the first: the use of local anesthesia. The second is the patient. The courageous candidate for surgery by Dr. Kane was Dr. Kane.

To prove his point, Dr. Kane operated on himself![13]

A wise move. The doctor became a patient in order to convince the patients to trust the doctor.

I've shared this story with several health professionals. They each gave me the same response: furrowed brow, suspicious grin, and the dubious words, "That's hard to believe."

Perhaps it is. But the story of the doctor who became his own patient is mild compared to the story of the God who became human. But Jesus did. So that you and I would believe that the Healer knows our hurts, he voluntarily became one of us. He placed himself in our position. He suffered our pains and felt our fears.

Rejection? He felt it. Temptation? He knew it. Loneliness? He experienced it. Death? He tasted it.

And stress? He could write a best-selling book about it.

Why did he do it? One reason. So that when you hurt, you will go to him—your Father and your Physician—and let him heal.

3

A
MOTHER'S
LOVE—
A
FRIEND'S
EMPATHY

*T*HERESA BRIONES IS A TENDER, loving mother. She also has a stout left hook that she used to punch a lady in a coin laundry. Why'd she do it?

Some kids were making fun of Theresa's daughter, Alicia.

Alicia is bald. Her knees are arthritic. Her nose is pinched. Her hips are creaky. Her hearing is bad. She has the stamina of a seventy-year-old. And she is only ten.

"Mom," the kids taunted, "come and look at the monster!"

Alicia weighs only twenty-two pounds and is shorter than most preschoolers. She suffers from progeria—a genetic aging disease that strikes one child in eight million. The life expectancy of progeria victims is twenty years. There are only fifteen known cases of this disease in the world.

"She is not an alien. She is not a monster," Theresa defended. "She is just like you and me."

Mentally, Alicia is a bubbly, fun-loving third grader. She has a long list of friends. She watches television in a toddler-sized rocking chair. She plays with Barbie dolls and teases her younger brother.

Theresa has grown accustomed to the glances and questions. She is patient with the constant curiosity. Genuine inquiries she accepts. Insensitive slanders she does not.

The mother of the finger-pointing children came to investigate. "I see 'it,'" she told the kids.

"My child is not an 'it,'" Theresa stated. Then she decked the woman.

Who could blame her? Such is the nature of parental love. Mothers and fathers have a God-given ability to love their children regardless of imperfections. Not because the parents are blind. Just the opposite. They see vividly.

Theresa sees Alicia's inability as clearly as anyone. But she also sees Alicia's value.

So does God.

God sees us with the eyes of a Father. He sees our defects, errors, and blemishes. But he also sees our value.

Two chapters ago, I closed with this question: What did Jesus know that enabled him to do what he did?

Here's part of the answer. He knew the value of people. He knew that each human being is a treasure. And because he did, people were not a source of stress, but a source of joy.

When Jesus lands on the shore of Bethsaida, he leaves the Sea of Galilee and steps into a sea of humanity. Keep in mind, he has crossed the sea to get *away* from the crowds. He needs to grieve. He longs to relax with his followers. He needs anything but another crowd of thousands to teach and heal.

But his love for people overcomes his need for rest.

When Jesus landed and saw a large crowd, he had compassion on them and healed their sick.[1]

He had compassion on them, because they were like sheep without a shepherd.[2]

He welcomed them and spoke to them about the kingdom of God, and healed those who needed healing.[3]

It is doubtful that anyone in the crowd thinks to ask Jesus how he is doing. There is no indication that anyone is concerned with how Jesus is feeling. No one has come to give; all have come to take.

In our house we call 5:00 P.M. the piranha hour. That's the time of day when everyone wants a piece of Mom. Sara, the baby, is hungry. Andrea wants Mom to read her a book. Jenna wants help with her homework. And I—the ever-loving, ever-sensitive husband—want Denalyn to drop everything and talk to me about my day.

When is your piranha hour? When do people in your world demand much and offer little?

Every boss has had a day in which the requests outnumber the results. There's not a businessperson alive who hasn't groaned as an armada of assignments docks at his or her desk. For the teacher, the piranha hour often begins when the first student enters and ends when the last student leaves.

Piranha hours: parents have them, bosses endure them, secretaries dread them, teachers are besieged by them, and Jesus taught us how to live through them successfully.

When hands extended and voices demanded, Jesus responded with love. He did so because the code within him disarmed the alarm. The code is worth noting: "People are precious."

I can hear somebody raising an objection at this point. "Yes, but it was easier for Jesus. He was God. He could do more than I can. After all, he was divine."

True, Jesus was equally God and man. But don't be too quick to dismiss what he did. Consider his loving response from another angle.

Consider that, along with his holy strength, he also had a holy awareness. There were no secrets on the mountain that day; Jesus knew the hearts of each person. He knew why they were there and what they would do.[4]

Matthew writes that Jesus "healed their sick."[5] Not *some* of their sick. Not the *righteous* among the sick. Not the *deserving* among the sick. But *"the sick."*

Surely, among the many thousands, there were a few people unworthy of good health.

The same divinity that gave Jesus the power to heal also gave him the power to perceive. I wonder if Jesus was tempted to say to the rapist, "Heal you? After what you've done?" Or to the child molester, "Why should I restore your health?" Or to the bigot, "Get out of here, buddy, and take your arrogance with you."

And he could see not only their past, he could see their future.

Undoubtedly, there were those in the multitude who would use their newfound health to hurt others. Jesus released tongues that would someday curse. He gave sight to eyes that would lust. He healed hands that would kill.

Many of those he healed would never say "thank you," but he healed them anyway. Most would be more concerned with being healthy than being holy, but he healed them anyway. Some of those who asked for bread today would cry for his blood a few months later, but he healed them anyway.

Jesus chose to do what you and I seldom, if ever, choose to do. He chose to give gifts to people, knowing full well that those gifts could be used for evil.

Don't be too quick to attribute Jesus' compassion to his divinity. Remember both sides. For each time Jesus healed, he had to overlook the future and the past.

Something, by the way, that he still does.

Have you noticed that God doesn't ask you to prove that you will put your salary to good use? Have you noticed that God doesn't turn off your oxygen supply when you misuse his gifts? Aren't you glad that God doesn't give you only that which you remember to thank him for? (Has it been a while since you thanked God for your spleen? Me, too. But I still have one.)

God's goodness is spurred by his nature, not by our worthiness.

Someone asked an associate of mine, "What biblical precedent do we have to help the poor who have no desire to become Christians?"

My friend responded with one word: "God."

God does it daily, for millions of people.

What did Jesus know that allowed him to do what he did? What internal code kept his calm from erupting into chaos? He knew the value of people.

Interestingly, the stress seen that day is not on Jesus' face, but on the faces of the disciples. "Send the crowds away,"[6] they demand. Fair request. "After all," they are saying, "you've taught them. You've healed them. You've accommodated them. And now they're getting hungry. If we don't send them away, they'll want you to feed them, too!"

I wish I could have seen the expression on the disciples' faces when they heard the Master's response. "They do not need to go away. You give them something to eat."[7]

I used to think that this was a rhetorical request. I used to think that Jesus knew the disciples couldn't feed the crowd, but that he asked them anyway. I used to think that it was a "test" to teach them to rely on God for what they couldn't do.

I don't see it like that anymore.

I still think it was a test—not a test to show them what they couldn't do, but a test to demonstrate what they could do. After all, they had just gone on tour achieving the impossible. Jesus is asking them to do it again. "You give them something to eat."[8]

I wish I could tell you that the disciples did it. I wish I could say that they knew God wouldn't ask them to do something he wouldn't empower them to do, so they fed the crowd. I wish I could tell you that the disciples miraculously fed the five thousand men plus women and children.

But I can't . . . because they didn't.

Rather than look to God, they looked in their wallets. "That would take eight months of a man's wages! Are we to go and spend that much on bread and give it to them to eat?"[9]

"Y-y-y-you've got to be kidding."

"He can't be serious."

"It's one of Jesus' jokes."

"Do you know how many people are out there?"

Eyes watermelon-wide. Jaws dangling open. One ear hearing the din of the crowd, the other the command of God.

Don't miss the contrasting views. When Jesus saw the people, he saw an opportunity to love and affirm value. When the disciples saw the people, they saw thousands of problems.

Also, don't miss the irony. In the midst of a bakery—in the presence of the Eternal Baker—they tell the "Bread of Life" that there is no bread.

How silly we must appear to God.

Here's where Jesus should have given up. This is the point in the pressure-packed day where Jesus should have exploded. The sorrow, the life threats, the exuberance, the crowds, the interruptions, the demands, and now this. His own disciples can't do what he asks them. In front of five thousand men, they let him down.

"Beam me up, Father," should have been Jesus' next words. But they weren't. Instead he inquires, "How many loaves do you have?"

The disciples bring him a little boy's lunch. A lunch pail becomes a banquet, and all are fed. No word of reprimand is given. No furrowed brow of anger is seen. No "I-told-you-so" speech is delivered. The same compassion Jesus extends to the crowd is extended to his friends.

Look at this day one more time. Review what our Lord faced.

Intense sorrow—the death of a dear friend and relative.

Immediate threat—his name is on the wanted poster.

Immeasurable joy—a homecoming with his followers.

Immense crowds—a Niagara of people followed him everywhere.

Insensitive interruptions—he sought rest and got people.

Incredible demands—crowds of thousands clamored for his touch.

Inept assistance—the one and only time he asked for help, he got a dozen "you're-pulling-my-leg" expressions.

But the calm within Christ never erupted. The alarm never sounded. What did Jesus know that enabled him to do what he did? He knew the incredible value of people. As a result:

- He didn't stamp his feet and demand his own way.
- He didn't tell the disciples to find another beach where there were no people.
- He didn't ask the crowds why they hadn't brought their own food.
- He didn't send the apostles back into the field for more training.
- Most important, he stayed calm in the midst of chaos. He even paused, in the midst of it all, to pray a prayer of thanks.[10]

A boy went into a pet shop, looking for a puppy. The store owner showed him a litter in a box. The boy looked at the puppies. He picked each one up, examined it, and put it back into the box.

After several minutes, he walked back to the owner and said, "I picked one out. How much will it cost?"

The man gave him the price, and the boy promised to be back in a few days with the money. "Don't take too long," the owner cautioned. "Puppies like these sell quickly."

The boy turned and smiled knowingly, "I'm not worried," he said. "Mine will still be here."

The boy went to work—weeding, washing windows, cleaning yards. He worked hard and saved his money. When he had enough for the puppy, he returned to the store.

He walked up to the counter and laid down a pocketful of wadded bills. The store owner sorted and counted the cash. After verifying the amount, he smiled at the boy and said, "All right, son, you can go get your puppy."

The boy reached into the back of the box, pulled out a skinny dog with a limp leg, and started to leave.

The owner stopped him.

"Don't take that puppy," he objected. "He's crippled. He can't play. He'll never run with you. He can't fetch. Get one of the healthy pups."

"No thank you, sir," the boy replied. "This is exactly the kind of dog I've been looking for."

As the boy turned to leave, the store owner started to speak but remained silent. Suddenly he understood. For extending from the bottom of the boy's trousers was a brace—a brace for his crippled leg.

Why did the boy want the dog? Because he knew how it felt. And he knew it was very special.

What did Jesus know that enabled him to do what he did? He knew how the people felt, and he knew that they were special.

I hope you never forget that.

Jesus knows how you feel. You're under the gun at work? Jesus knows how you feel. You've got more to do than is humanly possible? So did he. You've got children who make a "piranha hour" out of your dinner hour? Jesus knows what that's like. People take more from you than they give? Jesus understands. Your teenagers won't listen? Your students won't try? Your employees give you blank stares when you assign tasks? Believe me, friend, Jesus knows how you feel.

You are precious to him. So precious that he became like you so that you would come to him.

When you struggle, he listens. When you yearn, he responds. When you question, he hears. He has been there. You've heard that before, but you need to hear it again.

He loves you with the love of a Theresa Briones.

He understands you with the compassion of the crippled boy.

Like Theresa, he battles with hell itself to protect you.

And, like the boy, he paid a great price to take you home.

4

WHEN FISHERMEN DON'T FISH

They were like sheep without a shepherd. So he began teaching them many things.[1]

When Jesus landed and saw a large crowd, he had
compassion on them and healed their sick.[2]

*I*T'S A GOOD THING THOSE VERSES weren't written about me.
It's a good thing thousands of people weren't depend-
ing on Max for their teaching and nourishment. Especially
on a day when I'd just heard of the death of a dear friend.
Especially on a day when I wanted to be alone with my
friends. Especially after I'd gotten into a boat to escape
the crowds. Had that been me in Jesus' sandals on that
Bethsaida beach, the verses would read something like:

They were like sheep without a shepherd. So Max told
them to quit grazing on his pasture and to head back
to their pens.

When Max landed and saw a large crowd, he mumbled
something about how hard it was to get a day off and
radioed for the helicopter. Then he and the disciples
escaped to a private retreat.

It's a good thing I wasn't responsible for those people.
I would have been in no mood to teach them, no mood to
help them. I would have had no desire even to be with them.

But, as I think about it, Jesus had no desire to be with them either. After all, he did leave them, didn't he? He had every intention of getting away and being alone. So what happened? Why didn't he tell them to get lost? What made him change his mind and spend the day with the people he was trying to avoid?

Answer? Take a look at five words in Matthew 14:14: "He had compassion on them."

The Greek word used for compassion in this passage is *splanchnizomai*, which won't mean much to you unless you are in the health professions and studied "splanchnology" in school. If so, you remember that "splanchnology" is a study of the visceral parts. Or, in contemporary jargon, a study of the gut.

When Matthew writes that Jesus had compassion on the people, he is not saying that Jesus felt casual pity for them. No, the term is far more graphic. Matthew is saying that Jesus felt their hurt in his gut:

- He felt the limp of the crippled.
- He felt the hurt of the diseased.
- He felt the loneliness of the leper.
- He felt the embarrassment of the sinful.

And once he felt their hurts, he couldn't help but heal their hurts. He was moved in the stomach by their needs. He was so touched by their needs that he forgot his own needs. He was so moved by the people's hurts that he put his hurts on the back burner.

Maybe that's why God brings hurting people into your world, too. All solitude and no service equals selfishness. Some solitude and some service, however, equals perspective.

Here's a story to illustrate my point.

When I was in high school, our family used to fish every year during spring break. One year my brother and my mom couldn't go, so my dad let me invite a friend. I asked Mark. He was a good pal and a great sport. He got permission from his parents, and we began planning our trip.

Days before leaving, we could already anticipate the vacation. We could feel the sun warming our bodies as we floated in the boat. We could feel the yank of the rod and hear the spin of the reel as we wrestled the white bass into the boat. And we could smell the fish frying in an open skillet over an open fire.

We could hardly wait. Days passed like cold molasses. Finally spring break arrived. We loaded our camper and set out for the lake.

We arrived late at night, unfolded the camper, and went to bed—dreaming of tomorrow's day in the sun. But during the night, an unseasonably strong norther blew in. It got cold fast! The wind was so strong that we could barely open the camper door the next morning. The sky was gray. The lake was a mountain range of white-topped waves. There was no way we could fish in that weather.

"No problem," we said. "We'll spend the day in the camper. After all, we have Monopoly. We have *Reader's Digest*. We all know a few jokes. It's not what we came to do, but we'll make the best of it and fish tomorrow."

So, huddled in the camper with a Coleman stove and a Monopoly board, we three fishermen passed the day— indoors. The hours passed slowly, but they did pass. Night finally came, and we crawled into the sleeping bags dreaming of angling.

Were we in for a surprise. The next morning it wasn't the wind that made the door hard to open, it was the ice!

We tried to be cheerful. "No problem," we mumbled. "We can play Monopoly . . . again. We can reread the stories in *Reader's Digest*. And surely we know another joke or two." But as courageous as we tried to be, it was obvious that some of the gray had left the sky and entered our camper.

I began to notice a few things I hadn't seen before. I noticed that Mark had a few personality flaws. He was a bit too cocky about his opinions. He was easily irritated and constantly edgy. He couldn't take any constructive criticism. Even though his socks did stink, he didn't think it was my business to tell him.

"Just looking out for the best interest of my dad's camper," I defended, expecting Dad to come to my aid.

But Dad just sat over in the corner, reading. *Humph*, I thought, *where is he when I need him?* And then, I began to see Dad in a different light. When I mentioned to him that the eggs were soggy and the toast was burnt, he invited me to try my hand at the portable stove. *Touchy, touchy*, I said to myself. *Nothing like being cooped up in a camper with someone to help you see his real nature.*

It was a long day. It was a long, cold night.

When we awoke the next morning to the sound of sleet slapping the canvas, we didn't even pretend to be cheerful. We were flat-out grumpy. Mark became more of a jerk with each passing moment; I wondered what spell of ignorance I must have been in when I invited him. Dad couldn't do anything right; I wondered how someone so irritable could have such an even-tempered son. We sat in misery the whole day, our fishing equipment still unpacked.

The next day was even colder. "We're going home" were my father's first words. No one objected.

I learned a hard lesson that week. Not about fishing, but about people.

When those who are called to fish don't fish, they fight. When energy intended to be used outside is used inside, the result is explosive. Instead of casting nets, we cast stones. Instead of extending helping hands, we point accusing fingers. Instead of being fishers of the lost, we become critics of the saved. Rather than helping the hurting, we hurt the helpers.

The result? Church Scrooges. "Bah humbug" spirituality. Beady eyes searching for warts on others while ignoring the warts on the nose below. Crooked fingers that bypass strengths and point out weaknesses.

Split churches. Poor testimonies. Broken hearts. Legalistic wars.

And, sadly, poor go unfed, confused go uncounseled, and lost go unreached.

When those who are called to fish don't fish, they fight.

But note the other side of this fish tale: When those who are called to fish, fish—they flourish!

Nothing handles a case of the gripes like an afternoon service project. Nothing restores perspective better than a visit to a hospital ward. Nothing unites soldiers better than a common task.

Leave soldiers inside the barracks with no time on the front line and see what happens to their attitude. The soldiers will invent things to complain about. Bunks will be too hard. Food will be too cold. Leadership will be too tough. The company will be too stale. Yet place those same soldiers in the trench and let them duck a few bullets, and what was a boring barracks will seem like a haven. The beds will feel great. The food will be almost ideal. The leadership will be courageous. The company will be exciting.

When those who are called to fish, fish—they flourish!

Jesus knew that.

When he arrived at Bethsaida, he was sorrowful, tired, and anxious to be alone with the disciples. No one would have blamed him had he dismissed the crowds a second time. No one would have criticized him had he waved away the people. But he didn't. Later he would. Later he would demand their departure and seek solitude.

But not before he "healed their sick"[3] and taught them "many things."[4] Self was forgotten . . . others were served . . . and stress was relieved.

Make a note of that. The next time the challenges "outside" tempt you to shut the door and stay inside, stay long enough to get warm. Then get out. When those who are called to fish don't fish, they fight.

5

THE
JOY
IN
THE
JOURNEY

*S*HE SAT IN 14E, and I sat in 14D.

She was rural, and I was urban. She was backward, and I was sophisticated. She was homey, and I was "professional." But she could see, and I was blind.

"They sure do put these seats close up against each other, don't they," she said as I sat down.

Her face was ten inches from mine. She had basset-hound cheeks; her eyebrows peaked over her nose; and her jowls sagged. She smiled so widely you could see the cavity on her upper side. Her neck seemed to lean out of her shoulders at a forty-five-degree angle, leaving her head in front of her shoulders rather than above them. She wore a Dutch-bob haircut and a blue, velour pants suit.

I don't know if she was old or just looked old. But I do know one thing: She'd never flown.

"I don't do this too much, do you?"

When I told her I did, her eyes widened. "Oooh, that must be fu-un." (She could add a syllable to any word.)

I groaned to myself. I already had a bad attitude. My week had been hectic. The plane was late and overbooked. I had a toothache and had left the tooth medicine at the hotel. I wanted to sleep, but I had work to do. And now I was sitting next to Gomer Pyle's mother.

"Oooh, boy, look at that one!"

She pointed at the plane ahead of us on the runway.

"Is this one that big?"

"Yes." I hoped my brief response would show her that I wasn't up for chitchat. It didn't.

"I'm going to see my boy in Dallas. Do you ever go to Dallas? I hope he's OK. He had a stomach flu last week. He's got a new dog. I can't wait to see it. It's a Labrador. Do you know what that is? They are big and lovable and . . ."

She was uncanny. Not only could she add a syllable to every word, she could answer her own questions.

As we were taking off, however, she got quiet. For several moments she said nothing. Then she suddenly let out a sound that would have called the pigs for dinner.

"Oooooeeee, those trees down there look like peat moss!"

People seated around us turned and stared like I was E. F. Hutton.

"What river is that?"

I told her I didn't know, so she flagged down a stewardess.

When the drinks came around, I asked for a Coke; she asked for the list.

"Tell me again?" So the stewardess told her again. "Oh, it's so hard to choose," she giggled. But she finally chose.

When they brought her the drink, she exclaimed that she didn't know apple juice came in cans. And when they brought her a sandwich, she opened the box and proclaimed loud enough for the pilot to hear, "Why, they even put mayonnaise in here."

When I pulled out my laptop computer, she was enthralled. "Now isn't that clever."

And that went on . . . the whole flight. She didn't miss a thing. If she wasn't staring out the window, she was amazed by a magazine. If she wasn't talking, she was "ooohing." She played with her fan. She turned her light on and off. She toyed with her seat belt. She savored her lunch. When we went through turbulence, I looked over at her to be sure she was all right, and she was grinning. You'd have thought she was riding the Ferris wheel at the county fair!

It occurred to me, about mid-journey, that she was the only person enjoying the trip.

The rest of us, the "sophisticated," were too mature to have fun. The man in front of me was discussing business trips to Japan, dropping more names than the U.S. Bureau of the Census. The fellow behind me was ordering beers—two at a time. The lady to my right was up to her eyebrows in paperwork. And I was staring at a computer screen—eyes tired, mouth hurting, stressed-out, trying to find a message for stress-filled people and never noticing that the message was sitting beside me.

And I might never have noticed had she not leaned over and said to me at the end of the flight. "Son, I may be out of place in saying this, but you've worked the entire trip. You need to relax, boy. You need to put that machine up and enjoy the journey."

Gulp.

I smiled weakly and mumbled some excuse about needing to get the work done before tomorrow. But she wasn't listening. She was squeezing her hands together in excitement as we landed.

"Wasn't that a fu-un trip?" she asked as we were leaving the plane.

I didn't say anything. I just nodded and smiled. Off she walked, bouncing down the concourse as curious as a six-year-old. I watched her as long as I could, then turned to go to my next flight with a lesson learned.

I resolved to keep my eyes open.

It does little good, I decided, to make the trip and miss the journey.

6

REMARKABLE

SOMETHING HAPPENED A FEW weeks ago that could be filed in the folder labeled "Remarkable."

I was playing basketball at the church one Saturday morning. (A good number of guys show up each week to play.) Some are flat-bellies—guys in their twenties who can touch their toes when they stretch and touch the rim when they jump. The rest of us are fat-bellies—guys who are within eyesight of, if not over the top of, the hill. Touching our toes is no longer an option. Looking down and *seeing* our toes is the current challenge. We never touch the rim when we jump and seldom touch it when we shoot.

But the flat-bellies don't mind if the fat-bellies play. (They don't have a choice. We have the keys to the building.)

Anyway, a few Saturdays back we were in the middle of a game when I went up for a rebound. I must have been pretty slow because, just as I was going up for the ball, someone else was already coming down with it. And the only thing I got from the jump was a finger in the eye.

When I opened my eye, everything was blurry. I knew my contact lens was not where it used to be. I thought I felt it in the corner of my eye, so I waved out of the game and ran to the rest room. But after I looked in the mirror, I realized that it must have fallen out on the floor somewhere.

I ran back onto the court. The guys were at the opposite end, leaving the goal under which I had lost my contact lens vacant.

I hurried out, got down on my knees, and began to search. No luck. When the fellows started bringing the ball downcourt, they saw what I was doing and came to help. All ten of us were down on our knees, panting like puppies and sweating like Pony Express horses.

But no one could find the silly lens.

We were just about to give up when one fellow exclaimed, "There it is." I looked up. He was pointing at a player's shoulder. The same guy whose finger had explored my cornea.

There, on his shoulder, was my lens. It had fallen on him . . . stuck to his skin . . . stayed on his back all the way down the court while he jumped and bounced . . . and then ridden all the way back.

Remarkable.

Even more remarkable when you consider that the contact lens made this round trip on the back of a flat-belly. One of the guys who can touch the rim and his toes. Had it landed on the shoulder of one of the "top-of-the-hill guys," no one would have been impressed. Some of us have the mobility of grazing buffalo. But when you think of the ride the tiny piece of plastic took, when you think of the odds of it being found, you have only one place to put this event: in the folder labeled "Remarkable."

The more I thought about this event, the more remarkable it became.

The more remarkable it became, the more I learned about remarkable things.

I learned that remarkable things usually occur in unremarkable situations, i.e., Saturday morning basketball games.

I also noticed that there are more remarkable things going on than those I usually see. In fact, as I began to look around, I found more and more things that I'd labeled "To be expected" that deserve to be labeled "Well what do you know."

Examples?

My money is in a bank with at least several thousand other folks' money. Who knows how many transactions are made every day? Who knows how much money goes into that place and is taken out? But somehow, if I want some money or just want to know how much money I have, the bank teller can give me what I want.

Remarkable.

Each morning I climb into a truck that weighs half a ton and take it out on an interstate where I—and a thousand other drivers—turn our vehicles into sixty-mile-per-hour missiles. Although I've had a few scares and mishaps, I still whistle while I drive at a speed that would have caused my great-grandfather to pass out.

Remarkable.

Every day I have the honor of sitting down with a book that contains the words of the One who created me. Every day I have the opportunity to let him give me a thought or two on how to live.

If I don't do what he says, he doesn't burn the book or cancel my subscription. If I disagree with what he says, lightning doesn't split my swivel chair or an angel doesn't mark my name off the holy list. If I don't understand what he says, he doesn't call me a dummy.

In fact, he calls me "Son," and on a different page explains what I don't understand.

Remarkable.

At the end of the day when I walk through the house, I step into the bedrooms of three little girls. Their covers are usually kicked off, so I cover them up. Their hair usually hides their faces, so I brush it back. And one by one, I bend over and kiss the foreheads of the angels God has loaned me. Then I stand in the doorway and wonder why in the world he would entrust a stumbling, fumbling fellow like me with the task of loving and leading such treasures.

Remarkable.

Then I go and crawl into bed with a woman far wiser than I . . . a woman who deserves a man much better looking than I . . . but a woman who would argue that fact and tell me from the bottom of her heart that I'm the best thing to come down her pike.

After I think about the wife I have, and when I think that I get to be with her for a lifetime, I shake my head and thank the God of grace for grace and think, *Remarkable.*

In the morning, I'll do it all again. I'll drive down the same road. Go to the same office. Call on the same bank. Kiss the same girls. And crawl into bed with the same woman. But I'm learning not to take these everyday miracles for granted.

Just think, it all came out of a basketball game. Ever since I found that contact, I've seen things a lot clearer.

I'm discovering many things: traffic jams eventually clear up, sunsets are for free, Little League is a work of art, and most planes take off and arrive on time. I'm learning that most folks are good folks who are just as timid as I am about starting a conversation.

I'm meeting people who love their country and their God and their church and would die for any of the three.

I'm learning that if I look . . . if I open my eyes and observe . . . there are many reasons to take off my hat, look at the Source of it all, and just say thanks.

7

THANKS FOR THE BREAD

*D*EAR FRIEND,
   I'm writing to say thanks. I wish I could thank you personally, but I don't know where you are. I wish I could call you, but I don't know your name. If I knew your appearance, I'd look for you, but your face is fuzzy in my memory. But I'll never forget what you did.

There you were, leaning against your pickup in the West Texas oil field. An engineer of some sort. A supervisor on the job. Your khakis and clean shirt set you apart from us roustabouts. In the oil field pecking order, we were at the bottom. You were the boss. We were the workers. You read the blueprints. We dug the ditches. You inspected the pipe. We laid it. You ate with the bosses in the shed. We ate with each other in the shade.

Except that day.

I remember wondering why you did it.

We weren't much to look at. What wasn't sweaty was oily. Faces burnt from the sun; skin black from the grease. Didn't bother me, though. I was there only for the summer. A high-school boy earning good money laying pipe. For me, it was a summer job. For the others, it was a way of life. Most were illegal immigrants from Mexico. Others were drifters, bouncing across the prairie as rootless as tumbleweeds.

We weren't much to listen to, either. Our language was sandpaper coarse. After lunch, we'd light the cigarettes and begin the jokes. Someone always had a deck of cards with lacy-clad girls on the back. For thirty minutes in the heat of the day, the oil patch became Las Vegas—replete with foul language, dirty stories, blackjack, and barstools that doubled as lunch pails.

In the middle of such a game, you approached us. I thought you had a job for us that couldn't wait another few minutes. Like the others, I groaned when I saw you coming.

You were nervous. You shifted your weight from one leg to the other as you began to speak.

"Uh, fellows," you started.

We turned and looked up at you.

"I, uh, I just wanted, uh, to invite . . ."

You were way out of your comfort zone. I had no idea what you might be about to say, but I knew that it had nothing to do with work.

"I just wanted to tell you that, uh, our church is having a service tonight and, uh . . ."

"What?" I couldn't believe it. "He's talking church? Out here? With us?"

"I wanted to invite any of you to come along."

Silence. Screaming silence. The same silence you'd hear if a nun asked a madam if she could use the brothel for a mass. The same silence you'd hear if an IRS representative invited the Mafia to a seminar on tax integrity.

Several guys stared at the dirt. A few shot glances at the others. Snickers rose just inches from the surface.

"Well, that's it. Uh, if any of you want to go . . . uh, let me know."

After you turned and left, we turned and laughed. We called you "reverend," "preacher," and "the pope." We poked fun at each other, daring one another to go. You became the butt of the day's jokes.

I'm sure you knew that. I'm sure you went back to your truck knowing the only good you'd done was to make a good fool out of yourself. If that's what you thought, then you were wrong.

That's the reason for this letter.

I thought of you this week. I thought of you when I read about someone else who took a risk at lunch. I thought of you when I read the story of the little boy who gave his lunch to Jesus.[1]

His lunch wasn't much. In fact, it wasn't anything compared to what was needed for more than five thousand people.

He probably wrestled with the silliness of it all. What was one lunch for so many? He probably asked himself if it was even worth the effort.

How far could one lunch go?

I think that's why he didn't give the lunch to the crowd. Instead he gave it to Jesus. Something told him that if he would plant the seed, God would grant the crop.

So he did.

He summoned his courage, got up off the grass, and walked into the circle of grownups. He was as out of place in that cluster as you were in ours. He must have been nervous. No one likes to appear silly.

Someone probably snickered at him, too.

If they didn't snicker, they shook their heads. "The little fellow doesn't know any better."

If they didn't shake their heads, they rolled their eyes. "Here we have a hunger crisis, and this little boy thinks that a sack lunch will solve it."

But it wasn't the men's heads or eyes that the boy saw; he saw only Jesus.

You must have seen Jesus, too, when you made your decision. Most people would have considered us to be unlikely deacon material. Most would have saved their seeds for softer soil. And they'd have been almost right. But Jesus said to give . . . so you gave.

As I think about it, you and the little boy have a lot in common:

- You both used your lunch to help others.
- You both chose faith over logic.
- You both brought a smile to your Father's face.

There's one difference, though. The boy got to see what Jesus did with his gift, and you didn't. That's why I'm writing. I want you to know that at least one of the seeds fell into a fertile crevice.

—————————————————————

Some five years later, a college sophomore was struggling with a decision. He had drifted from the faith given to him by his parents. He wanted to come back. He wanted to come home. But the price was high. His friends might laugh. His habits would have to change. His reputation would have to be overcome.

Could he do it? Did he have the courage?

That's when I thought of you. As I sat in my dorm room late one night, looking for the guts to do what I knew was right, I thought of you.

I thought of how your love for God had been greater than your love for your reputation.

I thought of how your obedience had been greater than your common sense.

I remembered how you had cared more about making disciples than about making a good first impression. And when I thought of you, your memory became my motivation.

So I came home.

I've told your story dozens of times to thousands of people. Each time the reaction is the same: The audience becomes a sea of smiles, and heads bob in understanding. Some smile because they think of the "clean-shirted engineers" in their lives. They remember the neighbor who brought the cake, the aunt who wrote the letter, the teacher who listened . . .

Others smile because they have done what you did. And they, too, wonder if their "lunchtime loyalty" was worth the effort.

You wondered that. What you did that day wasn't much. And I'm sure you walked away that day thinking that your efforts had been wasted.

They weren't.

So I'm writing to say thanks. Thanks for the example. Thanks for the courage. Thanks for giving your lunch to God. He did something with it; it became the Bread of Life for me.

Gratefully,
Max

P.S. If by some remarkable coincidence you read this and remember that day, please give me a call. I owe you lunch.

8

MUSINGS
IN
MINNEAPOLIS

*I*T'S A LONG WAY FROM BOSTON, Massachusetts to Edmonton, Canada. No matter how you cut it or route it, it's a long way.

My journey today began around 1:30 P.M. I spoke where I was supposed to speak and changed into my Reeboks just in time to fight traffic all the way to Logan Airport.

The plane was overbooked; some folks were mad. The plane was also designed by a five-foot, four-inch engineer who hates tall people. (I ate my knees for lunch.) The plane arrived late into Minneapolis, where I was to change planes.

Now, I know I'm not supposed to complain. I've heard myself preach sermons on gratitude. And I know that a million people in the world would love to have the airline peanuts I threw away today. But still, I got off the plane with a cramp in my leg, an empty stomach, a bad attitude, and three more hours of travel to go.

On the way to my next plane, I saw a McDonald's. Looked good. Did I have time? Then I saw something better: a phone.

I walked over, set down my bags, and called home. Denalyn answered. I love it when she answers. She's always glad when I call. When she gets to heaven, Saint Peter will give her the receptionist job at the gate.

We spent twenty minutes talking about major Pentagon-level topics like the weather in New England and the weather in San Antonio. We talked about the fact that Jenna had a friend coming over to spend the night and that Sara might have a fever. I told her about the Canadian, French-speaking English teacher I sat next to on the plane, and she told me about the new elementary school.

We made no decisions. We solved no problems. We resolved no major conflicts. We just talked. And I felt better.

Jenna got on the phone and asked me when I was coming home, and it felt good to be wanted.

Andrea got on the phone and told me she loved me, and it felt good to be loved.

Jenna put the phone next to baby Sara's ear, and I talked baby talk in the middle of the airport. (Some people turned to stare.) But I didn't care because Sara cooed, and it felt good to be cooed at.

Denalyn got back on the phone and said, "I'm glad you called." And I hung up happy.

Now I'm back on the plane and my attitude is back on track. The plane is delayed because the runway is backed up, which means I'll get into Edmonton an hour later than I planned. I don't know who is going to pick me up, and I can't remember to whom I'm supposed to speak tomorrow. But that's OK.

I can handle being a pilgrim as long as I know that I can call home whenever I want.

Jesus could . . . and he did.

Maybe that's the rationale behind verse 19 of Matthew 14: "Taking the five loaves and the two fish and looking up to heaven, he gave thanks and broke the loaves." I'd always chalked this prayer up to, at best, a good example—at worst, a good habit.

Until now.

Now it occurs to me that Jesus needed to call home in the middle of the hassles as much as I did. He was surrounded by people who wanted food and disciples who wanted a break. His heart was heavy from the death of John the Baptist.

He needed a minute with someone who would understand.

Maybe he, like me, got a bit weary of the hassles of getting a job done in a distant land and needed to call home.

So he did. He chatted with the One he loved. He heard the sound of the home he missed. And he was reminded that when all hell breaks loose, all heaven draws near.

Maybe you should call home, too. God will be glad when you do—but not half as glad as you will be.

9

FENDING OFF THE VOICES

Y OU WANT SUCCESS? Here's your model. You want achievement? Here's your prototype. You want bright lights, pageants, and media attention? Consider the front-page, center article of the nation's largest daily newspaper.

It is a caricature of "Miss America." The "vital" data of the fifty-one participants has been compiled to present the perfect woman. She has brown hair. She has brown eyes. She knows how to sing and has a perfect figure: 35–24–35. She is Miss America. She is the ideal.

The message trumpets off the page: "This is the standard for American women." The implication is clear: Do what it takes to be like her. Firm your thighs. Deepen your cleavage. Pamper your hair. Improve your walk.

No reference is made to her convictions . . . to her honesty . . . to her faith . . . or to her God. But you are told her hip size.

In a small photo, four inches to the left, is another woman. Her face is thin. Her skin is wrinkled, almost leathery. No makeup . . . no blush . . . no lipstick. There is a faint smile on her lips and a glint in her eyes.

She looks pale. Perhaps it's my imagination or perhaps it's true. The caption reads, "Mother Teresa: In serious condition."[1]

Mother Teresa. You know her story. When she won the Nobel Peace Prize in 1985, she gave the two hundred thousand dollars to the poor of Calcutta. When a businessman bought her a new car, she sold it and gave the money to the underprivileged. She owns nothing. She owes nothing.

Two women: Miss America and Mother Teresa. One walks the boardwalk; the other works the alley. Two voices. One promises crowns, flowers, and crowds. The other promises service, surrender, and joy.

Now, I have nothing against beauty pageants (although I have my reservations about them). But I do have something against the lying voices that noise our world.

You've heard them. They tell you to swap your integrity for a new sale. To barter your convictions for an easy deal. To exchange your devotion for a quick thrill.

They whisper. They woo. They taunt. They tantalize. They flirt. They flatter. "Go ahead, it's OK." "Just wait until tomorrow." "Don't worry, no one will know." "How could anything that feels so right be so wrong?"

The voices of the crowd.

Our lives are Wall Streets of chaos, stock markets loud with demands. Grown men and women barking in a frenzied effort to get all they can before time runs out. "Buy. Sell. Trade. Swap. But whatever you do, do it fast—and loud."

A carnival of gray-flannel suits where no one smiles and everyone dashes.

An endless chorus of booming voices: some offering, some taking, and all screaming.

What do we do with the voices?

As I work on this manuscript, I'm seated at a desk in a hotel room. I'm away from home. Away from people who know me. Away from family members who love me.

Voices that encourage and affirm are distant.

But voices that tantalize and entice are near. Although the room is quiet, if I listen, their voices are crystal clear.

A placard on my nightstand invites me to a lounge in the lobby, where I can "make new friends in a relaxing atmosphere." An advertisement on top of the television promises me that with the request of a late-night adult movie my "fantasies will come true." In the phone book, several columns of escort services offer "love away from home." An attractive, gold-lettered volume in the drawer of the nightstand beckons: *The Book of Mormon—Another Testament of Jesus Christ.* On television a talk-show host discusses the day's topic: "How to succeed at sex in the office."

Voices. Some for pleasure. Some for power.

Some promise acceptance. Some promise tenderness. But all promise something.

───────────────

Even the voices that Jesus heard promised something.

"After the people saw the miraculous sign that Jesus did, they began to say, 'Surely this is the Prophet who is to come into the world.'"[2]

To the casual observer, these are the voices of victory. To the untrained ear, these are the sounds of triumph. What could be better? Five thousand men plus women and children proclaiming Christ to be the prophet. Thousands of voices swelling into a roar of revival, an ovation of adulation.

The people have everything they need for a revolution.

They have an enemy: Herod. They have a martyr: John the Baptist. They have leadership: the disciples. They have ample supplies: Jesus the bread maker. And they have a king: Jesus of Nazareth.

Why wait? The time has come. Israel will be restored. God's people have heard God's voice.

"King Jesus!" someone proclaims. And the crowd chimes in.

And don't think for a minute that Christ didn't hear their chant.

A chorus promising power intoxicates. No cross needed. No sacrifice required. An army of disciples at his fingertips. Power to change the world without having to die doing it.

Revenge would be sweet. *The one who took the head of John the Baptist is only a few miles away. I wonder if he has ever felt a cold blade on his neck.*

Yes, Jesus heard the voices. He heard the lurings. But he also heard someone else.

And when Jesus heard him, he sought him.

"Jesus, knowing that they intended to come and make him king by force, withdrew again to a mountain by himself."[3]

Jesus preferred to be alone with the true God rather than in a crowd with the wrong people.

Logic didn't tell him to dismiss the crowds. Conventional wisdom didn't tell him to turn his back on a willing army. No, it wasn't a voice from without that Jesus heard. It was a voice from within.

The mark of a sheep is its ability to hear the Shepherd's voice.

"The sheep listen to his voice. He calls his own sheep by name and leads them out."[4]

The mark of a disciple is his or her ability to hear the Master's voice.

"Here I am! I stand at the door and knock. If anyone hears my voice and opens the door, I will come in and eat with him, and he with me."[5]

The world rams at your door; Jesus taps at your door. The voices scream for your allegiance; Jesus softly and tenderly requests it. The world promises flashy pleasure;

Jesus promises a quiet dinner . . . with God. "I will come in and eat."

Which voice do you hear?

Let me state something important. There is never a time during which Jesus is not speaking. Never. There is never a place in which Jesus is not present. Never. There is never a room so dark . . . a lounge so sensual . . . an office so sophisticated . . . that the ever-present, ever-pursuing, relentlessly tender Friend is not there, tapping gently on the doors of our hearts—waiting to be invited in.

Few hear his voice. Fewer still open the door.

But never interpret our numbness as his absence. For amidst the fleeting promises of pleasure is the timeless promise of his presence.

"Surely I am with you always, to the very end of the age."[6]

"'Never will I leave you; never will I forsake you.'"[7]

There is no chorus so loud that the voice of God cannot be heard . . . if we will but listen.

That's true in this hotel room.

It took me a few minutes to find it, but I did. It wasn't as visible as the lounge placard or the movie advertisement. But it was there. It wasn't as fancy as the Mormon Bible or as attention-grabbing as the escort ads. But I'd give up those lies every time for the peace I've found in this treasure.

A Bible. A simple, hard-covered, Gideon-placed, King James Version Bible. It took me a few minutes to find it, but I did. And when I did, I opened it to one of my favorite voice passages:

A time is coming when all who are in their graves will hear his voice and come out—those who have done good will rise to live, and those who have done evil will rise to be condemned.[8]

Interesting. A day is coming when everyone will hear his voice. A day is coming when all the other voices will be silenced; his voice—and his voice only—will be heard.

Some will hear his voice for the very first time. It's not that he never spoke, it's just that they never listened. For these, God's voice will be the voice of a stranger. They will hear it once—and never hear it again. They will spend eternity fending off the voices they followed on earth.

But others will be called from their graves by a familiar voice. For they are sheep who know their shepherd. They are servants who opened the door when Jesus knocked.

Now the door will open again. Only this time, it won't be Jesus who walks into our house; it will be we, who walk into his.

10

THE PHOTO AND THE FILE

*E*ACH JUNE I PUT MY CALENDAR together for the coming year. June is the month of D-Day. I don't mean D-Day as in Normandy invasion. I mean D-Day as in decisions to be made.

This morning I began the process of decision. I opened the "Decision File" and began reading the speaking invitations. A church planter in Wyoming wonders if I could spend time with his church. A church camp in Washington invites me to speak to its campers. A missionary in India has read my books and asks, "If I can come up with the money, can you spend a week with us?"

Something happens as a person fields the invitations of others. He or she begins to feel important.

As I looked at the letters, it dawned on me how vital I was to the progress of humanity.

I wondered how the earth stayed on its axis before I was born. I nodded my head in understanding at the letter that read, "You are the one for this meeting." I put my hand under my shirt and rubbed the S on the red jersey—"Super Max."

I was feeling puffy and proud when I read the last letter. But as I put down the file, I noticed another request. One that didn't make it into the folder. One that was lying on my desk.

It had no date, no signature, no deadline. It wasn't a letter or a phone message. It was a photograph—a photograph so recent that it had no frame. It was a portrait of a mom and a dad encircled by three little girls. Our family portrait.

The positioning of the photo and the file struck me. There was something symbolic about the way I'd unintentionally placed the letters next to the family picture. The singular photo lying in the shadow of the stack of requests seemed to whisper a question that only I could answer:

"Max, who will win?"

There is only so much sand in the hourglass. Who gets it?

You know what I'm talking about, don't you? Since you don't stockpile your requests until June, your situation may not be as graphic as mine. But it's every bit as real.

"The PTA needs a new treasurer. With your background and experience and talent and wisdom and love for kids and degree in accounting, YOU are the perfect one for the job!"

"There's going to be some shuffling in the ranks. With the retirement of the branch manager, *somebody* will move up. The company is looking for a bright, young salesman— someone like you—who is willing to demonstrate his dedication to the organization by taking on some extra projects . . . and working some late hours."

"I apologize that I have to ask you again, but you are such a good Sunday-school teacher. If you could only take one more quarter . . ."

"I just lost my hygienist. Will you come back to work for me? I know you don't want to go back to work until your children start school. But it's only four hours a day and there's a day-care center just a few blocks from my office now. Wouldn't the extra money be nice?"

"Would I be willing to serve as chapter president? Well, to be honest, I was going to sit out this term because our youngest goes to college next fall. Yes, I realize this is a critical year for the organization. . . . Oh, no, I wouldn't want the club to falter. . . . Yes, we have made great progress over the last few months. It's just that . . ."

It's tug-of-war, and you are the rope.

On one side are the requests for your time and energy. They call. They compliment. They are valid and good. Great opportunities to do good things. If they were evil, it'd be easy to say no. But they aren't, so it's easy to rationalize.

On the other side are the loved ones in your world. They don't write you letters. They don't ask you to consult your calendar. They don't offer to pay your expenses. They don't use terms like "appointment," "engagement," or "do lunch." They don't want you for what you can do for them; they want you for who you are.

Clovis Chappell, a minister from a century back, used to tell the story of two paddleboats. They left Memphis about the same time, traveling down the Mississippi River to New Orleans. As they traveled side by side, sailors from one vessel made a few remarks about the snail's pace of the other.

Words were exchanged. Challenges were made. And the race began. Competition became vicious as the two boats roared through the Deep South.

One boat began falling behind. Not enough fuel. There had been plenty of coal for the trip, but not enough for a race. As the boat dropped back, an enterprising young sailor took some of the ship's cargo and tossed it into the ovens. When the sailors saw that the supplies burned as well as the coal, they fueled their boat with the material they had been assigned to transport. They ended up winning the race, but burned their cargo.

God has entrusted cargo to us, too: children, spouses, friends. Our job is to do our part in seeing that this cargo reaches its destination.

Yet when the program takes priority over people, people often suffer.

How much cargo do we sacrifice in order to achieve the number one slot? How many people never reach the destination because of the aggressiveness of a competitive captain?

A world of insight is hidden in four words in Matthew 14:22: "He dismissed the crowd." This wasn't just *any* crowd that Jesus dismissed.

These weren't casually curious.

These weren't coincidental bystanders.

This was a multitude with a mission. They had heard the disciples. They had left their homes. They had followed Jesus around the sea. They had heard him teach and had seen him heal. They had eaten the bread. And they were ready to make him king.

Surely Jesus will commandeer the crowd and focus their frenzy. Surely he will seize the chance to convert the thousands. Surely he will spend the night baptizing the willing followers. No one would turn down an opportunity to minister to thousands of people, right?

Jesus did.

"He dismissed the crowd." Why? Read verse 23: "After he had dismissed them, he went up on a mountainside by himself to pray."

He said no to the important in order to say yes to the vital.

He said no to a good opportunity in order to say yes to a better opportunity. It wasn't a selfish decision. It was a deliberate choice to honor priorities. If Jesus thought it necessary to say no to the demands of the crowds in order to pray, don't you think you and I should, too?

"Blessed are the meek,"[1] Jesus said. The word *meek* does not mean weak. It means focused. It is a word used to describe a domesticated stallion. Power under control. Strength with a direction.

Blessed are those who are harnessed. Blessed are those who recognize their God-given responsibilities. Blessed are those who acknowledge that there is only one God and have quit applying for his position. Blessed are those who know what on earth they are on earth to do and set themselves about the business of doing it. Blessed are those who are able to "discern what is best."[2]

As I looked at the photo and the file, I decided to try something. I decided to make a list of what I would lose by saying no to my family one night. It wasn't hard to do; I just made a list of what I would have missed by not being home with my family last night.

I could have been out of town this week. I had an invitation to be in the Midwest at a church. I turned it down. What if I hadn't? If I had gone, I would have had the attention of a thousand people for an hour. I would have had the opportunity to speak about Jesus to some people who don't know him. Is a Tuesday evening at home with three children and a spouse more important than preaching to an audience?

Read my list of what I would have missed. Then you decide.

I would have missed a trip to the swimming pool in which I saw Jenna climb onto her inner tube for the first time.

I would have missed fifteen minutes of bouncing up and down in the shallow end of the pool, with Andrea clinging to my neck singing the theme from "Sleeping Beauty."

I would have missed seeing Denalyn get sentimental as she unpacked a box of baby clothes.

I wouldn't have gone on a walk with the girls during which Jenna found ten "special" rocks.

I wouldn't have been there to hold Andrea when her finger got slammed in the door.

I wouldn't have been there to answer Jenna's question: "Daddy, what is a handicapped person?"

I would have missed seeing Andrea giggle as she took Jenna's straw when Jenna's back was turned.

I wouldn't have heard Jenna tell the story of Jesus on the cross during our family devotional (when she assured us, "But he didn't stay dead!").

I wouldn't have seen Andrea make a muscle with her arm and sing, "Our God is so BIIIIIIG!"

What do you think? I know my vote. There are a hundred speakers who could have addressed that crowd, but my girls just have one daddy.

After I made my list, just for the fun of it I picked up the phone and called the church that had asked me to come and speak this week. The minister wasn't in, but his secretary was. "Isn't this the week of your seminar?" I asked.

"Oh, yes! It has been a wonderful success!"

They didn't even miss me.

Now I've got a better idea what to do with my stack of requests.

STORMS
OF
DOUBT

11

SEEING GOD THROUGH SHATTERED GLASS

*T*HERE IS A WINDOW IN YOUR heart through which you can see God. Once upon a time that window was clear. Your view of God was crisp. You could see God as vividly as you could see a gentle valley or hillside. The glass was clean, the pane unbroken.

You knew God. You knew how he worked. You knew what he wanted you to do. No surprises. Nothing unexpected. You knew that God had a will, and you continually discovered what it was.

Then, suddenly, the window cracked. A pebble broke the window. A pebble of pain.

Perhaps the stone struck when you were a child and a parent left home—forever. Maybe the rock hit in adolescence when your heart was broken. Maybe you made it into adulthood before the window was cracked. But then the pebble came.

Was it a phone call? "We have your daughter at the station. You'd better come down."

Was it a letter on the kitchen table? "I've left. Don't try to reach me. Don't try to call me. It's over. I just don't love you anymore."

Was it a diagnosis from the doctor? "I'm afraid our news is not very good."

Was it a telegram? "We regret to inform you that your son is missing in action."

Whatever the pebble's form, the result was the same—
a shattered window. The pebble missiled into the pane and
shattered it. The crash echoed down the halls of your heart.
Cracks shot out from the point of impact, creating a spider
web of fragmented pieces.

And suddenly God was not so easy to see. The view
that had been so crisp had changed. You turned to see God,
and his figure was distorted. It was hard to see him through
the pain. It was hard to see him through the fragments of
hurt.

You were puzzled. God wouldn't allow something like
this to happen, would he? Tragedy and travesty weren't on
the agenda of the One you had seen, were they? Had you
been fooled? Had you been blind?

The moment the pebble struck, the glass became a
reference point for you. From then on, there was life before
the pain and life after the pain. Before your pain, the view
was clear; God seemed so near. After your pain, well,
he was harder to see. He seemed a bit distant . . . harder
to perceive. Your pain distorted the view—not eclipsed it,
but distorted it.

Maybe these words don't describe your situation. There
are some people who never have to redefine or refocus their
view of God. Most of us do.

Most of us know what it means to feel disappointed
by God.

Most of us have a way of completing this sentence: "If
God is God, then . . ." Call it an agenda, a divine job description. Each of us has an unspoken, yet definitive, expectation of what God should do. "If God is God, then . . ."

• There will be no financial collapse in my family.

• My children will never be buried before me.

• People will treat me fairly.

• This church will never divide.

• My prayer will be answered.

These are not articulated criteria. They are not written down or notarized. But they are real. They define the expectations we have of God. And when pain comes into our world—when the careening pebble splinters the window of our hearts—these expectations go unmet and doubts may begin to surface.

We look for God, but can't find him. Fragmented glass hinders our vision. He is enlarged through this piece and reduced through that one. Lines jigsaw their way across his face. Large sections of shattered glass opaque the view.

And now you aren't quite sure what you see.

———————————

The disciples weren't sure what they saw, either.

Jesus failed to meet their expectations. The day Jesus fed the five thousand men he didn't do what they wanted him to do.

The Twelve returned from their mission followed by an army. They finished their training. They recruited the soldiers. They were ready for battle. They expected Jesus to let the crowds crown him as king and attack the city of Herod. They expected battle plans . . . strategies . . . a new era for Israel.

What did they get?

Just the opposite.

Instead of weapons, they got oars. Rather than being sent to fight, they were sent to float. The crowds were sent away. Jesus walked away. And they were left on the water with a storm brewing in the sky.

What kind of Messiah would do this?

Note carefully the sequence of the stormy evening as Matthew records it:

> Immediately Jesus made the disciples get into the boat and go on ahead of him to the other side, while he dismissed the crowd. After he had dismissed them, he went up on a mountainside by himself to pray. *When evening came* [emphasis mine], he was there alone, but the boat was already a considerable distance from land, buffeted by the waves because the wind was against it.[1]

Matthew is specific about the order of events. Jesus sent the disciples to the boat. Then he dismissed the crowd and ascended a mountainside. It was evening, probably around 6:00 P.M. The storm struck immediately. The sun had scarcely set before typhoon-like winds began to roar.

Note that Jesus sent the disciples out into the storm *alone.* Even as he was ascending the mountainside, he could feel and hear the gale's force. Jesus was not ignorant of the storm. He was aware that a torrent was coming that would carpet-bomb the sea's surface. But he didn't turn around. The disciples were left to face the storm . . . alone.

The greatest storm that night was not in the sky; it was in the disciples' hearts. The greatest fear was not from seeing the storm-driven waves; it came from seeing the back of their leader as he left them to face the night with only questions as companions.

It was this fury that the disciples were facing that night. Imagine the incredible strain of bouncing from wave to wave in a tiny fishing vessel. One hour would weary you. Two hours would exhaust you.

Surely Jesus will help us, they thought. They'd seen him still storms like this before. On this same sea, they had awakened him during a storm, and he had commanded the skies to be silent. They'd seen him quiet the wind and soothe the waves. *Surely he will come off the mountain.*

But he doesn't. Their arms begin to ache from rowing. Still no sign of Jesus. Three hours. Four hours. The winds rage. The boat bounces. Still no Jesus. Midnight comes. Their eyes search for God—in vain.

By now the disciples have been on the sea for as long as six hours.

All this time they have fought the storm and sought the Master. And, so far, the storm is winning. And the Master is nowhere to be found.

"Where is he?" cried one.

"Has he forgotten us?" yelled another.

"He feeds thousands of strangers and yet leaves us to die?" muttered a third.

The Gospel of Mark adds compelling insight into the disciples' attitude. "They had not understood about the loaves; their hearts were hardened."[2]

What does Mark mean? Simply this. The disciples were mad. They began the evening in a huff. Their hearts were hardened toward Jesus because he fed the multitude. Their preference, remember, had been to "send the crowds away."[3] And Jesus had told them to feed the people. But they wouldn't try. They said it couldn't be done. They told Jesus to let the people take care of themselves.

Also keep in mind that the disciples had just spent some time on center stage. They'd tasted stardom. They were celebrities. They had rallied crowds. They had recruited an army. They were, no doubt, pretty proud of themselves. With chests a bit puffy and heads a bit swollen, they'd told Jesus, "Just send them away."

Jesus didn't. Instead, he chose to bypass the reluctant disciples and use the faith of an anonymous boy. What the disciples said couldn't be done was done—in spite of them, not through them.

They pouted. They sulked. Rather than being amazed at the miracle, they became mad at the Master. After all, they had felt foolish passing out the very bread they said could not be made. Add to that Jesus' command to go to the boat when they wanted to go to battle, and it's easier to understand why these guys are burning!

"Now what is Jesus up to, leaving us out on the sea on a night like this?"

It's 1:00 A.M., no Jesus.

It's 2:00 A.M., no Jesus.

Peter, Andrew, James, and John have seen storms like this. They are fishermen; the sea is their life. They know the havoc the gale-force winds can wreak. They've seen the splintered hulls float to shore. They've attended the funerals. They know, better than anyone, that this night could be their last. "Why doesn't he come?" they sputter.

Finally, he does. "During the fourth watch of the night [3:00 to 6:00 A.M.] Jesus went out to them, walking on the lake."[4]

Jesus came. He finally came. But between verse 24—being buffeted by waves—and verse 25—when Jesus appeared—a thousand questions are asked.

Questions you have probably asked, too. Perhaps you know the angst of being suspended between verses 24 and 25. Maybe you're riding a storm, searching the coastline for a light, a glimmer of hope. You know that Jesus knows what you are going through. You know that he's aware of your storm. But as hard as you look to find him, you can't see him. Maybe your heart, like the disciples' hearts, has been hardened by unmet expectations. Your pleadings for help are salted with angry questions.

The first section of this book spoke of stress; the second is about storms. Stress attacks your nerves. Storms attack your faith. Stress interrupts. Storms destroy. Stress comes like a siren. Storms come like a missile. Stress clouds the day. Storms usher in the night.

The question of stress is, *"How can I cope?"* The question of storms is, *"Where* is God and *why* would he do this?"

The second section of this book is for you if the pebble of pain has struck the window of your heart, if you've known the horror of looking for God's face and seeing only his back as he ascends a mountainside.

In the following pages, you will discover hopeful chronicles to help you deal with your doubts. Let me introduce you to a few friends who learned to see through shattered glass.

- An entrepreneur, stripped of treasures, who found one treasure that no one could take.

- A father who learned of trust during a six-hour drive with three children.

- A mother superior in New Mexico who discovered that prayer—her last resort—was her best resort.

- A woodsman who taught a village the virtue of patience.

- God's son—dog-tired and heartsore—who found strength through heaven's friends.

Some stories are fiction, some are fact. Some are legendary, others are biblical. Some are humorous, others are serious. But all have a message for those who know the anxiety of searching for God in a storm.

The message? When you can't see him, trust him. The figure you see is not a ghost. The voice you hear is not the wind.

Jesus is closer than you've ever dreamed.

12

TWO FATHERS, TWO FEASTS

I DROVE THE FAMILY TO Grandma's last night for Thanksgiving. Three hours into the six-hour trip, I realized that I was in a theology lab.

A day with a car full of kids will teach you a lot about God. Transporting a family from one city to another is closely akin to God transporting us from our home to his. And some of life's stormiest hours occur when the passenger and the Driver disagree on the destination.

A journey is a journey, whether the destination be the Thanksgiving table or the heavenly one. Both demand patience, a good sense of direction, and a driver who knows that the feast at the end of the trip is worth the hassles in the midst of the trip.

The fact that my pilgrims were all under the age of seven only enriched my learning experience.

As minutes rolled into hours and our car rolled through the hills, I began to realize that what I was saying to my kids had a familiar ring. I had heard it before—from God. All of a sudden, the car became a classroom. I realized that I was doing for a few hours what God has done for centuries: encouraging travelers who'd rather rest than ride.

I shared the idea with Denalyn. We began to discover similarities between the two journeys. Here are a few we noted.

In order to reach the destination, we have to say no to some requests.

Can you imagine the outcome if a parent honored each request of each child during a trip? We'd inch our bloated bellies from one ice-cream store to the next. Our priority would be popcorn and our itinerary would read like a fast-food menu. "Go to the Cherry Malt and make a right. Head north until you find the Chili Cheeseburger. Stay north for 1,300 calories and bear left at the Giant Pizza. When you see the two-for-one Chili Dog Special, take the Pepto-Bismol Turnpike east for five convenience stores. At the sixth toilet . . ."

Can you imagine the chaos if a parent indulged every indulgence?

Can you imagine the chaos if God indulged each of ours?

No is a necessary word to take on a trip. Destination has to reign over Dairy Deluxe Ice Cream Sundae.

"For God has not *destined* us [emphasis mine] to the terrors of judgement, but to the full attainment of salvation through our Lord Jesus Christ."[1]

Note God's destiny for your life. Salvation.

God's overarching desire is that you reach that destiny. His itinerary includes stops that encourage your journey. He frowns on stops that deter you. When his sovereign plan and your earthly plan collide, a decision must be made. Who's in charge of this journey?

If God must choose between your earthly satisfaction and your heavenly salvation, which do you hope he chooses?

Me, too.

When I'm in the driver's seat as the father of my children, I remember that I'm in charge. But when I'm in the passenger's seat as a child of my Father, I forget that he's in charge. I forget that God is more concerned with my destiny than my belly (although my belly hasn't done too badly). And I complain when he says no.

The requests my children made last night on the road to Grandma's weren't evil. They weren't unfair. They weren't rebellious. In fact, we had a couple of cones and Cokes. But most of the requests were unnecessary.

My four-year-old daughter would argue that fact. From her viewpoint, another soft drink is indispensable to her happiness. I know otherwise, so I say no.

A forty-year-old adult would argue that fact. From his standpoint, a new boss is indispensable to his happiness. God knows otherwise and says no.

A thirty-year-old woman would argue that fact. From her standpoint, *that* man with *that* job and *that* name is exactly who she needs to be happy. Her Father, who is more concerned that she arrive at his City than at the altar, says, "Wait a few miles. There's a better option down the road."

"Wait!" she protests. "How long do I have to wait?"

Which takes us to a second similarity between the two journeys.

Children have no concept of minutes or miles.
"We'll be there in three hours," I said.

"How long is three hours?" Jenna asked. (How do you explain time to a child who can't tell time?)

"Well, it's about as long as three Sesame Streets," I ventured.

The children groaned in unison. "Three Sesame Streets?! That's forever!"

And to them, it is.

And to us, it seems that way, too.

He who "lives forever"[2] has placed himself at the head of a band of pilgrims who mutter, "How long, O Lord? How long?"[3]

"How long must I endure this sickness?"

"How long must I endure this spouse?"

"How long must I endure this paycheck?"

Do you really want God to answer? He could, you know. He could answer in terms of the here and now with time increments we know. "Two more years on the illness." "The rest of your life in the marriage." "Ten more years for the bills."

But he seldom does that. He usually opts to measure the *here and now* against the *there and then.* And when you compare *this* life to *that* life, this life ain't long.

Our days on earth are like a shadow.[4]

Each man's life is but a breath.[5]

You are a mist that appears for a little while and then vanishes.[6]

As for man, his days are like grass, he flourishes like a flower of the field; the wind blows over it and it is gone, and its place remembers it no more.[7]

"It's a short journey," I offer to the children. "We're almost there."

I know. I've been there before. I've driven this road. I've covered this territory. For me, it's no challenge. Ah, but for the children, it's eternal.

So I try another approach. "Just think how good it will be," I depict. "Turkey, dressing, pie . . . I promise you, when you get there, the trip will have been worth it."

But they still groan.

Which takes us to the third similarity.

=====

Children can't envision the reward.

For me, six hours on the road is a small price to pay for my mom's strawberry cake. I don't mind the drive because I know the reward. I have three decades of Thanksgivings under my belt, literally. As I drive, I can taste the turkey. Hear the dinner-table laughter. Smell the smoke from the fireplace.

I can endure the journey because I know the destiny.

My daughters have forgotten the destiny. After all, they are young. Children easily forget. Besides, the road is strange, and the dark night has come. They can't see where we're going. It's my job, as their father, to guide them.

I try to help them see what they can't see.

I tell them how we'll feed the ducks at the lake. How we'll play on the swings. How they can spend the night with their cousins. We speak of sleeping on the floor in sleeping bags and staying up late since there is no school.

And it seems to work. Their grumbling decreases as their vision clears—as their destiny unfolds.

Perhaps that's how the apostle Paul stayed motivated. He had a clear vision of the reward.

Therefore we do not lose heart. Though outwardly we are wasting away, yet inwardly we are being renewed day by day. For our light and momentary troubles are achieving for us an eternal glory that far outweighs them all. So we fix our eyes not on what is seen, but on what is unseen.[8]

It's not easy to get three girls under the age of seven to see a city they can't see. But it's necessary.

It's not easy for us to see a City we've never seen, either, especially when the road is bumpy . . . the hour is late . . . and companions are wanting to cancel the trip and take up residence in a motel. It's not easy to fix our eyes on what is unseen. But it's necessary.

One line in the 2 Corinthians passage you just read makes me smile: "our light and momentary troubles."

I wouldn't have called them that if I were Paul. Read what he called *light and momentary,* and I think you'll agree:

- Imprisoned.
- Beaten with a whip five times.
- Faced death.
- Beaten with rods three times.
- Stoned once.
- Shipwrecked three times.
- Stranded in the open sea.
- Left homeless.
- In constant danger.
- Hungry and thirsty.[9]

Long and trying ordeals, perhaps. *Arduous and deadly afflictions,* OK. But *light and momentary troubles?* How could Paul describe endless trials with that phrase?

He tells us. He could see "an eternal glory that far outweighs them all."

Can I speak candidly for a few lines?

For some of you, the journey has been long. Very long and stormy. In no way do I wish to minimize the difficulties that you have had to face along the way. Some of you have shouldered burdens that few of us could ever carry. You have bid farewell to life-long partners. You have been robbed of life-long dreams. You have been given bodies that can't sustain your spirit. You have spouses who can't tolerate your faith. You have bills that outnumber the paychecks and challenges that outweigh the strength.

And you are tired.

It's hard for you to see the City in the midst of the storms. The desire to pull over to the side of the road and get out entices you. You want to go on, but some days the road seems so long.

Let me encourage you with one final parallel between your life's journey and the one our family took last night.

It's worth it.

As I write, the Thanksgiving meal is over. My legs are propped up on the hearth. My tablet is on my lap.

I have every intention of dozing off as soon as I finish this chapter.

The turkey has been attacked. The giblet gravy has been gobbled. The table is clear. The kids are napping. And the family is content.

As we sat around the table today, no one spoke of the long trip to get here. No one mentioned the requests I didn't honor. No one grumbled about my foot being on the accelerator when their hearts were focused on the banana splits. No one complained about the late hour of arrival.

Yesterday's challenges were lost in today's joy.

That's what Paul meant. God never said that the journey would be easy, but he did say that the arrival would be worthwhile.

Remember this: God may not do what you want, but he will do what is right . . . and best. He's the Father of forward motion. Trust him. He will get you home. And the trials of the trip will be lost in the joys of the feast.

Now, if you'll excuse me, I'll close my eyes. I'm a bit tired from the journey, and it feels good to rest.

13

DOUBTSTORMS

*T*HERE ARE SNOWSTORMS. There are hailstorms. There are rainstorms. And there are doubtstorms.

Every so often a doubtstorm rolls into my life, bringing with it a flurry of questions and gale-force winds of fear. And, soon after it comes, a light shines through it.

Sometimes the storm comes after the evening news. Some nights I wonder why I watch it. Some nights it's just too much. From the steps of the Supreme Court to the steppes of South Africa, the news is usually gloomy . . . thirty minutes of bite-sized tragedies. A handsome man in a nice suit with a warm voice gives bad news. They call him the anchorman. Good title. One needs an anchor in today's tempestuous waters.

Sometimes I wonder, *How can our world get so chaotic?*

Sometimes the storm comes when I'm at work. Story after story of homes that won't heal and hearts that won't melt. Always more hunger than food. More needs than money. More questions than answers. On Sundays I stand before a church with a three-point outline in my hand, thirty minutes on the clock, and a prayer on my lips. I do my best to say something that will convince a stranger that an unseen God still hears.

And I sometimes wonder why so many hearts have to hurt.

Do you ever get doubtstorms? Some of you don't, I know. I've talked to you. Some of you have a "Davidish" optimism that defies any Goliath. I used to think that you were naive at best and phony at worst.

I don't think that anymore.

I think you are gifted. You are gifted with faith. You can see the rainbow before the clouds part. If you have this gift, then skip this chapter. I won't say anything you need to hear.

But others of you wonder . . .

You wonder what others know that you don't. You wonder if you are blind or if they are. You wonder why some proclaim "Eureka" before the gold is found. You wonder why some shout "Land ho" before the fog has cleared. You wonder how some people believe so confidently while you believe so reluctantly.

As a result, you are a bit uncomfortable on the padded pew of blind belief. Your Bible hero is Thomas. Your middle name is Caution. Your queries are the bane of every Sunday school teacher.

"If God is so good, why do I sometimes feel so bad?"

"If his message is so clear, why do I get so confused?"

"If the Father is in control, why do good people have gut-wrenching problems?"

You wonder if it is a blessing or a curse to have a mind that never rests. But you would rather be a cynic than a hypocrite, so you continue to pray with one eye open and wonder:

- about starving children
- about the power of prayer
- about the depths of grace
- about Christians in cancer wards
- about who you are to ask such questions anyway.

Tough questions. Throw-in-the-towel questions. Questions the disciples must have asked in the storm.

All they could see were black skies as they bounced in the battered boat. Swirling clouds. Wind-driven white caps. Pessimism that buried the coastline. Gloom that swamped the bow. What could have been a pleasant trip became a white-knuckled ride through a sea of fear.

Their question—What hope do we have of surviving a stormy night?

My question—Where is God when his world is stormy?

Doubtstorms: turbulent days when the enemy is too big, the task too great, the future too bleak, and the answers too few.

Every so often a storm will come, and I'll look up into the blackening sky and say, "God, a little light, please?"

The light came for the disciples. A figure came to them walking on the water. It wasn't what they expected. Perhaps they were looking for angels to descend or heaven to open. Maybe they were listening for a divine proclamation to still the storm. We don't know what they were looking for. But one thing is for sure, they weren't looking for Jesus to come walking on the water.

"'It's a ghost,' they said and cried out in fear" (Matt. 14:26).

And since Jesus came in a way they didn't expect, they almost missed seeing the answer to their prayers.

And unless we look and listen closely, we risk making the same mistake. God's lights in our dark nights are as numerous as the stars, if only we'll look for them.

Can I share a few lights with you that have illuminated my world recently?

A friend and I sat in front of my house in his car and talked about his dilemma. His chief client pulled out on him, leaving him big bills and few solutions. What the client did wasn't right, but he did it anyway. The client's company was big and my friend's was small, and there wasn't a lot he could do. My friend was left with a den of hungry lions wanting six figures' worth of satisfaction.

"I called my uncle and told him what had happened. I told him I was thinking of filing for bankruptcy."

"What did he say?" I asked.

"He didn't say anything," my friend responded. "After he was silent for a long time, I said it for him. 'We don't do it like that, do we?'"

" 'No, we don't,' he told me. So I'll pay the bills. If I have to sell my house, I'll pay my bills."

I was encouraged. Somebody still believed that if he did what was right, God would do what was best. There was still some we-don't-do-it-like-that faith in the world. The sky began to clear.

Light number two came from a cancer ward.

"We will celebrate forty-four years tomorrow," Jack said, feeding his wife.

She was bald. Her eyes were sunken, and her speech was slurred. She looked straight ahead, only opening her mouth when he brought the fork near. He wiped her cheek. He wiped his brow.

"She has been sick for five years," he told me. "She can't walk. She can't take care of herself. She can't even feed herself, but I love her. And," he spoke louder so she could hear, "we are going to beat this thing, aren't we, Honey?"

He fed her a few bites and spoke again, "We don't have insurance. When I could afford it, I thought I wouldn't need it. Now I owe this hospital more than $50,000." He was quiet for a few moments as he gave her a drink. Then he continued. "But they don't pester me. They know I can't pay, but they admitted us with no questions asked. The doctors treat us like we are their best-paying patients. Who would've imagined such kindness?"

I had to agree with him. Who would've imagined such kindness? In a thorny world of high-tech, expensive, often criticized health care, it was reassuring to find professionals who would serve two who had nothing to give in return.

Jack thanked me for coming, and I thanked God that once again a sinew of light reminded me of the sun behind the clouds.

Then, a few days later, another light.

Larry Brown is the coach of the San Antonio Spurs, the local professional basketball team. I don't know him personally (although rumor has it that he wants me to sign a multi-year contract and play point guard for the team . . . nice fantasy).

Coach Brown recently spent an afternoon at a local men's store, signing autographs. He was scheduled to spend two hours, but ended up spending three. Pencil-and-pad-toting kids besieged the place, asking him questions and shaking his hand.

When he was finally able to slip out, he climbed into his car, only to notice a touching sight. A late-arriving youngster pedaled up, jumped off his bike, and ran to the window to see if the coach was still in the store. When he saw he wasn't, he turned slowly and sadly, walked over to his bike, and began to ride off.

Coach Brown turned off the ignition, climbed out of the car, and walked over to the boy. They chatted a few minutes, went next door to a drugstore, sat down at a table, and had a soft drink.

No reporters were near. No cameras were on. As far as these two knew, no one knew. I'm sure Larry Brown had other things to do that afternoon. No doubt he had other appointments to keep. But it's doubtful that anything he might have done that afternoon was more important than what he did.

In a world of big-bucked, high-glossed professional sports, it did me good to hear of one coach who is still a coach at heart. Hearing what he did was enough to blow away any lingering clouds of doubt and to leave me warmed by God's light . . . his gentle light.

Gentle lights. God's solutions for doubtstorms. Gold-flecked glows that amber hope into blackness. Not thunderbolts. Not explosions of light. Just gentle lights. A businessman choosing honesty. A hospital choosing compassion. A celebrity choosing kindness.

Visible evidence of the invisible hand.

Soft reminders that optimism is not just for fools.

Funny. None of the events were "religious." None of the encounters occurred in a ceremony or a church service. None will make the six o'clock news.

But such is the case with gentle lights.

When the disciples saw Jesus in the middle of their stormy night, they called him a ghost. A phantom. A hallucination. To them, the glow was anything but God.

When we see gentle lights on the horizon, we often have the same reaction. We dismiss occasional kindness as apparitions, accidents, or anomalies. Anything but God.

"When Jesus comes," the disciples in the boat may have thought, "he'll split the sky. The sea will be calm. The clouds will disperse."

"When God comes," we doubters think, "all pain will flee. Life will be tranquil. No questions will remain."

And because we look for the bonfire, we miss the candle. Because we listen for the shout, we miss the whisper.

But it is in burnished candles that God comes, and through whispered promises he speaks: "When you doubt, look around; I am closer than you think."

14

THE
MIRACLE
OF
THE
CARPENTER

*I*T'S NO ACCIDENT THAT NEW MEXICO is called the "Land of Enchantment." Sprawling deserts spotted with sage. Purple mountains wreathed with clouds. Adobe homes hidden on hillsides. Majestic pines. Endless artifacts. A cloverleaf of cultures from the conquistador to the Comanche to the cowboy. New Mexico enchants.

And in this land of enchantment, there is a chapel of wonder.

A block south of the La Fonda Hotel in Santa Fe, on the corner of Water Street and Old Santa Fe Trail, you will find Loretto Chapel. As you step through its iron gate, you enter more than a chapel courtyard. You enter another era. Pause for a moment under the sprawling branches of the ancient trees. Imagine what it was like when the Mexican carpenters completed the chapel in 1878.

Can you see the settlers stomping through the muddy streets? Can you hear the donkeys braying? The wagon wheels groaning? And can you see the early morning sun spotlighting this gothic chapel—so simple, so splendid—as it sits against the backdrop of the desert hills?

Loretto Chapel took five years to complete. Modeled after the Sainte-Chapelle in Paris, its delicate sanctuary contains an altar, a rose window, and a choir loft.

The choir loft is the reason for wonder.

Were you to stand in the newly built chapel in 1878, you might see the Sisters of Loretto looking forlornly at the balcony. Everything else was complete: the doors had been hung, the pews had been placed, the floor had been laid. Everything was finished. Even the choir loft. Except for one thing. No stairs.

The chapel was too small to accommodate a conventional stairway. The best builders and designers in the region shook their heads when consulted. "Impossible," they murmured. There simply wasn't enough room. A ladder would serve the purpose, but mar the ambiance.

The Sisters of Loretto, whose determination had led them from Kentucky to Santa Fe, now faced a challenge greater than their journey: a stairway that couldn't be built.

What they had dreamed of and what they could do were separated by fifteen impossible feet.

So what did they do? The only thing they could do. They ascended the mountain. Not the high mountains near Santa Fe. No, they climbed even higher. They climbed the same mountain that Jesus climbed 1,800 years earlier in Bethsaida. They climbed the mountain of prayer.

"He went up on a mountainside by Himself to pray."[1]

Jesus faced an impossible task. More than five thousand people were ready to fight a battle he had not come to fight. How could he show them that he didn't come to be a king, but to be a sacrifice? How could he take their eyes off an earthly kingdom so that they would see the spiritual one? How could they see the eternal when they only had eyes for the temporal?

What Jesus dreamed of doing and what he seemed able to do were separated by an impossible gulf. So Jesus prayed.

We don't know what he prayed about. But I have my guesses:

- He prayed that eyes blinded by power could see God's truth.

- He prayed that disciples dizzied by success could endure failure.

- He prayed that leaders longing for power would follow him to a cross.

- He prayed that people desiring bread for the body would hunger for bread for the soul.

He prayed for the impossible to happen.

Or maybe I'm wrong. Maybe he didn't ask for anything. Maybe he just stood quietly in the presence of Presence and basked in the Majesty. Perhaps he placed his war-weary self before the throne and rested.

Maybe he lifted his head out of the confusion of earth long enough to hear the solution of heaven. Perhaps he was reminded that hard hearts don't faze the Father. That problem people don't perturb the Eternal One.

We don't know what he did or what he said. But we do know the result. The hill became a steppingstone; the storm became a path. And the disciples saw Jesus as they had never seen him before.

During the storm, Jesus prayed. The sky darkened. The winds howled. Yet he prayed. The people grumbled. The disciples doubted. Yet he prayed. When forced to choose between the muscles of men and the mountain of prayer, he prayed.

Jesus did not try to do it by himself. Why should you?

There are crevasses in your life that you cannot cross alone. There are hearts in your world that you cannot change without help. There are mountains that you cannot climb until you climb His mountain.

Climb it. You will be amazed.

The Sisters of Loretto were.

━━━━━━━━━━━━━━━━

As the story goes, the nuns prayed for nine days. On the last day of the novena, a Mexican carpenter with a beard and a wind-burned face appeared at the convent. He explained that he had heard they needed a stairway to a chapel loft. He thought he could help.

The mother superior had nothing to lose, so she gave him permission.

He went to work with crude tools, painstaking patience, and uncanny skill. For eight months he worked.

One morning the Sisters of Loretto entered the chapel to find their prayers had been answered. A masterpiece of carpentry spiraled from the floor to the loft. Two complete three-hundred-sixty-degree turns. Thirty-three steps held together with wooden pegs and no central support. The wood is said to be a variety of hard fir, one nonexistent in New Mexico!

When the sisters turned to thank the craftsman, he was gone. He was never seen again. He never asked for money. He never asked for praise. He was a simple carpenter who did what no one else could do so singers could enter a choir loft and sing.

See the stairway for yourself, if you like. Journey into the land of Enchantment. Step into this chapel of amazement and witness the fruit of prayer.

Or, if you prefer, talk to the Master Carpenter yourself. He has already performed one impossible feat in your world. He, like the Santa Fe carpenter, built a stairway no one else could build. He, like the nameless craftsman, used material from another place. He, like the visitor to Loretto, came to span the gap between where you are and where you long to be.

Each year of his life is a step. Thirty-three paces. Each step of the stair is an answered prayer. He built it so you can climb it.

And sing.

15

THE
WOODCUTTER'S
WISDOM

WOULD YOU BUY A HOUSE IF you were only allowed to see one of its rooms? Would you purchase a car if you were permitted to see only its tires and a taillight? Would you pass judgment on a book after reading only one paragraph?

Nor would I.

Good judgment requires a broad picture. Not only is that true in purchasing houses, cars, and books, it's true in evaluating life. One failure doesn't make a person a failure; one achievement doesn't make a person a success.

"The end of the matter is better than its beginning,"[1] penned the sage.

"Be . . . patient in affliction,"[2] echoed the apostle Paul.

"Don't judge a phrase by one word," stated the woodcutter.

The woodcutter? Oh, you may not know him. Let me present him to you.

I met him in Brazil. He was introduced to me by a friend who knew that I needed patience. Denalyn and I were six months into a five-year stint in Brazil, and I was frustrated. My fascination with Rio de Janeiro had turned into exasperation with words I couldn't speak and a culture I didn't understand.

"Tenha paciência," Maria would tell me. "Just be patient." She was my Portuguese instructor. But, more than that, she was a calm voice in a noisy storm. With maternal persistence, she corrected my pronunciation and helped me learn to love her homeland.

Once, in the midst of a frustrating week of trying to get our goods out of customs (which eventually took three months), she gave me this story as a homework assignment. It helped my attitude far more than it helped my Portuguese.

It's a simple fable. Yet for those of us who try to pass judgment on life with only one day's evidence, the message is profound. I've done nothing to embellish it; I've only translated it. I pray that it will remind you, as it did me, that patience is the greater courage.

———————————————

Once there was an old man who lived in a tiny village. Although poor, he was envied by all, for he owned a beautiful white horse. Even the king coveted his treasure. A horse like this had never been seen before—such was its splendor, its majesty, its strength.

People offered fabulous prices for the steed, but the old man always refused. "This horse is not a horse to me," he would tell them. "It is a person. How could you sell a person? He is a friend, not a possession. How could you sell a friend?" The man was poor and the temptation was great. But he never sold the horse.

One morning he found that the horse was not in the stable. All the village came to see him. "You old fool," they scoffed, "we told you that someone would steal your horse. We warned you that you would be robbed. You are so poor.

How could you ever hope to protect such a valuable animal? It would have been better to have sold him. You could have gotten whatever price you wanted. No amount would have been too high. Now the horse is gone, and you've been cursed with misfortune."

The old man responded, "Don't speak too quickly. Say only that the horse is not in the stable. That is all we know; the rest is judgment. If I've been cursed or not, how can you know? How can you judge?"

The people contested, "Don't make us out to be fools! We may not be philosophers, but great philosophy is not needed. The simple fact that your horse is gone is a curse."

The old man spoke again. "All I know is that the stable is empty, and the horse is gone. The rest I don't know. Whether it be a curse or a blessing, I can't say. All we can see is a fragment. Who can say what will come next?"

The people of the village laughed. They thought that the man was crazy. They had always thought he was a fool; if he wasn't, he would have sold the horse and lived off the money. But instead, he was a poor woodcutter, an old man still cutting firewood and dragging it out of the forest and selling it. He lived hand to mouth in the misery of poverty. Now he had proven that he was, indeed, a fool.

After fifteen days, the horse returned. He hadn't been stolen; he had run away into the forest. Not only had he returned, he had brought a dozen wild horses with him. Once again the village people gathered around the woodcutter and spoke. "Old man, you were right and we were wrong. What we thought was a curse was a blessing. Please forgive us."

The man responded, "Once again, you go too far. Say only that the horse is back. State only that a dozen horses returned with him, but don't judge. How do you know if this is a blessing or not? You see only a fragment. Unless you know the whole story, how can you judge? You read only one page of a book. Can you judge the whole book? You read only one word of a phrase. Can you understand the entire phrase?

"Life is so vast, yet you judge all of life with one page or one word. All you have is a fragment! Don't say that this is a blessing. No one knows. I am content with what I know. I am not perturbed by what I don't."

"Maybe the old man is right," they said to one another. So they said little. But down deep, they knew he was wrong. They knew it was a blessing. Twelve wild horses had returned with one horse. With a little bit of work, the animals could be broken and trained and sold for much money.

The old man had a son, an only son. The young man began to break the wild horses. After a few days, he fell from one of the horses and broke both legs. Once again the villagers gathered around the old man and cast their judgments.

"You were right," they said. "You proved you were right. The dozen horses were not a blessing. They were a curse. Your only son has broken his legs, and now in your old age you have no one to help you. Now you are poorer than ever."

The old man spoke again. "You people are obsessed with judging. Don't go so far. Say only that my son broke his legs. Who knows if it is a blessing or a curse? No one knows. We only have a fragment. Life comes in fragments."

It so happened that a few weeks later the country engaged in war against a neighboring country. All the young men of the village were required to join the army. Only the son of the old man was excluded, because he was injured. Once again the people gathered around the old man, crying and screaming because their sons had been taken. There was little chance that they would return. The enemy was strong, and the war would be a losing struggle. They would never see their sons again.

"You were right, old man," they wept. "God knows you were right. This proves it. Your son's accident was a blessing. His legs may be broken, but at least he is with you. Our sons are gone forever."

The old man spoke again. "It is impossible to talk with you. You always draw conclusions. No one knows. Say only this: Your sons had to go to war, and mine did not. No one knows if it is a blessing or a curse. No one is wise enough to know. Only God knows."

———

The old man was right. We only have a fragment. Life's mishaps and horrors are only a page out of a grand book. We must be slow about drawing conclusions. We must reserve judgment on life's storms until we know the whole story.

I don't know where the woodcutter learned his patience. Perhaps from another woodcutter in Galilee. For it was the Carpenter who said it best:

"Do not worry about tomorrow, for tomorrow will worry about itself."[3]

He should know. He is the Author of our story. And he has already written the final chapter.

16

LAWS
OF
THE
LIGHTHOUSE

*T*HE FIRST OF THE YEAR IS known for three things: black-eyed peas, bowl games, and lists. Some don't eat black-eyed peas. Others hate football. But everybody likes lists. Lists are reassuring. They comfort us. They suggest that the crazy, zooming, blooming chaos of the universe can be mastered and tamed within the cage of a tidy column. To list is to understand, solve, and even control. For that reason we can't resist the urge, at the end of the year, to spew out lists like Washington, D.C. spews out documents.

We list the best movies . . . the best books . . . the worst dressed . . . the most used . . . the least popular . . . the most mysterious . . . the highest paid. We salute the good. We satire the bad. And we sum up the year on lists—"end-list" lists.

Although New Year's Day ranks at the top of the list of list-producing days, the rest of the year is by no means "list-less."

- Your grocery list makes a trip to the market manageable.

- Your calendar probably has a "to do" space, where you organize and number things you'd like to do but probably won't.

- Your syllabus tells you which books to buy.

- Your itinerary tells you which plane to take.

- Your telephone book tells you which numbers to dial.

The Bible certainly has its share of lists. Moses brought one down from the mountain. Noah might have used one as he loaded the ark. Jesus gave a list of principles in the Sermon on the Mount. (Paul gave his version in Romans 12.) Matthew and Luke listed the genealogies of Jesus. John listed the splendors of heaven.

There are lists of the gifts of the Spirit. Lists of good fruit and bad. Lists of salutations and greetings. Even the disciples' boat got into the action as it listed in the stormy Sea of Galilee. (If you smiled at that, then I've got a list of puns you'd enjoy.)

But the greatest day of lists is still New Year's Day. And the number one list is the list I call the Laws of the Lighthouse.

The Laws of the Lighthouse list contains immutable, immovable truths. Candidates for this inventory only qualify if they have lighthouse characteristics:

- They warn you of potential danger.
- They signal safe harbor.
- They are stronger than the storm.
- They shine brightest in the fog.

The Laws of the Lighthouse contain more than good ideas, personal preferences, and honest opinions. They are God-given, time-tested truths that define the way you should navigate your life. Observe them and enjoy secure passage. Ignore them and crash against the ragged rocks of reality.

In *U.S. Naval Institute Proceedings,* the magazine of the Naval Institute, Frank Koch illustrates the importance of obeying the Laws of the Lighthouse.[1]

> Two battleships assigned to the training squadron had been at sea on maneuvers in heavy weather for several days. I was serving on the lead battleship and was on watch on the bridge as night fell. The visibility was poor with patchy fog, so the captain remained on the bridge keeping an eye on all activities.
>
> Shortly after dark, the lookout on the wing reported, "Light, bearing on the starboard bow."
>
> "Is it steady or moving astern?" the captain called out.
>
> The lookout replied, "Steady, Captain," which meant we were on a dangerous collision course with that ship.
>
> The captain then called to the signalman, "Signal that ship: 'We are on a collision course, advise you change course twenty degrees.'"
>
> Back came the signal, "Advisable for you to change course twenty degrees."
>
> The captain said, "Send: 'I'm a captain, change course twenty degrees.'"
>
> "I'm a seaman second-class," came the reply. "You had better change course twenty degrees."
>
> By that time the captain was furious. He spat out, "Send: 'I'm a battleship. Change course twenty degrees.'"
>
> Back came the flashing light, "I'm a lighthouse."
>
> We changed course.

Smart move. The wise captain shifts the direction of his craft according to the signal of the lighthouse. A wise person does the same.

Herewith, then, are the lights I look for and the signals I heed:

- Love God more than you fear hell.
- Once a week, let a child take you on a walk.
- Make major decisions in a cemetery.
- When no one is watching, live as if someone is.
- Succeed at home first.
- Don't spend tomorrow's money today.
- Pray twice as much as you fret.
- Listen twice as much as you speak.
- Only harbor a grudge when God does.
- Never outgrow your love of sunsets.
- Treat people like angels; you will meet some and help make some.
- 'Tis wiser to err on the side of generosity than on the side of scrutiny.
- God has forgiven you; you'd be wise to do the same.
- When you can't trace God's hand, trust his heart.
- Toot your own horn and the notes will be flat.
- Don't feel guilty for God's goodness.
- The book of life is lived in chapters, so know your page number.
- Never let the important be the victim of the trivial.

• Live your liturgy.

To sum it all up:
Approach life like a voyage on a schooner. Enjoy the view. Explore the vessel. Make friends with the captain. Fish a little. And then get off when you get home.

17

HE
SPEAKS
THROUGH
THE
STORM

I HAD HEARD ABOUT YOU BEFORE, *but now I have seen you."*[1]
It all happened in one day. One day he could choose his tee time at the nicest golf course in the country; the next he couldn't even be the caddie. One day he could Lear jet across the country to see the heavyweight bout at the Las Vegas Mirage. The next he couldn't afford a city bus across town.

Talk about calm becoming chaos . . .

The first thing to go is his empire. The market crashes; his assets tumble. What is liquid goes dry. What has been up goes down. Stocks go flat, and Job goes broke. There he sits in his leather chair and soon-to-be-auctioned-off mahogany desk when the phone rings with news of calamity number two:

The kids were at a resort for the holidays when a storm blew in and took them with it.

Shell-shocked and dumbfounded, Job looks out the window into the sky that seems to be getting darker by the minute. He starts praying, telling God that things can't get any worse . . . and that's exactly what happens. He feels a pain in his chest that is more than last night's ravioli. The next thing he knows, he is bouncing in an ambulance with wires stuck to his chest and needles stuck in his arm.

He ends up tethered to a heart monitor in a community hospital room. Next to him lies an illegal immigrant who can't speak English.

Not, however, that Job lacks for conversation.

First there is his wife. Who could blame her for being upset at the week's calamities? Who could blame her for telling Job to curse God? But to curse God *and die?* If Job doesn't already feel abandoned, you know he does the minute his wife tells him to pull the plug and be done with it.

Then there are his friends. They have the bedside manner of a drill sergeant and the compassion of a chain-saw killer. A revised version of their theology might read like this: "Boy, you must have done something really bad! We know that God is good, so if bad things are happening to you, then you have been bad. Period."

Does Job take that lying down? Not hardly.

"You are doctors who don't know what they are doing," he says. "Oh, please be quiet! That would be your highest wisdom."[2]

Translation? "Why don't you take your philosophy back to the pigpen where you learned it."

"I'm not a bad man," Job argues. "I paid my taxes. I'm active in civic duties. I'm a major contributor to United Way and a volunteer at the hospital bazaar."

Job is, in his eyes, a good man. And a good man, he reasons, deserves a good answer.

"Your suffering is for your own good," states Elihu, a young minister fresh out of seminary who hasn't lived long enough to be cynical and hasn't hurt enough to be quiet. He paces back and forth in the hospital room, with his Bible under his arm and his finger punching the air.

"God does all these things to a man—twice, even three times—to turn back his soul from the pit, that the light of life may shine on him."[3]

Job follows his pacing like you'd follow a tennis player, head turning from side to side. What the young man says isn't bad theology, but it isn't much comfort, either. Job steadily tunes him out and slides lower and lower under the covers. His head hurts. His eyes burn. His legs ache. And he can't stomach any more hollow homilies.

Yet his question still hasn't been answered:

"God, why is this happening to me?"

So God speaks.

Out of the thunder, he speaks. Out of the sky, he speaks. For all of us who would put ditto marks under Job's question and sign our names to it, he speaks.

- For the father who holds a rose taken off his son's coffin, he speaks.

- For the wife who holds the flag taken off her husband's casket, he speaks.

- For the couple with the barren womb and the fervent prayers, he speaks.

- For any person who has tried to see God through shattered glass, he speaks.

- For those of us who have dared to say, "If God is God, then . . . ," God speaks.

He speaks out of the storm and into the storm, for that is where Job is. That is where God is best heard.

God's voice thunders in the room. Elihu sits down. Job sits up. And the two will never be the same again.

"Who is this that darkens my counsel with words without knowledge?"[4]

Job doesn't respond.

"Brace yourself like a man; I will question you, and you shall answer me."[5]

"Where were you when I laid the foundations of the earth? Tell me, if you know so much."[6]

One question would have been enough for Job, but it isn't enough for God.

"Do you know how its dimensions were determined and who did the surveying?" God asks. "What supports its foundations, and who laid its cornerstone, as the morning stars sang together and all the angels shouted for joy?"[7]

Questions rush forth. They pour like sheets of rain out of the clouds. They splatter in the chambers of Job's heart with a wildness and a beauty and a terror that leave every Job who has ever lived drenched and speechless, watching the Master redefine who is who in the universe.

> Have you ever once commanded the morning to appear, and caused the dawn to rise in the east? Have you ever told the daylight to spread to the ends of the earth, to end the night's wickedness?[8]

God's questions aren't intended to teach; they are intended to stun. They aren't intended to enlighten; they are intended to awaken. They aren't intended to stir the mind; they are intended to bend the knees.

> Has the location of the gates of Death been revealed to you? Do you realize the extent of the earth? Tell me about it if you know! Where does the light come from, and how do you get there? Or tell me about the darkness. Where does it come from? Can you find its boundaries, or go to its source? But of course you know all this! For you were born before it was all created, and you are so very experienced![9]

Finally Job's feeble hand lifts, and God stops long enough for him to respond. "I am nothing—how could I ever find the answers? I lay my hand upon my mouth in silence. I have said too much already."[10]

God's message has connected:

- Job is a peasant, telling the King how to run the kingdom.
- Job is an illiterate, telling e. e. cummings to capitalize his personal pronouns.
- Job is the bat boy, telling Babe Ruth to change his batting stance.
- Job is the clay, telling the potter not to press so hard.

"I owe no one anything," God declares in the crescendo of the wind. "Everything under the heaven is mine."[11]

Job couldn't argue. God owes no one anything. No explanations. No excuses. No help. God has no debt, no outstanding balance, no favors to return. God owes no man anything.

Which makes the fact that he gave us everything even more astounding.

How you interpret this holy presentation is key. You can interpret God's hammering speech as a divine "in-your-face" tirade if you want. You can use the list of unanswerable questions to prove that God is harsh, cruel, and distant. You can use the Book of Job as evidence that God gives us questions and no answers. But to do so, you need some scissors. To do so, you need to cut out the rest of the Book of Job.

For that is not how Job heard it. All his life, Job had been a good man. All his life, he had believed in God. All his life, he had discussed God, had notions about him, and had prayed to him.

But in the storm Job sees him!

He sees Hope. Lover. Destroyer. Giver. Taker. Dreamer. Deliverer.

Job sees the tender anger of a God whose unending love is often received with peculiar mistrust. Job stands as a blade of grass against the consuming fire of God's splendor. Job's demands melt like wax as God pulls back the curtain and heaven's light falls uneclipsed across the earth.

Job sees God.

God could turn away at this point. The gavel has been slammed, the verdict has been rendered. The Eternal Judge has spoken.

Ah, but God is not angry with Job. Firm? Yes. Direct? No doubt. Clear and convincing? Absolutely. But angry? No.

God is never irritated by the candle of an honest seeker.

If you underline any passage in the Book of Job, underline this one: "I had heard about you before, but now I have seen you."[12]

Job sees God—and that is enough.

But it isn't enough for God.

The years to come find Job once again sitting behind his mahogany desk with health restored and profits up. His lap is once again full of children and grandchildren and great-grandchildren—for four generations!

If Job ever wonders why God doesn't bring back the children he had taken away, he doesn't ask. Maybe he doesn't ask because he knows that his children could never be happier than they are in the presence of this One he has seen so briefly.

Something tells me that Job would do it all again, if that's what it took to hear God's voice and stand in the Presence. Even if God left him with his bedsores and bills, Job would do it again.

For God gave Job more than Job ever dreamed. God gave Job Himself.

18

PILGRIM
PONDERINGS

After six days Jesus took with him Peter, James and John the brother of James, and led them up a high mountain by themselves. There he was transfigured before them. His face shone like the sun, and his clothes became as white as the light. Just then there appeared before them Moses and Elijah, talking with Jesus.

Peter said to Jesus, "Lord, it is good for us to be here. If you wish, I will put up three shelters—one for you, one for Moses, and one for Elijah." While he was still speaking, a bright cloud enveloped them, and a voice from the cloud said, "This is my Son, whom I love; with him I am well pleased. Listen to him!"[1]

---

*T*HE YOUNG WOMAN, EIGHT MONTHS heavy with child, waddles into her mother's house. Flops onto the sofa. Kicks off her tennis shoes. Props her puffy feet on the coffee table. And groans, "I don't think I can make it."

Wise from the years, the mother picks up a photo album and sits down beside her daughter. She opens the album to photos of her children in diapers and ankle-high walking shoes. Slowly the two turn the memory-filled pages. They smile at the kids blowing out candles and sitting in front of Christmas trees.

As the mother sees yesterday, the daughter sees tomorrow.

And, for just a moment, the daughter is changed. The *here and now* becomes the *there and then*. Her child is born. She sees the first stumbling step taken. She hears the first word, discernible only to Mommy. She places the shiny, black, patent-leather shoes on the stockinged feet and Karo-syrups a ribbon on the nearly bald but ever-so-precious head.

A transformation occurs. The pain in her back is now overshadowed by the joy approaching. The hand that had rubbed the neck now rests on her stomach. For the first time that day, she smiles.

———————————————————

A snowstorm in Chicago. Stranded at O'Hare. No place to sit in the lobby, so he walks to the coffee shop. No place to sit in the coffee shop, so he buys a cup to go, wanders back to the lobby, sits on his briefcase, and drapes his overcoat over his lap.

He looks at his watch. *Should I go to a hotel for the night?* he wonders. *It's nearly midnight! I should be halfway home by now. Who knows when I'll be able to leave?*

He sighs, leans back against a wall, and waits. He unbuttons his collar. Loosens his tie. Rubs his whiskered neck. His thoughts drift back over the week. Many calls made. Few orders placed. Blame it on the economy. Blame it on the system. Blame it on God. But blame doesn't put money in the bank.

There's an executive lobby across the hall with empty couches, snacks, and a television. In better times, he could afford the membership; now that money goes toward college tuition and braces for the kids.

A flight is announced. He pulls his boarding pass out of his overcoat breast pocket. The flight isn't his. He sticks the pass back into the coat that stretches across his lap. A leather calendar tumbles out. He picks it up and, for no real reason, looks inside.

There, amidst taxi receipts and credit cards, is a laminated photo of a family—his family. Teenage daughter with eyes like her mom's and the metallic smile. College-bound son wearing a necktie and blue jeans, mid-step between adolescence and adulthood. And his wife. My, has it been twenty-five years? Take away a few wrinkles and pounds, and he can see her in the white gown again.

For just a moment, he is home. The television is off. The kids are in bed. The dog is outside. The doors are locked. The fire is golden. His wife is asleep on the couch. For just a moment, the world of O'Hare, hotels, and sales calls are a world away. He is where it's all worthwhile. He is home.

Someone taps him on the shoulder, and he hears a kind voice. "Is that your flight?" He looks up into the half-empty lobby . . . sees the line forming at the gate . . . and smiles.

"Yeah," the salesman says, standing. "It's my flight home."

Four people snake their way up the mountain. The trip has been long; the hour is late. A level place on the hillside is reached, and they sit down. They're tired. Their muscles hurt. The grayness of twilight settles over them like a soft cloth.

The quartet of pilgrims longs to sleep, but only three do.

The fourth sits in the shadows. Legs crossed. Face skyward. The stars wink at their Maker. Winds waft over the shoulders of their Designer, cooling his neck. He slips off his sandals and rubs his sore feet and reflects on the wildness of it all.

A God with sore legs? Holiness with hunger? Divinity with thirst? A World Maker made weary by his world?

His thoughts drift homeward. *Nazareth. How good it would be to be home again.*

The memories surface so easily. Sawdust-covered workbench. Friends stopping to talk. Dinner-table laughter. Wrestling with his brothers. The synagogue. The house. The home.

What I'd give to go home.

But Nazareth would never be home again. They tried to kill him the last time he was there. Neighbors, friends, teachers, schoolmates . . . they squeezed the stones intended for his body. Even his brothers and sisters considered him insane. They wanted to hide him, to put him away. They were ashamed to be known as his family.

No, Nazareth can never be home again.

What about Galilee? He could go back to Galilee. There the crowds listened. There the people followed. But he shook his head. *As long as I made them bread . . . As long as I said what they wanted to hear . . .* He remembered the crowds as they turned away. He heard their jeering. He felt their rejection.

No, I can never go back to Galilee.

He thinks of Jerusalem. She offers no comfort. He knows what she will do to him. A foreboding pain stabs his wrists. He winces at the slicing of his brow. He sees the world around him growing darker, darker . . . *My God!* a premonition inside him cries.

He shakes his head and breathes a staggered breath. His thoughts return to the present.

He plucks a shoot of grass, puts it into his mouth, and sits in the shadow of his fear.

He looks at his followers, as asleep as they are naive. They have no idea. They just can't understand. He speaks of suffering; they think of conquering. He speaks of sacrifice; they think of celebration. He's an artist painting for the color-blind. He's a singer singing for the deaf. They nod their heads and clap their hands. They think they see. They think they hear. But they don't.

They can't see. No one sees.

Part of him knew it would be like this. And part of him never knew it would be so bad.

Part of him wonders, *Would it be so bad to give up?* After all, there might be a better era. There will be other generations . . . other people.

He has given his best, and what does he have? A ragged band of good-hearted but hardheaded followers who are destined to fall face-flat over promises they can't keep. He puts his face into his cupped hands and closes his eyes and prays. It's all he knows to do.

Sounds familiar, doesn't it, seeker? Was it so long ago that you were on a quest for truth—Galahad in search of the grail? But the forest of questions was deep. The thicket of perplexities thick. It was easier to say nothing than to ask why. So you stopped.

Sounds familiar, doesn't it, dreamer? You wanted so badly to change the world. Sure the mountain was high, but you were brave. Then the winds came. Sharp rocks of reality cut your feet, breaking your stride . . . breaking your heart. And you found that the role of the cynic was less costly than the role of the dreamer. So you sat down.

You need to know something: Jesus sat down, too.

Oh, sure, there were moments when he stood tall. There were hours of splendor. There were dynamic days during which the lepers leapt and the dead came alive and the people worshiped. Those days came.

But his plateaus of popularity were gorged by canyons of isolation.

And on this day, the crevasse is deep. Steep walls mock an easy escape. Rocky abutments imprison his vision. His strength has reached its solstice.

He sits down and puts a tear-streaked face into cupped palms and prays. It's all he can do.

And when his Father sees him, it's all his Father can take.

From another dimension, a light comes. It enters the solitary figure and glows.

"As he was praying," Luke writes, "the appearance of his face changed, and his clothes became as bright as a flash of lightning."[2]

Jesus implodes with glory. For just a moment, he is transfigured; a roaring radiance pours from him. He becomes as he was before he came. For one brief, shining moment, the burden of his humanity is lifted. "Decarnation" occurs. He is elevated above earth's horizon and escorted into the eternal. He is home again. Familiar sounds surround him. Those who understand welcome him. And the One who sent him . . . holds him.

Dusty trails and hard hearts are, literally, a world away.

The One who felt weary is reminded: the weariness will soon pass.

Moses and Elijah, aflame with eternal robes, stand beside their King. When Jesus was preparing himself in the desert for the work of life, angels came to encourage him. Now, on the mountain, preparing himself for the work of death, Moses and Elijah draw near: Moses, the Lawgiver whose grave no man knew; Elijah, the prophet who side-stepped death in a fiery chariot.

The One who saw death is reminded: the grave is impotent.

And then, the voice thunders. God inhabits a cloud. It becomes a bonfire, puffy with brilliance. It consumes the shadows. It transforms the nightened mountain into a shining monument. And from the belly of the cloud, the Father speaks:

"This is my Son, whom I love; with him I am well pleased. Listen to him!"[3]

The One who had despaired is affirmed. "What people think doesn't matter," God shouts. "What I think does. And I'm proud."

By now Jesus is standing. By now the apostles are awake.

For Peter, James, and John, the scene is bizarre: dazzling white clouds, a voice from the sky, living images from the past. But for Jesus, it is a view of home. A view into yesterday. A glimpse into tomorrow.

He is the mother—pregnant with new life, dreading the pains of childbirth.

He is the father—on a long journey in a cold place.

He is—as they were, as we are—given a glimpse of home.

And tomorrow's dream becomes today's courage.

19

OUR STORM WAS HIS PATH

S UPPOSE ONE OF JESUS' DISCIPLES *kept a journal. And suppose that disciple made an entry in the journal on the morning after the storm. And suppose we discovered that journal. Here is how it would read . . . I suppose.*

Only minutes before, chaos had erupted.

Oh, how the storm roared. Stars were hidden by a black ceiling. Clouds billowed like smoke. Bolts of lightning were the conductor's baton that cued the kettledrums of thunder to rumble.

And rumble they did. The clouds seemed to rise as a bear on hind legs and growl. The booms shook everything: the heavens, the earth, and—most of all—the sea. It was as if the Sea of Galilee were a bowl in the hands of a dancing giant. From the bowels of the lake the waves came, turning the glassy surface into a mountain range of snow-topped waves. Five, ten, even fifteen feet into the air they mounted, rising and falling like swallows chasing mosquitoes.

In the midst of the sea, our boat bounced. The waves slapped it as easily as children would a ball. Our straining at the oars scarcely budged it. We were at the storm's mercy. The waves lifted us up so high that we felt like we were in midair. Then down into the valley we plunged.

We were a twig in a whirlpool . . . a leaf in the wind. We were helpless.

That's when the light appeared. At first I thought it was a reflection of the moon, a gleam on the surface of the water. But the night held no moon. I looked again. The light was moving toward us, not over the waves but through them. I wasn't the only one who saw it.

"A ghost," someone screamed. Fear of the sea was eclipsed by a new terror. Thoughts raced as the specter drew near. *Was it a figment of our imagination? Was it a vision? Who? How? What was this mystical light that appeared so . . . ?*

A flash of lightning illuminated the sky. For a second I could see its face . . . his face. A second was all I needed.

It was the Master!

He spoke:

"Take courage! It is I. Don't be afraid."[1]

Nothing had changed. The storm still raged. The wind still shrieked. The boat still pitched. The thunder still boomed. The rain still slapped. But in the midst of the tumult, I could hear his voice. Although he was still far away, it was like he was by my side. The night was ferocious, yet he spoke as though the sea were placid and the sky silent.

And, somehow, courage came.

"Lord, if it's you, . . . tell me to come to you on the water."[2]

The voice was Peter's. He wasn't being cocky. He wasn't demanding proof. He was scared. Like me, he knew what this storm could do. He knew that the boat would soon go down. He knew that Jesus was standing up. And he knew where he wanted to be . . . where we all wanted to be.

"Come on," Jesus invited.

So Peter climbed over the side and stepped onto the sea. Before him opened a trail through a forest of waves. He stepped quickly. Water splashed. But he kept going. This path to Jesus was a ribbon of calm. It was peaceful. Serene.

Jesus radiated light at the end of the trail. Smiling.

Peter stepped toward the light like it was his only hope. He was halfway there when we all heard the thunder. It boomed, and he stopped. I saw his head turn. He looked up at the sky. He looked up at the clouds. He felt the wind. And down he went.

Boy did he yell!

A hand came through the water sheets and grabbed Peter. Lightning flashed again, and I could see the face of Jesus. I noticed that his smile was gone. Hurt covered his face. It was like he couldn't believe that we couldn't believe. Danger to us was just a detour to him. I wanted to ask him, "Aren't you afraid, Jesus? Aren't you afraid?"

But I said nothing. Before I knew it, he was in the boat with us.

The sea stilled as silk.

The winds hushed.

A canyon opened in the clouds; soft moonlight fell over the water.

It happened instantaneously. It didn't take the rest of the night. It didn't take an hour. It didn't take a minute. It happened in a blink.

From chaos to calm. From panic to peace. The sky was so suddenly silent that I could hear my heart pounding. I thought I was dreaming. Then I saw the wide eyes of the others and felt my clothing soaked against my skin. This was no dream. I looked at the water. I looked at Peter. I looked at the others. And then I looked at him.

And I did the only thing I could have done. With the stars as my candles and the stilled boat as my altar, I fell at his feet and worshiped.

There are times in a person's life when, even in the midst of them, you know you'll never be the same. Moments that forever serve as journey posts. This was one.

I had never seen Jesus as I saw him then. I had seen him as powerful. I had seen him as wise. I had witnessed his authority and marveled at his abilities. But what I witnessed last night, I know I'll never forget.

I saw God. The God who can't sit still when the storm is too strong. The God who lets me get frightened enough to need him and then comes close enough for me to see him. The God who uses my storms as his path to come to me.

I saw God. It took a storm for me to see him. But I saw him. And I'll never be the same.

20

THEY'D
DO
IT
AGAIN

*T*HEY'D DO IT AGAIN. I'm confident they would. The disciples would get into the same boat and ride through the same storm. They'd do it again in a heartbeat. Why?

Because through the storm they saw the Savior.

Read this verse: "Then those who were in the boat worshiped him, saying, 'Truly you are the Son of God.'"[1]

After the storm, they worshiped him. They had never, as a group, done that before. Never. Check it out. Open your Bible. Search for a time when the disciples corporately praised him.

You won't find it.

You won't find them worshiping when he heals the leper. Forgives the adulteress. Preaches to the masses. They were willing to follow. Willing to leave family. Willing to cast out demons. Willing to be in the army.

But only after the incident on the sea did they worship him. Why?

Simple. This time, they were the ones who were saved. This time, their necks were removed from the noose. Their bodies were plucked from the deep. One minute, they were dangling over the edge of the abyss, staring into the throat of the slack-jawed canyon. The next, they were bottomplopped and wide-eyed on the deck of a still boat on a placid sea.

So they worshiped. They did the only thing that they could do when their death sentence was stayed at the eleventh hour: They looked to the Eternal Governor who gave the pardon and thanked him.

─────────────────────────

When you recognize God as Creator, you will admire him. When you recognize his wisdom, you will learn from him. When you discover his strength, you will rely on him. But only when he saves you will you worship him.

It's a "before and after" scenario. Before your rescue, you could easily keep God at a distance. Comfortably dismissed. Neatly shelved. Sure he was important, but so was your career. Your status. Your salary. He was high on your priority list, but he shared the spot with others.

Then came the storm . . . the rage . . . the fight . . . the ripped moorings . . . the starless night. Despair fell like a fog; your bearings were gone. In your heart, you knew there was no exit.

Turn to your career for help? Only if you want to hide from the storm . . . not escape it. Lean on your status for strength? A storm isn't impressed with your title. Rely on your salary for rescue? Many try . . . many fail.

Suddenly you are left with one option: God.

And when you ask . . . genuinely ask . . . he will come.

And from that moment on, he is not just a deity to admire, a teacher to observe, or a master to obey. He is the Savior. The Savior to be worshiped.

That's why I'm convinced that the disciples would do it again. They'd endure the storm another night . . . a thousand other nights . . . if that's what it took.

A season of suffering is a small price to pay for a clear view of God.

STING
OF
FAILURE

21

CASTLES
OF
SORROW

S ARAH WAS RICH. SHE HAD inherited twenty million dollars. Plus she had an additional income of one thousand dollars a day.

That's a lot of money any day, but it was immense in the late 1800s.

Sarah was well known. She was the belle of New Haven, Connecticut. No social event was complete without her presence. No one hosted a party without inviting her.

Sarah was powerful. Her name and money would open almost any door in America. Colleges wanted her donations. Politicians clamored for her support. Organizations sought her endorsement.

Sarah was rich. Well known. Powerful. And miserable.

Her only daughter had died at five weeks of age. Then her husband had passed away. She was left alone with her name, her money, her memories, . . . and her guilt.

It was her guilt that caused her to move west. A passion for penance drove her to San Jose, California. Her yesterdays imprisoned her todays, and she yearned for freedom.

She bought an eight-room farmhouse plus one hundred sixty adjoining acres. She hired sixteen carpenters and put them to work. For the next thirty-eight years, craftsmen labored every day, twenty-four hours a day, to build a mansion.

Observers were intrigued by the project. Sarah's instructions were more than eccentric . . . they were eerie.

The design had a macabre touch. Each window was to have thirteen panes, each wall thirteen panels, each closet thirteen hooks, and each chandelier thirteen globes.

The floor plan was ghoulish. Corridors snaked randomly, some leading nowhere. One door opened to a blank wall, another to a fifty-foot drop. One set of stairs led to a ceiling that had no door. Trapdoors. Secret passageways. Tunnels. This was no retirement home for Sarah's future; it was a castle for her past.

The making of this mysterious mansion only ended when Sarah died. The completed estate sprawled over six acres and had six kitchens, thirteen bathrooms, forty stairways, forty-seven fireplaces, fifty-two skylights, four hundred sixty-seven doors, ten thousand windows, one hundred sixty rooms, and a bell tower.

Why did Sarah want such a castle? Didn't she live alone? "Well, sort of," those acquainted with her story might answer. "There were the visitors . . ."

And the visitors came each night.

Legend has it that every evening at midnight, a servant would pass through the secret labyrinth that led to the bell tower. He would ring the bell . . . to summon the spirits. Sarah would then enter the "blue room," a room reserved for her and her nocturnal guests. Together they would linger until 2:00 A.M., when the bell would be rung again. Sarah would return to her quarters; the ghosts would return to their graves.

Who comprised this legion of phantoms?

Indians and soldiers killed on the U.S. frontier. They had all been killed by bullets from the most popular rifle in America—the Winchester. What had brought millions of dollars to Sarah Winchester had brought death to them.

So she spent her remaining years in a castle of regret, providing a home for the dead.

You can see this poltergeist place in San Jose, if you wish. You can tour its halls and see its remains.

But to see what unresolved guilt can do to a human being, you don't have to go to the Winchester mansion. Lives imprisoned by yesterday's guilt are in your own city. Hearts haunted by failure are in your own neighborhood. People plagued by pitfalls are just down the street . . . or just down the hall.

There is, wrote Paul, a "worldly sorrow" that "brings death."[1] A guilt that kills. A sorrow that's fatal. A venomous regret that's deadly.

How many Sarah Winchesters do you know? How far do you have to go to find a soul haunted by ghosts of the past? Maybe not very far.

Maybe Sarah's story is your story.

If so, I'm especially grateful that this book has made its way into your hands. This final section has been written with you in mind. In these final chapters, I have assembled thoughts on failure and forgiveness.

For in the twilight hours during the storm's black night, there is a story of grace.

It is the story of Peter: recognizing the Master's voice . . . seeing the Master's face . . . scrambling to safety from the storm.

It is also another story of Peter: hearing the winds . . . seeing the torrent . . . sinking into the water.

But most of all, it is the story of Jesus. It is the story of God extending his hand during stormy seas. It is the answer to the question every person asks: "What does God do when I fail?"

The answers to guilt's questions are not found in a new house.

The answer is found in the foundation of the one you have.

22

FEAR
THAT
BECOMES
FAITH

"They saw Jesus . . . walking on the water; and they were terrified."[1]

*F*AITH IS OFTEN the child of fear.
Fear propelled Peter out of the boat. He'd ridden these waves before. He knew what these storms could do. He'd heard the stories. He'd seen the wreckage. He knew the widows. He knew the storm could kill. And he wanted out.

All night he wanted out. For nine hours he'd tugged on sails, wrestled with oars, and searched every shadow on the horizon for hope. He was soaked to the soul and bone weary of the wind's banshee wail.

Look into Peter's eyes and you won't see a man of conviction. Search his face and you won't find a gutsy grimace. Later on, you will. You'll see his courage in the garden. You'll witness his devotion at Pentecost. You'll behold his faith in his epistles.

But not tonight. Look into his eyes tonight and see fear—a suffocating, heart-racing fear of a man who has no way out.

But out of this fear would be born an act of faith, for faith is often the child of fear.

"The fear of the Lord is the beginning of wisdom,"[2] wrote the wise man.

Peter could have been his sermon illustration.

r had seen Jesus walking on the water during a
eful day, do you think that he would have walked
n?

Nor do I.

Had the lake been carpet smooth and the journey pleasant, do you think that Peter would have begged Jesus to take him on a stroll across the top of the water? Doubtful.

But give a man a choice between sure death and a crazy chance, and he'll take the chance . . . every time.

Great acts of faith are seldom born out of calm calculation.

It wasn't logic that caused Moses to raise his staff on the bank of the Red Sea.[3]

It wasn't medical research that convinced Naaman to dip seven times in the river.[4]

It wasn't common sense that caused Paul to abandon the Law and embrace grace.[5]

And it wasn't a confident committee that prayed in a small room in Jerusalem for Peter's release from prison.[6] It was a fearful, desperate, band of backed-into-a-corner believers. It was a church with no options. A congregation of have-nots pleading for help.

And never were they stronger.

At the beginning of every act of faith, there is often a seed of fear.

Biographies of bold disciples begin with chapters of honest terror. Fear of death. Fear of failure. Fear of loneliness. Fear of a wasted life. Fear of failing to know God.

Faith begins when you see God on the mountain and you are in the valley and you know that you're too weak to make the climb. You see what you need . . . you see what you have . . . and what you have isn't enough to accomplish anything.

Peter had given it his best. But his best wasn't enough.

Moses had a sea in front and an enemy behind. The Israelites could swim or they could fight. But neither option was enough.

Naaman had tried the cures and consulted the soothsayers. Traveling a long distance to plunge into a muddy river made little sense when there were clean ones in his backyard. But what option did he have?

Paul had mastered the Law. He had mastered the system. But one glimpse of God convinced him that sacrifices and symbols were not enough.

The Jerusalem church knew that they had no hope of getting Peter out of prison. They had Christians who would fight, but too few. They had clout, but too little. They didn't need muscle. They needed a miracle.

So does Peter. He is aware of two facts: He is going down, and Jesus is staying up. He knows where he would rather be.

There's nothing wrong with this response. Faith that begins with fear will end up nearer the Father.

I went to West Texas some time back to speak at the funeral of a godly, family friend. He had raised five children. One son, Paul, told a story about his earliest memory of his father.

It was spring in West Texas—tornado season. Paul was only three or four years old at the time, but he remembers vividly the day that a tornado hit their small town.

His father hustled the kids indoors and had them lie on the floor while he laid a mattress over them. But his father didn't climb under the protection. Paul remembers peeking out from under the mattress and seeing him standing by an open window, watching the funnel cloud twist and churn across the prairie.

When Paul saw his father, he knew where he wanted to be. He struggled out of his mother's arms, crawled out from under the mattress, and ran to wrap his arms around his dad's leg.

"Something told me," Paul said, "that the safest place to stand in a storm was next to my father."

Something told Peter the same thing.

"Lord, if it's you," Peter says, "tell me to come to you on the water."[7]

Peter is not testing Jesus; he is pleading with Jesus. Stepping onto a stormy sea is not a move of logic; it is a move of desperation.

Peter grabs the edge of the boat. Throws out a leg . . . follows with the other. Several steps are taken. It's as if an invisible ridge of rocks runs beneath his feet. At the end of the ridge is the glowing face of a never-say-die friend.

We do the same, don't we? We come to Christ in an hour of deep need. We abandon the boat of good works. We realize, like Moses, that human strength won't save us. So we look to God in desperation. We realize, like Paul, that all the good works in the world are puny when laid before the Perfect One. We realize, like Peter, that spanning the gap between us and Jesus is a feat too great for our feet.

So we beg for help. Hear his voice. And step out in fear, hoping that our little faith will be enough.

Faith is not born at the negotiating table where we barter our gifts in exchange for God's goodness. Faith is not an award given to the most learned. It's not a prize given to the most disciplined. It's not a title bequeathed to the most religious.

Faith is a desperate dive out of the sinking boat of human effort and a prayer that God will be there to pull us out of the water. Paul wrote about this kind of faith in the letter to the Ephesians:

"For it is by grace you have been saved, through faith—and this not from yourselves, it is the gift of God—not by works, so that no one can boast."[8]

Paul is clear. The supreme force in salvation is God's grace. Not our works. Not our talents. Not our feelings. Not our strength.

Salvation is God's sudden, calming presence during the stormy seas of our lives. We hear his voice; we take the step.

We, like Paul, are aware of two things: We are great sinners and we need a great Savior.

We, like Peter, are aware of two facts: We are going down and God is standing up. So we scramble out. We leave behind the *Titanic* of self-righteousness and stand on the solid path of God's grace.

And, surprisingly, we are able to walk on water. Death is disarmed. Failures are forgivable. Life has real purpose. And God is not only within sight, he is within reach.

With precious, wobbly steps, we draw closer to him. For a season of surprising strength, we stand upon his promises. It doesn't make sense that we are able to do this. We don't claim to be worthy of such an incredible gift. When people ask how in the world we can keep our balance during such stormy times, we don't boast. We don't brag. We point unabashedly to the One who makes it possible. Our eyes are on him.

"Nothing in my hand I bring; Simply to Thy cross I cling,"[9] we sing.

"Dressed in His righteousness alone, Faultless to stand before the throne,"[10] we declare.

" 'Twas grace that taught my heart to fear, And grace my fears relieved,"[11] we explain.

Some of us, unlike Peter, never look back.

Others of us, like Peter, feel the wind and are afraid.[12]

Maybe we face the wind of pride: "I'm not such a bad sinner after all. Look at what I can do."

Perhaps we face the wind of legalism: "I know that Jesus is doing part of this, but I have to do the rest."

Most of us, though, face the wind of doubt: "I'm too bad for God to treat me this well. I don't deserve such a rescue."

And downward we plunge. Heavied by mortality's mortar, we sink. Gulping and thrashing, we fall into a dark, wet world. We open our eyes and see only blackness. We try to breathe, and no air comes. We kick and fight our way back to the surface.

With our heads barely above the water, we have to make a decision.

The prideful ask: "Do we 'save face' and drown in pride? Or do we scream for help and take God's hand?"

The legalists ask: "Do we sink under the lead-heavy weight of the Law? Or do we abandon the codes and beg for grace?"

The doubters ask: "Do we nurture doubt by mumbling, 'I've really let him down this time?' Or do we hope that the same Christ who called us out of the boat will call us out of the sea?"

We know Peter's choice.

"[As he was] beginning to sink, [he] cried out, 'Lord, save me!'"[13]

"Immediately Jesus reached out his hand and caught him."[14]

———

We also know the choice of another sailor in another storm.

Although separated by seventeen centuries, this sailor and Peter are drawn together by several striking similarities:

- Both made their living on the sea.
- Both met their Savior after a nine-hour battle in a storm.
- Both met the Father in fear and then followed him in faith.
- Both walked away from their boats and became preachers of the Truth.

You know the story of Peter, the first sailor. Let me tell you about the second, whose name was John.

He had served on the seas since he was eleven years old. His father, an English shipmaster in the Mediterranean, took him aboard and trained him well for a life in the Royal Navy.

Yet what John gained in experience, he lacked in discipline. He mocked authority. Ran with the wrong crowd. Indulged in the sinful ways of a sailor. Although his training would have qualified him to serve as an officer, his behavior caused him to be flogged and demoted.

In his early twenties, he made his way to Africa, where he became intrigued with the lucrative slave trade. At age twenty-one, he made his living on the *Greyhound,* a slave ship crossing the Atlantic Ocean.

John ridiculed the moral and poked fun at the religious. He even made jokes about a book that would eventually help reshape his life: *The Imitation of Christ.* In fact, he was degrading that book a few hours before his ship sailed into an angry storm.

That night the waves pummeled the *Greyhound,* spinning the ship one minute on the top of a wave. Plunging her the next into a watery valley.

John awakened to find his cabin filled with water. A side of the *Greyhound* had collapsed. Ordinarily such damage would have sent a ship to the bottom in a matter of minutes. The *Greyhound,* however, was carrying buoyant cargo and remained afloat.

John worked at the pumps all night. For nine hours, he and the other sailors struggled to keep the ship from sinking. But he knew that it was a losing cause. Finally, when his hopes were more battered than the vessel, he threw himself on the saltwater-soaked deck and pleaded, "If this will not do, then Lord have mercy on us all."

John didn't deserve mercy, but he received it. The *Greyhound* and her crew survived.

John never forgot God's mercy shown on that tempestuous day in the roaring Atlantic. He returned to England where he became a prolific composer. You've sung his songs, like this one:

> Amazing grace! how sweet the sound,
> That saved a wretch like me!
> I once was lost, but now am found,
> was blind, but now I see.[15]

This slave-trader-turned-songwriter was John Newton.

Along with his hymn writing, he also became a power-ful pulpiteer. For nearly fifty years, he filled pulpits and churches with the story of the Savior who meets you and me in the storm.

A year or two before his death, people urged him to give up preaching because of his failing sight. "What!" he ex-plained. "Shall the old African blasphemer stop while he can yet speak?"

He wouldn't stop. He couldn't stop. What had begun as a prayer of fear resulted in a lifetime of faith. During his last years, someone asked him about his health. He confessed that his powers were failing. "My memory is al-most gone," he said, "but I remember two things: I am a great sinner, and Jesus is a great Savior."

What more do you and I need to remember?

———————————

Two sailors and two seas. Two vessels in two storms. Two prayers of fear and two lives of faith. Uniting them is one Savior—one God who'll walk through hell or high water to extend a helping hand to a child who cries for help.

23

WHY
GOD
SMILES

I HAVE A SKETCH OF JESUS LAUGHING. It hangs on the wall across from my desk.

It's quite a drawing. His head is back. His mouth is open. His eyes are sparkling. He isn't just grinning. He isn't just chuckling. He's roaring. He hasn't heard or seen one like that in quite a while. He's having trouble catching his breath.

It was given to me by an Episcopal priest who carries cigars in his pocket and collects portraits of Jesus smiling. "I give them to anyone who might be inclined to take God too seriously," he explained as he handed me the gift.

He pegged me well.

I'm not one who easily envisions a smiling God. A weeping God, yes. An angry God, OK. A mighty God, you bet. But a chuckling God? It seems too . . . too . . . too unlike what God should do—and be. Which just shows how much I know—or don't know—about God.

What do I think he was doing when he stretched the neck of the giraffe? An exercise in engineering? What do I think he had in mind when he told the ostrich where to put his head? Spelunking? What do I think he was doing when he designed the mating call of an ape? Or the eight legs of the octopus? And what do I envision on his face when he saw Adam's first glance at Eve? A yawn?

Hardly.

As my vision improves and I'm able to read without my stained glasses, I'm seeing that a sense of humor is perhaps the only way God has put up with us for so long.

Is that him with a smile as Moses does a double take at the burning bush that speaks?

Is he smiling again as Jonah lands on the beach, dripping gastric juices and smelling like whale breath?

Is that a twinkle in his eye as he watches the disciples feed thousands with one boy's lunch?

Do you think that his face is deadpan as he speaks about the man with a two-by-four in his eye who points out a speck in a friend's eye?

Can you honestly imagine Jesus bouncing children on his knee with a somber face?

No, I think that Jesus smiled. I think that he smiled a bit at people and a lot with people.

Let me explain with an example.

We don't know a thing about her. We don't know her name . . . her background . . . her looks . . . her hometown. She came from nowhere and went nowhere. She disappeared the same way that she appeared, like a puff of smoke.

But what a delightful puff she was.

The disciples, during two years of training, hadn't done what she did in a few moments of conversing. She impressed God with her faith. The disciples' hearts may have been good. Their desire may have been sincere. But their faith didn't turn God's head.

Hers did. For all we don't know about her, we do know one remarkable truth: She impressed God with her faith. After that, anything else she ever did was insignificant.

"Woman, you have great faith!"[1] Jesus stated.

Some statement. Especially when you consider God said it. The God who can put a handful of galaxies into his palm. The One who creates Everests as a hobby. The One who paints rainbows without a canvas. The One who can measure the thickness of mosquito wings with one hand and level a mountain with the other.

One would think that the Creator would not be easily impressed. But something about this woman brought a sparkle to his eyes and . . . most likely . . . a smile to his face.

Matthew called her a "Canaanite woman" and, in doing so, called strikes one and two. Strike one? A Canaanite. An outsider. A foreigner. An apple in a family tree of oranges. Strike two? A woman. Might as well have been a junkyard dog. She lived in a culture that had little respect for women outside the bedroom and kitchen.

But she met the Teacher, who had plenty of respect for her.

Oh, it doesn't appear that way. In fact, the dialogue between the two seems harsh. It's not an easy passage to understand unless you're willing to concede that Jesus knew how to smile. If you have trouble with the sketch of the smiling Jesus hanging in my office, you'll have trouble with this story. But if you don't, if the thought of God smiling brings you a bit of relief, then you'll like the next few paragraphs.

Here's my interpretation.

The woman is desperate. Her daughter is demon possessed.

The Canaanite woman has no right to ask anything of Jesus. She is not a Jew. She is not a disciple. She offers no money for the ministry. She makes no promises to devote herself to missionary service. You get the impression that she knows as well as anybody that Jesus doesn't owe her anything, and she is asking him for everything. But that doesn't slow her down. She persists in her plea.

"Have mercy on me!"[2]

Matthew notes that Jesus says nothing at first. Nothing. He doesn't open his mouth. Why?

To test her? Most commentators suggest this. Maybe, they say, he is waiting to see how serious she is about her plea. My dad used to make me wait a week from the day I asked him for something to the day he gave me his answer. Most of the time, I forgot that I ever made the request. Time has a way of separating whims from needs. Is Jesus doing that?

I have another opinion. I think that he was admiring her. I think that it did his heart good to see some spunky faith for a change. I think that it refreshed him to see someone asking him to do the very thing he came to do—give great gifts to unworthy children.

How strange that we don't allow him to do it more often for us.

Perhaps the most amazing response to God's gift is our reluctance to accept it. We want it. But on our terms. For some odd reason, we feel better if we earn it. So we create religious hoops and hop through them—making God a trainer, us his pets, and religion a circus.

The Canaanite woman knew better. She had no re-sume. She claimed no heritage. She had no earned degrees. She knew only two things: Her daughter was weak, and Jesus was strong.

The disciples are annoyed. As Jesus sits in silence, they grow more smug. "Send her away," they demand. The spotlight is put on Jesus. He looks at the disciples, then looks at the woman. And what follows is one of the most intriguing dialogues in the New Testament.

"I was sent only to the lost sheep of Israel,"[3] he says.

"Lord, help me!"[4]

"It is not right to take the children's bread and toss it to their dogs,"[5] he answers.

"But even the dogs eat the crumbs that fall from their masters' table,"[6] she responds.

Is Jesus being rude? Is he worn-out? Is he frustrated? Is he calling this woman a dog? How do we explain this dialogue?

Bible commentaries give us three options.

Some say that Jesus was trapped. He could not help the woman because he had been sent first to the lost sheep of Israel. Neat theory, but full of problems. One is the Samaritan woman. Another is the centurion. Jesus had already helped Gentiles and stayed faithful to the focus of his mission. So why couldn't he do it now?

Others think that Jesus was rude. Who can blame him? He was tired. It had been a long trip. The disciples were coming along pretty slowly. And this request was the straw that broke the camel's back.

Like that explanation? I don't either. The one who had had compassion on the five thousand men . . . who had wept over the city of Jerusalem . . . who had come to seek and save ones like this one . . . would not snap so abruptly at such a needy woman.

The most popular theory is that he was testing her . . . again. Just to be sure that she was serious about her request. Just to make sure that her faith was real.

But by insinuating that she was a dog?

I don't think Jesus would do that, either. Let me suggest another alternative.

Could it be that Jesus' tongue is poking his cheek? Could it be that he and the woman are engaging in satirical banter? Is it wry exchange in which God's unlimited grace is being highlighted? Could Jesus be so delighted to have found one who is not bartering with a religious system or proud of a heritage that he can't resist a bit of satire?

He knows he can heal her daughter. He knows he isn't bound by a plan. He knows her heart is good. So he decides to engage in a humorous moment with a faithful woman. In essence, here's what they said:

"Now, you know that God only cares about Jews," he says smiling.

And when she catches on, she volleys back, "But your bread is so precious, I'll be happy to eat the crumbs."

In a spirit of exuberance, he bursts out, "Never have I seen such faith! Your daughter is healed."

This story does not portray a contemptuous God. It portrays a willing One who delights in a sincere seeker.

Aren't you glad he does?

The story is told about the time Napoleon's steed got away from him. An alert private jumped on his own horse and chased down the general's horse. When he presented the reins of the animal to Napoleon, the ruler took them, smiled at this willing private, and said, "Thank you, Captain."

The soldier's eyes widened at what he had heard. He then straightened. Saluted. And snapped, "Thank you, sir!"

He immediately went to the barracks. Got his bags. Moved into the officers' quarters. Took his old uniform to the quartermaster and exchanged it for that of a captain. By the general's word, he had become a private-turned-commissioned officer. He didn't argue. He didn't shrug. He didn't doubt. He knew that the one who had the power to do it had done it. And he accepted that.

If only we would do the same. If only we would have the faith of the private and the trust of the Canaanite woman. If only, when God smiles and says we are saved, we'd salute him, thank him, and live like those who have just received a gift from the commander in chief.

We seldom do that, though. We prefer to get salvation the old-fashioned way: We earn it. To accept grace is to admit failure, a step we are hesitant to take. We opt to impress God with how good we are rather than confessing how great he is. We dizzy ourselves with doctrine. Burden ourselves with rules. Think that God will smile on our efforts.

He doesn't.

God's smile is not for the healthy hiker who boasts that he made the journey alone. It is, instead, for the crippled leper who begs God for a back on which to ride.

Such were the woman's words. She knew that her request was ludicrous. But she also knew that Jesus was Lord.

Daniel's words could have been hers: "We do not make requests of you because we are righteous, but because of your great mercy."[7]

She came, banking on the hope that Jesus would answer her prayer based on his goodness and not her worthiness.

And he did. With a smile.

When I think about the prayers God has answered for me in spite of the life I've lived, I think he must be smiling still.

So I think I'll keep his picture on the wall.

24

THE
SACRIFICIAL
VISITOR

*L*ET ME DESCRIBE A SCENE to you and then ask you to come back to it at the end of the chapter.

An old man walks down a Florida beach. The sun sets like an orange ball on the horizon. The waves slap the sand. The smell of saltwater stings the air. The beach is vacant. No sun to entice the sunbathers. Not enough light for the fishermen. So, aside from a few joggers and strollers, the gentleman is alone.

He carries a bucket in his bony hand. A bucket of shrimp. It's not for him. It's not for the fish. It's for the sea gulls.

He walks to an isolated pier cast in gold by the setting sun. He steps out to the end of the pier. The time has come for the weekly ritual.

He stands and waits.

Soon the sky becomes a mass of dancing dots. The evening silence gives way to the screeching of birds. They fill the sky and then cover the moorings. They are on a pilgrimage to meet the old man.

For a half hour or so, the bushy-browed, shoulder-bent gentleman will stand on the pier, surrounded by the birds of the sea, until his bucket is empty.

But even after the food is gone, his feathered friends still linger. They linger as if they're attracted to more than just food. They perch on his hat. They walk on the pier. And they all share a moment together.

Got the scene? Now put it on the back burner for a few minutes.

———————————————

Jesus left there and went along the Sea of Galilee. Then he went up on a mountainside and sat down. Great crowds came to him, bringing the lame, the blind, the crippled, the mute and many others, and laid them at his feet; and he healed them. The people were amazed when they saw the mute speaking, the crippled made well, the lame walking and the blind seeing. And they praised the God of Israel.

Jesus called his disciples to him and said, "I have compassion for these people; they have already been with me three days and have nothing to eat. I do not want to send them away hungry, or they may collapse on the way."[1]

This is not the day that Jesus fed the five thousand men; it is the day he fed the *four* thousand. Although the events have much in common, they are different in several respects:

- When Jesus fed the five thousand, he was with Jews. When he fed the four thousand (plus women and children), he was in Decapolis, a Gentile region.

- When Jesus fed the five thousand, he taught and healed them. When he was with the four thousand, there is no record that he taught—only that he healed.

- When Jesus was with the five thousand, he was with them for one afternoon. When he was with the four thousand, he was with them for three days.

And for three days he did a most remarkable thing: He healed them. "The lame, the blind, the crippled, the mute and many others" came to him, Matthew wrote, "and he healed them."

Many times I wish that the New Testament writers had been a bit more descriptive. This is one of those times. "And he healed them" is too short a phrase to describe what must have been an astonishing sight.

Let your imagination go. Can you see the scene?

Can you see the blind husband seeing his wife for the first time? His eyes gazing into her tear-filled ones like she was the queen of the morning?

Envision the man who had never walked, now walking! Don't you know that he didn't want to sit down? Don't you know that he ran and jumped and did a dance with the kids?

And what about the mute who could speak? Can you picture him sitting by the fire late into the night and talking? Saying and singing everything and anything that he had ever wanted to say and sing.

And the deaf woman who could now hear. What was it like when she heard her child call her "Mamma" for the first time?

For three days it went on. Person after person. Mat after mat. Crutch after crutch. Smile after smile. No record is given of Jesus preaching or teaching or instructing or challenging. He just healed.

"The people," Matthew wrote, "were amazed when they saw the mute speaking, the crippled made well, the lame walking and the blind seeing." Four thousand amazed people, each telling a story grander than the other. In the midst of them all is Jesus. Not complaining. Not postponing. Not demanding. Just enjoying every minute.

Then Matthew, still the great economizer of words, gave us another phrase on which I wish he would have elaborated:

"They praised the God of Israel."

I wonder how they did that? I feel more certain of what they *didn't* do than of what they did do. I feel confident that they didn't form a praise committee. I feel confident that they didn't make any robes. I feel confident that they didn't sit in rows and stare at the back of each other's heads.

I doubt seriously if they wrote a creed on how they were to praise this God they had never before worshiped. I can't picture them getting into an argument over technicalities. I doubt if they felt it had to be done indoors.

And I know they didn't wait until the Sabbath to do it.

In all probability, they just did it. Each one—in his or her own way, with his or her own heart—just praised Jesus. Perhaps some people came and fell at Jesus' feet. Perhaps some shouted his name. Maybe a few just went up on the hillside, looked into the sky, and smiled.

I can picture a mom and dad standing speechless before the Healer as they hold their newly healed baby.

I can envision a leper staring in awe at the One who took away his terror.

I can imagine throngs of people pushing and shoving. Wanting to get close. Not to request anything or demand anything, but just to say "thank you."

Perhaps some tried to pay Jesus, but what payment would have been sufficient?

Perhaps some tried to return his gift with another, but what could a person give that would express the gratitude?

All the people could do was exactly what Matthew said they did. "They praised the God of Israel."

However they did it, they did it. And Jesus was touched, so touched that he insisted they stay for a meal before they left.

Without using the word *worship,* this passage defines it. Worship is when you're aware that what you've been given is far greater than what you can give. Worship is the awareness that were it not for his touch, you'd still be hobbling and hurting, bitter and broken. Worship is the half-glazed expression on the parched face of a desert pilgrim as he discovers that the oasis is not a mirage.

Worship is the "thank you" that refuses to be silenced.

We have tried to make a science out of worship. We can't do that. We can't do that any more than we can "sell love" or "negotiate peace."

Worship is a voluntary act of gratitude offered by the saved to the Savior, by the healed to the Healer, and by the delivered to the Deliverer. And if you and I can go days without feeling an urge to say "thank you" to the One who saved, healed, and delivered us, then we'd do well to remember what he did.

The old man on the pier couldn't go a week without saying "thank you."

His name was Eddie Rickenbacker. If you were alive in October 1942, you probably remember the day that he was reported missing at sea.

He had been sent on a mission to deliver a message to Gen. Douglas MacArthur. With a handpicked crew in a B-17 known as the "Flying Fortress," he set off across the South Pacific. Somewhere the crew became lost, the fuel ran out, and the plane went down.

All eight crew members escaped into the life rafts. They battled the weather, the water, the sharks, and the sun. But most of all, they battled the hunger. After eight days, their rations were gone. They ran out of options. It would take a miracle for them to survive.

And a miracle occurred.

After an afternoon devotional service, the men said a prayer and tried to rest. As Rickenbacker was dozing with his hat over his eyes, something landed on his head. He would later say that he knew it was a sea gull. He didn't know how he knew; he just knew. That gull meant food . . . if he could catch it. And he did.

The flesh was eaten. The intestines were used as fish bait. And the crew survived.

What was a sea gull doing hundreds of miles away from land?

Only God knows.

But whatever the reason, Rickenbacker was thankful. As a result, every Friday evening this old captain walked to the pier, his bucket full of shrimp and his heart full of thanks.

We'd be wise to do the same. We've much in common with Rickenbacker. We, too, were saved by a Sacrificial Visitor.

We, too, were rescued by One who journeyed far from only God knows where.

And we, like the captain, have every reason to look into the sky . . . and worship.

25

HOLINESS IN A BATHROBE

WHEN YOUR WORLD TOUCHES God's world, the result is a holy moment. When God's high hope kisses your earthly hurt, that moment is holy. That moment might happen on a Sunday during Communion or on a Thursday night at the skating rink. It might occur in a cathedral or in a subway, by a burning bush or by a feed trough. When and where don't matter. What matters is that holy moments occur. Daily. And I'd like to talk to you about the holiest of those moments—I'd like to talk to you about the holiest moment of your life.

No, not your birth. Not your wedding. Not the birth of a child. I'm talking about *the* holiest moment of your life. Those other moments are special. They sparkle with reverence. But compared to this moment, they are about as holy as a burp.

I'm talking about the sacred hour.

No, not your baptism or your christening. Not your first Communion or your first confession or even your first date. I know those moments are precious and certainly sacrosanct, but I've a different moment in mind.

It happened this morning. Right after you awoke. Right there in your house. Did you miss it? Let me recreate the scene.

The alarm rings. Your wife pokes you or your husband nudges you or your mom or dad shakes you. And you wake up.

You've already hit the sleeper button three times; hit it again and you'll be late. You've already asked for five more minutes . . . five different times; ask again and you'll get water poured on your head.

The hour has come. Daybreak has broken. So, with a groan and a grunt, you throw back the covers and kick a warm foot out into a cold world. It's followed by a reluctant companion.

You lean up and sit on the edge of the bed and stare at the back of your eyelids. You tell them to open, but they object. You pry them apart with your palms and peek into the room.

(The moment isn't holy yet, but it's almost here.)

You stand. At that moment, everything that will hurt during the course of the day hurts. It's as if the little person in your brain that's in charge of pain needs to test the circuits before you make it to the bathroom.

"Back pain?"

"Check."

"Stiff neck?"

"Check."

"High school football knee injury."

"Still hurting."

"Flaky scalp?"

"Still itching."

"Hay fever reaction?"

"Achoo!"

With the grace of a pregnant elephant, you step toward the bathroom. You wish there is some way to turn on the light slowly, but there isn't. So you slap on the spotlight, blink as your eyes adjust, and step up to the bathroom sink.

You are approaching the sacred. You may not know it, but you have just stepped on holy tile. You are in the inner sanctum. The burning bush of your world.

The holiest moment of your life is about to occur. Listen. You'll hear the fluttering of angels' wings signaling their arrival. Trumpets are poised on heaven's lips. A cloud of majesty encircles your bare feet. Heaven's hosts cease all motion as you raise your eyes and . . .

(Get ready. Here it comes. The holy moment is nigh.)

Cymbals clash. Trumpets echo in sacred halls. Heaven's children race through the universe scattering flower petals. Stars dance. The universe applauds. Trees sway in choreographed adulation. And well they should, for the child of the King has awakened.

Look in the mirror. Behold the holy one. Don't turn away. The image of perfection is looking back at you. The holy moment has arrived.

I know what you are thinking. *You call that "holy"? You call that "perfect"? You don't know what I look like at 6:30 A.M.*

No, but I can guess. Hair matted. Pajamas or nightgown wrinkled. Chunks of sleep stuck in the corners of your eyes. Belly bulging. Dried-out lips. Pudgy eyes. Breath that could stain a wall. A face that could scare a dog.

"Anything but holy," you say. "Give me an hour and I'll look holy. Give me some coffee, some makeup. Give me a toothbrush and a hairbrush, and I'll make this body presentable. A little perfume . . . a splash of cologne. Then take me into the Holy of Holies. Then I'll make heaven smile."

Ah, but there's where you're wrong. You see, what makes the morning moment so holy is its honesty. What makes the morning mirror hallowed is that you are seeing exactly who God sees.

And who God loves.

No makeup. No pressed shirts. No power ties. No matching shoes. No layers of images. No status jewelry. Just unkempt honesty.

Just you.

If people love you at 6:30 in the morning, one thing is sure: They love *you*. They don't love your title. They don't love your style. They don't love your accomplishments. They just love you.

"Love," wrote one forgiven soul, "covers over a multitude of sins."[1]

Sounds like God's love.

"He has made perfect forever those who are being made holy," wrote another.[2]

Underline the word *perfect*. Note that the word is not *better*. Not *improving*. Not *on the upswing*. God doesn't improve; he perfects. He doesn't enhance; he completes. What does the perfect person lack?

Now I realize that there's a sense in which we're imperfect. We still err. We still stumble. We still do exactly what we don't want to do. And that part of us is, according to the verse, "being made holy."

But when it comes to our position before God, we're perfect. When he sees each of us, he sees one who has been made perfect through the One who is perfect—Jesus Christ.

"All of you who were baptized into Christ have clothed yourselves with Christ."[3]

This morning I "put on" clothing to hide the imperfections I'd rather not display. When you see me, fully clothed, you can't see my moles, scars, or bumps. Those are hidden.

When we choose to be baptized, by lifestyle as much as by symbol, into Christ, the same shielding occurs. Our sins and faults are lost beneath the sheer radiance of his covering. "For you died, and your life is now hidden with Christ in God."[4] Please, don't miss the impact of this verse. When God sees us, he also sees Christ. He sees perfection! Not perfection earned by us, mind you, but perfection paid for by him.

Reflect on these words for a moment:

"God made him who had no sin to be sin for us so that *in him* [emphasis mine] we might become the righteousness of God."[5]

Now read these words in the Phillips translation:

"For God caused Christ, who himself knew nothing of sin, actually to *be* sin for our sakes, so that in Christ we might be made good with the goodness of God."

Note the last four words: "the goodness of God." God's goodness is your goodness. You are absolute perfection. Flawless. Without defects or mistakes. Unsullied. Unrivaled. Unmarred. Peerless. Virgin pure. Undeserved yet unreserved perfection.

No wonder heaven applauds when you wake up. A masterpiece has stirred.

"Shh," whisper the stars, "look at the wonder of that child."

"My!" gasp the angels, "what a prodigy God has created."

So while you groan, eternity gasps with wonder. As you stumble, angels are star struck. What you see in the mirror as morning disaster is, in reality, a morning miracle. Holiness in a bathrobe.

Go ahead and get dressed. Go ahead and put on the rings, shave the whiskers, comb the hair, and cover the moles. Do it for yourself. Do it for the sake of your image. Do it to keep your job. Do it for the benefit of those who have to sit beside you. But don't do it for God.

He has already seen you as you really are. And in his book, you are perfect.

26

THE
CHOICE

W HY DO I WANT TO DO BAD?" my daughter asked me, unknowingly posing a question asked by many seekers of truth. "Why do I do the thing I hate? What is this ape that gibbers within?" Or, perhaps a more basic question is being asked. "If sin separates me from God, why doesn't God separate me from sin? Why doesn't he remove from me the option to sin?"

To answer that, let's go to the beginning.

Let's go to the Garden and see the seed that both blessed and cursed. Let's see why God gave man . . . the choice.

Behind it all was a choice. A deliberate decision. An informed move. He didn't have to do it. But he chose to. He knew the price. He saw the implications. He was aware of the consequences.

We don't know when he decided to do it. We can't know. Not just because we weren't there. Because time was not there. *When* did not exist. Nor did *tomorrow* or *yesterday* or *next time*. For there was no time.

We don't know when he thought about making the choice. But we do know that he made it. He didn't have to do it. He chose to.

He chose to create.

"In the beginning God created . . ."[1]

With one decision, history began. Existence became measurable.

Out of nothing came light.

Out of light came day.

Then came sky . . . and earth.

And on this earth? A mighty hand went to work.

Canyons were carved. Oceans were dug. Mountains erupted out of flatlands. Stars were flung. A universe sparkled.

Our sun became just one of millions. Our galaxy became just one of thousands. Planets invisibly tethered to suns roared through space at breakneck speeds. Stars blazed with heat that could melt our planet in seconds.

The hand behind it was mighty. He is mighty.

And with this might, he created. As naturally as a bird sings and a fish swims, he created. Just as an artist can't not paint and a runner can't not run, he couldn't not create. He was the Creator. Through and through, he was the Creator. A tireless dreamer and designer.

From the pallet of the Ageless Artist came inimitable splendors. Before there was a person to see it, his creation was pregnant with wonder. Flowers didn't just grow; they blossomed. Chicks weren't just born; they hatched. Salmons didn't just swim; they leaped.

Mundaneness found no home in his universe.

He must have loved it. Creators relish creating. I'm sure his commands were delightful! "Hippo, you won't walk . . . you'll waddle!" "Hyena, a bark is too plain. Let me show you how to laugh!" "Look, raccoon, I've made you a mask!" "Come here, giraffe, let's stretch that neck a bit." And on and on he went. Giving the clouds their puff. Giving the oceans their blue. Giving the trees their sway.

Giving the frogs their leap and croak. The mighty wed with the creative, and creation was born.

He was mighty. He was creative.

And he was love. Even greater than his might and deeper than his creativity was one all-consuming characteristic:

Love.

Water must be wet. A fire must be hot. You can't take the wet out of water and still have water. You can't take the heat out of fire and still have fire.

In the same way, you can't take the love out of this One who lived before time and still have him exist. For he was . . . and is . . . Love.

Probe deep within him. Explore every corner. Search every angle. Love is all you find. Go to the beginning of every decision he has made and you'll find it. Go to the end of every story he has told and you'll see it.

Love.

No bitterness. No evil. No cruelty. Just love. Flawless love. Passionate love. Vast and pure love. He is love.

As a result, an elephant has a trunk with which to drink. A kitten has a mother from which to nurse. A bird has a nest in which to sleep. The same God who was mighty enough to carve out the canyon is tender enough to put hair on the legs of the Matterhorn Fly to keep it warm. The same force that provides symmetry to the planets guides the baby kangaroo to its mother's pouch before the mother knows it is born.

And because of who he was, he did what he did.

He created a paradise. A sinless sanctuary. A haven before fear. A home before there was a human dweller. No time. No death. No hurt. A gift built by God for his ultimate creation. And when he was through, he knew "it was very good."[2]

But it wasn't enough.

His greatest work hadn't been completed. One final masterpiece was needed before he would stop.

Look to the canyons to see the Creator's splendor. Touch the flowers and see his delicacy. Listen to the thunder and hear his power. But gaze on this—the zenith—and witness all three . . . and more.

Imagine with me what may have taken place on that day.

———————————

He placed one scoop of clay upon another until a form lay lifeless on the ground.

All of the Garden's inhabitants paused to witness the event. Hawks hovered. Giraffes stretched. Trees bowed. Butterflies paused on petals and watched.

"You will love me, nature," God said. "I made you that way. You will obey me, universe. For you were designed to do so. You will reflect my glory, skies, for that is how you were created. But this one will be like me. This one will be able to choose."

All were silent as the Creator reached into himself and removed something yet unseen. A seed. "It's called 'choice.' The seed of choice."

Creation stood in silence and gazed upon the lifeless form.

An angel spoke, "But what if he . . ."

"What if he chooses not to love?" the Creator finished. "Come, I will show you."

Unbound by today, God and the angel walked into the realm of tomorrow.

"There, see the fruit of the seed of choice, both the sweet and the bitter."

The angel gasped at what he saw. Spontaneous love. Voluntary devotion. Chosen tenderness. Never had he seen anything like these. He felt the love of the Adams. He heard the joy of Eve and her daughters. He saw the food and the burdens shared. He absorbed the kindness and marveled at the warmth.

"Heaven has never seen such beauty, my Lord. Truly, this is your greatest creation."

"Ah, but you've only seen the sweet. Now witness the bitter."

A stench enveloped the pair. The angel turned in horror and proclaimed, "What is it?"

The Creator spoke only one word: "Selfishness."

The angel stood speechless as they passed through centuries of repugnance. Never had he seen such filth. Rotten hearts. Ruptured promises. Forgotten loyalties. Children of the creation wandering blindly in lonely labyrinths.

"This is the result of choice?" the angel asked.

"Yes."

"They will forget you?"

"Yes."

"They will reject you?"

"Yes."

"They will never come back?"

"Some will. Most won't."

"What will it take to make them listen?"

The Creator walked on in time, further and further into the future, until he stood by a tree. A tree that would be fashioned into a cradle. Even then he could smell the hay that would surround him.

With another step into the future, he paused before another tree. It stood alone, a stubborn ruler of a bald hill. The trunk was thick, and the wood was strong. Soon it would be cut. Soon it would be trimmed. Soon it would be mounted on the stony brow of another hill. And soon he would be hung on it.

He felt the wood rub against a back he did not yet wear.

"Will you go down there?" the angel asked.

"I will."

"Is there no other way?"

"There is not."

"Wouldn't it be easier to not plant the seed? Wouldn't it be easier to not give the choice?"

"It would," the Creator spoke slowly. "But to remove the choice is to remove the love."

He looked around the hill and foresaw a scene. Three figures hung on three crosses. Arms spread. Heads fallen forward. They moaned with the wind.

Men clad in soldiers' garb sat on the ground near the trio. They played games in the dirt and laughed.

Men clad in religion stood off to one side. They smiled. Arrogant, cocky. They had protected God, they thought, by killing this false one.

Women clad in sorrow huddled at the foot of the hill. Speechless. Faces tear streaked. Eyes downward. One put her arm around another and tried to lead her away. She wouldn't leave. "I will stay," she said softly. "I will stay."

All heaven stood to fight. All nature rose to rescue. All eternity poised to protect. But the Creator gave no command.

"It must be done . . . ," he said, and withdrew.

But as he stepped back in time, he heard the cry that he would someday scream: "My God, my God, why have you forsaken me?"[3] He wrenched at tomorrow's agony.

The angel spoke again. "It would be less painful . . ."

The Creator interrupted softly. "But it wouldn't be love."

They stepped into the Garden again. The Maker looked earnestly at the clay creation. A monsoon of love swelled up within him. He had died for the creation before he had made him. God's form bent over the sculptured face and breathed. Dust stirred on the lips of the new one. The chest rose, cracking the red mud. The cheeks fleshened. A finger moved. And an eye opened.

But more incredible than the moving of the flesh was the stirring of the spirit. Those who could see the unseen gasped.

Perhaps it was the wind who said it first. Perhaps what the star saw that moment is what has made it blink ever since. Maybe it was left to an angel to whisper it:

"It looks like . . . it appears so much like . . . it is him!"

The angel wasn't speaking of the face, the features, or the body. He was looking inside—at the soul.

"It's eternal!" gasped another.

Within the man, God had placed a divine seed. A seed of his self. The God of might had created earth's mightiest. The Creator had created, not a creature, but another creator. And the One who had chosen to love had created one who could love in return.

Now it's our choice.

27

CAUGHT WITH YOUR PANTS DOWN, BUT YOUR HEAD UP

S TEVE LYONS WILL BE REMEMBERED as the player who dropped his pants.

He could be remembered as an outstanding infielder . . . as the player who played every position for the Chicago White Sox . . . as the guy who always dove into first base . . . as a favorite of the fans who high fived the guy who caught the foul ball in the bleachers. He could be remembered as an above-average player who made it with average ability.

But he won't. He'll be remembered as the player who dropped his pants on July 16, 1990.

The White Sox were playing the Tigers in Detroit. Lyons bunted and raced down the first-base line. He knew it was going to be tight, so he dove at the bag. Safe! The Tiger's pitcher disagreed. He and the umpire got into a shouting match, and Lyons stepped in to voice his opinion.

Absorbed in the game and the debate, Lyons felt dirt trickling down the inside of his pants. Without missing a beat he dropped his britches, wiped away the dirt, and . . . uh oh . . . twenty thousand jaws hit the bleachers' floor.

And, as you can imagine, the jokes began. Women behind the White Sox dugout waved dollar bills when he came onto the field. "No one," wrote one columnist, "had ever dropped his drawers on the field. Not Wally Moon. Not Blue

Moon Odom. Not even Heinie Manush."[1] Within twenty-four hours of the "exposure," he received more exposure than he'd gotten his entire career: seven live television and approximately twenty radio interviews.

"We've got this pitcher, Melido Perez, who earlier this month pitched a no-hitter," Lyons stated, "and I'll guarantee you he didn't do two live television shots afterwards. I pull my pants down, and I do seven. Something's pretty skewed toward the zany in this game."

Fortunately, for Steve, he was wearing sliding pants under his baseball pants. Otherwise the game would be rated "R" instead of "PG-13."

Now, I don't know Steve Lyons. I'm not a White Sox fan. Nor am I normally appreciative of men who drop their pants in public. But I think Steve Lyons deserves a salute.

I think anybody who dives into first base deserves a salute. How many guys do you see roaring down the baseline of life more concerned about getting a job done than they are about saving their necks? How often do you see people diving headfirst into anything?

Too seldom, right? But when we do . . . when we see a gutsy human throwing caution to the wind and taking a few risks . . . ah, now that's a person worthy of a pat on the . . . back.

So here's to all the Steve Lyons of the world.

Here's to the Miracles, a choral group out of Memphis, Tennessee, made up of the mentally retarded and the stouthearted. Just see if you can listen to them and still feel sorry for yourself.

Here's to the hero of the San Francisco marathon who crossed the finish line without seeing it. (He was blind.)

Here's to the woman whose husband left her with a nest of kids to raise and bills to pay, but who somehow tells me every Sunday that God has never been closer.

Here's to the single father of two girls who learned to braid their hair.

Here's to the grandparents whc came out of retirement to raise the children their children couldn't raise.

Here's to the foster parents who took in a child long enough for that child to take their hearts—then gave the child up again.

Here's to the girl, told by everyone to abort the baby, who chose to keep the baby.

Here's to the doctor who treats more than half of his patients for free.

Here's to the heroin-addict-turned-missionary.

Here's to the executive who every Tuesday hosts a 5:30 A.M. meeting for Bible study and prayer.

Here's to all of you reckless lovers of life and God, who stand on first base because you paid a price to get there.

So what if you forget about pleasing the crowd and get caught with your pants down? At least you're playing ball in the pros.

Most of us aren't even in your league.

28

LEMONADE AND GRACE

*L*EMONADE, *5¢"*

The *e* is larger than the *L*. The *m* is upper cased; all the other letters are lowered. The last two letters, *de,* curve downward because the artist ran out of room on the poster board.

Norman Rockwell would have loved it.

Two girls sit on the sidewalk in little chairs behind a little table. The six-year-old is the cashier. She monitors a plastic bowl of change. The four-year-old is the waitress. She handles the ice. Pours the drinks. Stacks and restacks the paper cups.

Behind them, seated on the grass, is Dad. He leans against an oak tree and smiles as he witnesses his daughters' inauguration into capitalism.

Business has been steady. The Saturday-afternoon stream of patrons has nearly emptied the pitcher. The bottom of the cashier's bowl is covered with thirty-five cents of change. With the exception of a few spills, the service has been exceptional. No complaints. Many compliments.

Part of the success, though, has been due to the marketing strategy.

Our street doesn't get much traffic, so we did a little advertising. As my daughters painted the sign, I called several families in the neighborhood and invited them to the grand opening of our lemonade stand. So all of our clients, thus far, had been partial.

I was proud of myself. I leaned back against the tree. Closed my eyes. Turned up the radio I had brought. And listened to the baseball game.

Then I heard an unfamiliar voice.

"I'll have a cup of lemonade, please."

I opened my eyes. It was a customer. A real customer. An unsolicited neighbor who had driven by, seen the sign, stopped, and ordered a drink.

Uh-oh, I thought. Our service was about to be tested.

Andrea, the four-year-old, grabbed a cup that had already been used.

"Get a clean cup," I whispered.

"Oh," she giggled, and got a clean cup.

She opened the ice bucket, looked in, and then looked back at me. "Daddy, we are out of ice."

The patron overheard her. "That's OK. I'll take it warm."

She picked up the pitcher and poured. Syrupy sugar oozed out of the pitcher. "Daddy, there's just a little bit."

Our customer spoke again. "That's fine. I don't want much."

"I hope you like it sweet," I said under my breath.

She handed the cup to the man and he handed her a dollar. She gave it to Jenna.

Jenna turned to me. "Daddy, what do I do?" (We weren't used to such big bills.)

I stuck my hands in my pockets; they were empty.

"Uh, we don't have any . . ." I began.

"No problem," he said, smiling. "Just keep the change."

I smiled sheepishly. He thanked the girls. Told them they were doing a great job. Climbed back into his car. And drove off.

Quite a transaction, I thought. *We give him a warm, partially filled cup of lemonade syrup, and he gives us a compliment and a payment twenty times too much.*

I had set out to teach the girls about free enterprise. They ended up with a lesson on grace.

And so had I. For all the theologizing we preachers do about God's grace, the kind stranger modeled it better than the best of sermons state it.

Perhaps the story of the stranger who brought grace to our street is a good place for us to wrap up this book. For this story is the story of each of us.

Each of us has seen our ice melt in the July sun of stress. Who hasn't attempted to serve the best, only to find that the best has already been served and that the pitcher needs to be refilled? And there's not a person alive who hasn't wondered what God does when what we promise and what we produce aren't even close to being the same.

Lemonade stands and living life would be high-risk endeavors were it not for the appearance of gentle strangers on our streets. But, thank God, they come.

And, thank God, He came.

For isn't God the stranger who became our friend after looking past the dregs and into our hearts?

And aren't we not much more than surprised children, amazed that what we receive is twenty times, yea, verily a million times, more than what we ask for?

The next time your calm becomes chaos, think of that. The next time you find yourself in a storm and can't see God on the horizon, reflect on the lemonade stand. And if your walking on the water becomes floundering in the deep like Peter's did, lift your eyes and look . . .

A Gentle Stranger may be bringing grace to your street . . . to your life.

CONCLUSION

I JUST DID WHAT YOU JUST DID. I just read this book. It goes in the mail tomorrow. The overnight-express package is on my desk, and the label is typed. The editors and their red pens are waiting. The printers and their presses are expectant. But I wasn't ready to send it off yet. So I sat on the couch with coffee, and highlighter and sipped and read and . . . gratefully. . . smiled.

I liked it. You might find that surprising. You might assume that every writer likes what he or she writes. They should and normally do, I suppose. But I always have that lingering fear that with all the work done, I might sit down to read what I wrote . . . and gag.

But I didn't. I was pleased.

I smiled at the right spots and was warmed at others. It was good to visit the seashore again and see the patient Master touching the people. It was fun to read about the woman who called my bluff on the plane. It did me good to read about the lost contact lens and the recovered vision, Rickenbacker's lost crew and the mysterious sea gull, the impossible stairway and the nameless carpenter.

It was good to be reminded again that this journey is a brief one. That Jesus knows how I feel and that he'd scramble off a mountain and walk through a storm to convince me of that.

It was good to hear God's gentle thunder. I hope it has been good for you. Thanks for reading my book. I realize that it took your time and money. I hope it has been worth both.

And I hope you never forget the last Lighthouse Law: Approach life like a voyage on a schooner. Enjoy the view. Explore the vessel. Make friends with the captain. Fish a little. And then get off when you get home.

Good sailing!

NOTES

Chapter 2 • God Under Pressure

1. Matthew 14:1–13.
2. Luke 9:9.
3. The wording of Matthew 14:1–13 has given rise to some discussion. At the beginning of the passage, it is clear that John the Baptist is already dead because Herod is concerned that Jesus might be "John the Baptist . . . risen from the dead." Jesus withdraws when he "heard what had happened." A fair question is, what news did Jesus hear? Did he hear that John had been killed? Or did he hear that Herod might be after him? Or a combination of both? Those scholars who argue that Jesus retreated solely out of sorrow over the death of John the Baptist suggest that Matthew simply forgot how he began the chapter with a reference to Herod. "[Matthew] . . . has forgotten the parenthetic nature of the story of John the Baptist" (R. Bultmann, *The History of the Synoptic Translation,* ed. John Marsh [New York: Harper & Row, 1963], 48). Other scholars argue that it was the awareness that Herod was looking for him that spurred Jesus' withdrawal. Lamar Cope reasons that Jesus withdrew due to fear that Herod would pursue him next. He writes, "In unpunctuated Greek there were only limited ways to mark off sections of thought" (Lamar Cope, *Catholic Bible Quarterly,* 37:4 [1976]: 515–18). He explains that the Greek indicates that the John the Baptist story was an insert and that the phrase "when Jesus heard" directly refers to Herod's acquaintance with Jesus. Hence Jesus left in peril. Most scholars,

however, are in general agreement that the phrase, "When Jesus heard what had happened," refers to a combination of sorrow and caution. For references see: *A Commentary Critical, Experimental and Practical of the Old and New Testaments; Matthew-John,* ed. David Brown, vol. 5 (Grand Rapids, Mich.: Eerdmans, 1948), 159; J. S. Exell, ed., *The Biblical Illustrator: Matthew* (Grand Rapids, Mich.: Baker Book House, 1955), 267; J. W. McGarvey, ed., *New Testament Commentary: Matthew and Mark,* vol. 1 (Delight, Ark.: Gospel Light Publishing, 1900), 130; Alan Hugh McNeile, *The Gospel According to St. Matthew, Greek Text* (London: Macmillan & Co., 1952), 212; C. E. Montefiore, *Synoptic Gospels* (London: Macmillan & Co., 1909), 60; J. B. Orchard, *A Synopsis of the Four Gospels in Greek* (Macon, Ga.: Mercer University Press, 1983), 30; Adam Clarke, *Clark's Commentary: Matthew-Acts,* vol. 5 (Nashville, Tenn.: Abingdon Press, 1831, 1967), 157; Frederick Dale Bruner, *Matthew: The Churchbook,* vol. 2 (Dallas, Tex.: Word Publishing, 1990), 526, 527; William Barclay, *The Gospel of Matthew,* vol. 2 (Philadelphia, Pa.: Westminster Press, 1975), 98; *The Expositors Bible Commentary,* vol. 8 (Grand Rapids, Mich.: Zondervan Publishing House, 1984), 340, 341; see especially William Hendricksen, *The Gospel of Matthew* (Grand Rapids, Mich.: Baker Book House, 1973), 593, 594.

4. Mark 6:30.

5. Mark 6:12.

6. Matthew 14:21.

7. John MacArthur, *The MacArthur Commentary: Matthew 8–15* (Chicago, Ill.: Moody Press, 1987), 427.

8. Mark 6:31.

9. Ibid.

10. Luke 9:11.

11. Max Lucado, *God Came Near* (Portland, Oreg.: Multnomah Press, 1987), 26.

12. How divinity and humanity could coexist in the same body is not easy to comprehend. Indeed, the paradox of the Incarnation has been a source of tension for theologians throughout

history. Discomfort with the mystery has driven thinkers to relegate the doctrine into one of two extremes, each of which is equally dangerous. One line of reasoning, known as Ebionitism, denies the full divinity of Christ. Those who embrace this position reject the presence of God in Christ. He is presented as a religious genius, a spiritual master, a guru, but not God himself. He was the "perfect religious personality, a spiritual life completely filled by the realization of God who is love." (Walter Rausenbusch, *A Theology for the Social Gospel,* 154, 155, as quoted by Bloesch in *Essentials of Evangelical Theology,* 1:135.) The other approach to the incarnation of Jesus begins with the deity of Christ, but never arrives at his humanity. "Docetism," (which comes from the Greek word *dokeo,* which means "to seem, to have the appearance of"), rejects God as a touchable, reachable human and relegates Jesus to the metaphysical. See Stephen Neill, *Jesus Through Many Eyes* (Philadelphia, Pa.: Fortress Press, 1976), 139. This form of Gnosticism, although comfortable with the overarching pattern or truth that is exemplified in Christ, is unable to endorse the complete indwelling of God in the man, Jesus. Both approaches, Ebionitism and Docetism, strain to exalt one nature at the expense of the other. Both are equally heretical. One leaves you with a good teacher who deceived the world with falsehood and tricks. . . . The other offers a god who simply masked himself in humanity, but never experienced it. The apostles John and Paul have strong words for both. "Every spirit that acknowledges that Jesus Christ has come in the flesh is from God, but every spirit that does not acknowledge Jesus is not from God" (1 John 4:2–3). "For in Christ all the fullness of the Deity lives in bodily form" (Col. 2:9). "In the beginning was the Word, and the Word was with God, and the Word was God" (John 1:1). It was this Word [Jesus] who assumed the human state and "made his dwelling among us . . . full of grace and truth" (John 1:14). Other Scriptures join the chorus. Jesus was "born of a woman, born under law" (Gal. 4:4). He shared in "their humanity" (Heb. 2:14). He "offered up prayers and petitions with loud cries and tears" (Heb. 5:7).

He grew in "wisdom and stature" (Luke 2:40, KJV). Yet, although human, he was divine. He is called "our great God and Savior" (Titus 2:13). He forgave sins (Mark 2:5, 7, 10). He raised the dead; he gave and gives life (John 5:21). He defeated death (2 Tim. 2:8). How do we justify the paradox? How do we explain "the Lord humbled for communion with man and likewise the Servant exalted to communion with God?" (Karl Barth, *The Humanity of Gods,* trans. Thomas Wieser and John Newton Thomas [Richmond, Va.: John Knox Press, 1964], 64). How do we explain that God was equally human and divine? We don't. It is a secret beyond our reach and, consequentially, worthy of our worship. Hence Paul wrote: "Great beyond all question is the mystery of our religion: 'He who was manifested in the body, vindicated in the spirit, seen by angels; who was proclaimed among the nations, believed in throughout the world, glorified in high heaven'" (1 Tim. 3:16, NEB).

13. *More of Paul Harvey's The Rest of the Story,* ed. Paul Aurandt (New York: Bantam Books, 1980), 79, 80.

Chapter 3 • A Mother's Love—A Friend's Empathy

1. Matthew 14:14.
2. Mark 6:34.
3. Luke 9:11.
4. See John 6:15, 26.
5. Matthew 14:14.
6. Matthew 14:15.
7. Matthew 14:16.
8. Mark 6:37.
9. Ibid.
10. Mark 6:41.

Chapter 4 • When Fishermen Don't Fish

1. Mark 6:34.
2. Matthew 14:14.

3. Ibid.
4. Mark 6:34.

Chapter 7 • Thanks for the Bread

1. John 6:1–14.

Chapter 9 • Fending Off the Voices

1. Ann Trebbe and Valerie Helmbreck, "'Ideal' is body beautiful and 'clean cut,'" *USA Today,* 15 September 1989.
2. John 6:14.
3. John 6:15.
4. John 10:3.
5. Revelation 3:20.
6. Matthew 28:20.
7. Hebrews 13:5.
8. John 5:28–29.

Chapter 10 • The Photo and the File

1. Matthew 5:5.
2. Philippians 1:10.

Chapter 11 • Seeing God Through Shattered Glass

1. Matthew 14:22–24.
2. Mark 6:52.
3. Matthew 14:15.
4. Ibid.

Chapter 12 • Two Fathers, Two Feasts

1. 1 Thessalonians 5:9, NEB.
2. Isaiah 57:15.
3. Psalm 74:10; 89:46.
4. 1 Chronicles 29:15.

5. Psalm 39:5.
6. James 4:14.
7. Psalm 103:15, 16.
8. 2 Corinthians 4:16–18.
9. 2 Corinthians 11:23–27.

Chapter 14 • The Miracle of the Carpenter

1. Matthew 14:23.

Chapter 15 • The Woodcutter's Wisdom

1. Ecclesiastes 7:8.
2. Romans 12:12.
3. Matthew 6:34.

Chapter 16 • Laws of the Lighthouse

1. As quoted by Stephen R. Covey, *The Seven Habits of Highly Effective People* (New York: Fireside—Simon & Schuster, 1989), 33.

Chapter 17 • He Speaks Through the Storm

1. Job 42:5, TLB.
2. Job 13:4, 5, TLB.
3. Job 33:29.
4. Job 38:2.
5. Job 38:3.
6. Job 38:4, TLB.
7. Job 38:5–7, TLB.
8. Job 38:12, 13, TLB.
9. Job 38:17–21, TLB.
10. Job 40:4, 5, TLB.
11. Job 41:11, TLB.
12. Job 42:5, TLB.

Chapter 18 • *Pilgrim Ponderings*

1. Matthew 17:1–5.
2. Luke 9:29.
3. Matthew 17:5.

Chapter 19 • *Our Storm Was His Path*

1. Matthew 14:27.
2. Matthew 14:28.

Chapter 20 • *They'd Do It Again*

1. Matthew 14:33.

Chapter 21 • *Castles of Sorrow*

1. 2 Corinthians 7:10.

Chapter 22 • *Fear That Becomes Faith*

1. John 6:19.
2. Proverbs 9:10.
3. Exodus 14:15, 16.
4. 2 Kings 5:13, 14.
5. Romans 3.
6. Acts 12:6–17.
7. Matthew 14:28.
8. Ephesians 2:8, 9.
9. "Rock of Ages, Cleft for Me," by Augustus M. Toplady.
10. "The Solid Rock," by Edward Mote.
11. "Amazing Grace," by John Newton.
12. Matthew 14:30.
13. Ibid.
14. Matthew 14:31.
15. "Amazing Grace," by John Newton.

Chapter 23 • Why God Smiles

1. Matthew 15:28.
2. Matthew 15:22.
3. Matthew 15:24.
4. Matthew 15:25.
5. Matthew 15:26.
6. Matthew 15:27.
7. Daniel 9:18.

Chapter 24 • The Sacrificial Visitor

1. Matthew 15:29–32.

Chapter 25 • Holiness in a Bathrobe

1. 1 Peter 4:8.
2. Hebrews 10:14.
3. Galatians 3:27.
4. Colossians 3:3.
5. 2 Corinthians 5:21.

Chapter 26 • The Choice

1. Genesis 1:1.
2. Genesis 1:31.
3. Mark 15:34.

Chapter 27 • Caught with Your Pants Down, But Your Head Up

1. "Moon Man," *Sports Illustrated,* 13 August 1990, 58–63.

STUDY
GUIDE

It is my hope that this book has given you encouragement to not only face and survive, but to grow through the storms of life. I hope it has given you encouragement to see Christ standing tall amidst the towering waves and step out toward his holy, helping hand.

This study guide is designed to help you move from encouraging thoughts to daring living in the eye of the storm. If you are reading through this book with a group, you might try to work through one study session a week. (Group leaders, please be sensitive to the personal nature of some of the questions in this guide. Sharing answers with the group should always be optional.)

Whether you use this study guide alone or with a group, I suggest that you have your Bible and notebook close at hand. Write down your thoughts and discoveries. Pray earnestly about how God would have you respond to his promises! Use this guide not as an end unto itself, but as a catalyst for further study—as a tool to further strengthen your faith against the fury of the storm.

SESSION 1

Chapter 1   *From Calm to Chaos*

1. Describe a moment when your life went from calm to chaos. When did it happen? What were the circumstances? Who was involved?

2. Afterwards, how did you feel about that sudden switch from calm to chaos? Did you recover quickly, or do you still bear scars from the trauma?

3. Think about the internal codes you might have used to deal with the chaos. Did you have the right ones? Did you know how to use them? What codes do you need to learn in order to keep cool in the pressure cooker?

Chapter 2   *God Under Pressure*

1. After learning about John the Baptist's murder and Herod's threat, and seeing how tired the disciples were, Jesus called a "time out." He and the disciples "withdrew by boat privately to a solitary place" (Luke 9:9).

When you are dealing with a difficult situation—when you reach your limit of stress, pain, rejection, loneliness— how do you take "time out"? Where do you go? What do you do?

2. The following passages describe some of God's promises that we can hold onto during times of stress: Psalm 33:20; 34:7; 145:18; Proverbs 30:5; Isaiah 41:10; 43:2; Matthew 28:20; John 16:33; Romans 8:17; Ephesians 6:10–17; Hebrews 13:6; 1 Peter 5:10. Select one that is most meaningful

to you and write it down or memorize it so that it will comfort you the next time your world goes from calm to chaos.

3. While Jesus and the disciples were in the boat, peace reigned. Suddenly, when they reached land, the crowd converged on them again and dashed their hopes of having a few hours alone.

Can you relate? Describe a time when what you *sought* and what you *got* were completely different. How did you feel at the time? How did you respond?

4. Read Hebrews 4:15. What is your initial response to the statement, "Jesus knows how you feel"? Is there even the slightest temptation to think, "He knows how I feel most of the time, but he doesn't *really* know what *this* feels like"?

As you review the experiences in your life, is it hard for you to believe that Jesus has fully experienced them? Which ones do you think Jesus may not have fully experienced?

Why do you think it is so hard to truly believe that Jesus knows how we feel? What difference does it make that Jesus shared fully in our experience of temptation—but never sinned?

What experiences and hurts do you need to take to Jesus—your understanding Father and Physician—so that he may heal you?

5. Write down or discuss what the following references tell us about Jesus: Mark 2:5, 7, 10; Luke 2:40; John 1:1, 14; John 5:21; Colossians 2:9; Titus 2:13; Hebrews 2:14a; Hebrews 5:7; 1 John 4:2b, 3a.

SESSION 2 ─────────────────────────────

Chapter 3   *A Mother's Love—A Friend's Empathy*

1. Consider this: "Jesus knew the value of people. He knew that each human being is a treasure. And because he did, people were not a source of stress, but a source of joy."

Could someone make the same statement about you? What do you think makes the difference between seeing people as a source of stress or a source of joy?

2. Try to place yourself in Jesus' position as the crowds surrounded him. Would you have healed all the sick that day, or only certain ones? By what criteria would you have made your decisions?

3. In your daily life, what criteria do you use to determine whether or not you will help someone? How does God's example of helping and healing out of his abundant goodness affect your decisions to help others? Under what conditions are you willing to help people who "have no desire to become Christians?"

4. If you had to list three areas of your life that God "overlooks" when he bestows his love on you, what would you list?

5. Irritated by the crowd, the disciples demanded that Jesus "send them away" (Matthew 14:15). Who in your life have you sent away when you could have meet the need in love?

6. How do you respond to the demands that people make on you? What has God asked you to do that left you

openmouthed and wondering whether or not he was kidding? Why do you think you assumed that God had asked you to do the impossible? Read Hebrews 11:1 and Romans 10:17. What is faith and where does it come from?

7. What has Jesus given you that could enable you to understand how another person feels? Is there someone in your life right now to whom you could reach out with Christ's love?

8. List three areas of your life in which you could use more peace and less chaos. How might the two inner codes— "Jesus knows how you feel" and "people are precious"— change how you handle the chaos?

SESSION 3

Chapter 4   *When Fishermen Don't Fish*

1. *Compassion* means to feel deep sorrow for a person who suffers misfortune and to desire to alleviate the suffering. Matthew 14:14 says that Jesus had compassion on the people, so he changed his agenda from that of quiet rest to offering healing for body and soul.

Has anyone ever shown this depth of compassion for you? If so, what was it like to be blessed by the compassion of another person?

When have you felt compassion for another person or group of people? What action did compassion prompt you to take?

2. When has God brought hurting people into your world to break the solitude and press you into service? Explain

how you did or did not find perspective when that occurred. Describe the balance between service and solitude that fosters a godly perspective in your life.

3. Read Mark 6:7–12, 30, 31. The disciples flourished when they went fishing, didn't they? They were so excited that the pressing crowd didn't dim their enthusiasm.

When do you flourish? What "miracles" do you do in Jesus' name that get you so excited that crowds don't bother you and you forget to eat?

4. Jesus' words in Luke 6:41–42 illustrate what happens when people stop fishing and flourishing and start fighting.

In practical terms, what steps can you take to focus more of your energy on fishing and flourishing? In what ways do you tend to complain about your friends' stinky socks in the camper?

Chapter 5 *The Joy in the Journey*

1. It's easy to judge people, isn't it? Read the following verses: Leviticus 19:15; Proverbs 24:23; Acts 10:34; Romans 10:12; Galatians 2:6.

When have you made judgments that you shouldn't have made about others and missed what you could have learned from them?

2. When has your journey been interrupted by a lesson you needed to learn? What lesson did you learn? Was it a lesson that you need to be reminded of frequently?

3. How might Jesus' words about an abundant life (John 10:10b) relate to your lifestyle? If you could do three

activities this week just for fun, what would they be? In what ways could you add joy to the routine activities in your life?

SESSION 4 ─────────────────────────────

Chapter 6 *Remarkable*

1. After reading this chapter, and its list of "remarkable" things, what remarkable aspects of your life do you tend to overlook? How might your life be different if you recognized more of the remarkable occurrences of everyday life?

2. Read Job 38:4–39:30; 40:9–41:11. How do these images expand your view of the remarkable?

3. Think back to the events surrounding the second most stressful day in Jesus' life (Matthew 14:1–21; Mark 6:7–44; Luke 9:1–17).

What remarkable things do you think the disciples could easily have overlooked on that day? If they had seen those things as truly remarkable, how might their responses have been different?

As you observe these events and the disciples' responses, what parallels do you see in your own life?

4. Read 1 Thessalonians 5:18. For what remarkable things can you now give thanks?

Chapter 7 *Thanks for the Bread*

1. This chapter shares the story of an engineer who took a risk that paid off. When has your life been touched by a person who took the risk to reach out to you?

2. Read John 6:1–14.

Have you, like the little boy, ever stood up and done something that might cause others to laugh at you? If so, how did you feel? What motivated you to do it, despite the risks?

What were the results of your action? If you don't know the results, what do you hope they were?

3. Jesus multiplied the little boy's lunch so that twelve baskets of food were left over. How might this illustration relate to your gifts? Do you believe that God can use you to accomplish great things for him? Why or why not?

4. People often say, "What you believe is fine for you, and what I believe is fine for me. So don't push what you believe on me." What does this chapter say about how God might have us take risks and share our faith with others?

5. Who in your life do you need to thank for taking a risk with you?

SESSION 5 ───────────────────────────────

Chapter 8   *Musings in Minnesota*

1. Who do you call when you "call home" as the author did in chapter eight? What makes calling home so special for you?

2. What do each of the following verses say about Jesus' willingness to listen and answer when we call? Psalm 91:15; Isaiah 55:6; 58:9; 65:24; Jeremiah 33:3; Luke 11:9.

3. When you, like Jesus in Matthew 14:19, face incredible pressure, how do you respond? Get angry? Shoo the crowds away? Take a moment to ask God for help?

Right now, close your eyes and—like Jesus—listen for the familiar, comforting sounds of heaven. Think about what you hear.

How might those sounds change the way you handle things if you were to stop and listen to them the next time the pressure builds?

Chapter 9   *Fending Off the Voices*

1. Tempting voices call out in hotel rooms, from the television, at the office . . . everywhere. Which voices clamor for your attention? What messages do they shout out to you?

2. Note how Jesus responded to the crowd's applause (John 6:14–15). List two temptations you face that on the surface seem positive and uplifting, but that really will lead you toward sin. How do you respond to the clamoring voices and temptations in your life?

3. In John 10:1–5, Jesus talks about how sheep listen to their shepherd's voice. In verses 7–17, he says that he is the Good Shepherd and that his sheep respond to his voice.

What does the voice of Jesus sound like to you? Can you always hear his voice? How can you seek his voice more intently so that you can be led by him?

4. Look up John 5:28, 29. When everyone hears God's voice, what will happen?

Chapter 10   *The Photo and the File*

1. Take a look at the activities you have planned for the coming weeks and months. What do they say about your priorities?

2. If you could make four things in your life a priority, what would you pick?

Now compare these four things to your calendar of events. What does the picture look like? Are your priorities and calendar in balance? What changes would bring your priorities and activities into better balance?

3. Read Philippians 1:9–11. How might these words help you set priorities in your life?

4. When people ask you to do certain things for them—things you are not really sure you should do—how do you typically respond?

Describe the last time someone used guilt and/or pride to try to entice you into making a wrong choice.

Read Matthew 14:22. Have you ever "dismissed the crowd" or said "no" in order to seek God? What did it feel like to make that decision?

5. Who in your life loves you for who you are rather than for what you can do? How does that person (or persons) fit into your priorities?

6. Did the story of the two paddleboats hit close to home? Have you ever won the race but burned the cargo? If so, describe that time.

SESSION 6 ————————————————————————

Chapter 11   *Seeing God Through Shattered Glass*

1. Can you remember a time when pain shattered your expectations of God, when he did something that didn't seem right to you or gave you the opposite of what you thought you should receive? If so, how did that experience affect your view of God?

2. Do you have a phrase (or even several) that is always ready to complete this sentence: "If God is God, then . . ."? What is it? How did that phrase develop in your thinking?

3. Read Matthew 14:22–24. Describe a time when you felt alone in the storm—abandoned by God's protection and care. Did you become weary, even exhausted?

How did you feel about God during that time? In what ways was your heart, like the hearts of the disciples, hardened against him? (See Mark 6:52.)

4. Has God ever used an exhausting, painful, or seemingly impossible circumstance to teach you something about himself or your relationship with him? If so, describe the circumstance and the lesson.

5. In what areas of your life could you trust God more, rather than questioning how he seems to be working?

When the next storm in your life appears, how can you be better prepared to see Jesus at work in the midst of the storm?

Chapter 12   *Two Fathers, Two Feasts*

1. According to 1 Thessalonians 5:9, what is God's ultimate destiny for your life? In what ways do you prefer to "rest rather than ride" toward the destiny God has for you?

2. When have you found yourself in an unlikely classroom, or on a "decision collision" with God regarding what stops should be made or which way to turn on your journey? Whose itinerary won out?

3. What requests has God said "no" to during your life's journey? Which "nos" were easier or more difficult to take? Why?

4. Reread 1 Chronicles 29:15, Psalm 39:5, James 4:14, and Psalm 103:15, 16. What do these verses say about our journey? About what should be important?

5. What will the eternal rewards be if you allow God to plan your earthly trip? What does "being renewed day by day" really mean? (See 2 Corinthians 4:16–18.)

What makes life's journey worth the hassles? Do you believe that God "will do what is right . . . and best" in your life? Why or why not?

6. As you anticipate the coming weeks, how do you feel? Tired? Strained? Angry? Joyful? Encouraged? What "light and momentary troubles" are you facing right now? In what ways might they be "achieving for you an eternal glory"? (See 2 Corinthians 4:16–18.)

7. Write down three requests that you wish God would honor this next week. Then pray honestly for the strength to follow the destiny he has chosen for you.

SESSION 7

Chapter 13   *Doubtstorms*

1. Jesus' disciples weren't the only ones in the Bible to have doubtstorms. Moses seemed to be plagued with them (see Exodus 3:7–4:17; 5:20–6:12; 6:28–7:6; 17:1–7—just to name a few). The entire book of Job is a doubtstorm. Some of Jesus' disciples faced doubtstorms after he died (Luke 24:13–32).

Can you envision the intensity of these doubtstorms? In what ways did God show his light? Do you think those glimmers of light were expected? Why or why not?

2. Describe your blackest doubtstorms. In what unexpected ways has God shown his light to you in the midst of those storms?

3. What gentle light from God have you seen recently? Did it appear in a way that you expected?

4. Have you ever missed—or almost missed—seeing God's gentle light in the midst of your doubtstorms? How can you train your heart to see his gentle light more clearly?

Chapter 14   *The Miracle of the Carpenter*

1. Write down or share a time when, like the Sisters of Loretto, you or someone close to you faced what seemed like an impossible situation and "ascended the mountain of prayer." Who, or what, did God bring into your life to meet the need?

2. When Jesus faced an impossible day, he took time out to pray. When times get tough for you, what do you do? Do you work harder or pray? Do you get angry or pray? What does it take for you to choose to pray when things get tough?

3. What are the impossible gulfs in your life that you cannot cross alone? Do you believe that Jesus came to span the gap between where you are and where you long to be? If so, write down how you plan to seek God's guidance and power in crossing the gulfs.

Chapter 15   *The Woodcutter's Wisdom*

1. Think about the woodcutter's story for a minute. How would you have responded to the events of the woodcutter's life? Would you have been quick to draw conclusions or content to see what unfolded?

Now consider the ways in which you pass judgment on the storms that blow into your own life. Could you benefit from adopting a perspective more like that of the woodcutter than that of the villagers? Explain your answer.

2. Why do you think it is so easy to pass judgment on life "with only one day's evidence"? What are the dangers of passing judgment too quickly?

3. Describe a time when you made judgments about a specific circumstance without realizing how limited your perspective really was. What was the result of your judgments? Did your judgments stand the test of time, or prove to be only fragments?

4. Read Matthew 6:33–34. What do you think Jesus was trying to communicate to his followers through those

words? How do those words provide perspective for your life?

SESSION 8

Chapter 16   *Laws of the Lighthouse*

1. Building on the Laws of the Lighthouse concept, where do most of your signals come from? Other ships on the sea? Friends on your ship? Lighthouses that shift position with the whims of culture? The time-tested lighthouse of God's Word?

2. Review the list of lights that the author looks for and the signals he heeds. Which ones stand out to you? Why?

Now make your own list. Write down the lights and signals that you believe are vital.

3. How carefully are you heeding the warnings of your lighthouse laws? In practical terms, what can you do to pay more attention to the Laws of the Lighthouse?

Chapter 17   *He Speaks Through the Storm*

1. Describe the most difficult circumstance you've ever faced. Who was involved? What happened? How long did it last?

Did you question or lash out at God during that time? What was the result?

What did you learn through that experience? How did it affect your view of yourself? Of God? Of others?

2. Think about friends who "advised" you during a difficult time. What type of wisdom did they give you? What kind of

advice have you given to others who have faced difficult times?

3. Do you sometimes receive God's unending love with mistrust? Name a situation in which you believed that God's love wasn't in your best interest. What was the outcome?

4. Read Job 1:8–12; 2:3–7. Why did God allow Job's difficult circumstances to occur? How does that knowledge add perspective to what happened to Job? Does that knowledge shed any light on the suffering in your life or in the life of someone you know? If so, explain.

5. The author writes that God is "best heard in the storm." Do you agree? Why or why not?

6. Read Job 38–41. What is God's message to you in his answer to Job's questions?

7. When God finished speaking, Job said, "I had heard about you before, but now I have seen you" (Job 42:5, TLB). What did Job gain as a result of seeing God?

Chapter 18 *Pilgrim Ponderings*

1. Why do you think God the Father spoke to Jesus on the mountain? (See Matthew 17:1–5.)

2. What kinds of experiences make you unbearably weary, leaving you sitting on the mountainside with your face in your hands? What does it take to encourage you during those times?

3. Describe a time when God transformed your desolation and met your need in a specific way.

SESSION 9

Chapter 19   *Our Storm Was His Path*

1. Has God ever used a storm "as his path to come to you"? What were the circumstances? What was the result in your life? In the lives of others around you?

2. What is your usual response when a storm lifts you up and then plunges you into a valley? Do you find it easier to sit in a tossing boat than to step out onto the water and walk toward Jesus? Why or why not?

3. When you have been desperately afraid in your life, and have seen an image coming toward you, have you ever cried out, "Lord, is it you?" If so, what was the answer? Was it as comforting as Jesus' response in Matthew 14:27?

4. Have you ever stepped out in faith like Peter did? (See Matthew 14:28—29.) Why did you do it? What was the result?

5. Write down a time in your life when God responded to your need in a special way and you knew you'd never be the same again. What did you discover about God in that situation that you had never seen before?

6. Most of us tend to look down on Peter's ill-fated walk on the water because he sank at the end. But at least he got out of the boat! In what ways can you take steps of faith and get out of the boat this week?

Chapter 20   *They'd Do It Again*

1. Have you, like the disciples, ever really worshiped God for who he is and for what he has done for you? If so, when? If not, why not?

2. What has Christ done that has touched you so deeply that your response could only be that of worship?

3. What kinds of "crutches" do you turn to when a raging storm erupts? How do they compare with God's strength?

4. At which times in your life have you found it easiest to turn to God when storms hit? Has it ever been difficult for you to worship God even after he has stilled a storm in your life? Explain your answer.

5. What price are you willing to pay for a clear view of God?

SESSION 10

Chapter 21 *Castles of Sorrow*

1. Which of your yesterdays imprisons your todays? What "haunting rooms in your castle" need to be opened to the light of day? What fears, failures, feelings of guilt, or dashed hopes need to be surrendered to God? You may need to work this answer out before the Lord during a special time with him.

2. Contrast the two types of sorrow mentioned in 2 Corinthians 7:10. What are the results of each kind of sorrow? Which kind of sorrow plays the greatest role in your life?

3. What kind of facades do you put up to hide your guilt, failures, or feelings of inadequacy? What hope does the story of Peter's encounter with Jesus on the water (Matthew 14:28–32) offer to you?

4. Read Psalm 1:1–2; Colossians 3:16; Ephesians 1:7; 2:8–9; James 1:22–25; 1 John 1:9; 2:12, 14. What is the foundation of your spiritual house? What can you do to strengthen it?

Chapter 22   *Fear That Becomes Faith*

1. How do you respond when you are backed into a corner? Does your faith flourish or flicker? Do you cling to God or your own self-sufficiency?

2. Would you agree that "faith is often the child of fear"? Why or why not?

What circumstances have produced greater faith in your life?

3. How would you define faith as it is portrayed in this chapter? Compare your answer to the description of faith in Hebrews 11:1, 6.

4. Matthew 14:28–31 tells about Peter's adventure on the water. What parallels do you see between this passage and aspects of your life? Describe a time when you took a small step of faith and were surprised by the way God met your need.

5. Read Matthew 21:21–22; Romans 1:17; 5:1, 2; Galatians 2:16; Ephesians 2:8. When we step out in faith, how does Jesus respond?

Write down three specific ways in which you will practice faith this week—at home, at work, with friends. Share your "faith steps" with a friend or family member.

SESSION 11 —————————————————————————

Chapter 23   *Why God Smiles*

1. How do you feel about a laughing Jesus? A smiling God? Do you feel comfortable with the idea? Is it difficult for you to imagine a Jesus who is that real? Explain your answers.

2. Think about the events in Jesus' life. In which ones can you imagine him flashing a smile or chuckling with a twinkle in his eye?

3. Jesus said that the woman mentioned in Matthew 15:21–28 had great faith. What, in your opinion, did he find so impressive about her faith? Is it what you would have expected him to be impressed with? Why or why not?

Read Hebrews 11:4–32. Make a list of other people in the Bible who impressed God by their faith. Is there a person you know whose faith impresses you? If so, what do you notice?

4. Read Matthew 14:23. How did the disciples feel toward the woman? How do you think they felt after Jesus spoke with her and honored her request?

Why, in our fast-paced culture, is it easy to respond to people the way the disciples did? In light of this biblical example, how might you change your responses to people?

5. Do you find that you prefer to get salvation the old-fashioned way, by earning it? If yes, list the ways in which you have tried to impress God. If not, describe the ways in which God has mercifully chosen to bless you.

Chapter 24   *The Sacrificial Visitor*

1. Matthew 15:29–32 records Jesus' healing of many
people and their praise for the "God of Israel." But Jesus
didn't preach at them; he just reached out to help them.
What does this teach you about what sharing Christ with
a hurting world really means?

2. Read Luke's version of this event (Luke 8:1–10). How
do Matthew's and Luke's versions differ? In which aspects
are they similar? What does Luke's account reveal about
the disciples' faith?

3. Read John 3:16; Matthew 1:21; John 10:9; John 1:29;
Revelation 5:12; Hebrews 7:26, 27. In what ways have you
been saved by a Sacrificial Visitor—Jesus Christ?

4. A miracle occurred in Rickenbacker's life that kept him
alive. What miracle has God done in your life or in the life
of someone you know?

Rickenbacker gives buckets of shrimp to sea gulls to
show his gratitude. What can you give to God to say "thank
you"?

5. The crowds were amazed when they saw what Jesus
had done (Matthew 15:31). How do you respond when God
does something special in your life? Write down four things
for which you can praise—or worship—God today.

Chapter 25   *Holiness in a Bathrobe*

1. Were you surprised by what the "holy moment" was?
Why or why not?

2. As you read this chapter, did you gain a new understanding of the relationship between *honesty* and *holiness,* the difference between *perfection earned* and *perfection paid?* (See also, Colossians 1:22 and 1 Corinthians 1:8.) Explain your answer.

3. Are you ready to take an honest look in the mirror? If so, what have you been trying to do to make yourself more presentable to God?

Read Hebrews 10:14. How has God made you perfect?

What effect does his love and your perfection in his eyes have on the way you feel about yourself? On the way you relate to others? On how you relate to him?

SESSION 12 ———————————————————————————

Chapter 26   *The Choice*

1. Read Genesis 1:1–26. When was the last time you took time to appreciate God's creation? Which of God's creations amaze you? What do they communicate about the character of God? How does it feel to be the creation that made all of God's creation complete?

2. Why is it so important that God gave Adam and Eve the opportunity to choose? (See Genesis 2:15–17; 3:1–13.) If God hadn't given us a choice, how would that have influenced our relationship with him? Why is our choice as to whether or not we'll love God so important?

What were the consequences of Adam's and Eve's choice? (See Genesis 3:14–19.)

3. What choice did Jesus make to deal with the sins of all mankind?

4. What choice is the author referring to when he writes, "Now it's our choice"?

Chapter 27   *Caught with Your Pants Down, But Your Head Up*

1. How do you think people will remember you? As a person who dove headfirst into life—and perhaps made some memorable mistakes? As a person who cheered from the sidelines? As a person who half-heartedly listened to the game on the radio? Be honest!

2. Read Jeremiah 29:11; Matthew 14:30–31; John 14:12; Romans 10:11. What effect should God's promises have on those of us who are afraid to risk?

3. Have you ever paid a price to "stand on first base"? If so, write down the experience. (If you're meeting with a group, share it with them.)

Would you do it again? Why or why not? How does a person's view of God determine the type of risks he or she will take?

4. Make a list of headlong heroes—those who haven't been afraid to go all-out for what was important to them. How do your heroes inspire you to "get in the game"?

Chapter 28   *Lemonade and Grace*

1. Did the lemonade story remind you of a time in your life when God's grace overlooked your flawed accomplishments? If so, describe what happened.

2. How does God respond to us, even though he knows that what we offer him may turn out to be a gooey mess? (See Romans 8:32, 35; Ephesians 2:4, 5; Hebrews 4:16.)

3. Is it possible, as the author writes, "that a Gentle Stranger may be bringing grace to your street . . . to your life"? In what ways?

Max Lucado is a preacher who writes or a writer who preaches. He is the father of three terrific daughters and the husband of a one-in-a-million wife.

He is convinced that Jesus' tomb is empty, that his promise is not and that the Easter sunrise will never fade. He speaks of this carpenter each week at the Oak Hills Church in San Antonio, Texas. He writes about him in his books. This is his sixth.

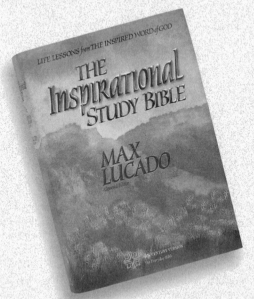

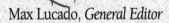

JOHN

*H*e's an old man, this one who sits on the stool and leans against the wall. Eyes closed and face soft, were it not for his hand stroking his beard, you'd think he was asleep.

Some in the room assume he is. He does this often during worship. As the people sing, his eyes will close and his chin will fall until it rests on his chest, and there he will remain motionless. Silent.

Those who know him well know better. They know he is not resting. He is traveling. Atop the music he journeys back, back, back until he is young again. Strong again. There again. There on the seashore with James and the apostles. There on the trail with the disciples and the women. There in the Temple with Caiaphas and the accusers.

It's been sixty years, but John sees him still. The decades took John's strength, but they didn't take his memory. The years dulled his sight, but they didn't dull his vision. The seasons may have wrinkled his face, but they didn't soften his love.

He had been with God. God had been with him. How could he forget?

❧ The wine that moments before had been water—John could still taste it.

❧ The mud placed on the eyes of the blind man in Jerusalem—John could still remember it.

❧ The aroma of Mary's perfume as it filled the room—John could still smell it.

And the voice. Oh, the voice. His voice. John could still hear it.

I am the light of the world, it rang ... I am the door ... I am the way, the truth, the life.

I will come back, it promised, and take you to be with me.

Those who believe in me, it assured, will have life even if they die.

John could hear him. John could see him. Scenes branded on his heart. Words seared into his soul. John would never forget. How could he? He had been there.

He opens his eyes and blinks. The singing has stopped. The teaching has begun. John looks at the listeners and listens to the teacher.

If only you could have been there, he thinks.

But he wasn't. Most weren't. Most weren't even born. And most who were there are dead. Peter is. So is James. Nathanael, Martha, Philip. They are all gone. Even Paul, the apostle who came late, is dead.

Only John remains.

He looks again at the church. Small but earnest. They lean forward to hear the teacher. John listens to him. What a task. Speaking of one he never saw. Explaining words he never heard. John is there if the teacher needs him.

But what will happen when John is gone? What will the teacher do then? When John's voice is silent and his tongue stilled? Who will tell them how Jesus silenced the waves? Will they hear how he fed the thousands? Will they remember how he prayed for unity?

How will they know? If only they could have been there.

Suddenly, in his heart he knows what to do.

Later, under the light of a sunlit shaft, the old fisherman unfolds the scroll and begins to write the story of his life ...

In the beginning there was the Word ...

LIFE LESSON

John 1:1-51

SITUATION ✒ The Greeks and the Jews were familiar with the concept of the *word*. For the Jews it was an expression of God's wisdom, and for the Greeks it meant reason and intellect.

OBSERVATION ✒ Leaving his heavenly home, Jesus put on human flesh to bring us God's Good News.

INSPIRATION ✒ It all happened in a moment, a most remarkable moment. . . . that was like none other. For through that segment of time a spectacular thing occurred. God became a man. While the creatures of earth walked unaware, Divinity arrived. Heaven opened herself and placed her most precious one in a human womb. . . .

God as a fetus. Holiness sleeping in a womb. The creator of life being created.

God was given eyebrows, elbows, two kidneys, and a spleen. He stretched against the walls and floated in the amniotic fluids of his mother.

God had come near. . . .

The hands that first held him were unmanicured, calloused, and dirty.

No silk. No ivory. No hype. No party. No hoopla.

Were it not for the shepherds, there would have been no reception. And were it not for a group of star-gazers, there would have been no gifts. . . .

Christ Comes to the World

*I*n the beginning there was the Word.[n] The Word was with God, and the Word was God. [2]He was with God in the beginning. [3]All things were made by him, and nothing was made without him. [4]In him there was life, and that life was the light of all people. [5]The Light shines in the darkness, and the darkness has not overpowered it.

[6]There was a man named John[n] who was sent by God. [7]He came to tell people the truth about the Light so that through him all people could hear about the Light and believe. [8]John was not the Light, but he came to tell people the truth about the Light. [9]The true Light that gives light to all was coming into the world!

[10]The Word was in the world, and the world was made by him, but the world did not know him. [11]He came to the world that was his own, but his own people did not accept him. [12]But to all who did accept him and believe in him he gave the right to become children of God. [13]They did not become his children in any human way—by any human parents or human desire. They were born of God.

[14]The Word became a human and lived among us. We saw his glory—the glory that belongs to the only Son of the Father—and he was full of grace and truth. [15]John tells the truth about him and cries out, saying, "This is the One I told you about: 'The One who comes after me is greater than I am, because he was living before me.'"

[16]Because he was full of grace and truth, from him we all received one gift after another. [17]The law was given through Moses, but grace and truth came through Jesus Christ. [18]No one has ever seen God. But God the only Son is very close to the Father,[n] and he has shown us what God is like.

John Tells People About Jesus

[19]Here is the truth John[n] told when the Jews in Jerusalem sent priests and Levites to ask him, "Who are you?"

[20]John spoke freely and did not refuse to answer. He said, "I am not the Christ."

[21]So they asked him, "Then who are you? Are you Elijah?"[n]

He answered, "No, I am not."

"Are you the Prophet?"[n] they asked.

He answered, "No."

[22]Then they said, "Who are you? Give us an answer to tell those who sent us. What do you say about yourself?"

[23]John told them in the words of the prophet Isaiah:

"I am the voice of one
    calling out in the desert:
'Make the road straight for the Lord.'"   *Isaiah 40:3*

Word   The Greek word is "logos," meaning any kind of communication; it could be translated "message." Here, it means Christ, because Christ was the way God told people about himself.
John   John the Baptist, who preached to people about Christ's coming (Matthew 3, Luke 3).
But . . . Father   This could be translated, "But the only God is very close to the Father." Also, some Greek copies say, "But the only Son is very close to the Father."
John   John the Baptist, who preached to people about Christ's coming (Matthew 3, Luke 3).
Elijah   A man who spoke for God. He lived hundreds of years before Christ and was expected to return before Christ (Malachi 4:5-6).
Prophet   They probably meant the prophet that God told Moses he would send (Deuteronomy 18:15-19).

²⁴Some Pharisees who had been sent asked John:²⁵"If you are not the Christ or Elijah or the Prophet, why do you baptize people?"

²⁶John answered, "I baptize with water, but there is one here with you that you don't know about. ²⁷He is the One who comes after me. I am not good enough to untie the strings of his sandals."

²⁸This all happened at Bethany on the other side of the Jordan River, where John was baptizing people.

²⁹The next day John saw Jesus coming toward him. John said, "Look, the Lamb of God,ⁿ who takes away the sin of the world! ³⁰This is the One I was talking about when I said, 'A man will come after me, but he is greater than I am, because he was living before me.' ³¹Even I did not know who he was, although I came baptizing with water so that the people of Israel would know who he is."

³²⁻³³Then John said, "I saw the Spirit come down from heaven in the form of a dove and rest on him. Until then I did not know who the Christ was. But the God who sent me to baptize with water told me, 'You will see the Spirit come down and rest on a man; he is the One who will baptize with the Holy Spirit.' ³⁴I have seen this happen, and I tell you the truth: This man is the Son of God."

The First Followers of Jesus

³⁵The next day Johnⁿ was there again with two of his followers. ³⁶When he saw Jesus walking by, he said, "Look, the Lamb of God!"ⁿ

³⁷The two followers heard John say this, so they followed Jesus. ³⁸When Jesus turned and saw them following him, he asked, "What are you looking for?"

They said, "Rabbi, where are you staying?" ("Rabbi" means "Teacher.")

³⁹He answered, "Come and see." So the two men went with Jesus and saw where he was staying and stayed there with him that day. It was about four o'clock in the afternoon.

⁴⁰One of the two men who followed Jesus after they heard John speak about him was Andrew, Simon Peter's brother. ⁴¹The first thing Andrew did was to find his brother Simon and say to him, "We have found the Messiah." ("Messiah" means "Christ.")

⁴²Then Andrew took Simon to Jesus. Jesus looked at him and said, "You are Simon son of John. You will be called Cephas." ("Cephas" means "Peter."ⁿ)

⁴³The next day Jesus decided to go to Galilee. He found Philip and said to him, "Follow me."

⁴⁴Philip was from the town of Bethsaida, where Andrew and Peter lived. ⁴⁵Philip found Nathanael and told him, "We have found the man that Moses wrote about in the law, and the prophets also wrote about him. He is Jesus, the son of Joseph, from Nazareth."

⁴⁶But Nathanael said to Philip, "Can anything good come from Nazareth?"

Philip answered, "Come and see."

⁴⁷As Jesus saw Nathanael coming toward him, he said, "Here is truly an Israelite. There is nothing false in him."

For thirty-three years he would feel everything you and I have ever felt. He felt weak. He grew weary. He was afraid of failure. He was susceptible to wooing women. He got colds, burped, and had body odor. His feelings got hurt. His feet got tired. And his head ached.

To think of Jesus in such a light is— well, it seems almost irreverent, doesn't it? It's not something we like to do; it's uncomfortable. It is much easier to keep the humanity out of the incarnation. He's easier to stomach that way. . . .

But don't do it. For heaven's sake, don't. Let him be as human as he intended to be. Let him into the mire and muck of our world. For only if we let him in can he pull us out.

(From *God Came Near* by Max Lucado)

APPLICATION 🖋 If people want to know what God is like, they can look at Jesus. If they want to know what Jesus is like, they should be able to look at his followers. Can people see Christ in you?

EXPLORATION 🖋 The Word is Born—John 14:6-7; 1 Corinthians 8:5-6; Galatians 4:4; Philippians 2:7, 8; 1 Timothy 3:16; Hebrews 2:14; 13:8; 1 John 1:1-2; 4:2.

Lamb of God   Name for Jesus. Jesus is like the lambs that were offered for a sacrifice to God.
Peter   The Greek name "Peter," like the Aramaic name "Cephas," means "rock."

HE STILL
MOVES
STONES

Other Books by Max Lucado

On the Anvil
No Wonder They Call Him the Savior
God Came Near
Six Hours One Friday
The Applause of Heaven
In the Eye of the Storm
Just in Case You Ever Wonder
And the Angels Were Silent
Tell Me the Story

HE STILL MOVES STONES

MAX LUCADO

WORD PUBLISHING
Dallas·London·Vancouver·Melbourne

Unless otherwise indicated, all Scripture references are from the New Century Version of the Bible, copyright © 1987, 1988, 1991, Word Publishing. Other Scripture quotations are from:

The New King James Version (NKJV), copyright © 1979, 1980, 1982, Thomas Nelson, Inc., Publisher.

The Holy Bible, New International Version (NIV), copyright © 1973, 1978, 1984 International Bible Society, and are used by permission of Zondervan Bible Publishers.

The Living Bible (TLB), copyright © 1971 by Tyndale House Publishers, Wheaton, Ill. Used by permission.

The New Testament in Modern English by J. B. Phillips (PHILLIPS), published by The Macmillan Company, © 1958, 1960, 1972 by J. B. Phillips.

Library of Congress Cataloging-in-Publication Data is available.

ISBN 0–8499–0864–7   LC 93–14512

6 7 8 9   RRD   10 9 8 7 6 5 4 3 2 1

Printed in the United States of America

A five-time divorcée.

A despondent cripple.

A sister at a funeral.

A father in an emergency.

These are not just Sunday school stories. Not romantic fables. Not somewhere-over-the-rainbow illusions. They are historic moments in which a real God met real pain so we could answer the question, "Where is God when I hurt?"

Author Max Lucado invites us to relive these stories with him. To be reminded that the God who spoke still speaks. To know that the God who forgave still forgives. The God who came still comes. He comes into your world. He comes to do what you can't. He comes to move the stones you can't budge.

He still moves stones.

Contents

Acknowledgments

Writing a book and traversing a desert have much in common. Long stretches of dry flatland marked with occasional pools of inspiration. Here's a salute to dear friends who made this journey so pleasant. Thanks for not complaining at the sand and celebrating at each oasis.

For my assistant, Karen Hill: You do more than organize my office and edit my writing. You preserve my sanity!

For my editor, Liz Heaney: Like a good surgeon, your judgment is keen and your scalpel sharp.

For the family at Word Publishing: To each of you—editors, artists, secretaries, receptionists, salespeople, and decision makers—you're the best.

For Roy and Barbie Johnston: Thanks for loaning me your Horseshoe Bay hideaway.

For UpWords Executive Director Steve Green: No one else could do what you do the way you do it. We are in your debt.

For my wife, Denalyn: What else can I say? You are starlight and I'm Galileo. Your sparkle still stuns.

And for you the reader, I reserve my final salute:

For some of you this book marks our tenth encounter (happy anniversary!). For others it's our first (glad to meet you). And for most, this is somewhere in between (good to be with you again).

You are about to entrust me with your most valuable asset—your time. I pledge to be a good steward. Though writing a book can be like a desert journey, reading a book shouldn't be. It should be a pause at the oasis. I hope it is.

Drink deeply.

Max Lucado

1

BRUISED REEDS AND SMOLDERING WICKS

A bruised reed he will not break,
and a smoldering wick he will not
snuff out.

Matthew 12:20 NIV

_I_magine it's a Saturday afternoon in October. What you needed to get done today, you've already done. Your afternoon lies before you with no obligations. Free afternoons don't come as often as they once did, so you consider your options for the day. You pick up a paper to get some ideas. A movie? Nothing good is showing. Television? You can do that any time. Wait. What's this? An ad catches your eye.

Special Art Exhibit
"Bruised Reeds and Smoldering Wicks"
2:00 to 4:00 Saturday Afternoon
Lincoln Library

Hmm . . . It's been a while since you've seen some good art. Bruised Reeds and Smoldering Wicks? Probably some nature stuff. Besides, the walk would be nice. You'll do it. You lay down the paper, put on a coat, and grab some gloves.

You're greeted by the musty odor of books as you walk through the library doors. Behind the counter sits a librarian with her hair in a bun and a pencil behind her ear. A student with a backpack at his feet stares into a drawer of cataloged cards. A table featuring old _Life_ magazines strikes you as interesting. You start to pick up the one with Truman on the cover when you see

13

a sign that reminds you why you came. "Bruised Reeds and Smoldering Wicks" it reads and points you toward a door. You walk across a hallway and open one of two heavy, wooden doors and step in.

It's an intimate room—no larger than a nice den. Bookshelves cover the walls, and books line the shelves. A fire crackles in a fireplace, and a couple of high wingback chairs invite you to spend the afternoon with a good book. *Maybe later,* you think. *First, the art.*

Placed around the room are the paintings. All framed. All in vivid color. All set on easels, in pairs, and always back to back. You put your gloves in your coat pocket, hang your coat on a hook, and move toward the first painting.

It's a portrait of a leper, the center figure on the canvas. He stoops like a hunchback. His fingerless hand, draped in rags, extends toward you, pleading. A tattered wrap hides all of his face except two pain-filled eyes. The crowd around the leper is chaotic. A father is grabbing a curious child. A woman trips over her own feet as she scrambles to get away. A man glares over his shoulder as he runs. The painting is entitled with the leper's plea, "If you will, you can . . ."

The next painting portrays the same leper, but the scene has changed dramatically. The title has only two words, "I will." In this sketch the leper is standing erect and tall. He is looking at his own outstretched hand—it has fingers! The veil is gone from his face and he is smiling. There is no crowd; only one other person is standing beside the leper. You can't see his face, but you can see his hand on the shoulder of the healed man.

"This is no nature exhibit," you whisper to yourself as you turn to the next painting.

In this one the artist's brush has captured a woman in midair, jumping from one side of a canyon to another. Her clothes are ragged. Her body is frail, and her skin is pale. She looks anemic. Her eyes are desperate as she reaches for the canyon wall with both hands. On the ledge is a man. All you see are his legs, sandals, and the hem of a robe. Beneath the painting are the woman's words, "If only . . ."

You step quickly to see the next scene. She is standing now. The ground beneath her bare feet is solid. Her face flushes with life. Her cautious eyes look up at the half-moon of people that surround her. Standing beside her is the one she sought to touch. The caption? His words. "Take heart . . ."

The next portrait is surrealistic. A man's contorted face dominates the canvas. Orange hair twists against a purple background. The face stretches downward and swells at the bottom like a pear. The eyes are perpendicular slits in which a thousand tiny pupils bounce. The mouth is frozen open in a scream. You notice something odd—it's inhabited! Hundreds of spiderish creatures claw over each other. Their desperate voices are captured by the caption, "Swear to God you won't torture me!"

Fascinated, you step to the next painting. It is the same man, but now his features are composed. His eyes, no longer wild, are round and soft. The mouth is closed, and the caption explains the sudden peace: "Released." The man is leaning forward as if listening intently. His hand strokes his chin. And dangling from his wrist is a shackle and a chain—a broken chain.

In another portrait a scantily clothed female cowers before an angry mob of men who threaten her with stones. In the next painting the stones lie harmlessly on the ground, littering the courtyard occupied by a surprised woman and a smiling man who stands over some pictures drawn in the dirt.

In one painting a paralytic on a pallet urges his friends not to give up as they stare at a house overflowing with people. In the next the pallet is on the boy's shoulders as he skips out the door of the house.

In one picture a blind man screams to a rabbi. In the next he bows before the one to whom he screamed.

Throughout the gallery the sequence repeats itself. Always two paintings, one of a person in trauma and one of a person in peace. "Before" and "after" testimonials to a life-changing encounter. Scene after scene of serenity eclipsing sorrow. Purpose defeating pain. Hope outshining hurt.

But alone in the center of the hall is a single painting. It is different from the others. There are no faces. No people. The artist has dipped his brush into ancient prophecy and sketched two simple objects—a reed and a wick.

> A bruised reed he will not break,
> and a smoldering wick he will not snuff out.
>
> Matthew 12:20 NIV

Is there anything more frail than a bruised reed? Look at the bruised reed at the water's edge. A once slender and tall stalk of sturdy river grass, it is now bowed and bent.

Are you a bruised reed? Was it so long ago that you stood so tall, so proud? You were upright and sturdy, nourished by the waters and rooted in the riverbed of confidence.

Then something happened. You were bruised . . .

by harsh words
by a friend's anger
by a spouse's betrayal
by your own failure
by religion's rigidity.

And you were wounded, bent ever so slightly. Your hollow reed, once erect, now stooped, and hidden in the bulrush.

And the smoldering wick on the candle. Is there anything closer to death than a smoldering wick? Once aflame, now flickering and failing. Still warm from yesterday's passion, but no fire. Not yet cold but far from hot. Was it that long ago you blazed with faith? Remember how you illuminated the path?

Then came the wind . . . the cold wind, the harsh wind. They said your ideas were foolish. They told you your dreams were too lofty. They scolded you for challenging the time-tested.

The constant wind wore down upon you. Oh, you stood strong for a moment (or maybe a lifetime), but the endless blast whipped your flickering flame, leaving you one pinch away from darkness.

The bruised reed and the smoldering wick. Society knows what to do with you. The world has a place for the beaten. The world will break you off; the world will snuff you out.

But the artists of Scripture proclaim that God won't. Painted on canvas after canvas is the tender touch of a Creator who has a special place for the bruised and weary of the world. A God who is the friend of the wounded heart. A God who is the keeper of your dreams. That's the theme of the New Testament.

And that's the theme of the gallery.

Let's stroll through the gallery together. Let's ponder the moments when Christ met people at their points of pain. We'll see the prophecy proved true. We'll see bruised reeds straightened and smoldering wicks ignited.

It's quite a collection of paintings. By the way, your portrait is in the gallery too. Go ahead. Look at it. It's there, to the side. Just like the others, there are two easels. But unlike the others, these canvases are white. Your name is at the bottom. Beside the easel is a table with paint and a brush . . .

THE BRUISED REED

It stood with assurance.
Head held high on strong stalk.
But that was before the careless bump, the harsh rain.
Now it's bruised, bent. Weakened.
It seeks gentle fingers to straighten and not break.
It needs a firm touch to heal and not to hurt.
Tender power.
Soft strength.
Is there such a hand?

2

NOT GUILTY

Overcoming Shame

Jesus went to the Mount of Olives. But early in the morning he went back to the Temple, and all the people came to him, and he sat and taught them. The teachers of the law and the Pharisees brought a woman who had been caught in adultery. They forced her to stand before the people. They said to Jesus, "Teacher, this woman was caught having sexual relations with a man who is not her husband. The law of Moses commands that we stone to death every woman who does this. What do you say we should do?" They were asking this to trick Jesus so that they could have some charge against him.

But Jesus bent over and started writing on the ground with his finger. When they continued to ask Jesus their question, he raised up and said, "Anyone here who has never sinned can throw the first stone at her." Then Jesus bent over again and wrote on the ground.

Those who heard Jesus began to leave one by one, first the older men and then the others. Jesus was left there alone with the woman standing before him. Jesus raised up again and asked her, "Woman, where are they? Has no one judged you guilty?"

She answered, "No one, sir."

Then Jesus said, "I also don't judge you guilty. You may go now, but don't sin anymore."

John 8:1–11

"I also don't judge you guilty."

John 8:11

---

*R*ebecca Thompson fell twice from the Fremont Canyon Bridge. She died both times. The first fall broke her heart; the second broke her neck.

She was only eighteen years of age when she and her eleven-year-old sister were abducted by a pair of hoodlums near a store in Casper, Wyoming. They drove the girls forty miles southwest to the Fremont Canyon Bridge, a one-lane, steel-beamed structure rising 112 feet above the North Platte River.

The men brutally beat and raped Rebecca. She somehow convinced them not to do the same to her sister Amy. Both were thrown over the bridge into the narrow gorge. Amy died when she landed on a rock near the river, but Rebecca slammed into a ledge and was ricocheted into deeper water.

With a hip fractured in five places, she struggled to the shore. To protect her body from the cold, she wedged herself between two rocks and waited until the dawn.

But the dawn never came for Rebecca. Oh, the sun came up, and she was found. The physicians treated her wounds, and the courts imprisoned her attackers. Life continued, but the dawn never came.

The blackness of her night of horrors lingered. She was never able to climb out of the canyon. So in September 1992, nineteen years later, she returned to the bridge.

Against her boyfriend's pleadings, she drove seventy miles-per-hour to the North Platte River. With her two-year-old daughter and boyfriend at her side, she sat on the edge of the Fremont Canyon Bridge and wept. Through her tears she retold the story. The boyfriend didn't want the child to see her mother cry, so he carried the toddler to the car.

That's when he heard her body hit the water.

And that's when Rebecca Thompson died her second death. The sun never dawned on Rebecca's dark night. Why? What eclipsed the light from her world?

Fear? Perhaps. She had testified against the men, pointing them out in the courtroom. One of the murderers had taunted her by smirking and sliding his finger across his throat. On the day of her death, the two had been up for parole. Perhaps the fear of a second encounter was too great.

Was it anger? Anger at her rapists? Anger at the parole board? Anger at herself for the thousand falls in the thousand nightmares that followed? Or anger at God for a canyon that grew ever deeper and a night that grew ever blacker and a dawn that never came?

Was it guilt? Some think so. Despite Rebecca's attractive smile and appealing personality, friends say that she struggled with the ugly fact that she had survived and her little sister had not.

Was it shame? Everyone she knew and thousands she didn't had heard the humiliating details of her tragedy. The stigma was tattooed deeper with the newspaper ink of every headline. She had been raped. She had been violated. She had been shamed. And try as she might to outlive and outrun the memory . . . she never could.

So nineteen years later she went back to the bridge.

Canyons of shame run deep. Gorges of never-ending guilt. Walls ribboned with the greens and grays of death. Unending echoes of screams. Put your hands over your ears. Splash water on your face. Stop looking over your shoulder. Try as you might to outrun yesterday's tragedies—their tentacles are longer than your hope. They draw you back to the bridge of sorrows to be shamed again and again and again.

If it was your fault, it would be different. If you were to blame, you could apologize. If the tumble into the canyon was your mistake, you could respond. But you weren't a volunteer. You were a victim.

Sometimes your shame is private. Pushed over the edge by an abusive spouse. Molested by a perverted parent. Seduced by a compromising superior. No one else knows. But you know. And that's enough.

Sometimes it's public. Branded by a divorce you didn't want. Contaminated by a disease you never expected. Marked by a handicap you didn't create. And whether it's actually in their eyes or just in your imagination, you have to deal with it—you are marked: a divorcee, an invalid, an orphan, an AIDS patient.

Whether private or public, shame is always painful. And unless you deal with it, it is permanent. Unless you get help— the dawn will never come.

You're not surprised when I say there are Rebecca Thompsons in every city and Fremont Bridges in every town. And there are many Rebecca Thompsons in the Bible. So many, in fact, that it almost seems that the pages of Scripture are stitched together with their stories. You've met many in this book. Each acquainted with the hard floor of the canyon of shame.

But there is one woman whose story embodies them all. A story of failure. A story of abuse. A story of shame.

And a story of grace.

That's her, the woman standing in the center of the circle. Those men around her are religious leaders. Pharisees, they are called. Self-appointed custodians of conduct. And the other man, the one in the simple clothes, the one sitting on the ground, the one looking at the face of the woman, that's Jesus.

Jesus has been teaching.

The woman has been cheating.

And the Pharisees are out to stop them both.

"Teacher, this woman was caught in the act of adultery" (John 8:4 NIV). The accusation rings off the courtyard walls.

"Caught in the act of adultery." The words alone are enough to make you blush. Doors slammed open. Covers jerked back.

"In the act." In the arms. In the moment. In the embrace.

"Caught." Aha! What have we here? This man is not your husband. Put on some clothes! We know what to do with women like you!

In an instant she is yanked from private passion to public spectacle. Heads poke out of windows as the posse pushes her through the streets. Dogs bark. Neighbors turn. The city sees. Clutching a thin robe around her shoulders, she hides her nakedness.

But nothing can hide her shame.

From this second on, she'll be known as an adulteress. When she goes to the market, women will whisper. When she passes, heads will turn. When her name is mentioned, the people will remember.

Moral failure finds easy recall.

The greater travesty, however, goes unnoticed. What the woman did is shameful, but what the Pharisees did is despicable. According to the law, adultery was punishable by death, but only if two people witnessed the act. There had to be two eyewitnesses.

Question: How likely are two people to be eyewitnesses to adultery? What are the chances of two people stumbling upon an early morning flurry of forbidden embraces? Unlikely. But if you do, odds are it's not a coincidence.

So we wonder. How long did the men peer through the window before they barged in? How long did they lurk behind the curtain before they stepped out?

And what of the man? Adultery requires two participants. What happened to him? Could it be that he slipped out?

The evidence leaves little doubt. It was a trap. She's been caught. But she'll soon see that she is not the catch—she's only the bait.

"The law of Moses commands that we stone to death every woman who does this. What do you say we should do?" (v. 5).

Pretty cocky, this committee of high ethics. Pretty proud of themselves, these agents of righteousness. This will be a moment they long remember, the morning they foil and snag the mighty Nazarene.

As for the woman? Why, she's immaterial. Merely a pawn in their game. Her future? It's unimportant. Her reputation? Who cares if it's ruined? She is a necessary, yet dispensable, part of their plan.

The woman stares at the ground. Her sweaty hair dangles. Her tears drip hot with hurt. Her lips are tight, her jaw is clenched. She knows she's been framed. No need to look up. She'll find no kindness. She looks at the stones in their hands. Squeezed so tightly that fingertips turn white.

She thinks of running. But where? She could claim mistreatment. But to whom? She could deny the act, but she was seen. She could beg for mercy, but these men offer none.

The woman has nowhere to turn.

You'd expect Jesus to stand and proclaim judgment on the hypocrites. He doesn't. You'd hope that he would snatch the woman and the two would be beamed to Galilee. That's not what happens either. You'd imagine that an angel would descend or heaven would speak or the earth would shake. No, none of that.

Once again, his move is subtle.

But, once again, his message is unmistakable.

What does Jesus do? (If you already know, pretend you don't and feel the surprise.)

Jesus writes in the sand.

He stoops down and draws in the dirt. The same finger that engraved the commandments on Sinai's peak and seared the warning on Belshazzar's wall now scribbles in the courtyard floor. And as he writes, he speaks: "Anyone here who has never sinned can throw the first stone at her" (v. 7).

The young look to the old. The old look in their hearts. They are the first to drop their stones. And as they turn to leave, the young who were cocky with borrowed convictions do the same. The only sound is the thud of rocks and the shuffle of feet.

Jesus and the woman are left alone. With the jury gone, the courtroom becomes the judge's chambers, and the woman awaits his verdict. *Surely, a sermon is brewing. No doubt, he's going to demand that I apologize.* But the judge doesn't speak. His head is down, perhaps he's still writing in the sand. He seems surprised when he realizes that she is still there.

"Woman, where are they? Has no one judged you guilty?"

She answers, "No one, sir."

Then Jesus says, "I also don't judge you guilty. You may go now, but don't sin anymore" (vv. 10–11).

If you have ever wondered how God reacts when you fail, frame these words and hang them on the wall. Read them. Ponder them. Drink from them. Stand below them and let them wash over your soul.

Or better still, take him with you to your canyon of shame. Invite Christ to journey with you back to the Fremont Bridge of your world. Let him stand beside you as you retell the events of the darkest nights of your soul.

And then listen. Listen carefully. He's speaking.

"I don't judge you guilty."

And watch. Watch carefully. He's writing. He's leaving a message. Not in the sand, but on a cross.

Not with his hand, but with his blood.

His message has two words: Not guilty.

3

DON'T MISS THE PARTY

The Dungeon of the Bitter

"The older son was in the field, and as he came closer to the house, he heard the sound of music and dancing. So he called to one of the servants and asked what all this meant. The servant said, 'Your brother has come back, and your father killed the fat calf, because your brother came home safely.' The older son was angry and would not go in to the feast. So his father went out and begged him to come in. But the older son said to his father, 'I have served you like a slave for many years and have always obeyed your commands. But you never gave me even a young goat to have at a feast with my friends. But your other son, who wasted all your money on prostitutes, comes home, and you kill the fat calf for him!' The father said to him, 'Son, you are always with me, and all that I have is yours. We had to celebrate and be happy because your brother was dead, but now he is alive. He was lost, but now he is found.'"

Luke 15:25–32

> "The older son was angry and would
> not go in to the feast."
>
> Luke 15:28

---

*T*he case of the elder brother.

A difficult one because he looked so good. He kept his room straight and his nose clean. He played by the rules and paid all his dues. His résumé? Impeccable. His credit? Squeaky clean. And loyalty? While his brother was sowing wild oats, he stayed home and sowed the crops.

On the outside he was everything a father could want in a son. But on the inside he was sour and hollow. Overcome by jealousy. Consumed by anger. Blinded by bitterness.

You remember the story. It's perhaps the best known of all the parables Jesus told. It's the third of three stories in Luke 15, three stories of three parties.

The first began after a shepherd found a sheep he'd lost. He had ninety-nine others. He could have been content to write this one off as a loss. But shepherds don't think like businessmen. So he searched for it. When he found the sheep, he carried it back to the flock, cut the best grass for the sheep to eat, and had a party to celebrate.

The second party was held in front of a house. A housewife had lost a coin. It wasn't her only coin, but you would have thought it was by the way she acted. She moved the furniture, got out the dust mop, and swept the whole house till she found it. And when she did, she ran shouting into the cul-de-sac and invited her neighbors over for a party to celebrate.

Then there is the story of the lost son. The boy who broke his father's heart by taking his inheritance and taking off. He trades his dignity for a whisky bottle and his self-respect for a pigpen. Then comes the son's sorrow and his decision to go home. He hopes his dad will give him a job on the farm and an apartment over the garage. What he finds is a father who has kept his absent son's place set at the table and the porch light on every night.

The father is so excited to see his son, you'll never guess what he does. That's right! He throws a party! We party-loving prodigals love what he did, but it infuriated the elder brother.

"The older son was angry" (v. 28). It's not hard to see why. "So, is this how a guy gets recognition in this family? Get drunk and go broke and you get a party?" So he sat outside the house and pouted.

I did that once. I pouted at a party. A Christmas party. I was in the fourth grade. Fourth graders take parties very seriously, especially when there are gifts involved. We had drawn names. Since you didn't know who had your name, you had to drop your hints very loudly. I didn't miss a chance. I wanted a "Sixth Finger"—a toy pistol that fit in the cleft of your hand and looked like a finger. (Honestly, it did exist!)

Finally the day came to open the gifts. I just knew I was going to get my pistol. Everyone in the class had heard my hints. I tore into the wrapping and ripped open the box and . . . know what I got? Stationery. Western stationery. Paper and envelopes with horses in the corners. Yuck! Probably left over from the Christmas before. Ten-year-old boys don't write letters! What was this person thinking? No doubt some mom forgot all about the present until this morning, so she went to the closet and rumbled about until she came out with stationery.

Tie my hands and feet and throw me in the river. I was distraught. I was upset. So I missed the party. I was present, but I pouted.

So did the big brother. He, too, felt he was a victim of inequity. When his father came out to meet him, the son started at the top, listing the atrocities of his life. To hear him say it, his woes began the day he was born.

"I have served you like a slave for many years and have always obeyed your commands. But you never gave me even a young goat to have at a feast with my friends. But your other son, who wasted all your money on prostitutes, comes home, and you kill the fat calf for him!" (v. 29–30).

Appears that both sons spent time in the pigpen. One in the pen of rebellion—the other in the pen of self-pity. The younger one has come home. The older one hasn't. He's still in the slop. He is saying the same thing you said when the kid down the street got a bicycle and you didn't. It's not fair!

That's what Wanda Holloway of Channelview, Texas, said. When it looked like her fourteen-year-old daughter wouldn't get elected to the cheerleading squad, Wanda got angry. She decided to get even. She hired a hit man to kill the mother of her daughter's chief competitor, hoping to so upset the girl that Wanda's daughter would make the squad. Bitterness will do that to you. It'll cause you to burn down your house to kill a rat.

Fortunately, her plan failed and Wanda Holloway was caught. She was sentenced to fifteen years. She didn't have to be put behind bars to be imprisoned, however. Bitterness is its own prison.

Black and cold, bitterness denies easy escape. The sides are slippery with resentment. A floor of muddy anger stills the feet. The stench of betrayal fills the air and stings the eyes. A cloud of self-pity blocks the view of the tiny exit above.

Step in and look at the prisoners. Victims are chained to the walls. Victims of betrayal. Victims of abuse. Victims of the government, the system, the military, the world. They lift their chains as they lift their voices and wail. Loud and long they wail.

They grumble. They're angry at others who got what they didn't.

They sulk. The world is against them.

They accuse. The pictures of their enemies are darted to the wall.

They boast. "I followed the rules. I played fairly . . . in fact, better than anybody else."

They whine. "Nobody listens to me. Nobody remembers me. Nobody cares about me."

Angry. Sullen. Accusatory. Arrogant. Whiny. Put them all together in one word and spell it b-i-t-t-e-r. If you put them all in one person, that person is in the pit—the dungeon of bitterness.

The dungeon, deep and dark, is beckoning you to enter.

You can, you know. You've experienced enough hurt. You've been betrayed enough times. You have a history of rejections, don't you? Haven't you been left out, left behind, or left out in the cold? You are a candidate for the dungeon.

You can choose, like many, to chain yourself to your hurt.

Or you can choose, like some, to put away your hurts before they become hates. You can choose to go to the party. You have a place there. Your name is beside a plate. If you are a child of God, no one can take away your sonship.

Which is precisely what the father said to the older son. "Son, you are always with me, and all that I have is yours" (v. 31).

And that is precisely what the Father says to you. How does God deal with your bitter heart? He reminds you that what you have is more important than what you don't have. You still have your relationship with God. No one can take that. No one can touch it.

Your health can be taken and your money stolen—but your place at God's table is permanent.

The brother was bitter because he focused on what he didn't have and forgot what he did have. His father reminded him—and us—that he had everything he'd always had. He had his job. His place. His name. His inheritance. The only thing he didn't have was the spotlight. And because he wasn't content to share it—he missed the party.

It takes courage to set aside jealousy and rejoice with the

achievements of a rival. Would you like an example of someone who did?

Standing before ten thousand eyes is Abraham Lincoln. An uncomfortable Abraham Lincoln. His discomfort comes not from the thought of delivering his first inaugural address but from the ambitious efforts of well-meaning tailors. He's unaccustomed to such attire—formal black dress coat, silk vest, black trousers, and a glossy top hat. He holds a huge ebony cane with a golden head the size of an egg.

He approaches the platform with hat in one hand and cane in the other. He doesn't know what to do with either one. In the nervous silence that comes after the applause and before the speech, he searches for a spot to place them. He finally leans the cane in a corner of the railing, but he still doesn't know what to do with the hat. He could lay it on the podium, but it would take up too much room. Perhaps the floor . . . no, too dirty.

Just then, and not a moment too soon, a man steps forward and takes the hat, returns to his seat, and listens intently to Lincoln's speech.

Who is he? Lincoln's dearest friend. The president said of him, "He and I are about the best friends in the world."

He was one of the strongest supporters of the early stages of Lincoln's presidency. He was given the honor of escorting Mrs. Lincoln in the inaugural grand ball. As the storm of the Civil War began to boil, many of Lincoln's friends left, but not this one. He amplified his loyalty by touring the South as Lincoln's peace ambassador. He begged Southerners not to secede and Northerners to rally behind the president.

His efforts were great, but the wave of anger was greater. The country did divide, and civil war bloodied the nation. Lincoln's friend never lived to see it. He died three months after Lincoln's inauguration. Wearied by his travels, he succumbed to a fever, and Lincoln was left to face the war alone.

Upon hearing the news of his friend's death, Lincoln wept openly and ordered the White House flag to be flown at half-staff. Some feel Lincoln's friend would have been chosen as his running mate in 1864 and would thus have become president following the assassination of the Great Emancipator.

No one will ever know about that. But we do know that Lincoln had one true friend. And we can only imagine the number of times the memory of him brought warmth to a cold Oval Office. He was a model of friendship.

He was also a model of forgiveness.

This friend could just as easily have been an enemy. Long before he and Lincoln were allies, they were competitors—politicians pursuing the same office. And unfortunately, their debates are better known than their friendship. The debates between Abraham Lincoln and his dear friend, Stephen A. Douglas.

But on Lincoln's finest day, Douglas set aside their differences and held the hat of the president. Unlike the older brother, Douglas heard a higher call. And unlike the older brother, he was present at the party.

Wise are we if we do the same. Wise are we if we rise above our hurts. For if we do, we'll be present at the Father's final celebration. A party to end all parties. A party where no pouters will be permitted.

Why don't you come and join the fun?

4

WHEN YOU AND YOUR KIN CAN'T

Dealing with Difficult Relatives

> "My true brother and sister and
> mother are those who do what God
> wants."
>
> Mark 3:35

Give me a word picture to describe a relative in your life who really bugs you."

I was asking the question of a half-dozen friends sitting around a lunch table. They all gave me one of those what-in-the-world? expressions. So I explained.

"I keep meeting people who can't deal with somebody in their family. Either their mother-in-law is a witch or their uncle is a bum or they have a father who treats them like they were never born."

Now their heads nodded. We were connecting. And the word pictures started coming.

"I've got a description," one volunteered. "A parasite on my neck. My wife has this brother who never works and always expects us to provide."

"A cactus wearing a silk shirt," said another. "It's my mother. She looks nice. Everyone thinks she's the greatest, but get close to her and she is prickly, dry, and . . . thirsty for life."

"A marble column," was the way another described an aunt. Dignified, noble, but high and hard.

"Tar baby in Brer Rabbit," someone responded. Everyone understood the reference except me. I didn't remember the story of Brer Rabbit. I asked for the short version. Wily Fox played a trick on Brer Rabbit. The fox made a doll out of tar and stuck it on the side of the road. When Rabbit saw the tar baby, he thought it was a person and stopped to visit.

It was a one-sided conversation. The tar baby's silence bothered the rabbit. He couldn't stand to be next to someone and not communicate with them. So in his frustration he hit the tar baby and stuck to it. He hit the tar baby again with the other hand and, you guessed it, the other hand got stuck.

"That's how we are with difficult relatives," my fable-using friend explained. "We're stuck to someone we can't communicate with."

Stuck is right. It's not as if they are a neighbor you can move away from or an employee you can fire. They are family. And you can choose your friends, but you can't . . . well, you know.

Odds are, you probably know very well.

You've probably got a tar baby in your life, someone you can't talk to and can't walk away from. A mother who whines, an uncle who slurps his soup, or a sister who flaunts her figure. A dad who is still waiting for you to get a real job or a mother-in-law who wonders why her daughter married you.

Tar-baby relationships—stuck together but falling apart.

It's like a crammed and jammed elevator. People thrust together by chance on a short journey, saying as little as possible. The only difference is you'll eventually get off the elevator and never see these folks again—not so with the difficult relative. Family reunions, Christmas, Thanksgiving, weddings, funerals— they'll be there.

And you'll be there sorting through the tough questions. Why does life get so *relatively* difficult? If we expect anyone to be sensitive to our needs, it is our family members. When we hurt physically, we want our family to respond. When we struggle emotionally, we want our family to know.

But sometimes they act like they don't know. Sometimes they act like they don't care.

In her book *Irregular People,* Joyce Landorf tells of a woman in her thirties who learned that she needed a mastectomy. She and her mother seldom communicated, so the daughter was apprehensive about telling her. One day over lunch, she decided to reveal the news. "Mother, I just learned that I am going to have a mastectomy."

The mother was silent. The daughter asked her if she had heard. The mother nodded her head. Then she calmly dismissed the subject by saying, "You know your sister has the best recipe for chicken enchiladas."

What can you do when those closest to you keep their distance? When you can get along with others, but you and your kin can't?

Does Jesus have anything to say about dealing with difficult relatives? Is there an example of Jesus bringing peace to a painful family? Yes, there is.

His own.

It may surprise you to know that Jesus had a difficult family. It may surprise you to know that Jesus had a family at all! You may not be aware that Jesus had brothers and sisters. He did. Quoting Jesus' hometown critics, Mark wrote, "[Jesus] is just the carpenter, the son of Mary and the brother of James, Joseph, Judas, and Simon. And his sisters are here with us" (Mark 6:3).

And it may surprise you to know that his family was less than perfect. They were. If your family doesn't appreciate you, take heart, neither did Jesus'. "A prophet is honored everywhere except in his hometown and with his own people and in his own home" (Mark 6:4).

I wonder what he meant when he said those last five words. He went to the synagogue where he was asked to speak. The people were proud that this hometown boy had done well—until they heard what he said. He referred to himself as the Messiah, the one to fulfill prophecy.

Their response? "Isn't this Joseph's son?" Translation? This is no Messiah! He's just like us! He's the plumber's kid from down the street. He's the accountant on the third floor. He's the construction worker who used to date my sister. God doesn't speak through familiar people.

One minute he was a hero, the next a heretic. Look what happens next. "They got up, forced Jesus out of town, and took him to the edge of the cliff on which the town was built. They planned to throw him off the edge, but Jesus walked through the crowd and went on his way" (Luke 4:29–30).

What an ugly moment! Jesus' neighborhood friends tried to kill him. But even uglier than what we see is what we don't see. Notice what is missing from this verse. Note what words should be there, but aren't. "They planned to throw him over the cliff, but Jesus' brothers came and stood up for him."

We'd like to read that, but we can't because it doesn't say that. That's not what happened. When Jesus was in trouble, his brothers were invisible.

They weren't always invisible, however. There was a time when they spoke. There was a time when they were seen with him in public. Not because they were proud of him but because they were ashamed of him. "His family . . . went to get him because they thought he was out of his mind" (Mark 3:21).

Jesus' siblings thought their brother was a lunatic. They weren't proud—they were embarrassed!

"He's off the deep end, Mom. You should hear what people are saying about him."

"People say he's loony."

"Yeah, somebody asked me why we don't do something about him."

"It's a good thing Dad isn't around to see what Jesus is doing."

Hurtful words spoken by those closest to Jesus.

Here are some more:

So Jesus' brothers said to him, "You should leave here and go to Judea so your followers there can see the miracles you do. Anyone who wants to be well known does not hide what he does. If you are doing these things, show yourself to the world." (Even Jesus' brothers did not believe in him.)

John 7:3–5

Listen to the sarcasm in those words! They drip with ridicule. How does Jesus put up with these guys? How can you believe in yourself when those who know you best don't? How can you move forward when your family wants to pull you back? When you and your family have two different agendas, what do you do?

Jesus gives us some answers.

It's worth noting that he didn't try to control his family's behavior, nor did he let their behavior control his. He didn't demand that they agree with him. He didn't sulk when they insulted him. He didn't make it his mission to try to please them.

Each of us has a fantasy that our family will be like the Waltons, an expectation that our dearest friends will be our next of kin. Jesus didn't have that expectation. Look how he defined his family: "My true brother and sister and mother are those who do what God wants" (Mark 3:35).

When Jesus' brothers didn't share his convictions, he didn't try to force them. He recognized that his spiritual family could provide what his physical family didn't. If Jesus himself couldn't force his family to share his convictions, what makes you think you can force yours?

We can't control the way our family responds to us. When it comes to the behavior of others toward us, our hands are tied. We have to move beyond the naive expectation that if we do good, people will treat us right. The fact is they may and they may not—we cannot control how people respond to us.

If your father is a jerk, you could be the world's best daughter and he still won't tell you so.

If your aunt doesn't like your career, you could change jobs a dozen times and still never satisfy her.

If your sister is always complaining about what you got and she didn't, you could give her everything and she still may not change.

As long as you think you can control people's behavior toward you, you are held in bondage by their opinions. If you think you can control their opinion and their opinion isn't positive, then guess who you have to blame? Yourself.

It's a game with unfair rules and fatal finishes. Jesus didn't play it, nor should you.

We don't know if Joseph affirmed his son Jesus in his ministry—but we know God did: "This is my Son, whom I love, and I am very pleased with him" (Matt. 3:17).

I can't assure you that your family will ever give you the blessing you seek, but I know God will. Let God give you what your family doesn't. If your earthly father doesn't affirm you, then let your heavenly Father take his place.

How do you do that? By emotionally accepting God as your father. You see, it's one thing to accept him as Lord, another to recognize him as Savior—but it's another matter entirely to accept him as Father.

To recognize God as Lord is to acknowledge that he is sovereign and supreme in the universe. To accept him as Savior is to accept his gift of salvation offered on the cross. To regard him as Father is to go a step further. Ideally, a father is the one in your life who provides and protects. That is exactly what God has done.

He has provided for your needs (Matt. 6:25–34). He has protected you from harm (Ps. 139:5). He has adopted you (Eph. 1:5). And he has given you his name (1 John 3:1).

God has proven himself as a faithful father. Now it falls to us to be trusting children. Let God give you what your family doesn't. Let him fill the void others have left. Rely upon him for your affirmation and encouragement. Look at Paul's words: "you are God's child, and *God will give you the blessing he promised,* because you are his child" (Gal. 4:7, emphasis added).

Having your family's approval is desirable but not necessary for happiness and not always possible. Jesus did not let the difficult dynamic of his family overshadow his call from God. And because he didn't, this chapter has a happy ending.

What happened to Jesus' family?

Mine with me a golden nugget hidden in a vein of the Book of Acts. "Then [the disciples] went back to Jerusalem from the Mount of Olives. . . . They all continued praying together with some women, *including Mary the mother of Jesus, and Jesus' brothers*" (Acts 1:12, 14, emphasis added).

What a change! The ones who mocked him now worship him. The ones who pitied him now pray for him. What if Jesus had disowned them? Or worse still, what if he'd suffocated his family with his demand for change?

He didn't. He instead gave them space, time, and grace. And because he did, they changed. How much did they change? One brother became an apostle (Gal. 1:19) and others became missionaries (1 Cor. 9:5).

So don't lose heart. God still changes families. A tar baby today might be your dearest friend tomorrow.

5

IT'S ALL RIGHT TO DREAM AGAIN

Facing Discouragement

At that time there was a strong earthquake. An angel of the Lord came down from heaven, went to the tomb, and rolled the stone away from the entrance. Then he sat on the stone. He was shining as bright as lightning, and his clothes were white as snow. The soldiers guarding the tomb shook with fear because of the angel, and they became like dead men.

The angel said to the women, "Don't be afraid. I know that you are looking for Jesus, who has been crucified. He is not here. He has risen from the dead as he said he would. Come and see the place where his body was. And go quickly and tell his followers, 'Jesus has risen from the dead. He is going into Galilee ahead of you, and you will see him there.'" Then the angel said, "Now I have told you."

The women left the tomb quickly. They were afraid, but they were also very happy. They ran to tell Jesus' followers what had happened. Suddenly, Jesus met them and said, "Greetings." The women came up to him, took hold of his feet, and worshiped him. Then Jesus said to them, "Don't be afraid. Go and tell my followers to go on to Galilee, and they will see me there."

Matthew 28:2–10

> "Don't be afraid. I know that you are looking for Jesus, who has been crucified. He is not here. He has risen from the dead as he said he would."
>
> Matthew 28:5

You know how you can read a story you think you know and then you read it again and see something you've never seen?

You know how you can read about the same event 100 times and then on the 101st hear something so striking and new that it makes you wonder if you slept through the other times?

Maybe it's because you started in the middle of the story instead of at the beginning. Or perhaps it's because someone else reads it aloud and pauses at a place where you normally wouldn't and POW! it hits you.

You grab the book and look at it, knowing that someone copied or read something wrong. But then you read it and well-how-do-you-do. Look at that!

Well, it happened to me. Today.

Only God knows how many times I've read the resurrection story. At least a couple of dozen Easters and a couple of hundred times in between. I've taught it. I've written about it. I've meditated on it. I've underlined it. But what I saw today I'd never seen before.

What did I see? Before I tell you, let me recount the story.

It's early dawn on Sunday morning and the sky is dark. Those, in fact, are John's words. "It was still dark . . ." (John 20:1).

It's a dark Sunday morning. It had been dark since Friday.

Dark with Peter's denial.
Dark with the disciples' betrayal.
Dark with Pilate's cowardice.
Dark with Christ's anguish.
Dark with Satan's glee.

The only ember of light is the small band of women standing at a distance from the cross—watching (Matt. 27:55).

Among them are two Marys, one the mother of James and Joseph and the other is Mary Magdalene. Why are they there? They are there to call his name. To be the final voices he hears before his death. To prepare his body for burial. They are there to clean the blood from his beard. To wipe the crimson from his legs. To close his eyes. To touch his face.

They are there. The last to leave Calvary and the first to arrive at the grave.

So early on that Sunday morning, they leave their pallets and walk out onto the tree-shadowed path. Theirs is a somber task. The morning promises only one encounter, an encounter with a corpse.

Remember, Mary and Mary don't know this is the first Easter. They are not hoping the tomb will be vacant. They aren't discussing what their response will be when they see Jesus. They have absolutely no idea that the grave has been vacated.

There was a time when they dared to dream such dreams. Not now. It's too late for the incredible. The feet that walked on water had been pierced. The hands that healed lepers had been stilled. Noble aspirations had been spiked into Friday's cross. Mary and Mary have come to place warm oils on a cold body and bid farewell to the one man who gave reason to their hopes.

But it isn't hope that leads the women up the mountain to the tomb. It is duty. Naked devotion. They expect nothing in return. What could Jesus give? What could a dead man offer? The two women are not climbing the mountain to receive, they are going to the tomb to give. Period.

There is no motivation more noble.

There are times when we, too, are called to love, expecting nothing in return. Times when we are called to give money to people who will never say thanks, to forgive those who won't forgive us, to come early and stay late when no one else notices.

Service prompted by duty. This is the call of discipleship.

Mary and Mary knew a task had to be done—Jesus' body had to be prepared for burial. Peter didn't offer to do it. Andrew didn't volunteer. The forgiven adulteress or healed lepers are nowhere to be seen. So the two Marys decide to do it.

I wonder if halfway to the tomb they had sat down and reconsidered. What if they'd looked at each other and shrugged, "What's the use?" What if they had given up? What if one had thrown up her arms in frustration and bemoaned, "I'm tired of being the only one who cares. Let Andrew do something for a change. Let Nathaniel show some leadership."

Whether or not they were tempted to, I'm glad they didn't quit. That would have been tragic. You see, we know something they didn't. We know the Father was watching. Mary and Mary thought they were alone. They weren't. They thought their journey was unnoticed. They were wrong. God knew. He was watching them walk up the mountain. He was measuring their steps. He was smiling at their hearts and thrilled at their devotion. And he had a surprise waiting for them.

> At that time there was a strong earthquake. An angel of the Lord came down from heaven, went to the tomb, and rolled the stone away from the entrance. Then he sat on the stone. He was shining bright as lightning, and his clothes were white as snow. The soldiers guarding the tomb shook with fear because of the angel, and they became like dead men.
>
> Matthew 28:2–4

(Now, read carefully, this is what I noticed for the first time today.)

51

Why did the angel move the stone? For whom did he roll away the rock?

For Jesus? That's what I always thought. I just assumed that the angel moved the stone so Jesus could come out. But think about it. Did the stone have to be removed in order for Jesus to exit? Did God have to have help? Was the death conqueror so weak that he couldn't push away a rock? ("Hey, could somebody out there move this rock so I can get out?")

I don't think so. The text gives the impression that Jesus was already out when the stone was moved! Nowhere do the Gospels say that the angel moved the stone for Jesus. For whom, then, was the stone moved?

Listen to what the angel says: "Come and see the place where his body was" (v. 6).

The stone was moved—not for Jesus—but for the women; not so Jesus could come out, but so the women could see in!

Mary looks at Mary and Mary is grinning the same grin she had when the bread and fish kept coming out of the basket. The old passion flares. Suddenly it's all right to dream again.

"Go quickly and tell his followers, 'Jesus has risen from the dead. He is going into Galilee ahead of you, and you will see him there'" (v. 7).

Mary and Mary don't have to be told twice. They turn and start running to Jerusalem. The darkness is gone. The sun is up. The Son is out. But the Son isn't finished.

One surprise still awaits them.

"Suddenly, Jesus met them and said, 'Greetings.' The women came up to him, took hold of his feet, and worshiped him. Then Jesus said to them, 'Don't be afraid. Go and tell my followers to go on to Galilee, and they will see me there'" (vv. 9–10).

The God of surprises strikes again. It's as if he said, "I can't wait any longer. They came this far to see me; I'm going to drop in on them."

God does that for the faithful. Just when the womb gets too old for babies, Sarai gets pregnant. Just when the failure is too great for grace, David is pardoned. And just when the road is too dark for Mary and Mary, the angel glows and the Savior shows and the two women will never be the same.

The lesson? Three words. Don't give up.

Is the trail dark? Don't sit.

Is the road long? Don't stop.

Is the night black? Don't quit.

God is watching. For all you know right at this moment he may be telling the angel to move the stone.

The check may be in the mail.

The apology may be in the making.

The job contract may be on the desk.

Don't quit. For if you do, you may miss the answer to your prayers.

God still sends angels. And God still moves stones.

6

SOUR MILK

Overcoming a Bad Attitude

While Jesus and his followers were traveling, Jesus went into a town. A woman named Martha let Jesus stay at her house. Martha had a sister named Mary, who was sitting at Jesus' feet and listening to him teach. But Martha was busy with all the work to be done. She went in and said, "Lord, don't you care that my sister has left me alone to do all the work? Tell her to help me."

But the Lord answered her, "Martha, Martha, you are worried and upset about many things. Only one thing is important. Mary has chosen the better thing, and it will never be taken away from her."

Luke 10:38–42

Do everything without complaining or
arguing. Then you will be innocent
and without any wrong.

Philippians 2:14–15

I love milk. I am a confessed milkaholic. One of the saddest
days of my life was when I learned that whole milk was un-
healthy. With great reluctance I have adapted to the watered-
down version—but on occasion I still allow myself the hallowed
ecstasy of a cold glass of whole milk and a hot, gooey, chocolate-
chip cookie.

In my years of appreciating the fine fruit of the cow I have
learned that a high price is paid for leaving milk out of the refrigerator. (On one occasion I spewed the spoiled stuff all over
the kitchen cabinet.) Sweet milk turns sour from being too warm
too long.

Sweet dispositions turn sour for the same reason. Let aggra-
vation stew without a period of cooling down, and the result? A
bad, bitter, clabberish attitude.

The tenth chapter of Luke describes the step-by-step process of the sweet becoming sour.

It's the story of Martha. A dear soul given to hospitality and
organization. More frugal than frivolous, more practical than
pensive, her household is a tight ship and she is a stern captain.
Ask her to choose between a book and a broom, and she'll take
the broom.

Mary, however, will take the book. Mary is Martha's sister.
Same parents, different priorities. Martha has things to do. Mary

has thoughts to think. The dishes can wait. Let Martha go to the market; Mary will go to the library.

Two sisters. Two personalities. And as long as they understand each other, it's hand in glove. But when the one resents the other, it's flint and stone.

Let's say we quietly step in the back door of Martha's kitchen and I'll show you what I mean. (One warning: Stay away from the milk; it's beginning to sour.)

Shhh, there she is. Over by the table. The one wearing the apron. My, look at her work! I told you this lady knows how to run a kitchen. How does she do that? Stirring with one hand, cracking eggs with the other. And nothing spills. She knows what she's doing.

Must be a big crowd. There's lots of food. That's them laughing in the next room. Sounds like they're having fun.

But Martha isn't. One look at the flour-covered scowl will tell you that.

"Stupid sister."

What? Did you hear her mumble something?

"That Mary. Here I am alone in the kitchen while she's out there."

Hmm. Seems the oven isn't the only thing hot in here.

"Wouldn't have invited Jesus over if I'd known he was gonna bring the whole army. Those guys eat like horses, and that Peter always belches."

Oh boy. She's miffed. Look at her glaring over her shoulder through the doorway. That's Mary she's staring at. The one seated on the floor, listening to Jesus.

"Little sweet sister . . . always ready to listen and never ready to work. I wouldn't mind sitting down myself. But all I do is cook and sew, cook and sew. Well, enough is enough!"

Watch out! There she goes. Someone's about to get it.

"Lord, don't you care that my sister has left me alone to do all the work? Tell her to help me" (v. 40).

Suddenly the room goes silent, deathly silent except for the tap-tap-tapping of Martha's foot on the stone floor and the slapping of a wooden spoon in her palm. She looms above the others—flour on her cheeks and fire in her eyes.

We have to chuckle at the expression on the faces of the disciples. They stare wide-eyed at this fury that hell hath not known. And poor Mary, flushed red with embarrassment, sighs and sinks lower to the floor.

Only Jesus speaks. For only Jesus understands the problem. The problem is not the large crowd. The problem is not Mary's choice to listen. The problem is not Martha's choice to host. The problem is Martha's heart, a heart soured with anxiety.

"Martha, Martha, you are worried and upset about many things" (v. 41). Bless her heart, Martha wanted to do right. But bless her heart, her heart was wrong. Her heart, Jesus said, was worried. As a result she turned from a happy servant into a beast of burden. She was worried: worried about cooking, worried about pleasing, worried about too much.

I like what my favorite theologian Erma Bombeck has to say about worrying:

> I've always worried a lot and frankly, I'm good at it. I worry about introducing people and going blank when I get to my mother. I worry about a shortage of ball bearings; a snake coming up through the kitchen drain. I worry about the world ending at midnight and getting stuck with three hours on a twenty-four hour cold capsule. I worry about getting into the *Guinness World Book of Records* under "Pregnancy: Oldest Recorded Birth." I worry what the dog thinks when he sees me coming out of the shower; that one of my children will marry an Eskimo who will set me adrift on an iceberg when I can no longer feed myself. I worry about salesladies following me into the fitting room, oil slicks, and Carol Channing going bald. I worry about scientists discovering someday that lettuce has been fattening all along.

Apparently Martha worried too much, too. So much so that she started bossing God around. Worry will do that to you. It makes you forget who's in charge.

What makes this case interesting, however, is that Martha is worried about something good. She's having Jesus over for dinner. She's literally serving God. Her aim was to please Jesus. But she made a common, yet dangerous mistake. As she began to work for him, her work became more important than her Lord. What began as a way to serve Jesus, slowly and subtly became a way to serve self.

Maybe the process went something like this. As she began to prepare the meal, she anticipated the compliments on the food. As she set the table, she imagined the approval. She could just picture it. Jesus would enter the house and thank her for all her work. He would tell the disciples to give her a standing ovation. John would cite her as an example of hospitality and dedicate a chapter in the Bible to her.

Then women would come from miles around to ask her how she learned to be such a kind and humble servant. The rest of her days would be spent directing a school of servanthood—with Jesus as the director and Martha as the professor.

But things didn't turn out like she'd planned. She didn't get the attention she sought. No standing ovation. No compliments. No adulations. No school. No one noticed. And that irritated her. Martha is long on anxiety and short on memory. She has forgotten that the invitation was her idea. She has forgotten that Mary has every right to be with Jesus. And most of all, she has forgotten that the meal is to honor Jesus, not Martha.

I know exactly how Martha feels. For I've been in Martha's kitchen. Or better, I've been in Max's office.

I know what it's like to set out to serve God and end up serving self. I've labored long and hard over sermons only to have my feelings hurt if they aren't complimented. I've pushed myself deeply into a manuscript only to catch myself daydreaming about the postpublication compliments. I've spoken to conference audiences about the sufferings of Christ and then gotten frustrated that the hotel room wasn't ready.

It's easy to forget who is the servant and who is to be served.

Satan knows that. This tool of distortion is one of Satan's slyest. Note: He didn't take Martha out of the kitchen; he took away her purpose in the kitchen. The adversary won't turn you against the church; he will turn you toward yourself in the church. He won't take you away from your ministry; he'll disillusion you in your ministry.

And when the focus is on yourself, you do what Martha did—you worry. You become anxious about many things. You worry that:

> Your co-workers won't appreciate you.
> Your leaders will overwork you.
> Your superintendent won't understand you.
> Your congregation won't support you.

With time, your agenda becomes more important than God's. You're more concerned with presenting self than pleasing him. And you may even find yourself doubting God's judgment.

"Lord, don't you care that my sister has left me alone to do all the work? Tell her to help me" (v. 40).

Don't you know Martha regretted saying that! I bet that after she cooled down, she would have loved to have those words back. I imagine she wished she'd heeded Solomon's counsel: "A rebel shouts in anger . . . a wise man holds his temper in and cools it" (Prov. 29:11 TLB).

There is a principle here. To keep an attitude from souring, treat it like you would a cup of milk. Cool it off.

Martha's life was cluttered. She needed a break. "Martha, Martha, you are worried and upset about many things," the Master explained to her. "Only one thing is important. Mary has chosen [it]" (v. 41–42).

What had Mary chosen? She had chosen to sit at the feet of Christ. God is more pleased with the quiet attention of a sincere servant than the noisy service of a sour one.

By the way, this story could easily have been reversed. Mary could have been the one to get angry. The sister on the floor could have resented the sister at the sink. Mary could have grabbed Jesus and dragged him into the kitchen and said, "Tell Martha to quit being so productive and to get reflective. Why do I have to do all the thinking and praying around here?"

What matters more than the type of service is the heart behind the service. A bad attitude spoils the gift we leave on the altar for God.

Maybe you've heard the joke about the fellow who prayed with a bad attitude?

"Why," he asked, "has my brother been blessed with wealth and I with nothing? All of my life I have never missed a single day without saying morning and evening prayers. My church attendance has been perfect. I have always loved my neighbor and given my money. Yet now, as I near the end of my life, I can hardly afford to pay my rent.

"My brother, on the other hand, drinks and gambles and plays all the time. Yet he has more money than he can count. I don't ask you to punish him, but tell me, why has he been given so much and I have been given nothing?"

"Because," God replied, "you're such a self-righteous pain in the neck."

Guard your attitude.

God has gifted you with talents. He has done the same to your neighbor. If you concern yourself with your neighbor's talents, you will neglect yours. But if you concern yourself with yours, you could inspire both.

7

A Crazy Hunch and a High Hope

Genuine Gestures of Faith

So Jesus went with him.

A large crowd followed Jesus and pushed very close around him. Among them was a woman who had been bleeding for twelve years. She had suffered very much from many doctors and had spent all the money she had, but instead of improving, she was getting worse. When the woman heard about Jesus, she came up behind him in the crowd and touched his coat. She thought, "If I can just touch his clothes, I will be healed." Instantly her bleeding stopped, and she felt in her body that she was healed from her disease.

At once Jesus felt power go out from him. So he turned around in the crowd and asked, "Who touched my clothes?"

His followers said, "Look at how many people are pushing against you! And you ask, 'Who touched me?'"

But Jesus continued looking around to see who had touched him. The woman, knowing that she was healed, came and fell at Jesus' feet. Shaking with fear, she told him the whole truth. Jesus said to her, "Dear woman, you are made well because you believed. Go in peace; be healed of your disease."

Mark 5:24–34

> "Daughter, your faith has made you well."
>
> Mark 5:34 NKJV

$\mathcal{A}$ clock for Christmas is not the kind of gift that thrills an eight-year-old boy, but I said thank you and took it to my bedroom, put it on the nightstand, and plugged it in.

It was a square-faced Bulova. It didn't have moving numbers—it had rotating hands. It didn't play tapes or CDs, but over the years it developed a slight, soothing hum that could be heard when the room was quiet.

Today you can buy clocks that sound like rain when it's time to sleep and like your mother when it's time to wake up. But not this one. Its alarm could make the dogs howl. Forget snooze buttons. Just pick it up and chunk it across the room. It was a Neanderthal model. It wouldn't net fifty cents at a garage sale in this day of digital clocks and musical alarms.

But still, over time, I grew attached to it. People don't usually get sentimental about electric clocks, but I did about this one. Not because of its accuracy, it was always a bit slow. Nor the hum, which I didn't mind. I liked it because of the light.

You see, this clock glowed in the dark.

All day, every day it soaked up the light. It sponged up the sun. The hands were little sticks of ticks and time and sunshine. And when the night came, the clock was ready. When I flicked off the light to sleep, the little clock flicked on its light and shined. Not much light, but when your world is dark, just a little seems like a lot.

Somewhat like the light a woman got when she met Jesus.

We don't know her name, but we know her situation. Her world was midnight black. Grope-in-the-dark-and-hope-for-help black. Read these two verses and see what I mean:

> A large crowd followed Jesus and pushed very close around him. Among them was a woman who had been bleeding for twelve years. She had suffered very much from many doctors and had spent all the money she had, but instead of improving, she was getting worse.
>
> Mark 5:24–26

She was a bruised reed: "bleeding for twelve years," "suffered very much," "spent all the money she had," and "getting worse."

A chronic menstrual disorder. A perpetual issue of blood. Such a condition would be difficult for any woman of any era. But for a Jewess, nothing could be worse. No part of her life was left unaffected.

Sexually . . . she could not touch her husband.

Maternally . . . she could not bear children.

Domestically . . . anything she touched was considered unclean. No washing dishes. No sweeping floors.

Spiritually . . . she was not allowed to enter the temple.

She was physically exhausted and socially ostracized.

She had sought help "under the care of many doctors" (v. 26 NIV). The Talmud gives no fewer than eleven cures for such a condition. No doubt she had tried them all. Some were legitimate treatments. Others, such as carrying the ashes of an ostrich egg in a linen cloth, were hollow superstitions.

She "had spent all she had" (v. 26 NIV). To dump financial strain on top of the physical strain is to add insult to injury. A friend battling cancer told me that the hounding of the creditors who demand payments for ongoing medical treatment is just as devastating as the pain.

"Instead of getting better she grew worse" (v. 26 NIV). She was a bruised reed. She awoke daily in a body that no one wanted. She is down to her last prayer. And on the day we encounter her, she's about to pray it.

By the time she gets to Jesus, he is surrounded by people. He's on his way to help the daughter of Jairus, the most important man in the community. What are the odds that he will interrupt an urgent mission with a high official to help the likes of her? Very few. But what are the odds that she will survive if she doesn't take a chance? Fewer still. So she takes a chance.

"If I can just touch his clothes," she thinks, "I will be healed" (v. 28).

Risky decision. To touch him, she will have to touch the people. If one of them recognizes her . . . hello rebuke, good-bye cure. But what choice does she have? She has no money, no clout, no friends, no solutions. All she has is a crazy hunch that Jesus can help and a high hope that he will.

Maybe that's all you have: a crazy hunch and a high hope. You have nothing to give. But you are hurting. And all you have to offer him is your hurt.

Maybe that has kept you from coming to God. Oh, you've taken a step or two in his direction. But then you saw the other people around him. They seemed so clean, so neat, so trim and fit in their faith. And when you saw them, they blocked your view of him. So you stepped back.

If that describes you, note carefully, only one person was commended that day for having faith. It wasn't a wealthy giver. It wasn't a loyal follower. It wasn't an acclaimed teacher. It was a shame-struck, penniless outcast who clutched onto her hunch that he could and her hope that he would.

Which, by the way, isn't a bad definition of faith: *A conviction that he can and a hope that he will.* Sounds similar to the definition of faith given by the Bible. "Without faith no one can please God. Anyone who comes to God must believe that he is real and that he rewards those who truly want to find him" (Heb. 11:6).

Not too complicated is it? Faith is the belief that God is real and that God is good. Faith is not a mystical experience or a midnight vision or a voice in the forest . . . it is a choice to believe that the one who made it all hasn't left it all and that he still sends light into shadows and responds to gestures of faith.

There was no guarantee, of course. She hoped he'd respond . . . she longed for it . . . but she didn't know if he would. All she knew was that he was there and that he was good. That's faith.

Faith is not the belief that God will do what you want. Faith is the belief that God will do what is right.

"Blessed are the dirt-poor, nothing-to-give, trapped-in-a-corner, destitute, diseased," Jesus said, "for theirs is the kingdom of heaven" (Matt. 5:6, my translation).

God's economy is upside down (or rightside up and ours is upside down!). God says that the more hopeless your circumstance, the more likely your salvation. The greater your cares, the more genuine your prayers. The darker the room, the greater the need for light.

Which takes us back to my clock. When it was daylight, I never appreciated my little Bulova's capacity to glow in the dark. But as the shadows grew, so did my gratitude.

A healthy lady never would have appreciated the power of a touch of the hem of his robe. But this woman was sick . . . and when her dilemma met his dedication, a miracle occurred.

Her part in the healing was very small. All she did was extend her arm through the crowd.

"If only I can touch him."

What's important is not the form of the effort but the fact of the effort. The fact is, she did something. She refused to settle for sickness another day and resolved to make a move.

Healing begins when we do something. Healing begins when we reach out. Healing starts when we take a step.

God's help is near and always available, but it is only given to those who seek it. Nothing results from apathy. The great work in this story is the mighty healing that occurred. But the great truth is that the healing began with her touch. And with that small, courageous gesture, she experienced Jesus' tender power.

Compared to God's part, our part is minuscule but necessary. We don't have to do much, *but we do have to do something.*

Write a letter.

Ask forgiveness.

Call a counselor.

Confess.

Call Mom.

Visit a doctor.

Be baptized.

Feed a hungry person.

Pray.

Teach.

Go.

Do something that demonstrates faith. For faith with no effort is no faith at all. *God will respond.* He has never rejected a genuine gesture of faith. Never.

God honors radical, risk-taking faith.

When arks are built, lives are saved. When soldiers march, Jerichos tumble. When staffs are raised, seas still open. When a lunch is shared, thousands are fed. And when a garment is touched—whether by the hand of an anemic woman in Galilee or by the prayers of a beggar in Bangladesh—Jesus stops. He stops and responds.

Mark can tell you. When this woman touched Christ, two things happened that happen nowhere else in the Bible. He recorded them both.

First, Jesus heals before he knows it. The power left automatically and instantaneously. It's as if the Father short-circuited the system and the divinity of Christ was a step ahead of the humanity of Christ.

Her need summoned his help. No neon lights or loud shouts. No razzle-dazzle. No fanfare. No hoopla. No splash. Just help.

Just like my dark room brought the light out of my clock, our dark world brings out the light of God.

Second, he calls her *daughter*. "Daughter, your faith has made you well" (v. 34 NKJV) It's the only time Jesus calls *any* woman *anywhere* daughter. Imagine how that made her feel! Who could remember the last time she received a term of affection? Who knew the last time kind eyes had met hers?

Leo Tolstoy, the great Russian writer, tells of the time he was walking down the street and passed a beggar. Tolstoy reached into his pocket to give the beggar some money, but his pocket was empty. Tolstoy turned to the man and said, "I'm sorry, my brother, but I have nothing to give."

The beggar brightened and said, "You have given me more than I asked for—you have called me brother."

To the loved, a word of affection is a morsel, but to the love-starved, a word of affection can be a feast.

And Jesus gave this woman a banquet.

Tradition holds that she never forgot what Jesus did. Legend states that she stayed with Jesus and followed him as he carried his cross up Calvary. Some believe she was Veronica, the woman who walked the road to the cross with him. And when the sweat and blood were stinging his eyes, she wiped his forehead.

She, at an hour of great need, received his touch—and he, at an hour of pain, received hers. We don't know if the legend is true, but we know it could be. And I don't know if the same has happened to you, but I know it can.

8

FOREVER YOUNG

How to Love Growing Old

"Whoever tries to keep his life safe will lose it, and the man who is prepared to lose his life will preserve it."

Luke 17:33 PHILLIPS

---

*D*on't you hate it when someone else reminds you?

The barber: "Getting a little thin on top here, Joe."

The stylist: "Next time you come in, Sue, we'll do something about these gray streaks."

The invitation: "You are invited to your thirtieth high school reunion."

Your kids: "Tell me again, who were the Rolling Stones?"

Your doctor: "Nothing to worry about, Bill. Your condition is common for folks in their mid-age."

The dawning of old age. The first pages of the final chapters. A golden speck appears on the green leaves of your life, and you are brought face to wrinkled face with the fact that you are getting older.

And though we joke ("Old age is when you sink your teeth into a steak . . . and they stay there"), not everyone laughs. Especially one who has been taught to treasure youth.

And weren't we all?

For decades you worried about everything except getting old. Out of all the things you couldn't count on, there was one thing you could, and that was your youth. You could eat like a horse and not look like one. All the schoolteachers were older than you. Professional athletes were about the same age as your older brother. Life was an open highway, and death was a millennium away.

But then they came, the subtle messages of mortality:

> You buy your first life insurance policy and it includes burial and funeral expenses.
>
> Your carpool friends ask you why you squint when you read road signs.
>
> The kid carrying your groceries calls you "Ma'am."

At first it's just raindrop reminders splashing on your water-color convictions of perpetual youth. With time, however, the raindrops become steady and stronger.

Everything hurts when you wake up. What doesn't hurt, doesn't work.

Your parents begin acting like your children.

The smile lines don't go away when you stop smiling.

And then—boom! The rain becomes a torrent. The gentle taps become thunder. Cardiac arrest. Empty nest. Forty candles. Bifocals. Boom. Boom! BOOM!

Now there is no denial. Ponce de Leon didn't find the fountain of youth, and neither will you. Oh, but how we try. Barbells get pumped. Black hair gone gray goes black again, or better yet, blond. The van is traded in on a truck, a four-wheel-drive monster that will tackle the treacherous ravines of the interstate. The face gets stretched. The chin gets tucked. Breasts get a lift.

But try as we might, the calendar pages still turn. The clocks still tick. And the body still grows older. And with every new pill we take we are reminded that growing old is a pill that has to be swallowed.

But why does the pill go down so slowly? Why is it so hard to accept? What is it about birthdays that causes us to quiver so?

Certainly part of the problem is the mirror (or at least the reflection in it). What was tight now sags. What once swung now bounces. Time, as they say, is a great healer, but it's a lousy beautician.

Or, for others, there is failure. What you set out to do, you didn't. You set out to avoid the trap of suburbia; now you're making mortgage payments. You swore you'd never be a corporate puppet, but now your closet is full of gray flannels. You determined to leave a legacy, but all you've left so far is a trail of diapers and check stubs.

But the real pain is deeper. For some it is the hollowness of success. Life at the top of the ladder can be lonely. Mahogany desks grow cold. Sales awards tarnish. Diplomas fade. Sometimes a dream-come-true world has come true and it's less than you'd hoped.

Regret becomes a major pastime. The plumber wishes he'd gone to medical school and the doctor wishes he were a plumber. The woman who works regrets the time she didn't spend with her kids and the stay-at-home mom wishes she had a career.

It can get even worse. Regret can lead to rebellion. Rebellion against the demands. Rebellion against the mundane. Rebellion against the ho-hum. Rebellion against whatever ties you down: your job, your government, your station wagon, or worse still . . . your family.

Those who rebel—those who choose to roam the back alleys of escape—are prime candidates to stumble into one of Satan's oldest pits . . . adultery.

A pretty, young secretary from down the hall brings some papers as well as some sympathy into your office . . .

The man next door says he can't believe you've had four kids and kept your figure so trim . . .

The David in us calls for Bathsheba. Potiphar's wife looks at Joseph. A romp is taken in the greener grass and the hurt begins.

Let me be very clear with my point: Growing old can be dangerous. The trail is treacherous and the pitfalls are many. One is wise to be prepared. You know it's coming. It's not like God kept the process a secret. It's not like you are blazing a trail as you grow older. It's not as if no one has ever done it before. Look around you. You have ample opportunity to prepare and ample case studies to consider. If growing old catches you by surprise, don't blame God. He gave you plenty of warning. He also gave you plenty of advice.

Want some examples? Glad you asked. How about Luke 17:33?

"Whoever tries to keep his life safe will lose it, and the man who is prepared to lose his life will preserve it" (PHILLIPS).

"There are two ways to view life," Jesus is saying, "those who protect it or those who pursue it. The wisest are not the ones with the most years in their lives, but the most life in their years."

What Annie Dillard says about writing in *The Writing Life* is true about life: "One of the few things I know about writing is this: spend it all, play it, lose it all, right away, every time. Do not hoard what seems good for a later place in the book, or for another book; give it, give it all, give it now."

There is a rawness and a wonder to life. Pursue it. Hunt for it. Sell out to get it. Don't listen to the whines of those who have settled for a second-rate life and want you to do the same so they won't feel guilty. Your goal is not to live long; it's to live.

Jesus says the options are clear. On one side there is the voice of safety. You can build a fire in the hearth, stay inside, and stay warm and dry and safe. You can't get hurt if you never get out, right? You can't be criticized for what you don't try, right? You can't fall if you don't take a stand, right? You can't lose your balance if you never climb, right? So, don't try it. Take the safe route.

Or you can hear the voice of adventure—God's adventure. Instead of building a fire in your hearth, build a fire in your heart. Follow God's impulses. Adopt the child. Move overseas. Teach the class. Change careers. Run for office. Make a difference. Sure it isn't safe, but what is?

You think staying inside out of the cold is safe? Jesus disagrees. "Whoever tries to keep his life safe will lose it." I like the words of General Douglas MacArthur when he was seventy-eight: "Nobody grows old by merely living a number of years.

People grow old by deserting their ideals. Years may wrinkle the skin, but to give up interest wrinkles the soul."

Charles Lindbergh, the first pilot to fly across the Atlantic, had this to say about living safely:

> I decided that if I could fly for ten years before I was killed in a crash, it would be a worthwhile trade for an ordinary lifetime. . . . Who valued life more highly, the aviators who spent it on the art they loved, or the misers who doled it out like pennies through their antlike days?

Once again, read Jesus' admonition. "Whoever tries to keep his life safe will lose it, and the man who is prepared to lose his life will preserve it."

Reclaim the curiosity of your childhood. Just because you're near the top of the hill doesn't mean you've passed your peak.

Your last chapters can be your best. Your final song can be your greatest. It could be that all of your life has prepared you for a grand exit. God's oldest have always been among his choicest.

It was his octogenarian activities that got Moses into your Bible. Old and mellow Abraham was much wiser than young and brash Abram. Caleb still claimed his mountain when he was eighty-five. Anna was an eighty-five-year-old widow who had enough strength to pray for the Messiah and enough vision to recognize him when he came.

And look at John, the aged apostle John. The last of the apostles. The dear friend of Jesus. Surely his final years will be quiet and restful. Surely John has done what he came to do.

Nope. Don't tell that to John. And don't tell that to God. For neither of them was finished. John had one more chapter to write. What was intended to be an island of isolation became a place of inspiration, and in his final years John wrote the final book of the Bible. Could it be that all of John's life had led to this moment?

Such is the ring of Robert Browning's well-known words:

> Grow old along with me
> The best is yet to be
> The last of life,
> For which the first was made.

The final years can be your best. Ask Othmar Ammann. During his "retirement" he designed such structures as the Connecticut and New Jersey turnpikes, the Pittsburgh Civic Arena, Dulles Airport, the Throngs Neck Bridge, and the Verrazano Narrows Bridge.

Heinrich Schliemann would agree. He retired from business to look for Homer's legendary city of Troy. He found it.

Winston Churchill was worthy of taking a rest after World War II, but he didn't take it. Instead he took up a pen and won the Nobel Prize in literature at the age of seventy-nine.

Some get old and go fishing. Others get old and go hunting—they go hunting for what they always wanted to do. And they do it.

A friend of the late American jurist Oliver Wendell Holmes asked him why he had taken up the study of Greek at the age of ninety-four. Holmes replied, "Well, my good sir, it's now or never."

When J. C. Penney was ninety-five years old, he affirmed, "My eyesight may be getting weaker, but my vision is increasing."

As we get older, our vision should improve. Not our vision of earth but our vision of heaven. Those who have spent their life looking for heaven gain a skip in their step as the city comes into view. After Michelangelo died, someone found in his studio a piece of paper on which he had written a note to his apprentice. In the handwriting of his old age the great artist wrote: "Draw, Antonio, draw, and do not waste time."

Well-founded urgency, Michelangelo. Time slips. Days pass. Years fade. And life ends. And what we came to do must be done while there is time.

We would think it bizarre for a traveler not to be prepared for the end of the journey. We would pity the poor passenger who never read his itinerary. We'd be bewildered by someone who thought the purpose of the trip was the trip.

And for that person some of the saddest words in Scripture were penned. "The harvest is past, / The summer is ended, / And we are not saved" (Jer. 8:20 NKJV).

Others, however, are anticipating the destination. I hope you are. And I hope you'll be ready when you get home. For you, age is no enemy. Age is a mile-marker—a gentle reminder that home has never been so near.

Tell that to your barber.

9

READ THE STORY

When Others Let You Down

That same day two of Jesus' followers were going to a town named Emmaus, about seven miles from Jerusalem. They were talking about everything that had happened. While they were talking and discussing, Jesus himself came near and began walking with them, but they were kept from recognizing him. Then he said, "What are these things you are talking about while you walk?"

The two followers stopped, looking very sad. The one named Cleopas answered, "Are you the only visitor in Jerusalem who does not know what just happened there?"

Jesus said to them, "What are you talking about?"

They said, "About Jesus of Nazareth. He was a prophet who said and did many powerful things before God and all the people. Our leaders and the leading priests handed him over to be sentenced to death, and they crucified him. But we were hoping that he would free Israel. Besides this, it is now the third day since this happened. And today some women among us amazed us. Early this morning they went to the tomb, but they did not find his body there. They came and told us that they had seen a vision of angels who said that Jesus was alive! So some of our group went to the tomb, too. They found it just as the women said, but they did not see Jesus."

Then Jesus said to them, "You are foolish and slow to believe everything the prophets said. They said that the Christ must suffer these things before he enters his glory." Then starting with what Moses and all the prophets had said about him, Jesus began to explain everything that had been written about himself in the Scriptures.

They came near the town of Emmaus, and Jesus acted as if he were going farther. But they begged him, "Stay with us, because it is late; it is almost night." So he went in to stay with them.

When Jesus was at the table with them, he took some bread, gave thanks, divided it, and gave it to them. And then, they were allowed to recognize Jesus. But when they saw who he was, he disappeared. They said to each other, "It felt like a fire burning in us when Jesus talked to us on the road and explained the Scriptures to us."

So the two followers got up at once and went back to Jerusalem. There they found the eleven apostles and others gathered. They were saying, "The Lord really has risen from the dead! He showed himself to Simon."

Then the two followers told what had happened on the road and how they recognized Jesus when he divided the bread.

Luke 24:13–35

> They said to each other, "It felt like a fire burning in us when Jesus talked to us on the road and explained the Scriptures to us."
>
> Luke 24:32

$\mathcal{T}$en-year-old Phineas was up before the sun was. He'd scarcely slept the night before. And long before a sound was heard in the house, he was downstairs with his bag packed, ready to climb into the wagon.

The year was 1820. And Phineas was about to see an island. His island. The island promised to him at birth. The day he was born, his grandfather presented newborn Phineas with a deed, a sizable portion of Connecticut land called Ivy Island. And to-day, for the first time, Phineas was to see it.

Not every boy is born a proprietor. Phineas's parents were always quick to remind their son of this. They urged him not to forget them when he came of age. Neighbors feared that the young landowner wouldn't want to play with their children.

Their concerns were legitimate. Phineas was different from his playmates. While they dreamed of dragons and knights, his fantasies were of Ivy Island. Someday he would be lord of his own territory. He'd build a house. Start a farm. Raise cattle. Rule his domain.

When you own an island you feel important.

When you own an island, you want to see it. Phineas had yet to see his. He pleaded with his father to take him to the is-land and, finally, in the summer of 1820, his father agreed.

Three sleepless nights preceded the expedition. Then, early that morning, Phineas, his father, and a hired hand climbed into the buggy and began the long-anticipated journey. Finally, Phineas would see his land.

He could scarcely sit still. At the top of each hill he would ask, "Are we nearly there? Can I see it from here?" And his father would encourage him to be patient and assure him that they were drawing near.

Finally, his dad pointed north beyond a meadow to a row of tall trees stretching into the sky.

"There," he said. "There is Ivy Island."

Phineas was overcome. He jumped from the wagon and dashed through the meadow, leaving his father far behind. He raced to the row of trees into an opening from which Ivy Island was visible.

When he saw the land he stopped. His heart sank.

Ivy Island was five acres of snake-infested marshland. His grandfather had called it the most valuable land in Connecticut. But it was worthless. His father had told him it was a generous gift. It wasn't. It was a joke . . . a cruel joke. As stunned Phineas stared, the father and the hired hand roared with laughter.

Phineas was not the fortunate beneficiary of the family. He was the laughingstock of the family. Grandfather Taylor had played a joke on his heir.

Phineas didn't laugh. Nor did he forget. That disappointment shaped his life. He, the deceived, made a lifestyle out of deception. The little boy fooled made a career out of fooling people.

He even may have fooled you.

You don't know him as Phineas. You know him as P.T. You don't know him as a landowner; you know him as a promoter. You know him as the one who coined the phrase, "There's a sucker born every minute." He spent his life proving it. Such was the life of P.T.—P. T. Barnum.

And such is the life of many others, many others who have been told they'd be taken to the Promised Land only to find themselves taken to the swamp.

I shared a ride to the airport this week with a businessman who a decade ago had an income twenty times what he has today. That was before his industry slumped. That was before he went broke.

After last Sunday's sermon a woman from another town asked what to do with her memories. I asked her what she meant. "I want to go to church, but I was abused by a preacher as a young girl. And now, every time I go to church, I remember."

A friend tells me that her husband cares more about his golf game than he cares about her.

Even as I was writing, a co-worker stopped by to update me on the lawsuit he has filed against the builder who never finished his house.

Is there anything wrong with these people? No, their desires are healthy. One wants a strong business, another wants fulfilling worship. A husband who'll honor his promise, a builder who'll keep his word. Who would fault them for such dreams? Who would blame them for dreaming? Who would have thought their dreams would be crushed?

Certainly they didn't.

But now they are faced with a decision. What do they do with their disillusionment? What do they do with their broken hearts? We're not talking inconveniences or hassles. We're not discussing long lines or red lights or a bad game of tennis. We're talking heartbreak. We're talking about what two friends of Jesus were feeling a couple of days after his death. Their world has tumbled in on them. It's obvious by the way they walk. Their feet shuffle, their heads hang, their shoulders droop. The seven miles from Jerusalem to Emmaus must feel like seventy.

As they walk they talk "about everything that had happened" (v. 14). It's not hard to imagine their words.

"Why did the people turn against him?"

"He could have come down from the cross. Why didn't he?"

"He just let Pilate push him around."

"What do we do now?"

As they walk, a stranger comes up behind them. It is Jesus, but they don't recognize him. Disappointment will do that to you. It will blind you to the very presence of God. Discouragement turns our eyes inward. God could be walking next to us, but despair clouds our vision.

Despair does something else. Not only does it cloud our vision, it hardens our hearts. We get cynical. We get calloused. And when good news comes, we don't want to accept it for fear of being disappointed again. That's what happened to these two people.

Later on they say these words:

> And today some women among us amazed us. Early this morning they went to the tomb, but they did not find his body there. They came and told us that they had seen a vision of angels who said that Jesus was alive! So some of our group went to the tomb, too. They found it just as the women said, but they did not see Jesus.
>
> Luke 24:22–24

When reading Scripture we can't always tell in what tone the words were spoken. Sometimes we don't know if the speaker means to be jubilant or sad or peaceful. This time, however, there is no question about what they're thinking: *As if it's not bad enough that Jesus was killed, now some grave robber has taken the body and duped some of our friends.*

These two followers aren't about to believe the women. Fool me once, shame on you. Fool me twice, shame on me. Cleopas and his friend are putting their hearts in a shell. They won't take another risk. They won't be hurt again.

Common reaction—isn't it? Been hurt by love? Then don't love. Had a promise violated? Then don't trust. Had your heart broken? Then don't give it away. Do like P. T. Barnum. Settle the score by blaming the world and hardening your heart.

There is a line, a fine line, which once crossed can be fatal. It's the line between disappointment and anger. Between hurt and hate, between bitterness and blame. If you are nearing that line, let me urge you, don't cross it. Step back and ask this question: How long am I going to pay for my disappointment? How long am I going to go on nursing my hurt?

At some point you have to move on. At some point you have to heal. At some point you have to let Jesus do for you what he did for these men.

Know what he did? First of all, he came to them. I know we've already mentioned that, but it's worth repeating. He didn't sit back and cross his arms and say, "Why can't those two get with the program?" He didn't complain to the angel and say, "Why won't they believe the empty tomb? Why are they so hard to please?"

What did he do? He met them at their point of pain. Though death has been destroyed and sin annulled, he has not retired. The resurrected Lord has once again wrapped himself in flesh, put on human clothes, and searched out hurting hearts.

Read carefully their words and see if you can find their hurt:

> Jesus said to them, "What are you talking about?"
> They said, "About Jesus of Nazareth. He was a prophet who said and did many powerful things before God and all the people. Our leaders and the leading priests handed him over to be sentenced to death, and they crucified him. But we were hoping that he would free Israel."
>
> Luke 24:19–21

There it is. "But we were hoping . . ." The disciples had hoped Jesus would free Israel. They had hoped he'd kick out the Romans. They'd hoped Pilate would be out and Jesus would be in. But Pilate was still in, and Jesus was dead.

Unfulfilled expectations. God didn't do what they wanted him to.

They knew what they expected of Jesus. They knew what he was supposed to do. They didn't have to ask him. If Jesus is the Messiah, he won't sleep in my storm. He won't ever die. He won't defy tradition. He'll do what he is supposed to do.

But that's not what he did. And aren't we glad? Aren't we glad the prayer of Cleopas and his friend went unanswered? Aren't we glad God didn't adjust his agenda to fulfill the requests of these two disciples?

They were good disciples. With good hearts. And sincere prayers. They just had the wrong expectations.

When my oldest daughter was about six years old, she and I were having a discussion about my work. It seems she wasn't too happy with my chosen profession. She wanted me to leave the ministry. "I like you as a preacher," she explained. "I just really wish you sold snow cones."

An honest request from a pure heart. It made sense to her that the happiest people in the world were the men who drove the snow-cone trucks. You play music. You sell goodies. You make kids happy. What more could you want? (Come to think about it, she may have a point. I could get a loan, buy a truck and . . . Naw, I'd eat too much.)

I heard her request, but I didn't heed it. Why? Because I knew better. I know what I'm called to do and what I need to do. The fact is I know more about life than she does.

And the point is, God knows more about life than we do.

People wanted him to redeem Israel, but he knew better. He would rather his people be temporarily oppressed than eternally lost. When forced to choose between battling Pilate and battling Satan, he chose the battle we couldn't win. He said no to what they wanted and yes to what they needed. He said no to a liberated Israel and yes to a liberated humanity.

And once again, aren't we glad he did? And aren't we glad he does?

Now be honest. Are we glad he says no to what we want and yes to what we need? Not always. If we ask for a new marriage, and he says honor the one you've got, we aren't happy. If we ask for healing, and he says learn through the pain, we aren't happy. If we ask for more money, and he says treasure the unseen, we aren't always happy.

When God doesn't do what we want, it's not easy. Never has been. Never will be. But faith is the conviction that God knows more than we do about this life and he will get us through it.

Remember, disappointment is caused by unmet expectations. Disappointment is cured by revamped expectations.

I like that story about the fellow who went to the pet store in search of a singing parakeet. Seems he was a bachelor and his house was too quiet. The store owner had just the bird for him, so the man bought it. The next day the bachelor came home from work to a house full of music. He went to the cage to feed the bird and noticed for the first time that the parakeet had only one leg.

He felt cheated that he'd been sold a one-legged bird, so he called and complained.

"What do you want," the store owner responded, "a bird who can sing or a bird who can dance?"

Good question for times of disappointment. What do we want? That's what Jesus asks the disciples. What do you want? Do you want temporary freedom—or eternal freedom? Jesus sets about the task of restructuring their expectations.

You know what he did? He told them the story. Not just any story. He told them the story of God and God's plan for people. "Then starting with what Moses and all the prophets had said about him, Jesus began to explain everything that had been written about himself in the Scriptures" (v. 27).

Fascinating. Jesus' cure for the broken heart is the story of God. He started with Moses and finished with himself. Why did he do that? Why did he retell the ancient tale? Why did he go all the way back two thousand years to the story of Moses? I think I know the reason. I know because what they heard is what we all need to hear when we are disappointed.

We need to hear that God is still in control. We need to hear that it's not over until he says so. We need to hear that life's mishaps and tragedies are not a reason to bail out. They are simply a reason to sit tight.

Corrie ten Boom used to say, "When the train goes through a tunnel and the world gets dark, do you jump out? Of course not. You sit still and trust the engineer to get you through."

Why did Jesus tell the story? So we'd know the engineer still controls the train.

The way to deal with discouragement? The cure for disappointment? Go back to the story. Read it again and again. Be reminded that you aren't the first person to weep. And you aren't the first person to be helped.

Read the story and remember, their story is yours!

The challenge too great? Read the story. That's you crossing the Red Sea with Moses.

Too many worries? Read the story. That's you receiving heavenly food with the Israelites.

Your wounds too deep? Read the story. That's you, Joseph, forgiving your brothers for betraying you.

Your enemies too mighty? Read the story. That's you marching with Jehoshaphat into a battle already won.

Your disappointments too heavy? Read the story of the Emmaus-bound disciples. The Savior they thought was dead now walked beside them. He entered their house and sat at their table. And something happened in their hearts. "It felt like a fire burning in us when Jesus talked to us on the road and explained the Scriptures to us" (v. 31).

Next time you're disappointed, don't panic. Don't jump out. Don't give up. Just be patient and let God remind you he's still in control. It ain't over till it's over.

THE SMOLDERING WICK

Fibers interwoven for flame
Flame ignited for light
Cold gusts—hot blasts
Candle overcome by night
yet
Stubborn ember struggles
Duels with shadows and seeks
Brighter flame for power
Dancing fire for heat.

10

THE POWER OF
A TIMID PRAYER

---

*When You Wonder If Your
Prayers Matter*

When Jesus, Peter, James, and John came back to the other followers, they saw a great crowd around them and the teachers of the law arguing with them. But as soon as the crowd saw Jesus, the people were surprised and ran to welcome him.

Jesus asked, "What are you arguing about?"

A man answered, "Teacher, I brought my son to you. He has an evil spirit in him that stops him from talking. When the spirit attacks him, it throws him on the ground. Then my son foams at the mouth, grinds his teeth, and becomes very stiff. I asked your followers to force the evil spirit out, but they couldn't."

Jesus answered, "You people have no faith. How long must I stay with you? How long must I put up with you? Bring the boy to me."

So the followers brought him to Jesus. As soon as the evil spirit saw Jesus, it made the boy lose control of himself, and he fell down and rolled on the ground, foaming at the mouth.

Jesus asked the boy's father, "How long has this been happening?"

The father answered, "Since he was very young. The spirit often throws him into a fire or into water to kill him. If you can do anything for him, please have pity on us and help us."

Jesus said to the father, "You said, 'If you can!' All things are possible for the one who believes."

Immediately the father cried out, "I do believe! Help me to believe more!"

When Jesus saw that a crowd was quickly gathering, he ordered the evil spirit, saying, "You spirit that makes people unable to hear or speak, I command you to come out of this boy and never enter him again!"

The evil spirit screamed and caused the boy to fall on the ground again. Then the spirit came out. The boy looked as if he were dead, and many people said, "He is dead!" But Jesus took hold of the boy's hand and helped him to stand up.

When Jesus went into the house, his followers began asking him privately, "Why couldn't we force that evil spirit out?"

Jesus answered, "That kind of spirit can only be forced out by prayer."

Mark 9:14–29

"That kind of spirit can only be forced out by prayer."

Mark 9:29

---

*T*his chapter isn't for Concordes; it's for crop dusters.

Some of you pray like a Concorde jet—smooth, sleek, high, and mighty. Your words reverberate in the clouds and send sonic booms throughout the heavens. If you pray like a Concorde, I salute you. If you don't, I understand.

Maybe you are like me, more a crop duster than a Concorde. You aren't flashy, you fly low, you seem to cover the same ground a lot, and some mornings it's tough to get the old engine cranked up.

Most of us are like that. Most of our prayer lives could use a tune-up.

Some prayer lives lack consistency. They're either a desert or an oasis. Long, arid, dry spells interrupted by brief plunges into the waters of communion. We go days or weeks without consistent prayer, but then something happens—we hear a sermon, read a book, experience a tragedy—something leads us to pray, so we dive in. We submerge ourselves in prayer and leave refreshed and renewed. But as the journey resumes, our prayers don't.

Others of us need sincerity. Our prayers are a bit hollow, memorized, and rigid. More liturgy than life. And though they are daily, they are dull.

Still others lack, well, honesty. We honestly wonder if prayer makes a difference. Why on earth would God in heaven want to talk to me? If God knows all, who am I to tell him anything? If God controls all, who am I to do anything?

If you struggle with prayer, I've got just the guy for you. Don't worry, he's not a monastic saint. He's not a calloused-kneed apostle. Nor is he a prophet whose middle name is Meditation. He's not a too-holy-to-be-you reminder of how far you need to go in prayer. He's just the opposite. A fellow crop duster. A parent with a sick son in need of a miracle. The father's prayer isn't much, but the answer is and the result reminds us: The power is not in the prayer; it's in the one who hears it.

He prayed out of desperation. His son, his only son, was demon-possessed. Not only was he a deaf mute and an epileptic, he was also possessed by an evil spirit. Ever since the boy was young, the demon had thrown him into fires and water.

Imagine the pain of the father. Other dads could watch their children grow and mature; he could only watch his suffer. While others were teaching their sons an occupation, he was just trying to keep his son alive.

What a challenge! He couldn't leave his son alone for a minute. Who knew when the next attack would come? The father had to remain on call, on alert twenty-four hours a day. He was desperate and tired, and his prayer reflects both.

"If you can do anything for him, please have pity on us and help us."

Listen to that prayer. Does it sound courageous? Confident? Strong? Hardly.

One word would have made a lot of difference. Instead of *if,* what if he'd said *since?* "*Since* you can do anything for him, please have pity on us and help us."

But that's not what he said. He said *if.* The Greek is even more emphatic. The tense implies doubt. It's as if the man were saying, "This one's probably out of your league, but if you can . . ."

A classic crop-duster appeal. More meek than mighty. More timid than towering. More like a crippled lamb coming to a shepherd than a proud lion roaring in the jungle. If his prayer sounds like yours, then don't be discouraged, for that's where prayer begins.

It begins as a yearning. An honest appeal. Ordinary people staring at Mount Everest. No pretense. No boasting. No posturing. Just prayer. Feeble prayer, but prayer nonetheless.

We are tempted to wait to pray until we know how to pray. We've heard the prayers of the spiritually mature. We've read of the rigors of the disciplined. And we are convinced we've a long way to traverse.

And since we'd rather not pray than pray poorly, we don't pray. Or we pray infrequently. We are waiting to pray until we learn how to pray.

Good thing this man didn't make the same mistake. He wasn't much of a pray-er. And his wasn't much of a prayer. He even admits it! "I do believe," he implored. "Help me to believe more" (see Mark 9:24).

This prayer isn't destined for a worship manual. No Psalm will result from his utterance. His was simple—no incantation or chant. But Jesus responded. He responded, not to the eloquence of the man, but to the pain of the man.

Jesus had many reasons to disregard this man's request.

For one thing, Jesus was just returning from the mountain, the Mount of Transfiguration. While there his face had changed and his clothes had become as bright as a flash of lightning (see Luke 9:29). A roaring radiance had poured from him. The burdens of earth were replaced with the splendors of heaven. Moses and Elijah came and angels encouraged. He was lifted above the dusty horizon of Terra and invited into the sublime. He was transfigured. The journey up was exhilarating.

But the journey down was disheartening.

When we lived in Rio de Janeiro we would occasionally vacation in Teresopolis, a mountain village a couple of hours outside of the city. Teresopolis was everything Rio was not. It was quiet. It was clean. It was calm. And most of all it was cool. Rio was a sauna.

The trip down was always depressing. Poverty, heat, and pollution hit like a wave. We faced a herculean temptation to turn around and go back.

If Denalyn and I felt that way after a week in the mountains, imagine what Jesus must have felt after a glimpse into heaven!

Look at the chaos that greets him as he returns. The disciples and the religious leaders are arguing. A crowd of bystanders is gawking. A boy, who'd suffered all his life, is on public display. And a father who'd come for help is despondent, wondering why no one can help.

No wonder Jesus says, "You people have no faith. How long must I stay with you? How long must I put up with you?" (v. 19).

Never has the difference between heaven and earth been so stark.

Never has the arena of prayer been so poor. Where is the faith in this picture? The disciples have failed, the scribes are amused, the demon is victorious, and the father is desperate. You'd be hard-pressed to find a needle of belief in that haystack.

You may even be hard-pressed to find one in your own. Perhaps your life is a long way from heaven, too. Noisy household—screaming kids instead of singing angels. Divisive religion—your leaders squabble more than they minister. Overwhelming problems. You can't remember when you didn't wake up to this demon.

And yet out of the din of doubt comes your timid voice. "If you can do anything for me . . ."

Does such a prayer make a difference?

Let Mark answer that question.

> When Jesus saw that a crowd was quickly gathering, he ordered the evil spirit, saying, "You spirit that makes people unable to hear or speak, I command you to come out of this boy and never enter him again."

> The evil spirit screamed and caused the boy to fall on the ground again. Then the spirit came out. The boy looked as if he were dead, and many people said, "He is dead!" But Jesus took hold of the boy's hand and helped him to stand up.
>
> Mark 9:25–27

This troubled the disciples. As soon as they got away from the crowds they asked Jesus, "Why couldn't we force that evil spirit out?"

His answer? "That kind of spirit can only be forced out by prayer."

What prayer? What prayer made the difference? Was it the prayer of the apostles? No, they didn't pray. Must have been the prayers of the scribes. Maybe they went to the temple and interceded. No. The scribes didn't pray either. Then it must have been the people. Perhaps they had a vigil for the boy. Nope. The people didn't pray. They never bent a knee. Then what prayer led Jesus to deliver the demon?

There is only one prayer in the story. It's the honest prayer of a hurting man. And since God is more moved by our hurt than our eloquence, he responded. That's what fathers do.

That's exactly what Jim Redmond did.

His son Derek, a twenty-six-year-old Briton, was favored to win the four-hundred-meter race in the 1992 Barcelona Olympics. Halfway into his semifinal heat, a fiery pain seared through his right leg. He crumpled to the track with a torn hamstring.

As the medical attendants were approaching, Redmond fought to his feet. "It was animal instinct," he would later say. He set out hopping, pushing away the coaches in a crazed attempt to finish the race.

When he reached the stretch, a big man pushed through the crowd. He was wearing a t-shirt that read "Have you hugged your child today?" and a hat that challenged, "Just Do It." The man was Jim Redmond, Derek's father.

"You don't have to do this," he told his weeping son.

"Yes, I do," Derek declared.

"Well, then," said Jim, "we're going to finish this together."

And they did. Jim wrapped Derek's arm around his shoulder and helped him hobble to the finish line. Fighting off security men, the son's head sometimes buried in the father's shoulder, they stayed in Derek's lane to the end.

The crowd clapped, then stood, then cheered, and then wept as the father and son finished the race.

What made the father do it? What made the father leave the stands to meet his son on the track? Was it the strength of his child? No, it was the pain of his child. His son was hurt and fighting to complete the race. So the father came to help him finish.

God does the same. Our prayers may be awkward. Our attempts may be feeble. But since the power of prayer is in the one who hears it and not the one who says it, our prayers do make a difference.

11

BRIGHT LIGHTS ON DARK NIGHTS

When You Are Out of Choices

Later Jesus went to Jerusalem for a special Jewish feast. In Jerusalem there is a pool with five covered porches, which is called Bethzatha in the Jewish language. This pool is near the Sheep Gate. Many sick people were lying on the porches beside the pool. Some were blind, some were crippled, and some were paralyzed. Sometimes an angel of the Lord came down to the pool and stirred up the water. After the angel did this, the first person to go into the pool was healed from any sickness he had. A man was lying there who had been sick for thirty-eight years. When Jesus saw the man and knew that he had been sick for such a long time, Jesus asked him, "Do you want to be well?"

The sick man answered, "Sir, there is no one to help me get into the pool when the water starts moving. While I am coming to the water, someone else always gets in before me."

Then Jesus said, "Stand up. Pick up your mat and walk." And immediately the man was well; he picked up his mat and began to walk.

The day this happened was a Sabbath day. So the Jews said to the man who had been healed, "Today is the Sabbath. It is against our law for you to carry your mat on the Sabbath day."

But he answered, "The man who made me well told me, 'Pick up your mat and walk.'"

Then they asked him, "Who is the man who told you to pick up your mat and walk?"

But the man who had been healed did not know who it was, because there were many people in that place, and Jesus had left.

Later, Jesus found the man at the Temple and said to him, "See, you are well now. Stop sinning so that something worse does not happen to you."

Then the man left and told the Jews that Jesus was the one who had made him well.

Because Jesus was doing this on the Sabbath day, the Jews began to persecute him. But Jesus said to them, "My Father never stops working, and so I keep working, too."

This made the Jews try still harder to kill him. They said, "First Jesus was breaking the law about the Sabbath day. Now he says that God is his own Father, making himself equal with God!"

John 5:1–18

> Jesus asked him, "Do you want to be well?"
>
> The sick man answered, "Sir, there is no one to help me."
>
> John 5:6–7

$\mathcal{F}$or the longest time this story didn't make any sense to me. I couldn't figure it out. It's about a man who has barely enough faith to stand on, but Jesus treats him as if he'd laid his son on the altar for God. Martyrs and apostles deserve such honor, but not some pauper who doesn't know Jesus when he sees him. Or so I thought.

For the longest time I thought Jesus was too kind. I thought the story was too bizarre. I thought the story was too good to be true. Then I realized something. This story isn't about an invalid in Jerusalem. This story is about you. It's about me. The fellow isn't nameless. He has a name—yours. He has a face—mine. He has a problem—just like ours.

Jesus encounters the man near a large pool north of the temple in Jerusalem. It's 360 feet long, 130 feet wide, and 75 feet deep. A colonnade with five porches overlooks the body of water. It's a monument of wealth and prosperity, but its residents are people of sickness and disease.

It's called Bethesda. It could be called Central Park, Metropolitan Hospital, or even Joe's Bar and Grill. It could be the homeless huddled beneath a downtown overpass. It could be Calvary Baptist. It could be any collection of hurting people.

An underwater spring caused the pool to bubble occasionally. The people believed the bubbles were caused by the dipping of angels' wings. They also believed that the first person to touch the water after the angel did would be healed. Did healing occur? I don't know. But I do know crowds of invalids came to give it a try.

Picture a battleground strewn with wounded bodies, and you see Bethesda. Imagine a nursing home overcrowded and understaffed, and you see the pool. Call to mind the orphans in Bangladesh or the abandoned in New Delhi, and you will see what people saw when they passed Bethesda. As they passed, what did they hear? An endless wave of groans. What did they witness? A field of faceless need. What did they do? Most walked past, ignoring the people.

But not Jesus. He is in Jerusalem for a feast. He is alone. He's not there to teach the disciples or to draw a crowd. The people need him—so he's there.

Can you picture it? Jesus walking among the suffering.

What is he thinking? When an infected hand touches his ankle, what does he do? When a blind child stumbles in Jesus' path, does he reach down to catch the child? When a wrinkled hand extends for alms, how does Jesus respond?

Whether the watering hole is Bethesda or Bill's Bar . . . how does God feel when people hurt?

It's worth the telling of the story if all we do is watch him walk. It's worth it just to know he even came. He didn't have to, you know. Surely there are more sanitary crowds in Jerusalem. Surely there are more enjoyable activities. After all, this is the Passover feast. It's an exciting time in the holy city. People have come from miles around to meet God in the temple.

Little do they know that God is with the sick.

Little do they know that God is walking slowly, stepping carefully between the beggars and the blind.

Little do they know that the strong young carpenter who surveys the ragged landscape of pain is God.

"When they suffered, he suffered also" Isaiah wrote (Isa. 63:9). On this day Jesus must have suffered much.

On this day Jesus must have sighed often as he walked along the poolside of Bethesda . . . and he sighs when he comes to you and me.

Remember, I told you this story was about us? Remember, I said I found our faces in the Bible? Well, here we are, filling the white space between the letters of verse 5: "A man was lying there who had been sick for thirty-eight years."

Maybe you don't like being described like that. Perhaps you'd rather find yourself in the courage of David or the devotion of Mary. We all would. But before you or I can be like them, we must admit we are like the paralytic. Invalids out of options. Can't walk. Can't work. Can't care for ourselves. Can't even roll down the bank to the pool to cash in on the angel water.

You may be holding this book with healthy hands and reading with strong eyes, and you can't imagine what you and this four-decade invalid have in common. How could he be you? What do we have in common with him?

Simple. Our predicament and our hope. What predicament? It is described in Hebrews 12:14: "Anyone whose life is not holy will never see the Lord."

That's our predicament: Only the holy will see God. Holiness is a prerequisite to heaven. Perfection is a requirement for eternity. We wish it weren't so. We act like it isn't so. We act like those who are "decent" will see God. We suggest that those who try hard will see God. We act as if we're good if we never do anything too bad. And that goodness is enough to qualify us for heaven.

Sounds right to us, but it doesn't sound right to God. And he sets the standard. And the standard is high. "You must be perfect, just as your Father in heaven is perfect" (Matt. 5:48).

You see, in God's plan, God is the standard for perfection. We don't compare ourself to others; they are just as fouled up as we are. The goal is to be like him; anything less is inadequate.

That's why I say the invalid is you and me. We, like the invalid, are paralyzed. We, like the invalid, are trapped. We, like the invalid, are stuck; we have no solution for our predicament.

That's you and me lying on the ground. That's us wounded and weary. When it comes to healing our spiritual condition, we don't have a chance. We might as well be told to pole-vault the moon. We don't have what it takes to be healed. Our only hope is that God will do for us what he did for the man at Bethesda—that he will step out of the temple and step into our ward of hurt and helplessness.

Which is exactly what he has done.

Read slowly and carefully Paul's description of what God has done for you: "When you were spiritually dead because of your sins and because you were not free from the power of your sinful self, God made you alive with Christ, and he forgave all our sins. He canceled the debt, which listed all the rules we failed to follow. He took away that record with its rules and nailed it to the cross. God stripped the spiritual rulers and powers of their authority. With the cross, he won the victory and showed the world that they were powerless" (Col. 2:13–15).

As you look at the words above, answer this question. Who is doing the work? You or God? Who is active? You or God? Who is doing the saving? You or God? Who is the one with strength? And who is the one paralyzed?

Let's isolate some phrases and see. First, look at your condition. "When you were spiritually dead . . . and . . . you were not free."

The invalid was better off than we are. At least he was alive. Paul says that if you and I are outside of Christ, then we are dead. Spiritually dead. Corpses. Lifeless. Cadavers. Dead. What can a dead person do? Not much.

But look what God can do with the dead.

> "God made you alive."
> "God forgave."
> "He canceled the debt."
> "He took away that record."
> "God stripped the spiritual rulers."
> "He won the victory."
> "[He] showed the world."

Again, the question. Who is active? You and I—or God? Who is trapped and who comes to the rescue?

God has thrown life jackets to every generation.

Look at Jonah in the fish belly—surrounded by gastric juices and sucked-in seaweed. For three days God has left him there. For three days Jonah has pondered his choices. And for three days he has come to the same conclusion: He ain't got one. From where he sits (or floats) there are two exits—and neither are very appealing. But then again, neither is Jonah. He blew it as a preacher. He was a flop as a fugitive. At best he's a coward, at worst a traitor. And what he's lacked all along he now has in abundance—guts.

So Jonah does the only thing he can do: He prays. He says nothing about how good he is—but a lot about how good God is. He doesn't even ask for help, but help is what he gets. Before he can say amen, the belly convulses, the fish belches, and Jonah lands face first on the beach.

Look at Daniel in the lions' den; his prospects aren't much better than Jonah's. Jonah had been swallowed, and Daniel is about to be. Flat on his back with the lions' faces so close he can smell their breath. The biggest one puts a paw on Daniel's chest and leans down to take the first bite and . . . nothing happens. Instead of a chomp, there is a bump. Daniel looks down and sees the nose of another lion rubbing against his belly. The lion's lips are snarling, but his mouth isn't opening.

That's when Daniel hears the snickering in the corner. He doesn't know who the fellow is, but he sure is bright and he sure is having fun. In his hands is a roll of bailing wire and on his face is one of those gotcha-while-you-weren't-watching expressions.

Or look at Joseph in the pit, a chalky hole in a hot desert. The lid has been pulled over the top and the wool has been pulled over his eyes. Those are his brothers up there, laughing and eating as if they did nothing more than tell him to get lost (which is what they'd done for most of his life). Those are his brothers, the ones who have every intention of leaving him to spend his days with the spiders and the snakes and then to die in the pit.

Like Jonah and Daniel, Joseph is trapped. He is out of options. There is no exit. There is no hope. But because Jacob's boys are as greedy as they were mean, Joseph is sold to some southbound gypsies and he changes history. Though the road to the palace takes a detour through a prison, it eventually ends up at the throne. And Joseph eventually stands before his brothers—this time with their asking for his help. And he is wise enough to give them what they ask and not what they deserve.

Or look at Barabbas on death row. The final appeal has been heard. The execution has been scheduled. Barabbas passes the time playing solitaire in his cell. He's resigned to the fact that the end is near. Doesn't appeal. Doesn't implore. Doesn't demand. The decision has been made, and Barabbas is going to die.

Like Jonah, Daniel, and Joseph, it's all over but the crying. And like Jonah, Daniel, and Joseph, the time to cry never comes. The steps of the warden echo in the chamber. Barabbas thinks he's bringing handcuffs and a final cigarette. Wrong. The warden brings street clothes. And Barabbas leaves the prison a free man because someone he'd probably never even seen took his place.

Such are the stories in the Bible. One near-death experience after another. Just when the neck is on the chopping block, just when the noose is around the neck, Calvary comes.

> Angels pound on Lot's door—Genesis 19.
> The whirlwind speaks to Job's hurt—Job 38–42.
> The Jordan purges Naaman's plague—2 Kings 5.
> An angel appears in Peter's cell—Acts 12.

God's efforts are strongest when our efforts are useless.

Go back to Bethesda for a moment. I want you to look at the brief but revealing dialogue between the paralytic and the Savior. Before Jesus heals him, he asks him a question: "Do you want to be well?"

"Sir, there is no one to help me get into the pool when the water starts moving. While I am coming to the water, someone else always gets in before me" (v. 7).

Is the fellow complaining? Is he feeling sorry for himself? Or is he just stating the facts? Who knows. But before we think about it too much, look what happens next.

"'Stand up. Pick up your mat and walk.'"

"And immediately the man was well; he picked up his mat and began to walk."

I wish we would do that; I wish we would take Jesus at his word. I wish, like heaven, that we would learn that when he says something, it happens. What is this peculiar paralysis that confines us? What is this stubborn unwillingness to be healed? When Jesus tells us to stand, let's stand.

> When he says we're forgiven, let's unload the guilt.
> When he says we're valuable, let's believe him.
> When he says we're eternal, let's bury our fear.
> When he says we're provided for, let's stop worrying.
> When he says, "Stand up," let's do it.

I love the story of the private who ran after and caught the runaway horse of Alexander the Great. When he brought the animal back to the general, Alexander thanked him by saying, "Thank you, captain."

With one word the private was promoted. When the general said it, the private believed it. He went to the quartermaster, selected a new uniform, and put it on. He went to the officers' quarters and selected a bunk. He went to the officers' mess and had a meal.

Because the general said it, he believed it. Would that we would do the same.

Is this your story? It can be. All the elements are the same. A gentle stranger has stepped into your hurting world and offered you a hand.

Now it's up to you to take it.

12

THE HARDEST THING GOD EVER DID

Understanding God's Priority

A few days later, when Jesus came back to Capernaum, the news spread that he was at home. Many people gathered together so that there was no room in the house, not even outside the door. And Jesus was teaching them God's message. Four people came, carrying a paralyzed man. Since they could not get to Jesus because of the crowd, they dug a hole in the roof right above where he was speaking. When they got through, they lowered the mat with the paralyzed man on it. When Jesus saw the faith of these people, he said to the paralyzed man, "Young man, your sins are forgiven."

Some of the teachers of the law were sitting there, thinking to themselves, "Why does this man say things like that? He is speaking as if he were God. Only God can forgive sins."

Jesus knew immediately what these teachers of the law were thinking. So he said to them, "Why are you thinking these things? Which is easier: to tell this paralyzed man, 'Your sins are forgiven,' or to tell him, 'Stand up. Take your mat and walk'? But I will prove to you that the Son of Man has authority on earth to forgive sins." So Jesus said to the paralyzed man, "I tell you, stand up, take your mat, and go home." Immediately the paralyzed man stood up, took his mat, and walked out while everyone was watching him.

The people were amazed and praised God. They said, "We have never seen anything like this!"

Mark 2:1–12

> "Which is easier: to tell this paralyzed man, 'Your sins are forgiven,' or to tell him, 'Stand up. Take your mat and walk'?"
>
> Mark 2:9

---

*L*et's talk for a minute about lovebursts.

You've witnessed *sunbursts:* sunlight shafting into a shadowed forest. You've seen *starbursts:* shots of light soaring through a night sky. And you've heard *powerbursts:* raw energy booming in the silence. And you've felt *lovebursts.* You may not have called them such, but you've felt them.

Lovebursts. Spontaneous affection. Tender moments of radiant love. Ignited devotion. Explosions of tenderness. May I illustrate?

You and your husband are at a party. One of those stand-in-the-living-room-and-talk-and-eat parties. You are visiting with some women, and your husband is across the room in a circle of men. The topic in your group is husbands, and the collective opinion is negative. The women complain about the amount of golf, dirty socks, and late nights at work. But you're silent. You say little because you have little to say. The guy you married isn't perfect, but he isn't a pain either. In fact, compared to these guys, he sounds pretty special. He's changed more than his share of diapers, and his golf clubs haven't come down out of the attic since the last baby was born. You look across the room at your husband and smile at the way he tugs at the tie you convinced him to wear. Still as handsome as the day you met. A bit paunchier and balder perhaps, but you don't see that. All you see is the man who stole your heart. And all of a sudden you'd go to China in a rowboat to tell him how glad you are that he did.

That's a loveburst. Here is another.

It's been a while since you held a baby. It's been a while since you were near a baby. But now you're alone with the baby. Your kids dropped him off at the house for the evening, and your wife ran to the store to get some milk, and now it's just you and your grandson. He's only a few days old and wrapped tighter than the cigars you gave your friends. As you cradle him in your arms, you realize this is the first time the two of you have been alone. With all the fanfare and friends at the hospital, you haven't shared a private moment—till now. So you sit in your big chair and turn him so you can see his face. You ponder the future, his future: first steps, first kiss, football, college. You wonder what it's going to be like being a kid in a world where hurt seems to linger on every corner.

As you look into the little eyes and nose that came from the other side of the family, it hits you. Out of nowhere comes a bolt of devotion. You're suddenly aware that hell itself would have to get past you to get to this one who carries your name. "It's gonna be all right," you hear yourself pledge to the sleeping boy. "Whatever happens, just remember I'm here. It's gonna be all right."

May I share one more?

You came home cranky because a deadline got moved up. She came home grumpy because the day care forgot to give your five-year-old her throat medicine. Each of you was wanting a little sympathy from the other, but neither got any. So there you sit at the dinner table—cranky and grumpy—with little Emily. Emily folds her hands to pray (as she has been taught), and the two of you bow you heads (but not your hearts) and listen. From where this prayer comes, God only knows.

"God, it's Emily. How are you? I'm fine, thank you. Mom and Dad are mad. I don't know why. We've got birds and toys and mash potatoes and each other. Maybe you can get them to stop being mad? Please do, or it's just gonna be you and me having any fun tonight. Amen."

The prayer is answered before it's finished; you both look up in the middle and laugh at the end and shake your heads and say you're sorry. And you both thank God for the little voice who reminded you about what matters.

That's what lovebursts do. They remind you about what matters. A telegram delivered to the back door of the familiar, telling you to treasure the treasure you've got while you've got it. A whisper from an angel, or someone who sounds like one, reminding you that what you have is greater than what you want and that what is urgent is not always what matters.

Those are lovebursts. You have them. I have them. And this may surprise you: Jesus had them . . . lots of them.

One of them happened when Jesus met an invalid. The man couldn't walk. He couldn't stand. His limbs were bent and his body twisted. A waist-high world walked past as he sat and watched.

Perhaps he was palsied, his body ridden with disease since birth. While other children had jumped and run, he had labored to bring a spoon to his mouth. As his brothers and sisters spoke and sang, his words slurred and slipped. Maybe he had never known what it was to be whole.

Or maybe he had known. Maybe he had once been healthy. Was there a time when he was known for his ability, not his disability? Was there an era when he could outrun anyone? Was there a time when he was the strongest in the shop? Was there a day when every kid in the village wanted to be like him?

Then came the fall—a tumble down a canyon, perhaps a stumble down some stairs. The pain in his skull was unbearable, but the numbness in his legs and arms was far worse. His feet hung like ornaments on the ends of his legs. His hands dangled like empty sleeves from his sides. He could see his limbs, but he couldn't feel them.

Whether he was born paralyzed or became paralyzed—the end result was the same: total dependence on others. Someone

117

had to wash his face and bathe his body. He couldn't blow his nose or go on a walk. When he ran, it was in his dreams, and his dreams would always awaken to a body that couldn't roll over and couldn't go back to sleep for all the hurt the night dream had brought.

"What he needs is a new body," any man in half his mind would say. What he needs is a God in heaven to restore what tragedy has robbed: arms that swing, hands that grip, and feet that dance.

When people looked at him, they didn't see the man; they saw a body in need of a miracle. That's not what Jesus saw, but that's what the people saw. And that's certainly what his friends saw. So they did what any of us would do for a friend. They tried to get him some help.

Word was out that a carpenter-turned-teacher-turned-wonder-worker was in town. And as the word got out, the people came. They came from every hole and hovel in Israel. They came like soldiers returning from battle—bandaged, crippled, sightless. The old with prune faces and toothless mouths. The young with deaf babies and broken hearts. Fathers with sons who couldn't speak. Wives with wombs that wouldn't bear fruit. The world, it seemed, had come to see if he was real or right or both.

By the time his friends arrived at the place, the house was full. People jammed the doorways. Kids sat in the windows. Others peeked over shoulders. How would this small band of friends ever attract Jesus' attention? They had to make a choice: Do we go in or give up?

What would have happened had the friends given up? What if they had shrugged their shoulders and mumbled something about the crowd being big and dinner getting cold and turned and left? After all, they had done a good deed in coming this far. Who could fault them for turning back? You can only do so much for somebody. But these friends hadn't done enough.

One said that he had an idea. The four huddled over the paralytic and listened to the plan to climb to the top of the house, cut through the roof, and lower their friend down with their sashes.

It was risky—they could fall. It was dangerous—*he* could fall. It was unorthodox—de-roofing is antisocial. It was intrusive—Jesus was busy. But it was their only chance to see Jesus. So they climbed to the roof.

Faith does those things. Faith does the unexpected. And faith gets God's attention. Look what Mark says: "When Jesus saw the faith of these people, he said to the paralyzed man, 'Young man, your sins are forgiven'" (v. 5).

Finally, someone took him at his word! Four men had enough hope in him and love for their friend that they took a chance. The stretcher above was a sign from above—somebody believes! Someone was willing to risk embarrassment and injury for just a few moments with the Galilean.

Jesus was moved.

> Like the wife overwhelmed with love for her paunchy but precious husband.
>
> Like the grandfather determined to protect his grandson.
>
> Like the parents touched by the prayer of their child.

Jesus was moved by the scene of faith. So he applauds—if not with his hands, at least with his heart. And not only does he applaud, he blesses. And we witness a divine loveburst.

The friends want him to heal their friend. But Jesus won't settle for a simple healing of the body—he wants to heal the soul. He leapfrogs the physical and deals with the spiritual. To heal the body is temporal; to heal the soul is eternal.

The request of the friends is valid—but timid. The expectations of the crowd are high—but not high enough. They expect Jesus to say, "I heal you." Instead he says, "I forgive you."

They expect him to treat the body, for that is what they see.

He chooses to treat not only the body, but also the spiritual, for that is what he sees.

They want Jesus to give the man a new body so he can walk. Jesus gives grace so the man can live.

Remarkable. Sometimes God is so touched by what he sees that he gives us what we need and not simply that for which we ask.

It's a good thing. For who would have ever thought to ask God for what he gives? Which of us would have dared to say: "God, would you please hang yourself on a tool of torture as a substitution for every mistake I have ever committed?" And then have the audacity to add: "And after you forgive me, could you prepare me a place in your house to live forever?"

And if that wasn't enough: "And would you please live within me and protect me and guide me and bless me with more than I could ever deserve?"

Honestly, would we have the chutzpah to ask for that? No, we, like the friends, would have only asked for the small stuff.

We would ask for little things like a long life and a healthy body and a good job. Grand requests from our perspective, but from God's it's like taking the moped when he offers the limo.

So, knowing the paralytic didn't know enough to ask for what he needed, Jesus gave it anyway: "Young man, your sins are forgiven" (v. 5).

The Pharisees start to grumble. That's not kosher. Even a tenderfoot Jew knows, "Only God can forgive sins" (v. 7).

Their mumbling spawns one of Christ's greatest questions: "Which is easier: to tell this paralyzed man, 'Your sins are forgiven,' or to tell him, 'Stand up. Take your mat and walk'?" (v. 9).

You answer the question. Which is easier for Jesus? To forgive a soul or heal a body? Which caused Jesus less pain—providing this man with health or providing this man with heaven?

To heal the man's body took a simple command; to forgive the man's sins took Jesus' blood. The first was done in the house of friends; the second on a hill with thieves. One took a word; the other took his body. One took a moment; the other took his life.

Which was easier?

So strong was his love for this crew of faith that he went beyond their appeal and went straight to the cross.

Jesus already knows the cost of grace. He already knows the price of forgiveness. But he offers it anyway. Love burst his heart.

By the way, he hasn't changed. What happened then happens today. When we take a step of faith, God sees. The same face that beamed at the paralytic beams at the alcoholic refusing the bottle. The same eyes that danced at the friends dance at the mom and dad who will do whatever it takes to get their child to Jesus. And the same lips that spoke to the man in Capernaum speak to the man in Detroit, to the woman in Belfast, to the child in Moscow . . . to any person anywhere who dares to come into the presence of God and ask for help.

And though we can't hear it here, the angels can hear him there. All of heaven must pause as another burst of love declares the only words that really matter: "Your sins are forgiven."

13

WHAT ONLY GOD CAN DO

---

*When You're Trapped
by Legalism*

There was a man named Nicodemus who was one of the Pharisees and an important Jewish leader. One night Nicodemus came to Jesus and said, "Teacher, we know you are a teacher sent from God, because no one can do the miracles you do unless God is with him."

Jesus answered, "I tell you the truth, unless one is born again, he cannot be in God's kingdom."

Nicodemus said, "But if a person is already old, how can he be born again? He cannot enter his mother's body again. So how can a person be born a second time?"

But Jesus answered, "I tell you the truth, unless one is born from water and the Spirit, he cannot enter God's kingdom. Human life comes from human parents, but spiritual life comes from the Spirit. Don't be surprised when I tell you, 'You must all be born again.' The wind blows where it wants to and you hear the sound of it, but you don't know where the wind comes from or where it is going. It is the same with every person who is born from the Spirit."

Nicodemus asked, "How can this happen?"

Jesus said, "You are an important teacher in Israel, and you don't understand these things? I tell you the truth, we talk about what we know, and we tell about what we have seen, but you don't accept what we tell you. I have told you about things here on earth, and you do not believe me. So you will not believe me if I tell you about things of heaven. The only one who has ever gone up to heaven is the One who came down from heaven— the Son of Man.

"Just as Moses lifted up the snake in the desert, the Son of Man must also be lifted up. So that everyone who believes can have eternal life in him.

"God loved the world so much that he gave his one and only Son so that whoever believes in him may not be lost, but have eternal life. God did not send his Son into the world to judge the world guilty, but to save the world through him. People who

believe in God's Son are not judged guilty. Those who do not believe have already been judged guilty, because they have not believed in God's one and only Son. They are judged by this fact: The Light has come into the world, but they did not want light. They wanted darkness, because they were doing evil things. All who do evil hate the light and will not come to the light, because it will show all the evil things they do. But those who follow the true way come to the light, and it shows that the things they do were done through God."

John 3:1–21

But Jesus answered, "I tell you the truth, unless one is born from water and the Spirit, he cannot enter God's kingdom."

John 3:5

_I_t's a fact of the farm. The most fertile ground remains barren if no seed is sown.

Apparently Nicodemus didn't know that. He thought the soil could bear fruit with no seeds. He was big on the farmer's part but forgetful of the seed's part. He was a legalist. And that is how a legalist thinks. A legalist prepares the soil but forgets the seed.

Nicodemus came about his legalism honestly. He was a Pharisee.

Pharisees taught that faith was an outside job. What you wore, how you acted, the title you carried, the sound of your prayers, the amount of your gifts—all these were the Pharisees' measure of spirituality.

Had they been farmers, they would have had the most attractive acreage in the region—painted silos and sparkling equipment. The fences would have been whitewashed and clean. The soil overturned and watered.

Had they been farmers they would have spent hours in the coffee shop discussing the theory of farming. Is it best to fertilize before or after a rain? Do you fallow a field every other year or every third year? Should a farmer wear overalls or jeans? Cowboy hats or baseball caps?

The Pharisees had only one problem. For all their discussion about the right techniques, they harvested little fruit. In fact, one untrained Galilean had borne more fruit in a few short months than all the Pharisees had in a generation. This made them jealous. Angry. Condescending. And they dealt with him by ignoring his results and insulting his methods.

That is, all the Pharisees except Nicodemus. He was curious. No, more than curious, he was stirred; stirred by the way people listened to Jesus. They listened as if he were the only one with truth. As if he were a prophet.

Nicodemus was stirred by what he saw Jesus do. Like the time Jesus stormed into the temple and overturned the tables of the moneychangers. Nicodemus once knew such passion. But that was a long time ago—before the titles, before the robes, before the rules.

Nicodemus is drawn to the carpenter, but he can't be seen with him. Nicodemus is on the high court. He can't approach Jesus in the day. So Nicodemus goes to meet him at night. He goes in the darkness.

Appropriate. For legalism offers no light.

Nicodemus begins with courtesies, "Teacher, we know you are a teacher sent from God, because no one can do the miracles you do unless God is with him" (v. 2).

Jesus disregards the compliment. "I tell you the truth, unless one is born again, he cannot be in God's kingdom" (v. 3).

No chitchat here. No idle talk. Straight to the point. Straight to the heart. Straight to the problem. Jesus knows the heart of the legalist is hard. You can't crack it with feathery accolades. You need a chisel. So Jesus hammers away:

> You can't help the blind by turning up the light, Nicodemus.
>
> You can't help the deaf by turning up the music, Nicodemus.
>
> You can't change the inside by decorating the outside, Nicodemus.
>
> You can't grow fruit without seed, Nicodemus.

You must be born again.

Whack! Whack! Whack!

The meeting between Jesus and Nicodemus was more than an encounter between two religious figures. It was a collision between two philosophies. Two opposing views on salvation.

Nicodemus thought the person did the work; Jesus says God does the work. Nicodemus thought it was a tradeoff. Jesus says it is a gift. Nicodemus thought man's job was to earn it. Jesus says man's job is to accept it.

These two views encompass all views. All the world religions can be placed in one of two camps: legalism or grace. Humankind does it or God does it. Salvation as a wage based on deeds done—or salvation as a gift based on Christ's death.

A legalist believes the supreme force behind salvation is you. If you look right, speak right, and belong to the right segment of the right group, you will be saved. The brunt of responsibility doesn't lie within God; it lies within you.

The result? The outside sparkles. The talk is good and the step is true. But look closely. Listen carefully. Something is missing. What is it? Joy. What's there? Fear. (That you won't do enough.) Arrogance. (That you have done enough.) Failure. (That you have made a mistake.)

Legalism is a dark world.

Perhaps you didn't know that. You may be reading with a puzzled expression asking, "What is this story doing in this book, Max? I thought this was a book about Jesus meeting people at their point of pain. Nicodemus isn't hurting. He's got clout. He's got friends. He studies the Bible. He's not in pain, is he?"

If you asked that question, be thankful. If you have never known the crush of legalism, be grateful. You have been spared.

Others of you haven't. Others of you could answer the above question better than I. Legalism is slow torture, suffocation of the spirit, amputation of one's dreams. Legalism is just enough religion to keep you, but not enough to nourish you.

So you starve. Your teachers don't know where to go for food, so you starve together. Your diet is rules and standards. No vitamins. No taste. No zest. Just bland, predictable religion.

Reminds me of a group I was in as a youngster. When I was eight years old I was a part of a boys' choir. We met two evenings a week for two hours. We wore blazers and sang at banquets. We even went on the road.

Curiously, our instructor was an ex-drill sergeant. Before he ran a boys' choir, he ran a boot camp. And some of the previous spilled over into the latter. Every evening during rehearsals, we took a marching break. We'd go outside and march in formation. He gave the commands, and we did the turns.

"Hut, two, three, four. Hut, two, three, four."

At first, I didn't question the practice. I didn't have the courage. I was intimidated by the man. Finally, I summoned enough guts to ask the kid beside me to explain the marching.

"Why are we doing this?"

"I don't know."

"Where are we going?"

"I don't know."

No one did. For two years we marched two nights every week. But no one knew where we were going and no one knew why. We just knew that if we wanted to sing we'd better stay in step.

That's legalism.

It's rigid. It's uniform. It's mechanical—and it's not from God.

Can I give you the down and dirty about legalism?

Legalism doesn't need God. Legalism is the search for innocence—not forgiveness. It's a systematic process of defending self, explaining self, exalting self, and justifying self. Legalists are obsessed with self—not God.

Legalism:

> Turns my opinion into your burden. There is only room for one opinion in this boat. And guess who is wrong!

> Turns my opinion into your boundary. Your opposing opinion makes me question not only your right to have fellowship with me, but also your salvation.

Turns my opinion into your obligation. Christians must toe the company line. Your job isn't to think, it's to march.

If you want to be in the group, stay in step and don't ask questions.

Nicodemus knew how to march, but he longed to sing. He knew there was something more, but he didn't know where to find it. So he went to Jesus.

He went at night because he feared the displeasure of his peers. Legalism puts the fear of man in you. It makes you approval-hungry. You become keenly aware of what others will say and think, and you do what it takes to please them. Conformity is not fun, but it's safe. The uniform doesn't fit, but it's approved, so you wear it. You don't know why you are marching or where you are going—but who are you to ask questions? So you stay in step and plod down the path of least resistance.

And if you dare explore another trail, you must do so at night, like Nicodemus did. He snuck through the shadows and crept through the ebony streets until he stood in the presence of Christ. In the conversation, Nicodemus, the renowned teacher of the law, speaks only three times: once to compliment and twice to question. After a lifetime of weighing the tittles of Scripture in the scale of logic, the scholar becomes suddenly silent as Jesus opens the gate and the light of grace floods the catacomb.

Jesus begins by revealing the source of spirituality: "Human life comes from human parents, but spiritual life comes from the Spirit" (v. 6).

Spiritual life is not a human endeavor. It is rooted in and orchestrated by the Holy Spirit. Every spiritual achievement is created and energized by God.

Spirituality, Jesus says, comes not from church attendance or good deeds or correct doctrine, but from heaven itself. Such words must have set Nicodemus back on his heels. But Jesus was just getting started.

"The wind blows where it wants to and you hear the sound of it, but you don't know where the wind comes from or where it is going. It is the same with every person who is born from the Spirit" (v. 8).

Ever had a gust of wind come to you for help? Ever seen a windstorm on the side of the road catching its breath? No, you haven't. The wind doesn't seek our aid. Wind doesn't even reveal its destiny. It's silent and invisible and so is the Spirit.

By now Nicodemus was growing edgy. Such light is too bright for his eyes. We religious teachers like to control and manage. We like to define and outline. Structure and clarity are the friend of the preacher. But they aren't always the protocol of God.

Salvation is God's business. Grace is his idea, his work, and his expense. He offers it to whom he desires, when he desires. Our job in the process is to inform the people, not to screen the people.

The question must have been written all over Nicodemus's face. Why would God do this? What would motivate him to offer such a gift? What Jesus told Nicodemus, Nicodemus never could have imagined. The motive behind the gift of new birth? Love. "God loved the world so much that he gave his one and only Son so that whoever believes in him may not be lost, but have eternal life (v. 16).

Nicodemus has never heard such words. Never. He has had many discussions of salvation. But this is the first in which no rules were given. No system was offered. No code or ritual. "Everyone who believes can have eternal life in him," Jesus told him. Could God be so generous? Even in the darkness of night, the amazement is seen on Nicodemus's face. *Everyone who believes can have eternal life.* Not "everyone who achieves." Not "everyone who succeeds." Not "everyone who agrees." But "everyone who believes."

Note how God liberates the legalist. Observe the tender firmness of his touch. Like a master farmer, he shoveled away the crusty soil until a moist, fertile spot was found, and there he planted a seed, a seed of grace.

Did it bear fruit? Read the following and see for yourself.

Nicodemus, who earlier had come to Jesus at night, went with Joseph. He brought about seventy-five pounds of myrrh and aloes. These two men took Jesus' body and wrapped it with the spices in pieces of linen cloth, which is how Jewish people bury the dead. In the place where Jesus was crucified, there was a garden. In the garden was a new tomb that had never been used before. The men laid Jesus in that tomb.

John 19:39–42

Strange how a man can go full circle in the kingdom. The one who'd come at night now appears in the day. The one who crept through the shadows to meet Jesus now comes to the cross to serve Jesus. And the one who'd received the seed of grace now plants the greatest seed of all—the seed of eternal life.

14

GALILEAN GRACE

When You Let God Down

Later, Jesus showed himself to his followers again—this time at Lake Galilee. This is how he showed himself: Some of the followers were together: Simon Peter, Thomas (called Didymus), Nathanael from Cana in Galilee, the two sons of Zebedee, and two other followers. Simon Peter said, "I am going out to fish."

The others said, "We will go with you." So they went out and got into the boat. They fished that night but caught nothing.

Early the next morning Jesus stood on the shore, but the followers did not know it was Jesus. Then he said to them, "Friends, did you catch any fish?"

They answered, "No."

He said, "Throw your net on the right side of the boat, and you will find some." So they did, and they caught so many fish they could not pull the net back into the boat.

The follower whom Jesus loved said to Peter, "It is the Lord!" When Peter heard him say this, he wrapped his coat around himself. (Peter had taken his clothes off.) Then he jumped into the water. The other followers went to shore in the boat, dragging the net full of fish. They were not very far from shore, only about a hundred yards. When the followers stepped out of the boat and onto the shore, they saw a fire of hot coals. There were fish on the fire, and there was bread.

Then Jesus said, "Bring some of the fish you just caught."

Simon Peter went into the boat and pulled the net to the shore. It was full of big fish, one hundred fifty-three in all, but even though there were so many, the net did not tear.

John 21:1–11

> The follower whom Jesus loved said to Peter, "It is the Lord!" When Peter heard him say this, he wrapped his coat around himself. (Peter had taken his clothes off.) Then he jumped into the water.
>
> John 21:7

---

*T*he sun was in the water before Peter noticed it—a wavy circle of gold on the surface of the sea. A fisherman is usually the first to spot the sun rising over the crest of the hills. It means his night of labor is finally over.

But not for this fisherman. Though the light reflected on the lake, the darkness lingered in Peter's heart. The wind chilled, but he didn't feel it. His friends slept soundly, but he didn't care. The nets at his feet were empty, the sea had been a miser, but Peter wasn't thinking about that.

His thoughts were far from the Sea of Galilee. His mind was in Jerusalem, reliving an anguished night. As the boat rocked, his memories raced:

> the clanking of the Roman guard,
> the flash of a sword and the duck of a head,
> a touch for Malchus, a rebuke for Peter,
> soldiers leading Jesus away.

"What was I thinking?" Peter mumbled to himself as he stared at the bottom of the boat. *Why did I run?*

Peter had run; he had turned his back on his dearest friend and run. We don't know where. Peter may not have known where. He found a hole, a hut, an abandoned shed—he found a place to hide and he hid.

He had bragged, "Everyone else may stumble . . . but I will not" (Matt. 26:33). Yet he did. Peter did what he swore he wouldn't do. He had tumbled face first into the pit of his own fears. And there he sat. All he could hear was his hollow promise. *Everyone else may stumble . . . but I will not. Everyone else . . . I will not. I will not. I will not.* A war raged within the fisherman.

At that moment the instinct to survive collided with his allegiance to Christ, and for just a moment allegiance won. Peter stood and stepped out of hiding and followed the noise till he saw the torch-lit jury in the courtyard of Caiaphas.

He stopped near a fire and warmed his hands. The fire sparked with irony. The night had been cold. The fire was hot. But Peter was neither. He was lukewarm.

"Peter followed at a distance" Luke described (22:54 NIV).

He was loyal . . . from a distance. That night he went close enough to see, but not close enough to be seen. The problem was, Peter was seen. Other people near the fire recognized him. "You were with him," they had challenged. "You were with the Nazarene." Three times people said it, and each time Peter denied it. And each time Jesus heard it.

Please understand that the main character in this drama of denial is not Peter, but Jesus. Jesus, who knows the hearts of all people, knew the denial of his friend. Three times the salt of Peter's betrayal stung the wounds of the Messiah.

How do I know Jesus knew? Because of what he did. "Then the Lord turned and looked straight at Peter" (Luke 22:61 NIV). When the rooster crowed, Jesus turned. His eyes searched for Peter and they found him. At that moment there were no soldiers, no accusers, no priests. At that predawn moment in Jerusalem there were only two people—Jesus and Peter.

Peter would never forget that look. Though Jesus' face was already bloody and bruised, his eyes were firm and focused. They were a scalpel, laying bare Peter's heart. Though the look had lasted only a moment, it lasted forever.

And now, days later on the Sea of Galilee, the look still seared. It wasn't the resurrection that occupied his thoughts. It wasn't the empty tomb. It wasn't the defeat of death. It was the eyes of Jesus seeing his failure. Peter knew them well. He'd seen them before. In fact he'd seen them on this very lake.

This wasn't the first night that Peter had spent on the Sea of Galilee. After all, he was a fisherman. He, like the others, worked at night. He knew the fish would feed near the surface during the cool of the night and return to the deep during the day. No, this wasn't the first night Peter had spent on the Sea of Galilee. Nor was it the first night he had caught nothing.

There was that time years before . . .

Most mornings Peter and his partners would sell their fish, repair their nets, and head home to rest with a bag of money and a feeling of satisfaction. This particular morning there was no money. There was no satisfaction. They had worked all through the night but had nothing to show for it except weary backs and worn nets.

And, what's worse, everyone knew it. Every morning the shore would become a market as the villagers came to buy their fish, but that day there were no fish.

Jesus was there that morning, teaching. As the people pressed there was little room for him to stand, so he asked Peter if his boat could be a platform. Peter agreed, maybe thinking the boat might as well be put to some good use.

Peter listens as Jesus teaches. It's good to hear something other than the slapping of waves. When Jesus finishes with the crowd, he turns to Peter. He has another request. He wants to go fishing. "Take the boat into deep water, and put your nets in the water to catch some fish" (Luke 5:4).

Peter groans. The last thing he wants to do is fish. The boat is clean. The nets are ready to dry. The sun is up and he is tired. It's time to go home. Besides, everyone is watching. They've already seen him come back empty-handed once. And, what's more, what does Jesus know about fishing?

137

So Peter speaks, "Master, we worked hard all night trying to catch fish" (v. 5).

Mark the weariness in the words.

"We worked hard." Scraping the hull. Carrying the nets. Pulling the oars. Throwing the nets high into the moonlit sky. Listening as they slap on the surface of the water.

"All night." The sky had gone from burnt orange to midnight black to morning gold. The hours had passed as slowly as the fleets of clouds before the moon. The fishermen's conversation had stilled and their shoulders ached. While the village slept, the men worked. All . . . night . . . long.

"Trying to catch fish." The night's events had been rhythmic: net swung and tossed high till it spread itself against the sky. Then wait. Let it sink. Pull it in. Do it again. Throw. Pull. Throw. Pull. Throw. Pull. Every toss had been a prayer. But every drag of the empty net had come back unanswered. Even the net sighed as the men pulled it out and prepared to throw it again.

For twelve hours they'd fished. And now . . . now Jesus is wanting to fish some more? And not just off the shore, but in the deep?

Peter sees his friends shrug their shoulders. He looks at the people on the beach watching him. He doesn't know what to do. Jesus may know a lot about a lot, but Peter knows about fishing. Peter knows when to work and when to quit. He knows there is a time to go on and a time to get out.

Common sense said it was time to get out. Logic said cut your losses and go home. Experience said pack it up and get some rest. But Jesus said, *"We can try again if you want."*

The most difficult journey is back to the place where you failed.

Jesus knows that. That's why he volunteers to go along. "The first outing was solo; this time I'll be with you. Try it again, this time with me on board."

And Peter reluctantly agrees to try again. "But you say to put the nets in the water, so I will" (Luke 5:5). It didn't make any sense, but he'd been around this Nazarene enough to know that his presence made a difference. That wedding in Cana? That sick child of the royal ruler? It's as if Jesus carried his own deck to the table.

So the oars dip again and the boat goes out. The anchor is set and the nets fly once more.

Peter watches as the net sinks, and he waits. He waits until the net spreads as far as his rope allows. The fishermen are quiet. Peter is quiet. Jesus is quiet. Suddenly the rope yanks. The net, heavy with fish, almost pulls Peter overboard.

"John, James!" he yells. "Come quick!"

Soon the boats are so full of fish that the port side rim dips close to the surface. Peter, ankle deep in flopping silver, turns to look at Jesus, only to find that Jesus is looking at him.

That's when he realizes who Jesus is.

What an odd place to meet God—on a fishing boat on a small sea in a remote country! But such is the practice of the God who comes into our world. Such is the encounter experienced by those who are willing to try again . . . with him.

Peter's life was never again the same after that catch.

He had turned his back on the sea to follow the Messiah. He had left the boats thinking he'd never return. But now he's back. Full circle. Same sea. Same boat. Maybe even the same spot.

But this isn't the same Peter. Three years of living with the Messiah have changed him. He's seen too much. Too many walking crippled, vacated graves, too many hours hearing his words. He's not the same Peter. It's the same Galilee, but a different fisherman.

Why did he return? What brought him back to Galilee after the crucifixion? Despair? Some think so—I don't. Hope dies hard for a man who has known Jesus. I think that's what Peter has. That's what brought him back. Hope. A bizarre hope that on the sea where he knew him first, he would know him again.

So Peter is in the boat, on the lake. Once again he's fished all night. Once again the sea has surrendered nothing.

His thoughts are interrupted by a shout from the shore. "Catch any fish?" Peter and John look up. Probably a villager. "No!" they yell. "Try the other side!" the voice yells back. John looks at Peter. What harm? So out sails the net. Peter wraps the rope around his wrist to wait.

But there is no wait. The rope pulls taut and the net catches. Peter sets his weight against the side of the boat and begins to bring in the net; reaching down, pulling up, reaching down, pulling up. He's so intense with the task, he misses the message.

John doesn't. The moment is déjà vu. This has happened before. The long night. The empty net. The call to cast again. Fish flapping on the floor of the boat. Wait a minute. He lifts his eyes to the man on the shore. "It's him," he whispers.

Then louder, "It's Jesus."

Then shouting, "It's the Lord, Peter. It's the Lord!"

Peter turns and looks. Jesus has come. Not just Jesus the teacher, but Jesus the death-defeater, Jesus the king . . . Jesus the victor over darkness. Jesus the God of heaven and earth is on the shore . . . and he's building a fire.

Peter plunges into the water, swims to the shore, and stumbles out wet and shivering and stands in front of the friend he betrayed. Jesus has prepared a bed of coals. Both are aware of the last time Peter had stood near a fire. Peter had failed God, but God had come to him.

For one of the few times in his life, Peter is silent. What words would suffice? The moment is too holy for words. God is offering breakfast to the friend who betrayed him. And Peter is once again finding grace at Galilee.

What do you say at a moment like this?

What do *you* say at a moment such as this?

It's just you and God. You and God both know what you did. And neither one of you is proud of it. What do you do?

You might consider doing what Peter did. Stand in God's presence. Stand in his sight. Stand still and wait. Sometimes that's all a soul can do. Too repentant to speak, but too hopeful to leave—we just stand.

Stand amazed.
He has come back.
He invites you to try again. This time, with him.

15

THE TENDERNESS OF GOD

*When You Wonder If
God Cares*

Two days later there was a wedding in the town of Cana in Galilee. Jesus' mother was there, and Jesus and his followers were also invited to the wedding. When all the wine was gone, Jesus' mother said to him, "They have no more wine."

Jesus answered, "Dear woman, why come to me? My time has not yet come."

His mother said to the servants, "Do whatever he tells you to do."

In that place there were six stone water jars that the Jews used in their washing ceremony. Each jar held about twenty or thirty gallons.

Jesus said to the servants, "Fill the jars with water." So they filled the jars to the top.

Then he said to them, "Now take some out and give it to the master of the feast."

So they took the water to the master. When he tasted it, the water had become wine. He did not know where the wine came from, but the servants who had brought the water knew. The master of the wedding called the bridegroom and said to him, "People always serve the best wine first. Later, after the guests have been drinking awhile, they serve the cheaper wine. But you have saved the best wine till now."

So in Cana of Galilee Jesus did his first miracle. There he showed his glory, and his followers believed in him.

John 2:1–11

"People always serve the best wine first. Later, after the guests have been drinking awhile, they serve the cheaper wine. But you have saved the best wine till now."

John 2:10

---

*L*et's pretend you are an angel. (That may be a stretch for some of you, but let's give it a try.)

You are an angel in the era before the Messiah. God has not yet come to the earth, but he soon will and that's where you come in. You receive notice that you've been given a special assignment. A once-in-an-eternity opportunity. You've been asked to serve on a special committee. Quite an honor, don't you think?

Michael chairs the heavenly task force. "Let's begin by choosing the first miracle," he states. "The first miracle is crucial. It's the lead-off proclamation. It's the vanguard demonstration. It must be chosen carefully."

"Must be powerful," someone volunteers.

"Undeniable."

"Unforgettable," chimes a third.

"We are in agreement, then," affirms Michael. "The first miracle of God on earth must have clout. Any ideas?"

Angelic creativity begins to whir.

"Have him raise a person from the dead."

"Or a whole cemetery from the dead!"

"Yeah, vacate the place."

"What about feeding every hungry person one meal?"

"Too easy. How about removing all the disease from the planet?"

145

"Bingo. I like that idea."

"I know," the voice is yours. All the other angels turn to look at you. "What if he rids the earth of all evil? I mean, with one great swoop all the bad is gone and just the good remains."

The group is silent. "Not bad," says one.

"Good thinking," says another.

"Get it done once and for all," agrees Michael. "It's settled. The first miracle will obliterate evil from the earth!"

Wings rustle with approval and you smile with pride. (You may get a promotion out of this.)

"Now let's move on to the second miracle . . ."

Sound far-fetched? Maybe, but the story is not without a couple of threads of truth.

One is that Jesus did have a plan. You can tell by some phrases he uses.

> "The right time for me has not yet come" (John 7:6).
> "The time has come for the Son of Man to receive his glory" (John 12:23).
> "The chosen time is near" (Matt. 26:18).
> "The time has come for the Son of Man to be handed over to sinful people" (Mark 14:41).
> "He looked toward heaven and prayed, 'Father, the time has come . . .'" (John 17:1).

Look at those words. "The right time has not yet come." "The time has come." "The chosen time." "The time has come." What do those phrases imply? A schedule. They represent a definite order of events. The mission of Christ was planned. I doubt if a committee ever existed, but a plan did.

There is a second shred of truth in my little scenario. Not only was there a plan in Christ's ministry, there was also a first miracle. What was it?

The plot is almost too simple. Jesus and his disciples are at a wedding. The host runs out of wine. All the stores are closed, so Jesus, at his mother's urging, transforms six jugs of water into six jugs of wine.

146

That's it. That's the lead-off hitter. Pretty low key, don't you think? Certainly doesn't have the punch of calling a person from the dead or the flair of straightening a crippled leg.

Or does it? Maybe there is more to this than we think.

You see, a wedding in the day of Christ was no small event. It usually began with a sundown ceremony at the synagogue. People would then leave the synagogue and begin a long, candlelight procession through the city, winding their way through the soft evening sunlight of the city streets. The couple would be escorted past as many homes as possible so everyone could wish them well. After the processional, however, the couple didn't go on a honeymoon; the honeymoon was brought to them.

They would go home to a party. For several days there would be gift-giving, speechmaking, food-eating and—you guessed it!—wine-drinking. Food and wine were taken very seriously. The host honored the guests by keeping their plates full and their cups overflowing. It was considered an insult to the guests if the host ran out of food or wine.

Hospitality at a wedding was a sacred duty. So serious were these social customs that, if they were not observed, lawsuits could be brought by the injured parties!

"Without wine," said the rabbis, "there is no joy." Wine was crucial, not for drunkenness, which was considered a disgrace, but for what it demonstrated. The presence of wine stated that this was a special day and that all the guests were special guests.

The absence of wine, then, was a social embarrassment.

Mary, the mother of Jesus, is one of the first to notice that the wine has run out. She goes to her son and points out the problem: "They have no more wine."

Jesus' response? "Dear woman, why come to me? My time has not yet come" (v. 4).

There are those words again. "My time." Jesus is aware of the plan. He has a place and a time for his first miracle. And this isn't it.

About now the angelic committee on the miracles of the Messiah lets out a collective sigh of relief.

"Whew, for a minute there, I thought he was going to blow it."

"Me, too. Can you imagine Jesus inaugurating his ministry with a water-to-wine miracle?"

"That's it, Jesus, say no. Stick to the plan."

Jesus knows the plan. At first, it appears he is going to stay with it. But as he hears his mother and looks into the faces of the wedding party, he reconsiders. The significance of the plan is slowly eclipsed by his concern for the people. Timing is important, but people are more so.

As a result, he changes his plan to meet the needs of some friends. Incredible. The schedule of heaven is altered so some friends won't be embarrassed. The inaugural miracle is motivated—not by tragedy or famine or moral collapse—but by concern for friends who are in a bind.

Now if you're an angel on the committee of Messianic miracles, you don't like that one bit. No, sir. You don't like this move on the part of Jesus. Everything about it is wrong. Wrong time. Wrong place. Wrong miracle.

"Come on, Jesus. Remember the schedule," you urge. "Remember the strategy. This isn't the way we had it planned."

No, if you're an angel on the committee, you don't like this move.

But if you're a human who has ever been embarrassed, you like this very much. Why? Because this miracle tells you that what matters to you matters to God.

You probably think that's true when it comes to the big stuff. When it comes to the major-league difficulties like death, disease, sin, and disaster—you know that God cares.

But what about the smaller things? What about grouchy bosses or flat tires or lost dogs? What about broken dishes, late flights, toothaches, or a crashed hard disk? Do these matter to God?

I mean, he's got a universe to run. He's got the planets to keep balanced and presidents and kings to watch over. He's got wars to worry with and famines to fix. Who am I to tell him about my ingrown toenail?

I'm glad you asked. Let me tell you who you are. In fact, let me *proclaim* who you are.

> You are an heir of God and a co-heir with Christ (Rom. 8:17).
>
> You are eternal, like an angel (Luke 20:36).
>
> You have a crown that will last forever (1 Cor. 9:25).
>
> You are a holy priest (1 Pet. 2:5), a treasured possession (Exod. 19:5).
>
> You were chosen before the creation of the world (Eph. 1:4). You are destined for "praise, fame, and honor, and you will be a holy people to the LORD your God" (Deut. 26:19).

But more than any of the above—more significant than any title or position—is the simple fact that you are God's child. "The Father has loved us so much that we are called children of God. And we really are his children" (1 John 3:1).

I love that last phrase! "We really are his children." It's as if John knew some of us would shake our heads and say, "Naw, not me. Mother Teresa, maybe. Billy Graham, all right. But not me." If those are your feelings, John added that phrase for you.

"We *really* are his children."

As a result, if something is important to you, it's important to God.

If you are a parent you know that. Imagine if you noticed an infected sore on the hand of your five-year-old son. You ask him what's wrong, and he says that he has a splinter. You ask him when it happened. He says last week! You ask him why he didn't tell you, and he says, "I didn't want to bother you. I knew you had all those things to do running the household and all, I didn't want to get in your way."

"Get in my way? Get in my way! I'm your dad. You're my son. My job is to help. I hurt when you hurt."

I have a perfect example of this on videotape. My eight-year-old daughter Jenna sang a solo at an appreciation banquet.

I agreed to stay home with our other two daughters if my wife would film the performance. When they came home, they had quite a story to tell and quite a tape to show.

Jenna forgot her lines. As she stood onstage in front of a large audience, her mind went blank. Since Denalyn was filming the moment, I saw the crisis through her eyes, the eyes of a mom. You can tell Denalyn is getting nervous the minute Jenna is getting forgetful—the camera begins to shake. "It's OK, it's OK," Denalyn's voice assures. She begins singing the words so Jenna will remember. But it's too late. Jenna says "I'm sorry" to the audience, bursts into tears, and bolts off the stage.

At this point Mom drops the camera and runs after Jenna. The camera records the floor and Denalyn's voice saying, "Come here, honey."

Why did Denalyn do that? Why did she drop everything and run after her daughter? (By the way, Jenna recovered. Denalyn dried her tears. The two rehearsed the lyrics. And Jenna sang and received a loud ovation.)

Now, why did Denalyn go to all that trouble? In the great scheme of things, does a social embarrassment matter that much? You know the answer before I tell you. To an eight-year-old girl, it's crucial. And because it was important to Jenna, it was important to Mom.

And because you are God's child, if it's important to you, it's important to God.

Why did Jesus change the water to wine? To impress the crowd? No, they didn't even know he did it. To get the wedding master's attention? No, he thought the groom was being generous. Why did Jesus do it? What motivated his first miracle?

His friends were embarrassed. What bothered them bothered him. If it hurts the child, it hurts the father.

So go ahead. Tell God what hurts. Talk to him. He won't turn you away. He won't think it's silly. "For our high priest is *able to understand* our weaknesses. When he lived on earth, he was tempted in every way that we are, but he did not sin. Let us, then, feel very sure that we can come before God's throne where there is grace" (Heb. 4:15–16, emphasis added).

Does God care about the little things in our lives? You better believe it.

If it matters to you, it matters to him.

16

THE MADMAN TURNED MISSIONARY

When You Encounter Evil

Jesus and his followers went to the other side of the lake to the area of the Gerasene people. When Jesus got out of the boat, instantly a man with an evil spirit came to him from the burial caves. This man lived in the caves, and no one could tie him up, not even with a chain. Many times people had used chains to tie the man's hands and feet, but he always broke them off. No one was strong enough to control him. Day and night he would wander around the burial caves and on the hills, screaming and cutting himself with stones. While Jesus was still far away, the man saw him, ran to him, and fell down before him.

The man shouted in a loud voice, "What do you want with me, Jesus, Son of the Most High God? I command you in God's name not to torture me!" He said this because Jesus was saying to him, "You evil spirit, come out of the man."

Then Jesus asked him, "What is your name?"

He answered, "My name is Legion, because we are many spirits."

He begged Jesus again and again not to send them out of that area.

A large herd of pigs was feeding on a hill near there. The demons begged Jesus, "Send us into the pigs; let us go into them." So Jesus allowed them to do this. The evil spirits left the man and went into the pigs. Then the herd of pigs—about two thousand of them—rushed down the hill into the lake and were drowned.

The herdsmen ran away and went to the town and to the countryside, telling everyone about this. So people went out to see what had happened. They came to Jesus and saw the man who used to have the many evil spirits, sitting, clothed, and in his right mind. And they were frightened. The people who saw this told the others what had happened to the man who had the demons living in him, and they told about the pigs. Then the people began to beg Jesus to leave their area.

As Jesus was getting back into the boat, the man who was freed from the demons begged to go with him.

But Jesus would not let him. He said, "Go home to your family and tell them how much the Lord has done for you and how he has had mercy on you." So the man left and began to tell the people in the Ten Towns about what Jesus had done for him. And everyone was amazed.

Mark 5:1–20

> They came to Jesus and saw the man
> who used to have the many evil
> spirits, sitting, clothed, and in his right
> mind.
>
> Mark 5:15

---

*H*ere's a question for you trivia hounds. Who was the first missionary Jesus ever sent?

Someone well trained, right? Someone with an intimate relationship with Christ. A devoted follower. A close disciple. One with a thorough knowledge of Scripture and sacrifice, wouldn't you think?

Let me give you a hint. To find him don't go to the Great Commission. Don't turn to the names of the apostles. This vanguard spokesman was not on that list.

How about the seventy-two disciples sent out by Christ? Sorry, wrong again. The epistles? No. Long before Paul picked up a pen, this preacher was already at work.

Where did Jesus go to find his first missionary? (You won't believe this.) A cemetery.

Who was the first ambassador he commissioned? (You're not going to buy this either.) A lunatic. The man Jesus sent out was a madman turned missionary. His story is found in the fifth chapter of Mark's Gospel.

> When Jesus got out of the boat, instantly a man with an evil
> spirit came to him from the burial caves. This man lived in
> the caves, and no one could tie him up, not even with a
> chain. Many times people had used chains to tie the man's

hands and feet, but he always broke them off. No one was strong enough to control him. Day and night he would wander around the burial caves and on the hills, screaming and cutting himself with stones.

Mark 5:2–5

He's the man your mom told you to avoid. He's the fellow the police routinely lock up. He's the deranged man who stalks neighborhoods and murders families. This is the face that fills the screen during the evening news.

And this is the first missionary of the church.

Palestine didn't know what to do with him. They restrained him, but he broke the chains. He ripped off his clothes. He lived in caves. He cut himself with rocks. He was a rabid coyote on the loose, a menace to society. Of absolutely no good to anyone. No one had a place for him—except Jesus.

Even today the best that modern medicine could offer such a man is medication and extensive treatment. Maybe, with much time, expense, and professional help, such destructive behavior could be curtailed. But it would take years.

With Jesus it takes seconds.

The encounter is explosive. The disciples' boat beaches near a graveyard and a herd of pigs. Both are ritually and culturally unclean for Jews. As Jesus steps out, a crazy man storms out of a cavern.

Wild hair. Bloody wrists. Scratched skin. Fury encased in flesh. Naked bedlam. Arms flailing and voice screaming. The apostles gawk and gulp and put a foot back in the boat.

They are horrified. But Jesus isn't. Read the next few verses carefully, for they provide a rare privilege—a glimpse into the unseen warfare. For just a few minutes the invisible conflict becomes visible and we are offered a position overlooking the battlefield.

Jesus speaks first: "You evil spirit, come out of the man" (v. 8).

The spirit panics: "What do you want with me, Jesus, Son of the Most High God?" (v. 7).

Jesus wants the man back. The demons muster no challenge. They offer no threat. They've heard this voice before. When God demands, the demons have one response. They plead. They "begged Jesus again and again not to send them out of that area" (v. 10).

Jesus' mere appearance humbles the demons. Though they had dominated this man, they cower before God. Though they had laced a region with fear, they beg for mercy from Jesus. His words reduce them to sniveling, groveling weaklings.

Feeling safer in a herd of pigs than in the presence of God, the demons ask to be sent into the swine. Jesus consents, and two thousand possessed pigs hurl themselves into the sea.

And all the while the disciples do nothing. While Jesus fights, the followers stare. They don't know anything else to do.

Can you relate? Are you watching a world out of control and don't know what to do? If so, do what the disciples did: When the fighting is fierce, stand back and let the Father fight.

I have a picture in my mental scrapbook that illustrates this principle. In the scene, my father and I are battling a storm in a fishing boat. We are surrounded by a mountain range of white tops, most taller than either of us. The coastline is hidden, the fog is thickening, and we are honestly beginning to wonder if we will make it back to shore.

I am young, maybe nine. The boat is small, perhaps ten feet. And the waves are high, high enough to overturn our craft. The sky rumbles, the clouds billow, and the lightning zigzags.

Dad has directed the boat toward the nearest beach, taking us bow first into the waves. He sits in the rear with a hand on the throttle and his face into the wind. I sit in the front looking back toward him. Rain stings my bare neck and soaks my shirt. One wave after another picks us up and slaps us down. I grab both sides of the boat and hang on.

In vain I search for the coast. It's buried by fog. I look for the sun . . . it's hidden by the clouds. I look for other boats . . . I see only waves. Everything I see frightens me. There is only one reassuring sight, the face of my father. Rain-splattered and grimacing, he peers into the storm. Water drips off the bill of his baseball cap, and his shirt is stuck to his skin.

Right then I made a decision. I quit looking at the storm and watched only my father. It just made sense. Watching the waves brought fear; watching my father brought calm. So I focused on Dad. So intent was my gaze that three decades later I can still see him guiding us out of the billows.

God wants us to do the same. He wants us to focus our eyes on him. What good does it do to focus on the storm? Why study the enemy? We won't defeat him. Only God will. The disciples can't destroy Satan; only God can.

And that's what Jesus did.

As the stunned disciples look on, Jesus goes into action and God delivers a lunatic. Pigs are embodied by demons. And a disciple is made in a cemetery.

Outlandish story? Just wait. It's not over yet. If you think the reaction of the demons is bizarre, wait until you see the response of the people.

The pig herders ran to the city and told everyone what they had seen.

So the people went out to see for themselves.

They came to Jesus and saw the man who used to have the many evil spirits, sitting, clothed, and in his right mind. And they were frightened. The people who saw this told the others what had happened to the man who had the demons living in him, and they told about the pigs. Then the people began to beg Jesus to leave their area.

Mark 5:15–17

They did what? *The people began to beg Jesus to leave the area.*

You mean the people asked Jesus to leave? That's right. Rather than thank him, they dismissed him? You got it. What would cause people to do such a thing?

Good question. What would cause people to prefer pigs and lunatics over the presence of God?

Or better . . .

What would cause an alcoholic to prefer drunken misery over sobriety?

What would cause a church to prefer slumber over revival?

What would cause a nation to prefer slavery over freedom?

What would cause people to prefer yesterday's traditions over today's living God?

The answer? Fear of change. Change is hard work. It's easier to follow the same old path than to move out into uncharted territory.

So the people dismissed Jesus. And since Jesus never goes where he isn't invited, he steps back into the boat.

Now watch what happens next.

> As Jesus was getting back into the boat, the man who was freed from the demons begged to go with him.
> But Jesus would not let him.
>
> Mark 5:18

Strange way to treat a new believer, don't you think? Why wouldn't Jesus take him along? Simple. He had greater plans for him. "Go home to your family and tell them how much the Lord has done for you and how he has had mercy on you" (v. 19).

There it is. The commissioning of the first missionary. One minute insane, the next in Christ. No training. No teaching. All he knew was that Jesus could scare the hell out of hell and apparently that was enough.

But even more surprising than the man who was sent is the fact that *anyone* was sent. I wouldn't have sent a missionary to some people who had just given me the boot, would you? A plague perhaps, but not a missionary. But Christ did.

And Christ does. He still sends the message to the unworthy. And he still uses the unworthy as messengers.

After all, look who's reading this book.

And look who wrote it.

17

SEEING THE UNSEEN

---

*When You Are Afraid
of the Future*

When Jesus went in the boat back to the other side of the lake, a large crowd gathered around him there. A leader of the synagogue, named Jairus, came there, saw Jesus, and fell at his feet. He begged Jesus, saying again and again, "My daughter is dying. Please come and put your hands on her so she will be healed and will live." So Jesus went with him. . . .

While Jesus was still speaking, some people came from the house of the synagogue leader. They said, "Your daughter is dead. There is no need to bother the teacher anymore."

But Jesus paid no attention to what they said. He told the synagogue leader, "Don't be afraid; just believe."

Jesus let only Peter, James, and John the brother of James go with him. When they came to the house of the synagogue leader, Jesus found many people there making lots of noise and crying loudly. Jesus entered the house and said to them, "Why are you crying and making so much noise? The child is not dead, only asleep." But they laughed at him. So, after throwing them out of the house, Jesus took the child's father and mother and his three followers into the room where the child was. Taking hold of the girl's hand, he said to her, "Talitha, koum!" (This means, "Young girl, I tell you to stand up!") At once the girl stood right up and began walking. (She was twelve years old.) Everyone was completely amazed. Jesus gave them strict orders not to tell people about this. Then he told them to give the girl something to eat.

Mark 5:21–24, 35–43

Faith means . . . knowing that
something is real even if we do not
see it.

Hebrews 11:1

---

*L*ast night I tried to teach my daughters to see with their eyes closed.

I asked Jenna, the eight-year-old, to go to one side of the den. I had Andrea, the six-year-old, stand on the other. Three-year-old Sara and I sat on the couch in the middle and watched. Jenna's job was to close her eyes and walk. Andrea's job was to be Jenna's eyes and talk her safely across the room.

With phrases like, "Take two baby steps to the left" and "Take four giant steps straight ahead," Andrea successfully navigated her sister through a treacherous maze of chairs, a vacuum cleaner, and a laundry basket.

Then Jenna took her turn. She guided Andrea past her mom's favorite lamp and shouted just in time to keep her from colliding into the wall when she thought her right foot was her left foot.

After several treks through the darkness, they stopped and we processed.

"I didn't like it," Jenna complained. "It's scary going where you can't see."

"I was afraid I was going to fall," Andrea agreed. "I kept taking little steps to be safe."

I can relate, can't you? We grownups don't like the dark either. But we walk in it. We, like Jenna, often complain about how scary it is to walk where we can't see. And we, like Andrea, often take timid steps so we won't fall.

We've reason to be cautious: We are blind. We can't see the future. We have absolutely no vision beyond the present. I can't tell you with certainty that I will live long enough to finish this paragraph. (Whew, I did!) Nor can you tell me you'll live long enough to read the next one. (Hope you do!)

I'm not talking nearsightedness or obstructed view; I'm talking opaque blindness. I'm not talking about a condition that passes with childhood; I'm describing a condition that passes only with death. We are blind. Blind to the future.

It's one limitation we all share. The wealthy are just as blind as the poor. The educated are just as sightless as the unschooled. And the famous know as little about the future as the unknown.

None of us know how our children will turn out. None of us know the day we will die. No one knows whom he or she will marry or even if marriage lies before him or her. We are universally, absolutely, unalterably blind.

We are all Jenna with her eyes shut, groping through a dark room, listening for a familiar voice—but with one difference. Her surroundings are familiar and friendly. Ours can be hostile and fatal. Her worst fear is a stubbed toe. Our worst fear is more threatening: cancer, divorce, loneliness, death.

And try as we might to walk as straight as we can, chances are a toe is going to get stubbed and we are going to get hurt.

Just ask Jairus. He is a man who has tried to walk as straight as he can. But Jairus was a man whose path has taken a sudden turn into a cave—a dark cave. And he doesn't want to enter it alone.

Jairus is the leader of the synagogue. That may not mean much to you and me, but in the days of Christ the leader of the synagogue was the most important man in the community. The synagogue was the center of religion, education, leadership, and social activity. The leader of the synagogue was the senior religious leader, the highest-ranking professor, the mayor, and the best-known citizen all in one.

Jairus has it all. Job security. A guaranteed welcome at the coffee shop. A pension plan. Golf every Thursday and an annual all-expenses-paid trip to the national convention.

Who could ask for more? Yet Jairus does. He *has* to ask for more. In fact, he would trade the whole package of perks and privileges for just one assurance—that his daughter will live.

The Jairus we see in this story is not the clear-sighted, black-frocked, nicely groomed civic leader. He is instead a blind man begging for a gift. He fell at Jesus' feet, "saying again and again, 'My daughter is dying. Please come and put your hands on her so she will be healed and will live'" (Mark 5:23).

He doesn't barter with Jesus. ("You do me a favor, and I'll see you are taken care of for life.") He doesn't negotiate with Jesus. ("The guys in Jerusalem are getting pretty testy about your antics. Tell you what, you handle this problem of mine, and I'll make a few calls . . .") He doesn't make excuses. ("Normally, I'm not this desperate, Jesus, but I've got a small problem.")

He just pleads.

There are times in life when everything you have to offer is nothing compared to what you are asking to receive. Jairus is at such a point. What could a man offer in exchange for his child's life? So there are no games. No haggling. No masquerades. The situation is starkly simple: Jairus is blind to the future and Jesus knows the future. So Jairus asks for his help.

And Jesus, who loves the honest heart, goes to give it.

And God, who knows what it is like to lose a child, empowers his son.

But before Jesus and Jairus get very far, they are interrupted by emissaries from his house.

"Your daughter is dead. There is no need to bother the teacher anymore" (v. 35).

Get ready. Hang on to your hat. Here's where the story gets moving. Jesus goes from being led to leading, from being convinced by Jairus to *convincing* Jairus. From being admired to being laughed at, from helping out the people to casting out the people.

Here is where Jesus takes control.

"But Jesus paid no attention to what they said . . ." (v. 36).

I love that line! It describes the critical principle for seeing the unseen: Ignore what people say. Block them out. Turn them off. Close your ears. And, if you have to, walk away.

Ignore the ones who say it's too late to start over.

Disregard those who say you'll never amount to anything.

Turn a deaf ear toward those who say that you aren't smart enough, fast enough, tall enough, or big enough—ignore them.

Faith sometimes begins by stuffing your ears with cotton.

Jesus turns immediately to Jairus and pleads: "Don't be afraid; just believe" (v. 36).

Jesus compels Jairus to see the unseen. When Jesus says, "Just believe . . . ," he is imploring, "Don't limit your possibilities to the visible. Don't listen only for the audible. Don't be controlled by the logical. Believe there is more to life than meets the eye!"

"Trust me," Jesus is pleading. "Don't be afraid; just trust."

A father in the Bahamas cried out the same plea to his young son who was trapped in a burning house. The two-story structure was engulfed in flames, and the family—the father, mother, and several children—was on its way out when the smallest boy became terrified and ran back upstairs. His father, outside, shouted to him: "Jump, son, jump! I'll catch you." The boy cried: "But Daddy, I can't see you." "I know," his father called, "but I can see you."

The father could see, even though the son could not.

A similar example of faith was found on the wall of a concentration camp. On it a prisoner had carved the words:

> I believe in the sun, even though it doesn't shine,
> I believe in love, even when it isn't shown,
> I believe in God, even when he doesn't speak.

I try to imagine the person who etched those words. I try to envision his skeletal hand gripping the broken glass or stone that cut into the wall. I try to imagine his eyes squinting through the darkness as he carved each letter. What hand could have cut such a conviction? What eyes could have seen good in such horror?

There is only one answer: Eyes that chose to see the unseen.

As Paul wrote: "We set our eyes not on what we see but on what we cannot see. What we see will last only a short time, but what we cannot see will last forever" (2 Cor. 4:18).

Jesus is asking Jairus to see the unseen. To make a choice. Either to live by the facts or to see by faith. When tragedy strikes we, too, are left to choose what we see. We can see either the hurt or the Healer.

The choice is ours.

Jairus made his choice. He opted for faith and Jesus . . . and faith *in* Jesus led him to his daughter.

At the house Jesus and Jairus encounter a group of mourners. Jesus is troubled by their wailing. It bothers him that they express such anxiety over death. "Why are you crying and making so much noise? The child is not dead, only asleep" (v. 39).

That's not a rhetorical question. It's an honest one. From his perspective, the girl is not dead—she is only asleep. From God's viewpoint, death is not permanent. It is a necessary step for passing from this world to the next. It's not an end; it's a beginning.

As a young boy I had two great loves—playing and eating. Summers were made for afternoons on the baseball diamond and meals at Mom's dinner table. Mom had a rule, however. Dirty, sweaty boys could never eat at the table. Her first words to us as we came home were always, "Go clean up and take off those clothes if you want to eat."

Now no boy is fond of bathing and dressing, but I never once complained and defied my mom by saying, "I'd rather stink than eat!" In my economy a bath and a clean shirt were a small price to pay for a good meal.

169

And from God's perspective death is a small price to pay for the privilege of sitting at his table. "Flesh and blood cannot have a part in the kingdom of God. . . . This body that can be destroyed *must* clothe itself with something that can never be destroyed. And this body that dies *must* clothe itself with something that can never die" (1 Cor. 15:50, 53, emphasis added).

God is even more insistent than my mom was. In order to sit at his table, a change of clothing *must* occur. And we must die in order for our body to be exchanged for a new one. So, from God's viewpoint, death is not to be dreaded; it is to be welcomed.

And when he sees people crying and mourning over death, he wants to know, "Why are you crying?" (v. 39).

When we see death, we see disaster. When Jesus sees death, he sees deliverance.

That's too much for the people to take. "They laughed at him" (v. 40). (The next time people mock you, you might remember they mocked him, too.)

Now look closely because you aren't going to believe what Jesus does next. He throws the mourners out! That's what the text says, "after throwing them out of the house . . ." (v. 40). He doesn't just ask them to leave. He *throws* them out. He picks them up by collar and belt and sets them sailing. Jesus' response was decisive and strong. In the original text, the word used here is the same word used to describe what Jesus did to the moneychangers in the temple. It's the same verb used *thirty-eight* times to describe what Jesus did to the demons.

Why? Why such force? Why such intolerance?

Perhaps the answer is found by going back to last evening's living-room experience. After Jenna and Andrea had taken turns guiding each other through the den, I decided to add a diabolical twist. On the last trip, I snuck up behind Jenna, who was walking with her eyes shut, and began whispering, "Don't listen to her. Listen to me. I'll take care of you."

Jenna stopped. She analyzed the situation and made her choice between the two voices. "Be quiet, Daddy," she giggled and then continued in Andrea's direction.

Undeterred, I grabbed the lid of a pan, held it next to her ear, and banged it with a spoon. She jumped and stopped, startled by the noise. Andrea, seeing that her pilgrim was frightened, did a great thing. She ran across the room and threw her arms around her sister and said, "Don't worry, I'm right here."

She wasn't about to let the noise distract Jenna from the journey.

And God isn't going to let the noise distract you from yours. He's still busy casting out the critics and silencing the voices that could deter you.

Some of his work you have seen. Most of it you haven't. Only when you get home will you know how many times he has protected you from luring voices. Only eternity will reveal the time he:

> Interfered with the transfer, protecting you from involvement in unethical business.
>
> Fogged in the airport, distancing you from a shady opportunity.
>
> Flattened your tire, preventing you from checking into the hotel and meeting a seductive man.

And only heaven will show the times he protected you by:

> Giving you a mate who loves God more than you do.
>
> Opening the door for a new business so you could attend the same church.
>
> Having the right voice with the right message on the right radio station the day you needed his encouragement.

Mark it down: God knows you and I are blind. He knows living by faith and not by sight doesn't come naturally. And I think that's one reason he raised Jairus's daughter from the dead. Not for her sake—she was better off in heaven. But for our sake—to teach us that heaven sees when we trust.

One final thought from the seeing-with-your-eyes-closed experiment. I asked Jenna how she could hear Andrea's voice guiding her across the room when I was trying to distract her by whispering in her ear.

Her answer? "I just concentrated and listened as hard as I could."

18

JOSEPH'S PRAYER

---

*When You're Confused by
God's Actions*

Joseph . . . did what the Lord's
angel had told him to do.

Matthew 1:24

$\mathcal{T}$he white space between Bible verses is fertile soil for questions. One can hardly read Scripture without whispering, "I wonder . . ."

"I wonder if Eve ever ate any more fruit."

"I wonder if Noah slept well during storms."

"I wonder if Jonah liked fish or if Jeremiah had friends."

"Did Moses avoid bushes? Did Jesus tell jokes? Did Peter ever try water-walking again?"

"Would any woman have married Paul had he asked?"

The Bible is a fence full of knotholes through which we can peek but not see the whole picture. It's a scrapbook of snapshots capturing people in encounters with God, but not always recording the result. So we wonder:

When the woman caught in adultery went home, what did she say to her husband?

After the demoniac was delivered, what did he do for a living?

After Jairus's daughter was raised from the dead, did she ever regret it?

Knotholes and snapshots and "I wonders." You'll find them in every chapter about every person. But nothing stirs so many questions as does the birth of Christ. Characters appear and disappear before we can ask them anything. The innkeeper too busy to welcome God—did he ever learn who he turned away? The shepherds—did they ever hum the song the angels sang? The wise men who followed the star—what was it like to worship a toddler? And Joseph, especially Joseph. I've got questions for Joseph.

> Did you and Jesus arm wrestle? Did he ever let you win?
>
> Did you ever look up from your prayers and see Jesus listening?
>
> How do you say "Jesus" in Egyptian?
>
> What ever happened to the wise men?
>
> What ever happened to you?

We don't know what happened to Joseph. His role in Act I is so crucial that we expect to see him the rest of the drama—but with the exception of a short scene with twelve-year-old Jesus in Jerusalem, he never reappears. The rest of his life is left to speculation, and we are left with our questions.

But of all my questions, my first would be about Bethlehem. I'd like to know about the night in the stable. I can picture Joseph there. Moonlit pastures. Stars twinkle above. Bethlehem sparkles in the distance. There he is, pacing outside the stable.

What was he thinking while Jesus was being born? What was on his mind while Mary was giving birth? He'd done all he could do—heated the water, prepared a place for Mary to lie. He'd made Mary as comfortable as she could be in a barn and then he stepped out. She'd asked to be alone, and Joseph has never felt more so.

In that eternity between his wife's dismissal and Jesus' arrival, what was he thinking? He walked into the night and looked into the stars. Did he pray?

For some reason, I don't see him silent; I see Joseph animated, pacing. Head shaking one minute, fist shaking the next. This isn't what he had in mind. I wonder what he said . . .

This isn't the way I planned it, God. Not at all. My child being born in a stable? This isn't the way I thought it would be.

A cave with sheep and donkeys, hay and straw? My wife giving birth with only the stars to hear her pain?

This isn't at all what I imagined. No, I imagined family. I imagined grandmothers. I imagined neighbors clustered outside the door and friends standing at my side. I imagined the house erupting with the first cry of the infant. Slaps on the back. Loud laughter. Jubilation.

That's how I thought it would be.

The midwife would hand me my child and all the people would applaud. Mary would rest and we would celebrate. All of Nazareth would celebrate.

But now. Now look. Nazareth is five days' journey away. And here we are in a . . . in a sheep pasture. Who will celebrate with us? The sheep? The shepherds? The stars?

This doesn't seem right. What kind of husband am I? I provide no midwife to aid my wife. No bed to rest her back. Her pillow is a blanket from my donkey. My house for her is a shed of hay and straw.

The smell is bad, the animals are loud. Why, I even smell like a shepherd myself.

Did I miss something? Did I, God?

When you sent the angel and spoke of the son being born—this isn't what I pictured. I envisioned Jerusalem, the temple, the priests, and the people gathered to watch. A pageant perhaps. A parade. A banquet at least. I mean, this is the Messiah!

Or, if not born in Jerusalem, how about Nazareth? Wouldn't Nazareth have been better? At least there I have my house and my business. Out here, what do I have? A weary mule, a stack of firewood, and a pot of warm water. This is not the way I wanted it to be! This is not the way I wanted my son.

Oh my, I did it again. I did it again didn't I, Father? I don't mean to do that; it's just that I forget. He's not my son . . . he's yours.

The child is yours. The plan is yours. The idea is yours. And forgive me for asking but . . . is this how God enters the world?

The coming of the angel, I've accepted. The questions people asked about the pregnancy, I can tolerate. The trip to Bethlehem, fine. But why a birth in a stable, God?

Any minute now Mary will give birth. Not to a child, but to the Messiah. Not to an infant, but to God. That's what the angel said. That's what Mary believes. And, God, my God, that's what I want to believe. But surely you can understand; it's not easy. It seems so . . . so . . . so . . . bizarre.

I'm unaccustomed to such strangeness, God. I'm a carpenter. I make things fit. I square off the edges. I follow the plumb line. I measure twice before I cut once. Surprises are not the friend of a builder. I like to know the plan. I like to see the plan before I begin.

But this time I'm not the builder, am I? This time I'm a tool. A hammer in your grip. A nail between your fingers. A chisel in your hands. This project is yours, not mine.

I guess it's foolish of me to question you. Forgive my struggling. Trust doesn't come easy to me, God. But you never said it would be easy, did you?

One final thing, Father. The angel you sent? Any chance you could send another? If not an angel, maybe a person? I don't know anyone around here and some company would be nice. Maybe the innkeeper or a traveler? Even a shepherd would do.

I wonder. Did Joseph ever pray such a prayer? Perhaps he did. Perhaps he didn't.

But you probably have.

You've stood where Joseph stood. Caught between what God says and what makes sense. You've done what he told you to do only to wonder if it was him speaking in the first place. You've stared into a sky blackened with doubt. And you've asked what Joseph asked.

You've asked if you're still on the right road. You've asked if you were supposed to turn left when you turned right. And you've asked if there is a plan behind this scheme. Things haven't turned out like you thought they would.

Each of us knows what it's like to search the night for light. Not outside a stable, but perhaps outside an emergency room. On the gravel of a roadside. On the manicured grass of a cemetery. We've asked our questions. We questioned God's plan. And we've wondered why God does what he does.

The Bethlehem sky is not the first to hear the pleadings of a confused pilgrim.

If you are asking what Joseph asked, let me urge you to do what Joseph did. Obey. That's what he did. He obeyed. He obeyed when the angel called. He obeyed when Mary explained. He obeyed when God sent.

He was obedient to God.

He was obedient when the sky was bright.

He was obedient when the sky was dark.

He didn't let his confusion disrupt his obedience. He didn't know everything. But he did what he knew. He shut down his business, packed up his family, and went to another country. Why? Because that's what God said to do.

What about you? Just like Joseph, you can't see the whole picture. Just like Joseph your task is to see that Jesus is brought into your part of your world. And just like Joseph you have a choice: to obey or disobey. Because Joseph obeyed, God used him to change the world.

Can he do the same with you?

God still looks for Josephs today. Men and women who believe that God is not through with this world. Common people who serve an uncommon God.

Will you be that kind of person? Will you serve . . . even when you don't understand?

No, the Bethlehem sky is not the first to hear the pleadings of an honest heart, nor the last. And perhaps God didn't answer every question for Joseph. But he answered the most important one. "Are you still with me, God?" And through the first cries of the God-child the answer came.

"Yes. Yes, Joseph. I'm with you."

There are many questions about the Bible that we won't be

able to answer until we get home. Many knotholes and snap-shots. Many times we will muse, "I wonder . . ."

But in our wonderings, there is one question we never need to ask. Does God care? Do we matter to God? Does he still love his children?

Through the small face of the stable-born baby, he says yes.

Yes, your sins are forgiven.

Yes, your name is written in heaven.

Yes, death has been defeated.

And yes, God has entered your world.

Immanuel. God is with us.

19

THE GRAVE FACT

Understanding Death

A man named Lazarus was sick. He lived in the town of Bethany, where Mary and her sister Martha lived. Mary was the woman who later put perfume on the Lord and wiped his feet with her hair. Mary's brother was Lazarus, the man who was now sick. So Mary and Martha sent someone to tell Jesus, "Lord, the one you love is sick."

When Jesus heard this, he said, "This sickness will not end in death. It is for the glory of God, to bring glory to the Son of God." Jesus loved Martha and her sister and Lazarus. But when he heard that Lazarus was sick, he stayed where he was for two more days. Then Jesus said to his followers, "Let's go back to Judea."

The followers said, "But Teacher, the Jews there tried to stone you to death only a short time ago. Now you want to go back there?"

Jesus answered, "Are there not twelve hours in the day? If anyone walks in the daylight, he will not stumble, because he can see by this world's light. But if anyone walks at night, he stumbles because there is no light to help him see."

After Jesus said this, he added, "Our friend Lazarus has fallen asleep, but I am going there to wake him."

The followers said, "But Lord, if he is only asleep, he will be all right."

Jesus meant that Lazarus was dead, but his followers thought he meant Lazarus was really sleeping. So then Jesus said plainly, "Lazarus is dead. And I am glad for your sakes I was not there so that you may believe. But let's go to him now."

Then Thomas (the one called Didymus) said to the other followers, "Let us also go so that we can die with him."

When Jesus arrived, he learned that Lazarus had already been dead and in the tomb for four days. Bethany was about two miles from Jerusalem. Many of the Jews had come there to comfort Martha and Mary about their brother.

When Martha heard that Jesus was coming, she went out to meet him, but Mary stayed home. Martha said to Jesus, "Lord, if you had been here, my brother would not have died. But I know that even now God will give you anything you ask."

Jesus said, "Your brother will rise and live again."

Martha answered, "I know that he will rise and live again in the resurrection on the last day."

Jesus said to her, "I am the resurrection and the life. Those who believe in me will have life even if they die. And everyone who lives and believes in me will never die. Martha, do you believe this?"

Martha answered, "Yes, Lord. I believe that you are the Christ, the Son of God, the One coming to the world."

After Martha said this, she went back and talked to her sister Mary alone. Martha said, "The Teacher is here and he is asking for you." When Mary heard this, she got up quickly and went to Jesus. Jesus had not yet come into the town but was still at the place where Martha had met him. The Jews were with Mary in the house, comforting her. When they saw her stand and leave quickly, they followed her, thinking she was going to the tomb to cry there. But Mary went to the place where Jesus was. When she saw him, she fell at his feet and said, "Lord, if you had been here, my brother would not have died."

When Jesus saw Mary crying and the Jews who came with her also crying, he was upset and was deeply troubled. He asked, "Where did you bury him?"

"Come and see, Lord," they said.

Jesus cried.

So the Jews said, "See how much he loved him."

But some of them said, "If Jesus opened the eyes of the blind man, why couldn't he keep Lazarus from dying?"

Again feeling very upset, Jesus came to the tomb. It was a cave with a large stone covering the entrance. Jesus said, "Move the stone away."

Martha, the sister of the dead man, said, "But, Lord, it has been four days since he died. There will be a bad smell."

Then Jesus said to her, "Didn't I tell you that if you believed you would see the glory of God?"

So they moved the stone away from the entrance. Then Jesus looked up and said, "Father, I thank you that you heard me. I know that you always hear me, but I said these things because of the people here around me. I want them to believe that you sent me." After Jesus said this, he cried out in a loud voice, "Lazarus, come out!" The dead man came out, his hands and feet wrapped with pieces of cloth, and a cloth around his face.

Jesus said to them, "Take the cloth off of him and let him go."

John 11:1–44

Death, where is your victory?

1 Corinthians 15:55

You are leaving the church building. The funeral is over. The burial is next. Ahead of you walk six men who carry the coffin that carries the body of your son. Your only son.

You're numb from the sorrow. Stunned. You lost your husband, and now you've lost your son. Now you have no family. If you had any more tears, you'd weep. If you had any more faith, you'd pray. But both are in short supply, so you do neither. You just stare at the back of the wooden box.

Suddenly it stops. The pallbearers have stopped. You stop.

A man has stepped in front of the casket. You don't know him. You've never seen him. He wasn't at the funeral. He's dressed in a corduroy coat and jeans. You have no idea what he is doing. But before you can object, he steps up to you and says, "Don't cry."

Don't cry? Don't cry! This is a funeral. My son is dead. Don't cry? Who are you to tell me not to cry? Those are your thoughts, but they never become your words. Because before you can speak, he acts.

He turns back to the coffin, places his hand on it, and says in a loud voice, "Young man, I tell you, get up!"

"Now just a minute," one of the pallbearers objects. But the sentence is interrupted by a sudden movement in the casket. The men look at one another and lower it quickly to the ground. It's a good thing they do, because as soon as it touches the sidewalk the lid slowly opens . . .

Sound like something out of a science fiction novel? It's not. It's right out of the Gospel of Luke. "He went up and touched the coffin, and the people who were carrying it stopped. Jesus said, 'Young man, I tell you, get up!' And the son sat up and began to talk" (Luke 7:14–15).

Be careful now. Don't read that last line too fast. Try it again. Slowly.

"The son sat up and began to talk."

Incredible sentence, don't you think? At the risk of overdoing it, let's read it one more time. This time say each word aloud. "The son sat up and began to talk."

Good job. (Did everyone around you look up?) Can we do it again? This time read it aloud again, but very s-l-o-w-l-y. Pause between each word.

"The . . . son . . . sat . . . up . . . and . . . began . . . to . . . talk."

Now the question. What's odd about that verse?

You got it. Dead people don't sit up! Dead people don't talk! Dead people don't leave their coffins!

Unless Jesus shows up. Because when Jesus shows up, you never know what might happen.

Jairus can tell you. His daughter was already dead. The mourners were already in the house. The funeral had begun. The people thought the best Jesus could do was offer some kind words about Jairus's girl. Jesus had some words all right. Not about the girl, but for the girl.

"My child, stand up!" (Luke 8:54).

The next thing the father knew, she was eating, Jesus was laughing, and the hired mourners were sent home early.

Martha can tell you. She'd hoped Jesus would show up to heal Lazarus. He didn't. Then she'd hoped he'd show up to bury Lazarus. He didn't. By the time he made it to Bethany, Lazarus was four-days buried and Martha was wondering what kind of friend Jesus was.

She hears he's at the edge of town so she storms out to meet him. "Lord, if you had been here," she confronts, "my brother would not have died" (John 11:21).

There is hurt in those words. Hurt and disappointment. The one man who could have made a difference didn't, and Martha wants to know why.

Maybe you do, too. Maybe you've done what Martha did. Someone you love ventures near the edge of life, and you turn to Jesus for help. You, like Martha, turn to the only one who can pull a person from the ledge of death. You ask Jesus to give a hand.

Martha must have thought, *Surely he will come. Didn't he aid the paralytic? Didn't he help the leper? Didn't he give sight to the blind? And they hardly knew Jesus. Lazarus is his friend. We're like family. Doesn't Jesus come for the weekend? Doesn't he eat at our table? When he hears that Lazarus is sick, he'll be here in a heartbeat.*

But he didn't come. Lazarus got worse. She watched out the window. Jesus didn't show. Her brother drifted in and out of consciousness. "He'll be here soon, Lazarus," she promised. "Hang on."

But the knock at the door never came. Jesus never appeared. Not to help. Not to heal. Not to bury. And now, four days later, he finally shows up. The funeral is over. The body is buried, and the grave is sealed.

And Martha is hurt.

Her words have been echoed in a thousand cemeteries. "If you had been here, my brother would not have died."

If you were doing your part, God, my husband would have survived. If you'd done what was right, Lord, my baby would have lived.

If only you'd have heard my prayer, God, my arms wouldn't be empty.

The grave unearths our view of God.

When we face death, our definition of God is challenged. Which, in turn, challenges our faith. Which leads me to ask a grave question. Why is it that we interpret the presence of death as the absence of God? Why do we think that if the body is not healed then God is not near? Is healing the only way God demonstrates his presence?

Sometimes we think so. And as a result, when God doesn't answer our prayers for healing, we get angry. Resentful. Blame replaces belief. "If you had been here, doing your part, God, then this death would not have happened."

It's distressing that this view of God has no place for death.

Some time ago a visitor to our house showed my daughters some tricks. Magic acts. Simple sleight-of-hand stuff. I stood to the side and watched the girls' responses. They were amazed. When the coin disappeared, they gasped. When it reappeared, they were stunned. At first I was humored by their bewilderment.

But with time, my bewilderment became concern. Part of me didn't like what was happening. My kids were being duped. He was tricking them. They, the innocent, were being buffaloed by him, the sneak. I didn't like that. I didn't like seeing my children fooled.

So I whispered to my daughters. "It's in his sleeve." Sure enough it was. "It's behind his ear." And what do you know, I was right! Maybe I was rude to interfere with the show, but I don't enjoy watching a trickster pull one over on my children.

Neither does God.

Jesus couldn't bear to sit and watch the bereaved be fooled.

Please understand, he didn't raise the dead for the sake of the dead. He raised the dead for the sake of the living.

"Lazarus, come out!" (v. 43).

Martha was silent as Jesus commanded. The mourners were quiet. No one stirred as Jesus stood face to face with the rock-hewn tomb and demanded that it release his friend.

No one stirred, that is, except for Lazarus. Deep within the tomb, he moved. His stilled heart began to beat again. Wrapped eyes popped open. Wooden fingers lifted. And a mummied man in a tomb sat up. And want to know what happened next?

Let John tell you. "The dead man came out, his hands and feet wrapped with pieces of cloth, and a cloth around his face" (v. 44).

There it is again. Did you see it? Read the first five words of the verse again.

"The dead man came out."

Again. Slower this time.

"The dead man came out."

One more time. This time out loud and very slowly. (I know you think I'm crazy, but I really want you to get the point.)

"The . . . dead . . . man . . . came . . . out."

Can I ask the same questions? (Of course I can; I'm writing the book!)

Question: What's wrong with this picture?

Answer: Dead men don't walk out of tombs.

Question: What kind of God is this?

Answer: The God who holds the keys to life and death.

The kind of God who rolls back the sleeve of the trickster and reveals death for the parlor trick it is.

The kind of God you want present at your funeral.

He'll do it again, you know. He's promised he would. And he's shown that he can.

"The Lord himself will come down from heaven with a loud command" (1 Thess. 4:16).

The same voice that awoke the boy near Nain, that stirred the still daughter of Jairus, that awakened the corpse of Lazarus—the same voice will speak again. The earth and the sea will give up their dead. There will be no more death.

Jesus made sure of that.

20

LISTLESS CHRISTIANITY

*When Being Good Is
Not Enough*

When they came to a place called the Skull, the soldiers cruci-fied Jesus and the criminals—one on his right and the other on his left. Jesus said, "Father, forgive them, because they don't know what they are doing."

The soldiers threw lots to decide who would get his clothes. The people stood there watching. And the leaders made fun of Jesus, saying, "He saved others. Let him save himself if he is God's Chosen One, the Christ."

The soldiers also made fun of him, coming to Jesus and offering him some vinegar. They said, "If you are the king of the Jews, save yourself!" At the top of the cross these words were written: THIS IS THE KING OF THE JEWS.

One of the criminals on a cross began to shout insults at Jesus: "Aren't you the Christ? Then save yourself and us."

But the other criminal stopped him and said, "You should fear God! You are getting the same punishment he is. We are punished justly, getting what we deserve for what we did. But this man has done nothing wrong." Then he said, "Jesus, remember me when you come into your kingdom."

Luke 23:33–42

> "I tell you the truth, today you will be with me in paradise."
>
> Luke 23:43

She nearly missed the flight. In fact, I thought I had the row to myself when I looked up and saw her puffing down the aisle, dragging two large bags.

"I hate to fly," she blurted out as she fell into her seat. "I put off getting here as long as I can."

"You almost put it off too long," I smiled.

She was tall, young, blonde, tan, and talkative. Her jeans were fashionably ripped at the knees. And her black boots boasted silver tips. She really did hate to fly, I learned. And the way she coped with flying was by talking.

"I'm going home to see my dad. He'll really be amazed at my tan. He thinks I'm crazy living in California—me being single and all. I've got this new boyfriend, he's from Lebanon. He travels a lot though, so I only see him on weekends, which is fine with me because that gives me the house to myself. It isn't far from the beach and . . ."

I've learned what to do when a friendly, attractive woman sits beside me. As soon as possible I reveal my profession and marital status. It keeps us both out of trouble.

"My *wife* hates to fly, too," I jumped in when she took a breath, "so I know how you feel. And since I'm a *minister,* I know a section of the Bible you might like to read as we take off."

I pulled out my Bible from my briefcase and opened it to Psalm 23.

For the first time she was quiet. "The Lord is my shepherd," she read the words then looked up with a broad smile. "I remember this," she said as the plane was taking off. "I read it when I was young."

She turned to read some more. The next time she looked up there was a tear in her eye.

"It's been a long time. A long, long time." She told me how she believed . . . once. She became a Christian when she was young, but she couldn't remember the last time she'd been to church.

We talked some about faith and second chances. I asked her if I could ask her a question. She said I could.

"Do you believe in heaven?"

"Yeah."

"Do you think you'll go there?"

She looked away for a minute and then turned and answered confidently, "Yeah. Yeah, I'll be in heaven."

"How do you know?"

"How do I know I'm going to heaven?" She grew quiet as she formulated her response.

Somehow I knew what she was going to say before she said it. I could see it coming. She was going to give me her "list." (Everybody has one.)

"Well, I'm basically good. I don't smoke more than a pack a day. I exercise. I'm dependable at work and," she counted each achievement on a finger, "I made my boyfriend get tested for AIDS."

Ta-da. That was her list. Her qualifications. By her way of thinking, heaven could be earned by good health habits and safe sex. Her line of logic was simple—I keep the list on earth and I get the place in heaven.

Now lest we be too hard on her, let me ask you a question. What's on your list?

Most of us have one. Most of us are like the girl on the plane. We think we are "basically good." Decent, hardworking folk. Most of us have a list to prove it. Maybe yours doesn't include cigarettes or AIDS. But you have a list.

"I pay my bills."

"I love my spouse and kids."

"I attend church."

"I'm better than Hitler."

"I'm basically good."

Most of us have a list. There is a purpose for the list: to prove we are good. But there is a problem with the list: none of us is good enough.

Paul made this point when he placed two short-fused sticks of dynamite in the third chapter of his letter to the Romans. The first is in verse 10. "There is no one who always does what is right," he wrote, "not even one." No one. Not you. Not me. Not anyone. The second explosion occurs in verse 23. "All have sinned and are not good enough for God's glory."

Boom. So much for lists. So much for being "basically good."

Then how do you go to heaven? If no one is good, if no list is sufficient, if no achievements are adequate, how can a person be saved?

No question is more crucial. To hear Jesus answer it, let's ponder the last encounter he had before his death. An encounter between Jesus and two criminals.

All three are being crucified.

One might like to think that these two thieves are victims. Undeserving of punishment. Good men who got a bad rap. Patriots dying a martyr's death. But such is not the case. Matthew dispels any such notion with just one verse, "the robbers who were being crucified beside Jesus also insulted him" (Matt. 27:44).

Tragedy reveals a person's character. And the tragedy of this crucifixion reveals that these two thieves had none. They slander Jesus with their last breaths. Can you hear them? Voices—husky with pain—sneer at the Messiah.

"Some king of the Jews you are."

"Life is pretty tough on Messiahs these days, eh?"

"How about a little miracle, Galilean?"

"Ever see nails that size in Nazareth?"

You'd expect it from the Pharisees. You'd expect it from the crowd. Even the mocking of the soldiers isn't surprising. But from the thieves?

Crucified men insulting a crucified man? It's two men with nooses on their necks ridiculing the plight of a third. Two POWs before a firing squad taunting another's misfortune.

Could anyone be more blind?

Could anyone be more vile?

No wonder these two are on the cross! Rome deems them worthy of ugly torture. Their only value to society is to serve as a public spectacle. Strip them naked so all will know that evil cannot hide. Nail their hands so all will see that the wicked have no strength. Post them high so all will tell their children, "That's what happens to evil men."

Every muscle in their bodies screams for relief. Nails pulse fire through their arms. Legs contort and twist seeking comfort.

But there is no comfort on a cross.

Yet even the pain of the spike won't silence their spiteful tongues. These two will die as they lived, attacking the innocent. But in this case, the innocent doesn't retaliate.

The man they mocked wasn't much to look at. His body was whip-torn flesh, yanked away from the bone. His face was a mask of blood and spit; eyes puffy and swollen. "King of the Jews" was painted over his head. A crown of thorns pierced his scalp. His lip was split. Maybe his nose was bleeding or a tooth was loose.

The man they mocked was half-dead. The man they mocked was beaten. But the man they mocked was at peace. "Father, forgive them, because they don't know what they are doing" (Luke 23:34).

After Jesus' prayer, one of the criminals began to shout insults at him: "Aren't you the Christ? Then save yourself and us" (v. 39).

The heart of this thief remains hard. The presence of Christ crucified means nothing to him. Jesus is worthy of ridicule, so the thief ridicules. He expects his chorus to be harmonized from the other cross. It isn't. Instead, it is challenged.

"You should fear God! You are getting the same punishment he is. We are punished justly, getting what we deserve for what we did. But this man has done nothing wrong" (vv. 40–41).

Unbelievable. The same mouth that cursed Christ now defends Christ. What has happened? What has he seen since he has been on the cross? Did he witness a miracle? Did he hear a lecture? Was he read a treatise on the trinity?

No, of course not. According to Luke, all he heard was a prayer, a prayer of grace. But that was enough. Something happens to a man who stands in the presence of God. And something happened to the thief.

Read again his words. "We are punished justly, getting what we deserve. . . . But this man has done nothing wrong."

The core of the gospel in one sentence. The essence of eternity through the mouth of a crook:

I am wrong; Jesus is right.

I have failed; Jesus has not.

I deserve to die; Jesus deserves to live.

The thief knew precious little about Christ, but what he knew was precious indeed. He knew that an innocent man was dying an unjust death with no complaint on his lips. And if Jesus can do that, he just might be who he says he is.

So the thief asks for help: "Jesus, remember me when you come into your kingdom."

The heavy head of Christ lifts and turns, and the eyes of these two meet. What Jesus sees is a naked man. I don't mean in terms of clothes. I mean in terms of charades. He has no cover. No way to hide.

His title? Scum of the earth. His achievement? Death by crucifixion. His reputation? Criminal. His character? Depraved until the last moment. Until the final hour. Until the last encounter.

Until now.

Tell me, what has this man done to warrant help? He has wasted his life. Who is he to beg for forgiveness? He publicly scoffed at Jesus. What right does he have to pray this prayer?

Do you really want to know? The same right you have to pray yours.

You see, that is you and me on the cross. Naked, desolate, hopeless, and estranged. That is us. That is us asking, "In spite of what I've done, in spite of what you see, is there any way you could remember me when we all get home?"

We don't boast. We don't produce our list. Any sacrifice appears silly when placed before God on a cross.

It's more than we deserve. But we are desperate. So we plead. As have so many others: The cripple at the pool. Mary at the wedding. Martha at the funeral. The demoniac at Geresene. Nicodemus at night. Peter on the sea. Jairus on the trail. Joseph at the stable. And every other human being who has dared to stand before the Son of God and admit his or her need.

We, like the thief, have one more prayer. And we, like the thief, pray.

And we, like the thief, hear the voice of grace. *Today you will be with me in my kingdom.*

And we, like the thief, are able to endure the pain knowing he'll soon take us home.

21

THE STONE MOVER'S GALLERY

Quite a gallery, don't you think? A room of pain-to-peace portraits. A ward of renewed strength. A forest of restored vigor.

An exhibition of second chances.

Wouldn't it be incredible to visit a real one? Wouldn't it be great to walk through an actual collection of "Bruised Reeds and Smoldering Wicks"? What if you could see portrayal after portrayal of God meeting people at their points of pain? Not just biblical characters, but contemporary folks just like you? People from your generation and your world!

And what if this gallery contained not only their story, but yours and mine as well? What if there were a place where we could display our "before" and "after" experiences? Well, there might be one. I have an idea for such a gallery. It may sound far-fetched, but it's worth sharing.

Before I do, we need to discuss one final question. A crucial question. You've just read one story after another of God meeting people where they hurt. Tell me, why are these stories in the Bible? Why are the Gospels full of such people? Such hopeless people? Though their situations vary, their conditions don't. They are trapped. Estranged. Rejected. They have nowhere to turn. On their lips, a desperate prayer. In their hearts, desolate dreams. And in their hands, a broken rope. But before their eyes a never-say-die Galilean who majors in stepping in when everyone else steps out.

Surprisingly simple, the actions of this man. Just words of mercy or touches of kindness. Fingers on sightless eyes. A hand on a weary shoulder. Words for sad hearts . . . all fulfilling the prophecy: "A bruised reed he will not break, and a smoldering wick he will not snuff out."

Again I ask. Why are these portraits in the Bible? Why does this gallery exist? Why did God leave us one tale after another of wounded lives being restored? So we could be grateful for the past? So we could look back with amazement at what Jesus did?

No. No. No. A thousand times no. The purpose of these stories is not to tell us what Jesus *did*. Their purpose is to tell us what Jesus *does*.

"Everything that was written in the past was written to teach us," Paul penned. "The Scriptures give us patience and encouragement so that we can have hope" (Rom. 15:4).

These are not just Sunday school stories. Not romantic fables. Not somewhere-over-the-rainbow illusions. They are historic moments in which a real God met real pain so we could answer the question, "Where is God when I hurt?"

How does God react to dashed hopes? Read the story of Jairus. How does the Father feel about those who are ill? Stand with him at the pool of Bethesda. Do you long for God to speak to your lonely heart? Then listen as he speaks to the Emmaus-bound disciples. What is God's word for the shameful? Watch as his finger draws in the dirt of the Jerusalem courtyard.

He's not doing it just for them. He's doing it for me. He's doing it for you.

Which takes us to the final painting in the gallery—yours. Now that you've finished the book, pick up the brush. Now that you've read their stories, reflect on yours. Stand in front of the canvases that bear your name and draw your portraits.

It doesn't have to be on a canvas with paint. It could be on a paper with pencil, on a computer with words, in a sculpture with clay, in a song with lyrics. It doesn't matter how you do it, but I urge you to do it. Record your drama. Retell your saga. Plot your journey.

Begin with "before." What was it like before you knew him? Do you remember? Could be decades ago. Perhaps it was yesterday. Maybe you know him well. Maybe you've just met him. Again, that doesn't matter. What matters is that you never forget what life is like without him.

Remembering can hurt. Parts of our past are not pleasant to revisit. But the recollection is necessary. "Look at what you were when God called you," Paul instructed (1 Cor. 1:26). We, the adopted, can't forget what life was like as orphans. We, the liberated, should revisit the prison. We, the found, can't forget the despair of being lost.

Amnesia fosters arrogance. We can't afford to forget. We need to remember.

And we need to share our story. Not with everyone but with someone. There is someone who is like you were. And he or she needs to know what God can do. Your honest portrayal of your past may be the courage for another's future.

But don't just portray the past, depict the present. Describe his touch. Display the difference he has made in your life. This task has its challenges, too. Whereas painting the "before" can be painful, painting the "present" can be unclear. He's not finished with you yet!

Ah, but look how far you've come! I don't even know you, but I know you've come a long way. Wasn't there a time when you wouldn't even pick up a Christian book? And now look at you; you've almost finished one! God has begun a work in your heart. And what God begins, God completes. "God began doing a good work in you, and I am sure he will continue it until it is finished when Jesus Christ comes again" (Phil. 1:6).

So chronicle what Christ has done. If he has brought peace, sketch a dove. If joy, splash a rainbow on a wall. If courage, sing a song about mountain-movers. And when you're finished, don't hide it away. Put it where you can see it. Put it where you can be reminded, daily, of the Father's tender power.

And when we all get home, we'll make a gallery.

That's my idea. I know it's crazy, but what if, when we all get home, we make a gallery? I don't know if they allow this kind of stuff in heaven. But something tells me the Father won't mind. After all, there's plenty of space and lots of time.

And what an icebreaker! What a way to make friends! Can you envision it? There's Jonah with a life-size whale. Moses in front of a blazing bush. David is giving slingshot lessons. Gideon is letting people touch the fleece—*the* fleece—and Abraham is describing a painting entitled, "The Night with a Thousand Stars."

You can sit with Zacchaeus in his tree. A young boy shows you a basket of five loaves and two fishes. Martha welcomes you in her kitchen. The Centurion invites you to touch the cross.

Martin Luther is there with the Book of Romans. Susannah Wesley tells how she prayed for her sons—Charles and John. Dwight Moody tells of the day he left the shoe store to preach. And John Newton volunteers to sing "Amazing Grace" with an angelic backup.

Some are famous, most are not . . . but all are heroes. A soldier lets you sit in a foxhole modeled after the one he was in when he met Christ. A housewife shows you her tear-stained New Testament. Beside a Nigerian is the missionary who taught him. And behind the Brazilian is a drawing of the river in which he was baptized.

And somewhere in the midst of this arena of hope is your story. Person after person comes. They listen as if they have all the time in the world. (And they do!) They treat you as if you are royalty. (For you are!) Solomon asks you questions. Job compliments your stamina. Joshua lauds your courage. And when they all applaud, you applaud too. For in heaven, everyone knows that all praise goes to one source.

And speaking of the source, he's represented in the heavenly gallery as well. Turn and look. High above the others. In the most prominent place. Exactly in the middle. There is one display elevated high on a platform above the others. Visible from any point in the gallery is a boulder. It's round. It's heavy. It used to seal the opening of a tomb.

But not anymore. Ask Mary and Mary. Ask Peter. Ask Lazarus. Ask anyone in the gallery. They'll tell you. Stones were never a match for God.

Will there be such a gallery in heaven? Who knows? But I do know there used to be a stone in front of a tomb. And I do know it was moved. And I also know that there are stones in your path. Stones that trip and stones that trap. Stones too big for you.

Please remember, the goal of these stories is not to help us look back with amazement, but forward with faith. The God who spoke still speaks. The God who forgave still forgives. The God who came still comes. He comes into our world. He comes into your world. He comes to do what you can't. He comes to move the stones you can't budge.

Stones are no match for God. Not then and not now. He still moves stones.

Study Guide

Chapter 1 • *Bruised Reeds and Smoldering Wicks*

Looking Under the Stones:

1. Describe the appearance of a bruised reed and a smoldering wick. What makes them both so fragile, so close to death? In what way can people be like bruised reeds or smoldering wicks?

2. Describe a time you have felt like a bruised reed or a smoldering wick. What were the circumstances? How did things turn out?

3. Discuss Max's comments: "The world has a place for the beaten. The world will break you off; the world will snuff you out. But the artists of Scripture proclaim that God won't." Do you find his observations to be true? Explain your answer.

4. Max claims that God is "the friend of the wounded heart . . . the keeper of your dreams" and that he "has a special place for the bruised and weary of the world." What do you think he means by this? Describe a time in your life when you experienced the truth of his words.

5. Are there any "bruised reeds" or "smoldering wicks" in your life right now? If so, how do you handle them? What do you say? Do? How can the message of *He Still Moves Stones* instruct you on how to treat such fragile people?

6. Finish the following sentence: "The fact that Jesus doesn't break bruised reeds and doesn't snuff out smoldering wicks makes me _____."

Building on the Rock:

1. Read Matthew 12:15–21.

   a. How does verse 15 fulfill Isaiah's prophecy quoted in verse 20?

   b. How does verse 16 fulfill Isaiah's prophecy quoted in verse 19?

   c. In what way did Jesus fulfill Isaiah's prophecy quoted in verse 21? What does it mean to "find hope" in Jesus? Have you done this?

2. Read Luke 4:14–21.

   a. How is the prophecy quoted in verses 18–19 like the prophecy quoted in Matthew 12? How is it different?

   b. What did Jesus mean in verse 21? How had this prophecy been "fulfilled"? If it really had been fulfilled, what would this mean about the identity of Jesus?

Chapter 2 • Not Guilty

Looking Under the Stones:

1. In what way did Rebecca Thompson "die" twice? Do you know of anyone who has "died" as Rebecca did the first time? If so, describe the situation.

2. No one can know for sure why Rebecca jumped. What do you think drove her to suicide? Fear? Anger? Guilt? Shame? Explain your answer.

3. Max writes, "Whether private or public, shame is always painful. And unless you deal with it, it is permanent. Unless you get help—the dawn will never come." What do you think he

means? Do you agree with him? Why or why not?

4. What does the word *shame* mean to you? What does the word *grace* mean to you? Which is the stronger term? Why?

5. With what character in the story of John 8 do you identify most closely? The woman? The guilty (but absent) man? The Pharisees? The men in the crowd? Jesus? Explain your choice.

6. The Scripture doesn't say, but what do you think Jesus may have been writing in the sand?

7. Jesus told the woman, "I also don't judge you guilty. You may go now, but don't sin anymore" (John 8:11). Does any part of this statement bother you? Is it what you would have expected Jesus to say? Why?

8. Do the words "not guilty" apply to you? Explain your answer. How do those words make you feel?

Building on the Rock:

1. Read John 8:1–11.

   a. What was the trap the Pharisees were trying to lay for Jesus? What did they want him to do? How did he avoid their trap?

   b. Verse 9 says "those who heard [Jesus' answer] began to go away one at a time, the older ones first." Why do you think the older ones left first? Why is this an important detail?

2. Read Romans 8:1–9.

   a. In what way does this text explain the phrase "not guilty"? According to Romans 8, to whom does it apply?

b. How does verse 9 explain how the woman caught in adultery could comply with Jesus' command to her in John 8:11?

Chapter 3 • Don't Miss the Party

Looking Under the Stones:

1. What was the elder son's basic problem? Have you ever felt the way he did? If so, what were the circumstances?

2. Give your own definition of *bitterness*.

3. Do you know anyone whose life is marked by bitterness? If so, what is it like to be around that person? What lessons have you learned from him or her?

4. What does Max mean when he writes, "what you have is more important than what you don't have"? Is he right? Why or why not?

5. Did it surprise you to learn that Stephen A. Douglas was Abraham Lincoln's closest friend? If so, why? In what way is Lincoln a good example of the central truth of this chapter? In what way is he a good model for us?

6. Max writes that "no pouters are permitted" at God's final celebration. If God were to call us to his party today, would you be ready? Explain your answer.

7. Why don't some people "come and join the fun"? What reasons do they give? Did you ever give such reasons? If so, what were they? What convinced you to change your mind?

Building on the Rock:

1. Read Luke 15:11–32.

a. With whom do you most identify in this story? The younger son? The older son? The father? The servants? The fat calf? Explain your answer.

b. How did the father react to the younger son's speech in verse 21? How is this significant? What might it suggest to you about your own prayer life?

c. How does verse 32 help to color our understanding of Luke 15:10?

2. Read Hebrews 12:14–15.

a. What connection is there in verse 14 between living in peace with all people and being holy? Which one logically comes first?

b. What is the connection in verse 15 between "God's grace" and a "bitter root"? What does the grace of God do? What does a bitter root do?

c. In what ways do the story of Luke 15:11–32 illustrate the truths of Hebrews 12:14–15?

Chapter 4 • When You and Your Kin Can't

Looking Under the Stones:

1. Give a word picture to describe a relative in *your* life who really bugs you.

2. Do you have any "tar-baby relatives"? If so, what makes it hard to communicate with them?

3. Why *does* life get so "relatively difficult"? What can you do when those closest to you keep their distance?

4. How does it make you feel that Jesus himself had a difficult family? What was your reaction when you first read such a statement?

5. What do you think Jesus meant when he said, "A prophet is honored everywhere except in his hometown and in his own home" (Matt. 13:57)?

6. Go back through the chapter and list the many ways Jesus' family dishonored him. How did Jesus react to these insults? What can we learn from these incidents?

7. Max writes, "It's worth noting that [Jesus] didn't try to control his family's behavior, nor did he let their behavior control his." In what way is this an excellent principle for us?

8. How did the members of Jesus' family finally change in their appraisal of him? How can this give us hope?

Building on the Rock:

1. Read Psalm 139:5, Matthew 6:25–34, Galatians 4:7, Ephesians 1:5, and 1 John 3:1.

   a. What do these verses tell us about God as our Father? What does each one mean to you?

   b. If you have other favorite verses that describe God as your Father, list them. Why are these personal favorites?

2. Compare Romans 14:14–15:4 with 1 Corinthians 10:29–30.

   a. What light do these passages shed on our ability to withstand both our family's attempts to control us as well as our desire to control the behavior of our family?

b. In what way is Romans 14:19 generally a good prescription for harmony in the family? How about Romans 15:2? In what instances must other principles also be considered?

Chapter 5 • *It's All Right to Dream Again*

Looking Under the Stones:

1. Max writes, "there are times when we, too, are called to love, expecting nothing in return." What sort of times like this can you recall?

2. Discuss the following statement: "Service prompted by duty. This is the call of discipleship."

3. Does the fact that the angel rolled the stone away from the Lord's tomb imply anything significant for your own life? If so, what?

4. Describe some times in your life when God has proven to be a God of surprises.

5. What challenges face you right now in which the words "don't give up" are especially appropriate?

6. How does it make you feel that God is watching you and your circumstances?

7. In what ways does the resurrection breathe new life into your own hopes and dreams?

Building on the Rock:

1. Read Matthew 28:1–15.

a. Why do you think the angel not only rolled away the stone but then sat on it (v. 2)? Why do you think he spoke to the women and not to the guards?

b. Why would the women be "afraid but they were also very happy" as verse 8 tells us?

c. What logical flaws can you spot in the fabricated story described in verse 13?

2. Read Galatians 6:9.

   a. What command is given in this verse? Why does it seem so easy for us to ignore this command? What promise is given to us when we comply with the command?

   b. How are the two Marys good illustrations of the truth of this verse?

3. Read Hebrews 10:32–38.

   a. What is the purpose of the "history lesson" in verses 32–34? If the writer were describing your own experience rather than that of the Hebrews, what would he have written?

   b. What command is given in verse 35? What related promise is described? How is this promise further explained in verse 36?

   c. How is the prophecy of verse 37 intended to help us persevere? In what way does this prophecy encourage you?

Chapter 6 • Sour Milk

Looking Under the Stones:

1. Max writes, "Sweet milk turns sour from being too warm, too long. Sweet dispositions turn sour for the same reason." Explain what this means to you.

2. Are you more likely to follow Mary or Martha's example? Are you satisfied with this? Why? If you think you need to change, describe what you can do to bring about that change.

3. Do you know of a situation where someone's work for the Lord became more important than the Lord himself? Has this ever happened to you? If so, describe what happened.

4. Discuss the following statement: "God is more pleased with the quiet attention of a sincere servant than the noisy service of a sour one."

5. Why is it so easy for most of us to forget who is the servant and who is to be served?

6. What steps do you take to ensure that your focus doesn't become stuck on yourself?

7. When was the last time you took a break simply to "sit at the feet of Jesus"? Describe what you did and how it affected your behavior and attitudes afterward.

8. Discuss the joke about the fellow who prayed with a bad attitude on page 62. Have you ever prayed this prayer? What did you think of God's answer to the man's prayer?

Building on the Rock:

1. Read Luke 10:38–42.

   a. What was the Lord talking about when he told Martha that "only one thing is important" in verse 42? What is this "one thing"? Does it exist in your life?

   b. What is significant about the Lord's words, "Mary has *chosen* the better thing"? How does this comment relate to your own Christian walk?

c. What promise is made in verse 42? How does this promise also apply to us?

2. Read Matthew 21:28–32.

   a. What does this parable teach us about service? What lesson might Martha have learned from it?

   b. Which of the two sons do you resemble?

   c. What point is Jesus making in verses 31–32? Why does he sound so harsh here?

Chapter 7 • A Crazy Hunch and a High Hope

Looking Under the Stones:

1. What was the crazy hunch and the high hope of the woman in Mark 5? In specific terms, how can she be an example for us today?

2. Discuss Max's definition of faith: "A conviction that [God] can and a hope that he will."

3. Max writes, "Faith is not the belief that God will do what you want. Faith is the belief that God will do what is right." How should this change the way you pray? Does it?

4. Do you believe that "the more hopeless your circumstance, the more likely your salvation"? Why or why not?

5. Is it true that "faith with no effort is no faith at all"? Explain your answer.

6. Look over Max's "to do" list on page 69. Is there anything on the list that you need to do? Is there something that true faith would require you to do that isn't on that list? If so, what?

7. What is significant about the fact that Jesus called the afflicted woman "daughter"? Does this mean anything for your own relationship with Jesus?

Building on the Rock:

1. Read Mark 5:24–34.

   a. Why was it important for Jesus to find out who had touched his clothes? Why not just continue on his way?

   b. Why did the woman fall at Jesus' feet and tremble with fear? Is this the reaction you would expect? Why or why not?

2. Read Hebrews 11:1–6.

   a. How does the writer of Hebrews define faith? How would you describe it in your own terms?

   b. How are Abel and Enoch good examples of people of faith? How did they demonstrate their faith?

   c. How does the certainty of "reward" increase our faith (v. 6)?

3. Read James 2:14–26.

   a. Is it accurate to say that the writer of Hebrews *defines* faith and that James *illustrates* it? Explain your answer.

   b. Discuss the following: "Faith is not deeds, but faith produces deeds." Would James agree with this statement? Why or why not?

Chapter 8 • Forever Young

Looking Under the Stones:

1. When was the first time you specifically recall "the dawning of old age" in your own life? What happened? How does getting older make you feel?

2. Why does growing older sometimes spawn regrets? Try to name some examples of this.

3. How do regrets sometimes lead to rebellion? How can this process be short-circuited?

4. Max writes that there are two options as we grow older: safety vs. adventure. What does he mean and how do these two options play out in real life?

5. How can we "reclaim curiosity"? What advantages are there in doing so?

6. Max writes that Abraham, Moses, Caleb, Anna, and John all had one important thing in common. What was it? How can this be an encouragement to us?

7. When asked why he had taken up the study of Greek at the age of ninety-four, Oliver Wendell Holmes is reputed to have said, "Well, my good sir, it's now or never." What attitude do you suppose prompted Holmes to make such a statement? Do you admire him for it? Explain your answer.

8. Max writes, "As we get older, our vision should improve." What does this mean? Do you think it's true of your own experience? Why or why not?

Building on the Rock:

1. Read Luke 17:20–37.

   a. Jesus' saying, "Whoever tries to keep his life will lose it, and whoever loses his life will preserve it" is found in the middle of a discussion on planetary conditions as history draws to a close. Why is this significant? In what way does this seem especially significant for those who are growing older?

   b. How is Lot's wife a chilling example of Luke 17:33? (See Gen. 19:12–26.)

2. Read Titus 2:2–5.

   a. According to verse 2, what are the special duties of older men?

   b. According to verses 3–5, what are the special duties of older women?

Chapter 9 • Read the Story

Looking Under the Stones:

1. How does P. T. Barnum's saying, "There's a sucker born every minute," remind you of a hurt, heartbroken little boy?

2. Try to recall the first time you were heartbroken. How did you respond? How long did it take you to recover? What did friends or family do to help you recover?

3. Max writes, "Disappointment . . . will blind you to the very presence of God." How did this happen with the two men on the road to Emmaus? How does this happen with you?

4. In what ways does despair harden our hearts and make us cynical and calloused? Why is this dangerous?

5. Max writes that those with broken hearts are tempted to stop loving, stop trusting, and stop giving their hearts away. Have you ever seen people react in this way? If so, what did they do? Why do you suppose they did it?

6. Jesus did two things for the men on the road to Emmaus: (1) He came to them where they were; and (2) He told them the story of God. How is this formula still the cure for broken hearts? Does this mean the cure is easy? Explain.

7. Unfulfilled expectations are at the root of most heartbreaks. Why?

8. How can the knowledge that God is still in control affect our outlook when our heart is broken?

Building on the Rock:

1. Read Luke 24:13–35.

   a. ". . . but we were hoping," said Cleopas in verse 21. How does this phrase sum up his deep heartbreak?

   b. The most amazing Bible lesson in history is described in verse 27. What specific passages do you suppose Jesus quoted in this lesson?

2. Read Psalm 135:5–14 and Daniel 4:34–35.

   a. What picture of God do you get in Psalm 135?

   b. What picture of God do you get in Daniel 4?

   c. How do these pictures help us in times of heartbreak?

Chapter 10 • The Power of a Timid Prayer

Looking Under the Stones:

1. Are your prayers more of the Concorde or of the crop-duster variety? Explain.

2. Max writes that prayer begins as a yearning. A yearning for what? Is this true for you? If so, in what way?

3. What reasons do we give for not praying as we think we should? What reasons seem to be your "favorites"?

4. The man in Mark 9:24 prayed, "I do believe! Help me to believe more." Is this a prayer of faith? Is it an admirable prayer? Do you ever pray like this? Explain.

5. In what way did Jim Redmond's act at the 1992 Barcelona Olympics illustrate what our heavenly Father does for us? Describe the last time you received the Father's help in this way.

6. Discuss Max's statement that "the power of prayer is in the one who hears it and not the one who says it." What does this imply for our prayer life? Does it imply that our character makes no difference to God when it comes to answering our prayers? Explain.

7. Whether you're a crop duster or a Concorde, do you want to improve your prayer life? What specific steps can you take to do so?

Building on the Rock:

1. Read Mark 9:14–29.

   a. In what way was the man's comment, "*If* you can do anything" conditioned by his experience with Jesus' disciples? How do our actions affect unbelievers' opinions of Jesus?

b. How are Jesus' words in verse 25 specifically crafted to show his power and authority? How is this healing of a demoniac different from others recorded in Scripture?

2. Read Nehemiah 2:1–9.

a. Does the prayer alluded to in verse 4 belong to the Concorde or crop-duster variety? Was it answered? How is this significant?

b. What connection is there between the prayer of 2:4 and Nehemiah's actions in chapter 1? What should this teach us about our own prayer life?

Chapter 11 • Bright Lights on Dark Nights

Looking Under the Stones:

1. How often do you deliberately choose to be among the suffering? Is Jesus' presence at the pool of Bethesda an encouragement to you or a rebuke—or both? Explain.

2. In what way is the sick man's story really a tale about you and me?

3. Max writes, "we must admit we are like the paralytic. Invalids out of options." What does he mean by this? Do you agree with him? Why or why not?

4. Comment on this statement: "In God's plan, God is the standard for perfection . . . The goal is to be like him; anything less is inadequate." Identify some Scripture passages that say this in another way.

5. Why does it seem easier for an army private to believe the word of Alexander the Great (see page 111) than it does for us to believe the word of Jesus Christ?

6. Is Jesus telling you today, like the paralytic, to "stand up" in any area of your life? If so, what? If he is, what do you plan to do about it?

Building on the Rock:

1. Read Romans 3:9–23.

   a. What groups of people are included in this evaluation? What groups are excluded? Where do you fit?

   b. What does it mean to "are not good enough for God's glory" (v. 23)? How serious is this?

2. Read Colossians 2:13–15.

   a. What was your condition prior to coming to faith in Jesus Christ (v. 13)?

   b. List the things Jesus accomplished for you on the cross, based on this passage.

   c. According to verse 15, was the cross a victory for Jesus or a defeat? Explain how this can be.

Chapter 12 • The Hardest Thing God Ever Did

Looking Under the Stones:

1. Describe several examples of "lovebursts" you have enjoyed over the years.

2. Max writes that lovebursts remind you "that what you have is greater than what you want and that what is urgent is not

always what matters." How do lovebursts do this? Try to name a few examples from your own life where you have seen this principle at work.

3. Had the paralyzed man's friends given up when they saw the full house, what do you suppose would have happened to the man? Do you have any friends who would go as far to help you as this man's friends did for him? Are you such a friend for anyone else?

4. Max writes, "Faith does the unexpected. And faith gets God's attention." Acting in faith, have you ever done the unexpected? If so, what happened?

5. Comment on the following statement: "They want to give the man a new body so he can walk. Jesus gives grace so the man can live." What implications does this have for our day-to-day lives?

6. Are you glad that God often bypasses our requests and gives us what we need instead? Explain.

7. Try to list at least five implications of the fact that Jesus has the authority to forgive sins.

Building on the Rock:

1. Read Mark 2:1–12.

   a. Whose faith did Jesus respond to in his healing of the paralytic (v. 5)? What significance does this have in regard to many contemporary claims of faith healings (or the failure to heal)?

   b. It is obviously as easy to say, "Stand up, take your mat, and go home," as it is to say, "Your sins are forgiven," so why did Jesus ask the question in verse 9? By healing the paralytic right after he asked this question, what point was he making? What claim was he making for himself?

2. Read Psalm 50:15.

   a. What does God instruct us to do in this verse? What does he promise to do? How are we to respond?

3. Read Romans 8:26–27 and Ephesians 3:20–21.

   a. According to Romans 8:26, how accurate are we in what we pray for? What is God's solution to our problem?

   b. How does the Ephesians passage add to this understanding of prayer? How should we respond?

Chapter 13 • *What Only God Can Do*

Looking Under the Stones:

1. How would you define a "legalist"? Do most legalists consider themselves as such? Explain.

2. In what way does a legalist "prepare the soil but forget the seed"? What does this picture tell us about legalism?

3. Why do you think Jesus ignored Nicodemus's comment in John 3:2 and instead responded, "I tell you the truth, unless a man is born again, he cannot be in God's kingdom"? Was this polite?

4. What does Max mean when he writes, "All the world religions can be placed in one of two camps: legalism or grace"? In which camp does your religion fall? How do you know?

5. Comment on the following statement: "Legalism is slow torture, suffocation of the spirit, amputation of the dreams." If you have ever felt legalism's grip, describe your experience.

6. Do you agree with the statement that "every spiritual achievement is created and energized by God"? Why or why not?

7. In your own words, define the term *grace* (and don't say, "God's unmerited favor"!).

8. How does John 19:39–42 prove that Nicodemus finally escaped the trap of legalism? How did he escape its grip?

Building on the Rock:

1. Read Galatians 5:1–6.

   a. What danger does Paul warn us about in this passage? Why is it a real threat?

   b. How does this passage teach that salvation cannot be achieved through a mixture of faith and deeds?

2. Read Colossians 2:20–23.

   a. What reason does Paul give in verse 20 for refusing to submit to man-made rules? What does this mean?

   b. In what way do many human regulations "have an appearance of wisdom"? What makes them attractive?

   c. How effective are our rules at restraining sensual indulgence (v. 23)?

   d. Why do you think we are so easily drawn back into legalism? What is the only way to stay free of it?

Chapter 14 • Galilean Grace

Looking Under the Stones:

1. Why do you think Peter denied the Lord after Jesus was arrested? Have you ever "denied" him in a similar way? If so, describe the situation.

2. How was Peter's denial an illustration of Proverbs 16:18? How is his experience a lesson and a warning for us?

3. Have you ever been loyal to the Lord . . . from a distance? If so, what were the circumstances surrounding this event?

4. When Luke 22:61 says that Jesus "turned and looked straight at Peter," what sort of look do you think it was? Accusing? Condemning? Compassionate? Exasperated? Sorrowful? Explain your answer.

5. How do you think Peter felt at the moment he plunged into the lake to meet the Lord on the beach? What was going through his mind?

6. Max imagines a moment after we have sinned and writes, "It's just you and God. You and God both know what you did. And neither one of you is proud of it. What do you do?" How would you answer his question?

7. Comment on the following statement: "[God] invites you to try again. This time, with him." Exactly *how* do you try something again, this time with God? What do you do differently than you tried the first time around?

Building on the Rock:

1. Read John 21:14–19.

a. The restoration of Peter was not complete until he went through the encounter described in this passage. What was Jesus trying to accomplish in this meeting? How did he do it?

b. Notice Jesus' final charge to Peter in verse 19. How is this both different and the same as his original call recorded in Matthew 4:19? How is this significant?

Chapter 15 • The Tenderness of God

Looking Under the Stones:

1. Max writes that Jesus was referring to some kind of plan when he spoke phrases such as "the time has not yet come." What plan is he speaking of? A plan to do what?

2. Max writes, "The inaugural miracle is motivated—not by tragedy or famine or moral collapse—but by concern for friends who are in a bind." What does this say about Jesus? How does this knowledge affect the way you relate to him today?

3. Comment on the statement: "This miracle tells you that what matters to you, matters to God." How true is this? How do you know? What examples from your own life can you produce to demonstrate its truth?

4. How do you think God sees you? If he were to describe you to an angel, what would he say? What does he think of you?

5. How does Denalyn's response to her daughter Jenna illustrate how God responds to the pain of his own children?

6. Jesus' first miracle was turning water into wine at the wedding of some friends; his last miracle was to heal the ear of a man who had come to arrest him (see Luke 22:50–51). What does this tell you about Jesus' availability to listen to your requests?

Building on the Rock:

1. Read Hebrews 4:14–16.

   a. How is Jesus described in this passage? List each description.

   b. Based on the characteristics listed above, what should be our response? What are we encouraged to do?

2. Read Philippians 4:6–7.

   a. What things does this text instruct us to pray for? What elements of prayer does it mention?

   b. According to verse 7, what results can we expect from praying as we are instructed in verse 6?

3. Read 1 Peter 5:6–7.

   a. What are we instructed to do in verse 6? How do you do this? What promise is given?

   b. How is verse 7 dependent upon verse 6? What are we told to do in verse 7? What promise is given?

Chapter 16 • The Madman Turned Missionary

Looking Under the Stones:

1. Were you surprised to learn that the first missionary was a former lunatic? Explain your answer.

2. Max writes, "Jesus' mere appearance humbles the demons. Though they had dominated this man, they cower before God." How should this be a tremendous encouragement to us today?

3. The demons implore Jesus to send them into a herd of swine, and Jesus does so. But why would the demons make such a request if they immediately drove the pigs to their death? (See John 8:44; 10:10.) What does this tell you about demonic character?

4. How was a young Max able to get through the storm that threatened to capsize his fishing boat? How can we emulate his actions in regard to our relationship with our heavenly Father?

5. Max writes, "When the fighting is fierce, stand back and let the Father fight." Is this good advice? What does it mean in practical terms? How do you "stand back and let the Father fight"?

6. Why do you think the people asked Jesus to leave their territory after he had delivered the demoniac? Raw fear? Fear of change? Fear of further economic loss?

7. When Jesus told the formerly demon-possessed man to go home to his family and tell them how much God had done for him, it was one of the few times he instructed someone to broadcast the news of a healing. What was different in this man's case? Why did Jesus tell this man to testify, but the others to keep quiet (see Mark 1:40–45)?

Building on the Rock:

1. Read 1 Corinthians 15:8–11 and 1 Timothy 1:12–16.

   a. Why was Paul amazed that God called him to be a missionary? According to these passages, what were his credentials?

   b. According to 1 Timothy 1:16, why did God choose Paul to be an apostle? What does this suggest for you and me?

2. Read 2 Corinthians 10:3–5.

a. What insight does this passage give us into fighting in the spiritual realm?

b. How does this passage show that the only way to win the fight is by resting in the Father's strength?

Chapter 17 • Seeing the Unseen

Looking Under the Stones:

1. What did you think of Max's "faith experiment" with his daughters? What was he trying to teach them?

2. Do you ever wish you could see into the future? What would be the benefits of doing so? The drawbacks? If you could acquire the ability to see your whole future, would you do so? Explain.

3. Max writes, "There are times in life when everything you have to offer is nothing compared to what you are asking to receive." Describe a time in your life when this was true of you.

4. Have you ever tried to "barter" with the Lord? ("You do this for me and I'll . . .") What's wrong with bartering? Why isn't God at all interested in it?

5. Max claims that a critical principle for seeing the unseen is to ignore what people say. What does he mean? What sort of people do you ignore? What kinds of advice do you refuse to heed? Couldn't Max's advice be dangerous in some circumstances? In what kind of circumstances?

6. Comment on the concentration camp inmate's words: "I believe in the sun, even though it doesn't shine, I believe in love, even when it isn't shown, I believe in God, even when he doesn't speak." Do you have faith like this? Explain your answer.

7. Max writes, "Death is a small price to pay for the privilege of sitting at [God's] table." Do you agree with him? Why or why not?

8. Why did Jesus throw the people out of Jairus's home?

9. What did you learn about faith from Max's experiment with his daughters?

Building on the Rock:

1. Read 1 Corinthians 15:50–57.

    a. According to this passage, why cannot "flesh and blood" inherit the kingdom of God?

    b. What must occur for us to take our place at God's side? Who makes it possible for us to get there (v. 57)? How did he do this?

2. Read 2 Corinthians 4:16–18.

    a. What reason does Paul give in verse 16 for not giving up hope? How does he amplify this in verse 17?

    b. According to verse 18, how permanent is the world we see? How permanent is the world we do not see? How do you "Set our eyes" on Jesus?

Chapter 18 • Joseph's Prayer

Looking Under the Stones:

1. What questions do you have that were prompted by the Bible's silence?

2. What do you imagine Joseph thought about in the stable while Jesus was being born? If your guess is different from Max's, describe it.

3. Describe a time when you were caught between what God says and what seemed to make sense.

4. What does it mean to you to walk by faith, not by sight? How can you know for sure that you're on the right trail?

5. What is the connection between our obedience and divine guidance. Why is it pointless to ask God for direction for your life if you are disobeying some command of Scripture?

6. What instances in your past have caused you to question why God did what he did?

7. What generally happens to your attitude when you question God's handling of your life or circumstances? Is there a pattern you can discern?

8. How do you respond to Max's question: "Will you serve . . . even when you don't understand?"

Building on the Rock:

1. Read Hebrews 3:12–19.

   a. What advice is given in verse 13 to help us obey God to-gether?

   b. Note the close connection between obedience and belief in verses 18 and 19. What is this connection?

2. Read 1 Samuel 15:22–23.

a. Samuel delivered this speech to Saul after the king had disobeyed a direct divine command. To what does Samuel contrast obedience in verse 22? Which of these two things does God treasure the most?

b. To what does Samuel compare disobedience? What were the consequences for Saul's disobedience?

3. Read Job 42:1–6.

a. When Job comes face to face with God, what happens to his questions?

b. When Job finally gets a clear picture of God, how does he respond? How does the story end in 42:7–17? How is this important?

Chapter 19 • The Grave Fact

Looking Under the Stones:

1. How often do you think of death? What images does it create in your mind?

2. Describe what you felt and did the first time a loved one died.

3. As you get older, do you find yourself thinking more about death? Do you ever try to imagine your own funeral? If so, describe it.

4. How does death "unearth our view of God"?

5. Have you ever found yourself thinking or saying something like, "If you were doing your part, God, my husband would have survived." "If you'd done what was right, Lord, my baby would have lived"? Do you know anyone who has acted in this way? How did you respond in each case?

6. Do you agree that many of us "interpret the presence of death as the absence of God"? Explain your answer.

7. Max writes that Christians serve "the kind of God who rolls back the sleeve of the trickster and reveals death for the parlor trick it is." What does he mean? What hope can this give you?

Building on the Rock:

1. Read 1 Thessalonians 4:13–18.

   a. According to this passage, why are Christians not to grieve like the unbelieving world? What hope do Christians have that unbelievers don't?

   b. What promise is given in verse 17? How is this to encourage us?

2. Read John 14:1–3.

   a. What is the bedrock way to remove the fear of death, according to verse 1?

   b. What is the tremendous promise given to every believer in verses 2–3? How can this give us courage in the face of death?

3. Read Revelation 21:1–7, 9–22:5.

   a. List as many characteristics of our final home as you can find in this passage.

   b. For you personally, what is the greatest promise contained in this passage?

Chapter 20 • Listless Christianity

Looking Under the Stones:

1. Do most of your friends and acquaintances believe in heaven? What do they think it's like?

2. How do most of the people you know believe someone "makes it" to heaven? What is on their "list"?

3. What is on *your* list of what it takes to get to heaven? How can you be confident that your list is accurate?

4. How did one of the thieves crucified with Jesus go so quickly from reviling the Lord to asking for a reservation in paradise? Doesn't this sound like a contradiction?

5. Max imagines that the thief thought, "I am wrong; Jesus is right. I have failed; Jesus has not. I deserve to die; Jesus deserves to live." How do these statements constitute "the core of the gospel"?

6. How do you feel about Max's conviction that, "You see, that is you and me on the cross. Naked, desolate, hopeless, and estranged. That is us"? Is this insulting or accurate? Explain your answer.

7. Do you agree that "we, like the thief, are able to endure the pain knowing he'll soon take us home"? Why or why not?

8. If in heaven you could ask the thief on the cross any question at all, what would you ask him? Why?

Building on the Rock:

1. Read Romans 10:9–13.

a. How can we enter into a life-giving relationship with God, according to this passage? What "list" does this passage give?

b. How does the thief's story stack up against this passage? Is his conversion story a good illustration of what Paul wrote here?

c. Have you ever taken the steps Paul outlines here?

2. Read 2 Corinthians 5:1–5, 17–6:2.

a. For what purpose has God made us, according to verses 4 and 5? What guarantee has he given us that he will fulfill his promise to us?

b. How is verse 21 an excellent summary of the gospel message? According to 6:1–2, how do we apply the work of Christ to our own behalf?

Chapter 21 • The Stone Mover's Gallery

Looking Under the Stones:

1. Why do you think the Bible is full of stories of hurting men and women?

2. Max writes, "The goal of these stories is not to help us look back with amazement, but forward with faith." What is the difference between the two? Describe any times when you have made this mistake. How did you correct it?

3. Take some time, as Max says, to "record your drama. Retell your saga. Plot your journey." Follow his suggestion and:

a. Begin with your experience before you knew Jesus.

b. Then describe your present experience.

c. Last, share your story with someone else.

4. If you were to pick a single item that characterizes either your salvation experience or your subsequent Christian walk, what would that thing be? Explain your choice.

5. Discuss Max's comment, "Stones were never a match for God." What stones has he removed in your own life? What stones are even now blocking your way? How does it help to remember that "stones were never a match for God"?

6. What has been the most helpful insight to you in *He Still Moves Stones?* Has anything left you a little puzzled? Spend a few moments "debriefing" your reading experience.

Building on the Rock:

1. Read 1 Corinthians 1:26 and Philippians 1:6.

   a. According to 1 Corinthians 1:26, why did Paul think it was important for the Corinthians to remember their pre-Christian lives? Is it important for us to remember our own pre-Christian lives? Why or why not?

   b. According to Philippians 1:6, what two truths help to keep us on track in our Christian lives?

2. Read Romans 15:4 and 1 Corinthians 10:11–13.

   a. According to Romans 15:4, why were so many stories of hurting people included in the Bible? What two specific reasons are given?

   b. According to 1 Corinthians 10:11–13, what other specific reasons did God have in mind when he gave us these stories in the Bible? How are these stories supposed to help us today?

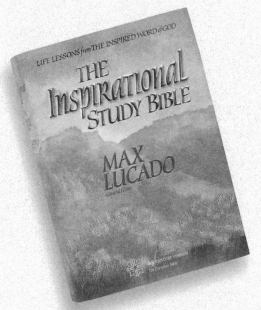

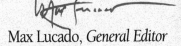

JOHN

INTRODUCTION

*H*e's an old man, this one who sits on the stool and leans against the wall. Eyes closed and face soft, were it not for his hand stroking his beard, you'd think he was asleep.

Some in the room assume he is. He does this often during worship. As the people sing, his eyes will close and his chin will fall until it rests on his chest, and there he will remain motionless. Silent.

Those who know him well know better. They know he is not resting. He is traveling. Atop the music he journeys back, back, back until he is young again. Strong again. There again. There on the seashore with James and the apostles. There on the trail with the disciples and the women. There in the Temple with Caiaphas and the accusers.

It's been sixty years, but John sees him still. The decades took John's strength, but they didn't take his memory. The years dulled his sight, but they didn't dull his vision. The seasons may have wrinkled his face, but they didn't soften his love.

He had been with God. God had been with him. How could he forget?

❀ The wine that moments before had been water—John could still taste it.

❀ The mud placed on the eyes of the blind man in Jerusalem—John could still remember it.

❀ The aroma of Mary's perfume as it filled the room—John could still smell it.

And the voice. Oh, the voice. His voice. John could still hear it.

I am the light of the world, it rang . . . I am the door . . . I am the way, the truth, the life.

I will come back, it promised, and take you to be with me.

Those who believe in me, it assured, will have life even if they die.

John could hear him. John could see him. Scenes branded on his heart. Words seared into his soul. John would never forget. How could he? He had been there.

He opens his eyes and blinks. The singing has stopped. The teaching has begun. John looks at the listeners and listens to the teacher.

If only you could have been there, he thinks.

But he wasn't. Most weren't. Most weren't even born. And most who were there are dead. Peter is. So is James. Nathanael, Martha, Philip. They are all gone. Even Paul, the apostle who came late, is dead.

Only John remains.

He looks again at the church. Small but earnest. They lean forward to hear the teacher. John listens to him. What a task. Speaking of one he never saw. Explaining words he never heard. John is there if the teacher needs him.

But what will happen when John is gone? What will the teacher do then? When John's voice is silent and his tongue stilled? Who will tell them how Jesus silenced the waves? Will they hear how he fed the thousands? Will they remember how he prayed for unity?

How will they know? If only they could have been there.

Suddenly, in his heart he knows what to do.

Later, under the light of a sunlit shaft, the old fisherman unfolds the scroll and begins to write the story of his life . . .

In the beginning there was the Word . . .

LIFE LESSON
John 1:1-51

SITUATION ✒ The Greeks and the Jews were familiar with the concept of the *word*. For the Jews it was an expression of God's wisdom, and for the Greeks it meant reason and intellect.

OBSERVATION ✒ Leaving his heavenly home, Jesus put on human flesh to bring us God's Good News.

INSPIRATION ✒ It all happened in a moment, a most remarkable moment.... that was like none other. For through that segment of time a spectacular thing occurred. God became a man. While the creatures of earth walked unaware, Divinity arrived. Heaven opened herself and placed her most precious one in a human womb....

God as a fetus. Holiness sleeping in a womb. The creator of life being created.

God was given eyebrows, elbows, two kidneys, and a spleen. He stretched against the walls and floated in the amniotic fluids of his mother.

God had come near....

The hands that first held him were unmanicured, calloused, and dirty.

No silk. No ivory. No hype. No party. No hoopla.

Were it not for the shepherds, there would have been no reception. And were it not for a group of star-gazers, there would have been no gifts....

Christ Comes to the World

*I*n the beginning there was the Word.*ⁿ* The Word was with God, and the Word was God. ²He was with God in the beginning. ³All things were made by him, and nothing was made without him. ⁴In him there was life, and that life was the light of all people. ⁵The Light shines in the darkness, and the darkness has not overpowered it.

⁶There was a man named John*ⁿ* who was sent by God. ⁷He came to tell people the truth about the Light so that through him all people could hear about the Light and believe. ⁸John was not the Light, but he came to tell people the truth about the Light. ⁹The true Light that gives light to all was coming into the world!

¹⁰The Word was in the world, and the world was made by him, but the world did not know him. ¹¹He came to the world that was his own, but his own people did not accept him. ¹²But to all who did accept him and believe in him he gave the right to become children of God. ¹³They did not become his children in any human way—by any human parents or human desire. They were born of God.

¹⁴The Word became a human and lived among us. We saw his glory—the glory that belongs to the only Son of the Father—and he was full of grace and truth. ¹⁵John tells the truth about him and cries out, saying, "This is the One I told you about: 'The One who comes after me is greater than I am, because he was living before me.'"

¹⁶Because he was full of grace and truth, from him we all received one gift after another. ¹⁷The law was given through Moses, but grace and truth came through Jesus Christ. ¹⁸No one has ever seen God. But God the only Son is very close to the Father,*ⁿ* and he has shown us what God is like.

John Tells People About Jesus

¹⁹Here is the truth John*ⁿ* told when the Jews in Jerusalem sent priests and Levites to ask him, "Who are you?"

²⁰John spoke freely and did not refuse to answer. He said, "I am not the Christ."

²¹So they asked him, "Then who are you? Are you Elijah?"*ⁿ*

He answered, "No, I am not."

"Are you the Prophet?"*ⁿ* they asked.

He answered, "No."

²²Then they said, "Who are you? Give us an answer to tell those who sent us. What do you say about yourself?"

²³John told them in the words of the prophet Isaiah:

"I am the voice of one
   calling out in the desert:
'Make the road straight for the Lord.'"   *Isaiah 40:3*

Word   The Greek word is "logos," meaning any kind of communication; it could be translated "message." Here, it means Christ, because Christ was the way God told people about himself.
John   John the Baptist, who preached to people about Christ's coming (Matthew 3, Luke 3).
But...Father   This could be translated, "But the only God is very close to the Father." Also, some Greek copies say, "But the only Son is very close to the Father."
John   John the Baptist, who preached to people about Christ's coming (Matthew 3, Luke 3).
Elijah   A man who spoke for God. He lived hundreds of years before Christ and was expected to return before Christ (Malachi 4:5-6).
Prophet   They probably meant the prophet that God told Moses he would send (Deuteronomy 18:15-19).

²⁴Some Pharisees who had been sent asked John:²⁵"If you are not the Christ or Elijah or the Prophet, why do you baptize people?"

²⁶John answered, "I baptize with water, but there is one here with you that you don't know about. ²⁷He is the One who comes after me. I am not good enough to untie the strings of his sandals."

²⁸This all happened at Bethany on the other side of the Jordan River, where John was baptizing people.

²⁹The next day John saw Jesus coming toward him. John said, "Look, the Lamb of God,ⁿ who takes away the sin of the world! ³⁰This is the One I was talking about when I said, 'A man will come after me, but he is greater than I am, because he was living before me.' ³¹Even I did not know who he was, although I came baptizing with water so that the people of Israel would know who he is."

³²⁻³³Then John said, "I saw the Spirit come down from heaven in the form of a dove and rest on him. Until then I did not know who the Christ was. But the God who sent me to baptize with water told me, 'You will see the Spirit come down and rest on a man; he is the One who will baptize with the Holy Spirit.' ³⁴I have seen this happen, and I tell you the truth: This man is the Son of God."

The First Followers of Jesus

³⁵The next day Johnⁿ was there again with two of his followers. ³⁶When he saw Jesus walking by, he said, "Look, the Lamb of God!"ⁿ

³⁷The two followers heard John say this, so they followed Jesus. ³⁸When Jesus turned and saw them following him, he asked, "What are you looking for?"

They said, "Rabbi, where are you staying?" ("Rabbi" means "Teacher.")

³⁹He answered, "Come and see." So the two men went with Jesus and saw where he was staying and stayed there with him that day. It was about four o'clock in the afternoon.

⁴⁰One of the two men who followed Jesus after they heard John speak about him was Andrew, Simon Peter's brother. ⁴¹The first thing Andrew did was to find his brother Simon and say to him, "We have found the Messiah." ("Messiah" means "Christ.")

⁴²Then Andrew took Simon to Jesus. Jesus looked at him and said, "You are Simon son of John. You will be called Cephas." ("Cephas" means "Peter."ⁿ)

⁴³The next day Jesus decided to go to Galilee. He found Philip and said to him, "Follow me."

⁴⁴Philip was from the town of Bethsaida, where Andrew and Peter lived. ⁴⁵Philip found Nathanael and told him, "We have found the man that Moses wrote about in the law, and the prophets also wrote about him. He is Jesus, the son of Joseph, from Nazareth."

⁴⁶But Nathanael said to Philip, "Can anything good come from Nazareth?"

Philip answered, "Come and see."

⁴⁷As Jesus saw Nathanael coming toward him, he said, "Here is truly an Israelite. There is nothing false in him."

For thirty-three years he would feel everything you and I have ever felt. He felt weak. He grew weary. He was afraid of failure. He was susceptible to wooing women. He got colds, burped, and had body odor. His feelings got hurt. His feet got tired. And his head ached.

To think of Jesus in such a light is—well, it seems almost irreverent, doesn't it? It's not something we like to do; it's uncomfortable. It is much easier to keep the humanity out of the incarnation. He's easier to stomach that way. . . .

But don't do it. For heaven's sake, don't. Let him be as human as he intended to be. Let him into the mire and muck of our world. For only if we let him in can he pull us out.

(From *God Came Near* by Max Lucado)

APPLICATION If people want to know what God is like, they can look at Jesus. If they want to know what Jesus is like, they should be able to look at his followers. Can people see Christ in you?

EXPLORATION The Word is Born—John 14:6-7; 1 Corinthians 8:5-6; Galatians 4:4; Philippians 2:7, 8; 1 Timothy 3:16; Hebrews 2:14; 13:8; 1 John 1:1-2; 4:2.

Lamb of God   Name for Jesus. Jesus is like the lambs that were offered for a sacrifice to God.
Peter   The Greek name "Peter," like the Aramaic name "Cephas," means "rock."

A Gentle Thunder

Max Lucado

A Gentle Thunder

Hearing God Through the Storm

WORD PUBLISHING
DALLAS LONDON VANCOUVER MELBOURNE

PUBLISHED BY WORD PUBLISHING
DALLAS, TEXAS

Unless otherwise indicated, Scripture quotations used in this book
are from the Holy Bible, New Century Version, copyright © 1987, 1988, 1991
by Word Publishing, Dallas, Texas 75234. Used by permission.

Other references are from the following sources: The Holy Bible,
New International Version (NIV). Copyright © 1973, 1978, 1984 International
Bible Society. Used by permission of Zondervan Bible Publishers. *The Living Bible*
(TLB), copyright 1971 by Tyndale House Publishers, Wheaton, Ill. Used by permis-
sion. The New English Bible (NEB). Copyright © 1961, 1970 by the Delegates of the
Oxford University Press and the Syndics of the Cambridge University Press.
Reprinted by permission. *The Message* (TM), copyright © 1993.
Used by permission of NavPress Publishing Group.

Anecdotes in this volume are based on fact; however in some instances
details have been changed to protect identities.

Book Design by Mark McGarry
Set in Janson

LIBRARY OF CONGRESS CATALOGING-IN-PUBLICATION DATA
Lucado, Max
A Gentle Thunder / Max Lucado.
p. cm.
ISBN 0–8499–1138–9 (HARDCOVER)
(INCLUDES BIBLIOGRAPHICAL REFERENCES).
1. Bible. N.T. John–Meditations. 2. Consolation. 3. Christian life. I. Title.

BS2615.4.L83 1995
242'.5–dc20 95-19816
CIP

5 6 7 8 9 0 1 2 3 9 BVG 9 8 7 6 5 4 3 2 1

Printed in the United States of America.

In honor of the past,
in anticipation of the future,
I dedicate this book to
Kip Jordon and Byron Williamson
of Word Publishing.

Contents

Contents

Contents

Acknowledgments

A BOOK should be a garden that fits in the hands. Word-petals of color. Stems of strength. Roots of truth. Turn a page and turn the seasons. Read the sentence and enjoy the roses.

No gardening is easy, however, especially that of words. Weeds sprout and ideas wilt. Some paragraphs need water; others need the shears. There are times when you wonder if this jungle can ever be trimmed. I am deeply grateful to some folks who rolled up their sleeves, got down in the soil, and joined me in the work.

Karen Hill: my assistant and dear friend. Loyal, creative, and always willing to help. You are invaluable.

Liz Heaney: my longtime editor. Though I wince when you prune, no shears are truer.

Steve Halliday: Another great job with the discussion guide.

The staff and members of the Oak Hills Church: What a field of faith!

The '94 edition of the Young Messiah Tour: Thanks for listening to these words before they were weeded.

Word Publishing: No team does better!

Lynn Anderson: My first purchase after leaving college was a set of your sermons on the Gospel of John. Because you loved John then, I love him today.

Steve and Cheryl Green: For doing all that you do so I could do this.

Lindsey Hill, Lois Jeane Davis, Jeanette Rudd, Becky Bryant, Tina Chisholm, and Francis Rose, the staff of UpWords Radio Ministry: angels on loan.

Sue Ann Jones: What a sharp eye and skillful pen!

Jenna, Andrea, and Sara: May you always be rooted in the soil of his love.

And for Denalyn, my wife: For making the grass so green on this side of the fence that the other side looks barren.

And finally, for you, the reader: Of the many gardens you could visit, you've chosen to visit this one. I'm honored. I hope your stay is delightful. May you find familiar things new, and new things familiar.

Stay as long as you like. If you find a rose worth keeping, feel free to clip it. If you find a few worth sharing, please do.

And who knows? Adam heard God speak in a garden; maybe the same will happen to you.

When you were in trouble, you called,
and I saved you.
I answered you with thunder.

Psalm 81:7

His Voice, Our Choice

A GOOD PILOT does what it takes to get his passengers home.

I saw a good example of this while flying somewhere over Missouri. The flight attendant told us to take our seats because of impending turbulence. It was a rowdy flight, and the folks weren't quick to respond; so she warned us again. "The flight is about to get bumpy. For your own safety, take your seats."

Most did. But a few didn't, so she changed her tone, "Ladies and gentlemen, for your own good, take your seats."

I thought everyone was seated. But apparently I was wrong, for the next voice we heard was that of the pilot. "This is Captain Brown," he advised. "People have gotten hurt by going to the bathroom instead of staying in their seats. Let's be very clear about our responsibilities. My job is to get you through the storm. Your job is to do what I say. Now sit down and buckle up!"

About that time the bathroom door opened, and a red-faced fellow with a sheepish grin exited and took his seat.

Was the pilot wrong in what he did? Was the pilot being insensitive or unthoughtful? No, just the opposite. He would rather the man be safe and embarrassed than uninformed and hurt.

Good pilots do what it takes to get their passengers home.

So does God. Here is a key question. How far do you want God to go in getting your attention? If God has to choose between your eternal safety and your earthly comfort, which do you hope he chooses? Don't answer too quickly. Give it some thought.

If God sees you standing when you should be sitting, if God sees you at risk rather than safe, how far do you want him to go in getting your attention?

What if he moved you to another land? (As he did Abraham.) What if he called you out of retirement? (Remember Moses?) How about the voice of an angel or the bowel of a fish? (À la Gideon and Jonah.) How about a promotion like Daniel's or a demotion like Samson's?

God does what it takes to get our attention. Isn't that the message of the Bible? Isn't that *the* message of the Bible? The relentless pursuit of God. God on the hunt. God in the search. Peeking under the bed for hiding kids, stirring the bushes for lost sheep. Cupping hand to mouth and shouting into the canyon. Wrestling with us Jacobs in the muddy Jabboks of life.

For all its peculiarities and unevenness, the Bible has a simple story. God made man. Man rejected God. God won't give up until he wins him back. From Moses in Moab to John on Patmos, the voice can be heard: "I'm the pilot. You're the passenger. My job is to get you home. Your job is to do what I say."

God is as creative as he is relentless. The same hand that sent manna to Israel sent Uzzah to his death. The same hand that set the children free from Israel also sent them captive to Babylon. Both kind and stern. Tender and tough. Faithfully firm. Patiently urgent. Eagerly tolerant. Softly shouting. Gently thundering.

Gentle thunder.

That's how John saw Jesus. John's Gospel has two themes: the voice of God and the choice of man. And since this book is based on John, you'll see the same tandem: His voice. Our choice.

Jesus said, "I am the bread that gives life. I am the light of the world. I am the resurrection and the life. I am the light of the world. I am the door. I am the way, the truth, and the life. I will come back and take you with me."

Jesus proclaiming—ever offering but never forcing:

> Standing over the crippled man: "Do you want to be well?" (John 5:6).
>
> Eye to eye with the blind man, now healed: "Do you believe in the Son of Man?" (John 9:35).
>
> Near the tomb of Lazarus, probing the heart of Martha: "Everyone who lives and believes in me will never die. Martha, do you believe this?" (John 11:26).
>
> Testing Pilate's motive: "Is that your own question, or did others tell you about me?" (John 18:34).

The first time John hears Jesus speak, Jesus asks a question, "What are you looking for?" (John 1:38). Among Jesus' last words is yet another: "Do you love me?" (21:17).

This is the Jesus John remembers. The honest questions. The thundering claims. The gentle touch. Never going where not invited, but once invited never stopping until he's finished, until a choice has been made.

God will whisper. He will shout. He will touch and tug. He will take away our burdens; he'll even take away our blessings. If there are a thousand steps between us and him, he will take all but one. But he will leave the final one for us. The choice is ours.

Please understand. His goal is not to make you happy. His goal is to make you his. His goal is not to get you what you want; it is to get you what you need. And if that means a jolt or two to get you in your seat, then be jolted. Earthly discomfort is a glad swap for heavenly peace. Jesus said, "In this world you will have trouble, but be brave! I have defeated the world" (John 16:33).

How could he speak with such authority? What gave him the right to take command? Simple. He, like the pilot, knows what we don't, and he can see what we can't.

What did the pilot know? He knew how to fly the plane.

What did the pilot see? Storm clouds ahead.

What does God know? He knows how to navigate history.

What does God see? I think you get the message.

God wants to get you home safely.

Just think of him as your pilot. Think of yourself as his passenger. Consider this book as in-flight reading—and think twice before you get up to go to the potty.

His Voice

Once there was a man who dared God to speak.

Burn the bush like you did for Moses, God.
   And I will follow.

Collapse the walls like you did for Joshua, God.
   And I will fight.

Still the waves like you did on Galilee, God.
   And I will listen.

And so the man sat by a bush, near a wall, close to the sea
   and waited for God to speak.

And God heard the man, so God answered.
He sent fire, not for a bush, but for a church.
      He brought down a wall, not of brick, but of sin.
            He stilled a storm, not of the sea, but of a soul.

And God waited for the man to respond.
And he waited . . .
      And he waited . . .
            And waited.

But because the man was looking at bushes, not hearts;
      bricks and not lives, seas and not souls,
            he decided that God had done nothing.
Finally he looked to God and asked, *Have you lost your power?*
And God looked at him and said, *Have you lost your hearing?*

In the beginning was the Word. . . .
The Word became a human and lived among us.

John 1:1, 14

The Author of Life
The God Who Dreamed

SEATED AT THE great desk, the Author opens the large book. It has no words. It has no words because no words exist. No words exist because no words are needed. There are no ears to hear them, no eyes to read them. The Author is alone.

And so he takes the great pen and begins to write. Like an artist gathers his colors and a woodcarver his tools, the Author assembles his words.

There are three. Three single words. Out of these three will pour a million thoughts. But on these three words, the story will suspend. He takes his quill and spells the first. *T-i-m-e*.

Time did not exist until he wrote it. He, himself, is timeless, but his story would be encased in time. The story would have a first rising of the sun, a first shifting of the sand. A beginning . . . and an end. A final chapter. He knows it before he writes it.

Time. A footspan on eternity's trail.

Slowly, tenderly, the Author writes the second word. A name. *A-d-a-m*.

As he writes, he sees him, the first Adam. Then he sees all the others. In a thousand eras in a thousand lands, the Author sees them. Each Adam. Each child. Instantly loved. Permanently loved. To each he assigns a time. To each he appoints a place. No accidents. No coincidences. Just design.

The Author makes a promise to these unborn: *In my image, I will make you. You will be like me. You will laugh. You will create. You will never die. And you will write.*

They must. For each life is a book, not to be read, but rather a story to be written. The Author starts each life story, but each life will write his or her own ending.

What a dangerous liberty. How much safer it would have been to finish the story for each Adam. To script every option. It would have been simpler. It would have been safer. But it would not have been love. Love is only love if chosen.

So the Author decides to give each child a pen. "Write carefully," he whispers.

Lovingly, deliberately, he writes the third word, already feeling the pain. *E-m-m-a-n-u-e-l.*

The greatest mind in the universe imagined time. The truest judge granted Adam a choice. But it was love that gave Emmanuel, God with us.

The Author would enter his own story.

The Word would become flesh. He, too, would be born. He, too, would be human. He, too, would have feet and hands. He, too, would have tears and trials.

And most importantly, he, too, would have a choice. Emmanuel would stand at the crossroads of life and death and make a choice.

The Author knows well the weight of that decision. He pauses as he writes the page of his own pain. He could stop. Even the Author has a choice. But how can a Creator not create? How can a Writer not write? And how can Love not love? So he chooses life, though it means death, with hope that his children will do the same.

And so the Author of Life completes the story. He drives the spike in the flesh and rolls the stone over the grave. Knowing the choice he will make, knowing the choice all Adams will make, he pens, "The End," then closes the book and proclaims the beginning.

"Let there be light!"

I saw the Spirit come down in the form of a dove and rest on him. Until then I did not know who the Christ was. But the God who sent me to baptize with water told me, "You will see the Spirit come down and rest on a man; he is the One who will baptize with the Holy Spirit." I have seen this happen, and I tell you the truth: This is the Son of God.

John 1:32–34

The Hound of Heaven
The God Who Pursues

JOHN THE BAPTIST saw a dove and believed. James Whittaker saw a sea gull and believed. Who's to say the one who sent the first didn't send the second?

James Whittaker was a member of the handpicked crew that flew the B-17 Flying Fortress captained by Eddie Rickenbacker. Anybody who remembers October of 1942 remembers the day Rickenbacker and his crew were reported lost at sea.

Somewhere over the Pacific, out of radio range, the plane ran out of fuel and crashed into the ocean. The nine men spent the next month floating in three rafts. They battled the heat, the storms, and the water. Sharks, some ten feet long, would ram their nine-foot boats. After only eight days their rations were eaten or destroyed by saltwater. It would take a miracle to survive.

One morning after their daily devotions, Rickenbacker leaned his head back against the raft and pulled his hat over his eyes. A bird landed on his head. He peered out from under his hat. Every eye was on him. He instinctively knew it was a sea gull.

Rickenbacker caught it, and the crew ate it. The bird's intestines were used for bait to catch fish . . . and the crew survived to tell the story. A story about a stranded crew with no hope or help in sight.

A story about prayers offered and prayers answered. A story about a visitor from an unknown land traveling a great distance to give his life as a sacrifice.

A story of salvation.

A story much like our own. Weren't we, like the crew, stranded? Weren't we, like the crew, praying? And weren't we, like the crew, rescued by a visitor we've never seen through a sacrifice we'll never forget?

You may have heard the Rickenbacker story before. You may have even heard it from me. You may have read it in one of my books. Coreen Schwenk did. She was engaged to the only crew member who did not survive, young Sgt. Alex Kacymarcyck. As a result of a 1985 reunion of the crew, Mrs. Schwenk learned that the widow of James Whittaker lived only eighty miles from her house. The two women met and shared their stories.

After reading this story in my book *In the Eye of the Storm*, Mrs. Schwenk felt compelled to write to me. The real miracle, she informed me, was not a bird on the head of Eddie Rickenbacker but a change in the heart of James Whittaker. The greatest event of that day was not the rescue of a crew but the rescue of a soul.

James Whittaker was an unbeliever. The plane crash didn't change his unbelief. The days facing death didn't cause him to reconsider his destiny. In fact, Mrs. Whittaker said her husband grew irritated with John Bartak, a crew member who continually read his Bible privately and aloud.

But his protests didn't stop Bartak from reading. Nor did Whittaker's resistance stop the Word from penetrating his soul. Unknown to Whittaker, the soil of his heart was being plowed. For it was one morning after a Bible reading that the sea gull landed on Captain Rickenbacker's head.

And at that moment Jim became a believer.

I chuckled when I read the letter. Not at the letter; I believe every word of it. Nor at James Whittaker. I have every reason to believe his conversion was real. But I had to chuckle at . . . please excuse me . . . I had to chuckle at God.

Isn't that just like him? Who would go to such extremes to save a soul? Such an effort to get a guy's attention. The rest of the world is occupied with Germany and Hitler. Every headline is reporting the actions of Roosevelt and Churchill. The globe is locked in a battle for freedom . . . and the Father is in the Pacific sending a missionary pigeon to save a soul. Oh, the lengths to which God will go to get our attention and win our affection.

In 1893 Francis Thompson, a Roman Catholic poet, described God as the "Hound of Heaven":

> I fled Him, down the nights and down the days;
> I fled Him, down the arches of the years;
> I fled Him, down the labyrinthian ways
>   Of my own mind; and in the mist of tears
> I hid from Him, and under running laughter,
>   Up vestaed hopes I sped
> And shot precipitated
> Adown Titanic glooms.[1]

Thompson speaks of Jesus as "that tremendous lover, pursuing me with his love." Jesus follows with "unhurrying chase and unperturbed pace, deliberate speed, majestic instancy." And in the end Jesus speaks, reminding us, "Alas, thou knowest not how little worthy of any love thou art. Whom wilt thou find to love ignoble thee, save me, save only me? For that which I took from thee I did but take, not for thy harm but that thou might seek it in my arms."[2]

Do you have room for such a picture of God? Can you see God as the "tremendous lover, pursuing us with his love"? During the first week of Jesus' ministry he calls his first disciples. Why do they come? Who influences their choice? Note the verbs associated with Jesus in John 1.

> Jesus turned . . . v. 38
> Jesus asked . . . v. 38
> Jesus answered . . . v. 39
> Jesus looked . . . v. 42

Jesus decided . . . v. 43

Jesus found . . . v. 43

It's clear who does the work. If anyone is in Christ, it is because Christ has called him or her. Christ may use a sermon. He may inspire a conversation. He may speak through a song. But in every case Christ is the One who calls.

Consider these examples:

One evening, John Wesley entered a brief account in his journal. He wrote of going unwillingly to a meeting of a society in Aldersgate Street in London where one of the group was reading the preface to Luther's *Commentary on the Epistle to the Romans*. Did you get the picture? He went unwillingly, a stranger to a small group, listening to a two-hundred-year-old piece of literature. And yet he wrote, "About a quarter before nine I felt my heart strangely warmed."[3]

In his classic work *Confessions*, Augustine tells of the turning point in his life. Torn between the temptation of a mistress and the quiet call of the Spirit of God, he was sitting on a bench under a fig tree, his Bible open, his eyesight fogged by tears. He heard a voice calling from a neighboring house, "Pick it up . . . Pick it up . . ."

The voice was not addressed to Augustine; no doubt children were calling to one another in a game. However, the voice stirred Augustine in his solitude, and he did what the voice commanded. He picked up his Bible and read it. The passage before him was Romans 13:13–14: "Let us live in a right way, like people who belong to the day. We should not have wild parties or get drunk. There should be no sexual sins of any kind, no fighting or jealousy. But clothe yourselves with the Lord Jesus Christ and forget about satisfying your sinful self."

He heard the voice of God, bade farewell to his mistress, and followed Christ.[4]

Novelist Frederick Buechner was twenty-seven years old and living alone in New York City, trying to write a book when he, a non-churchgoer, went to church. On impulse. The preacher spoke on the topic of crowning Christ in your heart. Jesus refused the crown of Satan in the wilderness but accepts the crown of his people when we confess him. The preacher went on for quite some time with words that sounded nice but didn't stick.

But then he said something that Buechner never forgot. I'll let him tell you:

> And then with his head bobbing up and down so that his glasses tittered, he said in his odd sandy voice, the voice of an old nurse, that the coronation of Jesus took place among confession and tears and, as God is my witness, great laughter, he said. Jesus is crowned among confession and tears and great laughter, and at that phrase great laughter, for reasons I have never satisfactorily understood, the great wall of China crumbled and Atlantis rose up out of the sea, and on Madison Avenue, at 73rd Street, tears leapt from my eyes as though I had been struck in the face.[5]

Too bizarre? Think for a moment about your world. Remember that voice, that face, that event? Wasn't there a time when the common bush of the wilderness was ablaze with a voice that left you stuttering? For Wesley it was a reading, for Augustine the voice of a child, and for Buechner a call to laughter.

And for you? The extended hand of a bag woman? The birth of your child? The tears of the widower? The explosion of a sunset? The impassioned sermon that moved all? The dull sermon that moved none—but you?

It isn't the circumstance that matters; it is God in the circumstance. It isn't the words; it is God speaking them. It wasn't the mud that healed the eyes of the blind man; it was the finger of God in the mud. The cradle and the cross were as common as grass. What made them holy was the One laid upon them. The dove and the gull weren't special. But the One who sent them was.

Amazing, the lengths to which God will go to get our attention.

Nathanael said to Philip, "Can anything good come from Nazareth?"
Philip answered, "Come and see."

John 1:46

Come and See

The God Who Came

THE FIRST ANSWER given the first doubter is the only one necessary.

When Nathanael doubted that anything good could come out of Nazareth, Philip's response was simply, "Come and see."

Nathanael's question remains: "Can anything good come out of Nazareth?" Have two thousand years of Christianity changed this world? Is the life of the young Nazarene carpenter really worth considering?

The question still lingers.

And the answer of Philip still suffices. Come and see.

Come and see the rock that has withstood the winds of time. Hear his voice.

The truth undaunted,
grace unspotted,
loyalty undeterred.

Come and see the flame that tyrants and despots have not extinguished.

Come and see the passion that oppression has not squelched.

Come and see the hospitals and orphanages rising beside the crumbling ruins of humanism and atheism. Come and see what Christ has done.

Come and see the great drama threading through twenty centuries of history and art.

> Handel weeping as he composes *The Messiah*.
>
> Da Vinci sighing as he portrays the Last Supper.
>
> Michelangelo stepping back from the rock-carved David and bidding the stone to speak.

Can anything good come out of Nazareth? Come and see.

> See Wilberforce fighting to free slaves in England—because he believed.
>
> See Washington at prayer in Valley Forge—because he believed.
>
> See Lincoln alone with a dog-eared Bible—because he believed.

Can anything good come out of Nazareth? Come and see.
Come and see the changed lives:
> the alcoholic now dry,
>> the embittered now joyful,
>>> the shamed now forgiven.

Come and see the marriages rebuilt, the orphans embraced, the imprisoned inspired.

Journey into the jungles and hear the drums beating in praise.

Sneak into the corners of communism and find believers worshiping under threat of death.

Walk on death row and witness the prisoner condemned by man yet liberated by God.

Venture into the gulags and dungeons of the world and hear the songs of the saved refusing to be silent.

Can anything good come out of Nazareth?

Come and see the pierced hand of God touch the most common heart, wipe the tear from the wrinkled face, and forgive the ugliest sin.

Come and see.

Come and see the tomb. The tomb once occupied, now vacant; the grave once sealed, now empty. Cynics have raised their theories, doubters have raised their questions. But their musings continue to melt in the bright light of Easter morning.

Come and see. He avoids no seeker. He ignores no probe. He fears no search. Come and see. Nathanael came. And Nathanael saw. And Nathanael discovered, "Teacher, you are the Son of God; you are the King of Israel."

It was dark now, and Jesus had not yet come to them.

John 6:17

Miracle at Midnight
The God of Perfect Timing

LET ME SHARE with you the thoughts of a young missionary. What follows are phrases excerpted from his journal during his first month on the mission field.

On the flight to the field he writes: "The next time this plane touches down, I will be a missionary. For good! Yes, finally. To God be the glory."

The second day he reflects: "I keep reminding myself that the homesickness is temporary—it comes with the weariness and adjustments. That doesn't remove it, though. I must remember the reason I'm here. Not for my own joy or gain, but for the growth of God's kingdom."

By day number three his spirits are up: "God, it's a grand blessing to serve you. The people are so friendly . . . the mountains are so pretty . . . our friends are so gracious."

But on the fourth day his spirits sag: "It's difficult for us to think about home. We cried this morning."

On the fifth day he doesn't rebound: "Today is not so clear. The clouds have buried the mountains. The sky is gray."

By day six, the storm is coming in: "Yesterday was the toughest day thus far. The newness is gone. I'm tired of this language. We were blue all day. We could hardly think of our family and friends without weeping."

On the eighth day the waves have crested, and the winds are blowing: "This hotel room which has been our home is cold and impersonal. The tall ceiling, the strange walls . . . the unfamiliar surroundings. I held my wife as she wept, and we both confessed the ugliness of the thought of spending the rest of our lives in this foreign country. It's hard. We're so far from home."

By the tenth day the gales are at full force: "Doggone it, I know God is guiding us, I know he has a plan for us, but it's so hard. When will we find a house? How will we learn this language? Lord, forgive my sorry attitude."

And just when you'd think it couldn't get any darker: "I wish I could say I'm thrilled to be here. I'm not. I'm only willing to be here. This last week was as tough as I've ever had anywhere. My commitment to be a missionary feels like a prison sentence."

I know well the frustration behind those words—I wrote them. I remember my confusion. Hadn't Denalyn and I obeyed God? Didn't God send us to Brazil? Wasn't this his plan? Weren't we just doing what we were told?

Doesn't peace always follow obedience? (Why are you smiling?)

Perhaps the disciples had the same expectation. They only did what they were told. Jesus told them to get into the boat, so they did. They didn't question the order; they simply obeyed it. They could have objected. After all, it was evening and darkness was only minutes away. But Jesus told them to get into the boat, so they did.

What was the result of their obedience? John's crisp description will tell you: "That evening Jesus' followers went down to

Lake Galilee. It was dark, and Jesus had not yet come to them. The followers got into a boat and started across the lake to Capernaum. By now a strong wind was blowing, and the waves on the lake were getting bigger" (John 6:16–17).

What a chilling phrase, "Jesus had not yet come to them." Caught in the storm of the "not yet." They did exactly what Jesus said, and look what it got them! A night on a storm-tossed sea with their Master somewhere on the shore.

It's one thing to suffer for doing wrong. Something else entirely to suffer for doing right. But it happens. And when the storm bursts, it washes away the naive assumption that if I do right, I will never suffer.

Just ask the faithful couple whose crib is empty and whose womb is barren.

Just ask the businessman whose honest work was rewarded with runaway inflation.

Just ask the student who took a stand for the truth and got mocked, the Sunday school teacher who took a class and got tired, the husband who took a chance and forgave his wife, only to be betrayed again.

And so the winds blow.

And so the boat bounces.

And so the disciples wonder, "Why the storm, and where is Jesus?" It's bad enough to be in the storm, but to be in the storm alone?

The disciples had been on the sea for about nine hours.[1] John tells us they rowed four miles (John 6:19). That's a long night. How many times did they search the darkness for their Master? How many times did they call out his name?

Why did he take so long?

Why does he take so long?

I think I hear the answer in the next room. As I write, I can hear my ten-year-old daughter playing the piano. She has just begun her second year. Her teacher recently upped the ante. No more rinky-dink songs; no more nursery rhymes. It's time to move on. Now the rhythm varies, the notes sharpen, and the key changes. It will be pleasant to the ear . . . someday.

But today the notes come slowly and the fingers drag and Jenna would quit if given the chance. Am I a cruel father for urging her to continue? Am I unfair in prodding her to practice? I'm not oblivious to her struggle. I can hear it. I'm not blind to her tears. I can see them. I know she'd be much happier swimming or reading or watching television.

Then why do I let her suffer?

Because I love her. And I know that a struggle today will result in music tomorrow.

Mark tells us that during the storm Jesus "saw his followers struggling" (Mark 6:48). Through the night he saw them. Through the storm he saw them. And like a loving father he waited. He waited until the right time, until the right moment. He waited until he knew it was time to come, and then he came.

What made it the right time? I don't know. Why was the ninth hour better than the fourth or fifth? I can't answer that. Why does God wait until the money is gone? Why does he wait until the sickness has lingered? Why does he choose to wait until the other side of the grave to answer the prayers for healing?

I don't know. I only know his timing is always right. I can only say he will do what is best. "God will always give what is right to his people who cry to him night and day, and he will not be slow to answer them" (Luke 18:7).

Though you hear nothing, he is speaking. Though you see nothing, he is acting. With God there are no accidents. Every incident is intended to bring us closer to him.

Can I give a great example? The direct route from Egypt to Israel would take only eleven days by foot.[2] But God took the Israelites on the long road, which took forty years. Why did he do that? Read carefully the explanation.

Remember how the LORD your God has led you in the
desert for these forty years, taking away your pride and
testing you, because he wanted to know what was in your
heart. He took away your pride when he let you get hungry, and then he fed you with manna, which neither you
nor your ancestors had ever seen. This was to teach you
that a person does not live by eating only bread, but by
everything the LORD says. During these forty years, your
clothes did not wear out, and your feet did not swell. Know
in your heart that the LORD your God corrects you as a
parent corrects a child. (Deut. 8:2–4)

Look what God did in the desert. He took away the Israelites'
pride. He tested their hearts. He proved that he would provide for
them. Did God want the children of Israel to reach the Promised
Land? Of course. But he was more concerned that they arrive prepared than that they arrive soon.

It reminds me of the often-told story of two maestros who attended a concert to hear a promising young soprano. One
commented on the purity of her voice. The other responded, "Yes,
but she'll sing better once her heart is broken." There are certain
passions only learned by pain. And there are times when God, knowing that, allows us to endure the pain for the sake of the song.

So what does God do while we are enduring the pain? What
does he do while we are in the storm? You'll love this. He prays for
us. Jesus wasn't in the boat because he had gone to the hills to pray
(see Mark 6:46). Jesus prayed. That is remarkable. It is even more
remarkable that Jesus didn't stop praying when his disciples were
struggling. When he heard their cries, he remained in prayer.

Why? Two possible answers. Either he didn't care, or he believed in prayer. I think you know the correct choice.

And you know what? Jesus hasn't changed. He still prays for
his disciples. "Because Jesus lives forever, he will never stop serving as priest. So he is able always to save those who come to God

through him because he always lives, asking God to help them" (Heb. 7:24–25).

So where does that leave us? While Jesus is praying and we are in the storm, what are we to do? Simple. We do what the disciples did. We row. The disciples rowed most of the night. Mark says they "struggled hard" to row the boat (Mark 6:48). The word *struggle* is elsewhere translated as "tormented." Wasn't easy. Wasn't glamorous.

Much of life is spent rowing. Getting out of bed. Fixing lunches. Turning in assignments. Changing diapers. Paying bills. Routine. Regular. More struggle than strut. More wrestling than resting.

When Denalyn and I went to Brazil, we thought the life of a missionary was one of daily charm and fascination. A Christian Indiana Jones. We learned otherwise.

You have, too? You thought marriage was going to be a lifelong date? You thought having kids was going to be like baby-sitting? You thought the company who hired you wanted to hear all the ideas you had in college?

Then you learned otherwise. The honeymoon ended. The IRS called, and the boss wanted you to spend the week in Muleshoe, Texas. Much of life is spent rowing.

Oh, there are moments of glamour, days of celebration. We have our share of feasts, but we also have our share of baloney sandwiches. And to have the first we must endure the second.

As things turned out, Denalyn and I had five wonderful years in Brazil. And we learned that at the right time, God comes. In the right way, he appears. So don't bail out. Don't give up! Don't lay down the oars! He is too wise to forget you, too loving to hurt you. When you can't see him, trust him. He is praying a prayer that he himself will answer.

Jesus knew that the father had given him power over everything and that he had come from God and was going back to God. So during the meal Jesus stood up and took off his outer clothing. Taking a towel, he wrapped it around his waist. Then he poured water into a bowl and began to wash the followers' feet, drying them with the towel that was wrapped around him.

John 13:3–5

The Secret of Forgiveness

The God of Great Grace

IT'S NOT EASY watching Jesus wash these feet.

To see the hands of God massaging the toes of men is, well . . . it's not right. The disciples should be washing his feet. Nathanael should pour the water. Andrew should carry the towel. But they don't. No one does. Rather than serve, they argue over which one is the greatest (Luke 22:24).

What disappointment their words must have brought Jesus.

"I'm the number one apostle."

"No, I'm much more spiritual than you."

"You guys are crazy. I brought more people to hear Jesus than anyone."

As they argue, the basin sits in the corner, untouched. The towel lies on the floor, unused. The servant's clothing hangs on the wall, unworn. Each disciple sees these things. Each disciple knows their purpose. But no one moves, except Jesus. As they bicker, he stands.

But he doesn't speak. He removes his robe and takes the servant's wrap off of the wall. Taking the pitcher, he pours the water into the basin. He kneels before them with the basin and sponge and begins to wash. The towel that covers his waist is also the towel that dries their feet.

It's not right.

Isn't it enough that these hands will be pierced in the morning? Must they scrub grime tonight? And the disciples . . . do they deserve to have their feet washed? Their affections have waned; their loyalties have wavered.

We want to say . . .

Look at John, Jesus. This is the same John who told you to destroy a city. The same John who demanded that you censure a Christ-follower who wasn't in your group. Why are you washing his feet?

And James! Skip James. He wanted the seat of honor. He and his brother wanted special treatment. Don't give it to him. Give him the towel. Let him wash his own feet. Let him learn a lesson.

And while you are at it, Jesus, you might as well skip Philip. He told you there wasn't enough food to feed the large crowd. You tested him, and he flunked. You gave him the chance, and he blew it.

And Peter? Sure, these are the feet that walked on water, but they're also the feet that thrashed about in the deep. He didn't believe you. Sure he confessed you as the Christ, but he's also the one who told you that you didn't have to die. He doesn't deserve to have his feet washed.

None of them do. When you were about to be stoned in Nazareth, did they come to your defense? When the Pharisees took up rocks to kill you, did they volunteer to take your place? You know what they have done.

And what's more, you know what they are about to do!

You can already hear them snoring in the garden. They say they'll stay awake, but they won't. You'll sweat blood; they'll saw logs.

You can hear them sneaking away from the soldiers. They make promises tonight. They'll make tracks tomorrow.

Look around the table, Jesus. Out of the twelve, how many will stand with you in Pilate's court? How many will share with you the Roman whip? And when you fall under the weight of the cross, which disciple will be close enough to spring to your side and carry your burden?

None of them will. Not one. A stranger will be called because no disciple will be near.

Don't wash their feet, Jesus. Tell them to wash yours.

That's what we want to say. Why? Because of the injustice? Because we don't want to see our King behaving as a servant? God on his hands and knees, his hair hanging around his face? Do we object because we don't want to see God washing feet?

Or do we object because we don't want to do the same?

Stop and think for a minute. Don't we have some people like the disciples in our world?

Double-tongued promise-breakers. Fair-weather friends. What they said and what they did are two different things. Oh, maybe they didn't leave you alone at the cross, but maybe they left you alone with the bills . . .

> or your question
>> or your illness.

Or maybe you were just left at the altar,
> or in the cold,
>> holding the bag.

Vows forgotten. Contract abandoned.

Logic says: "Put up your fists."

Jesus says: "Fill up the basin."

Logic says: "Bloody his nose."

Jesus says: "Wash his feet."

Logic says: "She doesn't deserve it."

Jesus says: "You're right, but you don't, either."

I don't understand how God can be so kind to us, but he is. He kneels before us, takes our feet in his hands, and washes them. Please understand that in washing the disciples' feet, Jesus is washing ours. You and I are in this story. We are at the table. That's us being cleansed, not from our dirt, but from our sins.

And the cleansing is not just a gesture; it is a necessity. Listen to what Jesus said: "If I don't wash your feet, you are not one of my people" (John 13:8).

Jesus did not say, "If you don't wash your feet." Why not? Because we cannot. We cannot cleanse our own filth. We cannot remove our own sin. Our feet must be in his hands.

Don't miss the meaning here. To place our feet in the basin of Jesus is to place the filthiest parts of our lives into his hands. In the ancient East, people's feet were caked with mud and dirt. The servant of the feast saw to it that the feet were cleaned. Jesus is assuming the role of the servant. He will wash the grimiest part of your life.

If you let him. The water of the Servant comes only when we confess that we are dirty. Only when we confess that we are caked with filth, that we have walked forbidden trails and followed the wrong paths.

We tend to be proud like Peter and resist. "I'm not that dirty, Jesus. Just sprinkle a few drops on me and I'll be fine."

What a lie! "If we say we have no sin, we are fooling ourselves, and the truth is not in us" (1 John 1:8).

We will never be cleansed until we confess we are dirty. We will never be pure until we admit we are filthy. And we will never be able to wash the feet of those who have hurt us until we allow Jesus, the one we have hurt, to wash ours.

You see, that is the secret of forgiveness. You will never forgive anyone more than God has already forgiven you. Only by letting him wash your feet can you have strength to wash those of another.

Still hard to imagine? Is it still hard to consider the thought of forgiving the one who hurt you?

If so, go one more time to the room. Watch Jesus as he goes from disciple to disciple. Can you see him? Can you hear the water splash? Can you hear him shuffle on the floor to the next person? Good. Keep that image.

John 13:12 says, "When he had finished washing their feet . . ."

Please note, he *finished* washing their feet. That means he left no one out. Why is that important? Because that also means he washed the feet of Judas. Jesus washed the feet of his betrayer. He gave his traitor equal attention. In just a few hours Judas's feet would guide the Roman guard to Jesus. But at this moment they are caressed by Christ.

That's not to say it was easy for Jesus.

That's not to say it is easy for you.

That is to say that God will never call you to do what he hasn't already done.

I am the bread that gives life.

John 6:35

The Bread of Life
The God Who Feeds My Soul

WHAT BREAD IS to hunger, Jesus claims to be for the soul.

Travel to almost any country and sit in any restaurant and they'll serve you bread. Bread is a staple. If the poor have nothing, they have bread. If the rich have everything, they still have bread. Bread is not a regional food nor a national dish. No country claims to be the exclusive source of bread. It may be in the form of a tortilla in Mexico or a bagel in New York, but bread is available everywhere. So is Christ. He is not bound by boundaries. No country claims him. No region owns him. No nation monopolizes him. He is everywhere at the same time. Universally available.

Bread is eaten daily. Some fruits are available only in season. Some drinks are made only at holidays. Not so with bread. And not so with Jesus. He should be brought to our table every day. We let him nourish our hearts, not just in certain months or on special events, but daily.

Bread is served in many forms. It's toasted, jellied, buttered, flattened, and grilled. It can be a sandwich, sweet roll, hot-dog bun, croissant, or dinner roll. Bread can meet many needs. So can Jesus. He adapts himself to meet our needs. He has a word for the lonely as well as for the popular. He has help for the physically ill and the emotionally ill. If your vision is clear, he can help you. If your vision is cloudy, he can help you. Jesus can meet each need.

Can you see why Jesus called himself the Bread of Life?

I can think of one other similarity. Consider how bread is made. Think about the process. Wheat grows in the field, then it is cut down, winnowed, and ground into flour. It passes through the fire of the oven and is then distributed around the world. Only by this process does bread become bread. Each step is essential. Eliminate the plant, and you have no wheat. Eliminate the winnowing, and you have no flour. Eliminate the fire, and you have no product. Eliminate the distribution, and you have no satisfaction. Each step is essential.

Now, consider Jesus. He grew up as a "small plant before the LORD" (Isa. 53:2). One of millions of boys on the planet. One of thousands in Israel. One of dozens in Nazareth. Indistinguishable from the person down the street or the child in the next chair. Had you seen him as a youngster, you wouldn't have thought he was the Son of God. You might have thought him polite or courteous or diligent, but God on earth? Not a chance. He was just a boy. One of hundreds. Like a staff of wheat in the wheat field.

But like wheat, he was cut down. Like chaff he was pounded and beaten. "He was wounded for the wrong we did; he was crushed for the evil we did" (Isa. 53:5). And like bread he passed through the fire. On the cross he passed though the fire of God's anger, not because of his sin, but because of ours. "The LORD has put on him the punishment for all the evil we have done" (Isa. 53:6).

Jesus experienced each part of the process of making bread: the growing, the pounding, the firing. And just as each is necessary for bread, each was also necessary for Christ to become the bread of life. "The Christ must suffer these things before he enters his glory" (Luke 24:26).

The next part of the process, the distribution, Christ leaves with us. We are the distributors. We can't force people to eat the bread, but we can make sure they have it. Yet, for some reason we are reluctant to do so. It's much easier to stay in the bakery than to get into the truck. As the following parable illustrates, we may not even know how to give the bread when someone requests it.

The Beggar and the Bread

A beggar came and sat before me. "I want bread," he said.

"How wise you are," I assured him. "Bread is what you need. And you have come to the right bakery." So I pulled my cookbook down from my shelf and began to tell him all I knew about bread.

I spoke of flour and wheat, of grain and barley. My knowledge impressed even me as I cited the measurements and recipe. When I looked up, I was surprised to see he wasn't smiling. "I just want bread," he said.

"How wise you are." I applauded his choice. "Follow me, and I'll show you our bakery." Down the hallowed halls I guided him, pausing to point out the rooms where the dough is prepared and the ovens where the bread is baked.

"No one has such facilities. We have bread for every need. But here is the best part," I proclaimed as I pushed open two swinging doors. "This is our room of inspiration." I knew he was moved as we stepped into the auditorium full of stained-glass windows.

The beggar didn't speak. I understood his silence. With my arm around his shoulder, I whispered, "It overwhelms me as well." I then leaped to the podium and struck my favorite pose behind the lectern. "People come from miles to hear me speak. Once a week my workers gather, and I read to them the recipe from the cookbook of life."

By now the beggar had taken a seat on the front row. I knew what he wanted. "Would you like to hear me?"

"No," he said, "but I would like some bread."

"How wise you are," I replied. And I led him to the front door of the bakery. "What I have to say next is very important," I told him as we stood outside. "Up and down this street you will find many bakeries. But take heed; they don't serve the true bread. I know of one who adds two spoons of salt rather than one. I know of another whose oven is three degrees too hot. They may call it bread," I warned, "but it's not according to the book."

The beggar turned and began walking away. "Don't you want bread?" I asked him.

He stopped, looked back at me, and shrugged, "I guess I lost my appetite."

I shook my head and returned to my office. "What a shame," I said to myself. "The world just isn't hungry for true bread anymore."

I don't know what is more incredible: that God packages the bread of life in the wrapper of a country carpenter or that he gives us the keys to the delivery truck. Both moves seem pretty risky. The carpenter did his part, however. And who knows—we may just learn to do ours.

He had always loved those who were his own in the world, and he loved them all the way to the end.

John 13:1

Give thanks to the LORD because he is good. His love continues forever.

Psalm 136:1

For Longer Than Forever
The God Who Loves Boldly

GOD, I HAVE a question: Why do you love your children? I don't want to sound irreverent, but only heaven knows how much pain we've brought you. Why do you tolerate us? You give us every breath we breathe, but do we thank you? You give us bodies beyond duplication, but do we praise you?

Seldom.

We complain about the weather. We bicker about our toys. We argue over who gets which continent and who has the best gender. Not a second passes when someone, somewhere, doesn't use your name to curse a hammered thumb or a bad call by the umpire. (As if it were your fault.)

You fill the world with food, but we blame you for hunger. You keep the earth from tilting and the arctics from thawing, but we accuse you of unconcern. You give us blue skies, and we demand rain. You give rain, and we demand sun. (As if we knew what was best anyway.)

We give more applause to a brawny ball-carrier than we do to the God who made us. We sing more songs to the moon than to the Christ who saved us. We are a gnat on the tail of one elephant in a galaxy of Africas, and yet we demand that you find us a parking place when we ask. And if you don't give us what we want, we say you don't exist. (As if our opinion matters.)

We pollute the world you loan us. We mistreat the bodies you gave us. We ignore the Word you sent us. And we killed the Son you became. We are spoiled babies who take and kick and pout and blaspheme.

You have every reason to abandon us.

I sure would! I would wash my hands of the whole mess and start over on Mars. But do you?

I see the answer in the rising of the sun. I hear the answer in the crashing of the waves. I feel the answer in the skin of a child.

Father, your love never ceases. Never. Though we spurn you, ignore you, disobey you, you will not change. Our evil cannot diminish your love. Our goodness cannot increase it. Our faith does not earn it anymore than our stupidity jeopardizes it. You don't love us less if we fail. You don't love us more if we succeed.

Your love never ceases.

How do we explain it?

Perhaps the answer is found in yet another question.

Moms: Why do you love your newborn? I know, I know; it's a silly question, but indulge me. Why do you?

For months this baby has brought you pain. She (or he!) made you break out in pimples and waddle like a duck. Because of her you craved sardines and crackers and threw up in the morning. She punched you in the tummy. She occupied space that wasn't hers and ate food she didn't fix.

You kept her warm. You kept her safe. You kept her fed. But did she say thank you?

Are you kidding? She's no more out of the womb than she starts to cry! The room is too cold, the blanket is too rough, the nurse is too mean. And who does she want? Mom.

Don't you ever get a break? I mean, who has been doing the work the last nine months? Why can't Dad take over? But no, Dad won't do. The baby wants Mom.

She didn't even tell you she was coming. She just came. And what a coming! She rendered you a barbarian. You screamed. You swore. You bit bullets and tore the sheets. And now look at you. Your back aches. Your head pounds. Your body is drenched in sweat. Every muscle strained and stretched.

You should be angry, but are you?

Far from it. On your face is a for-longer-than-forever love. She has done nothing for you; yet you love her. She's brought pain to your body and nausea to your morning, yet you treasure her. Her face is wrinkled and her eyes are dim, yet all you can talk about are her good looks and bright future. She's going to wake you up every night for the next six weeks, but that doesn't matter. I can see it on your face. You're crazy about her.

Why?

Why does a mother love her newborn? Because the baby is hers? Even more. Because the baby is her. Her blood. Her flesh. Her sinew and spine. Her hope. Her legacy. It bothers her not that the baby gives nothing. She knows a newborn is helpless, weak. She knows babies don't ask to come into this world.

And God knows we didn't either.

We are his idea. We are his. His face. His eyes. His hands. His touch. We are him. Look deeply into the face of every human being on earth, and you will see his likeness. Though some appear to be distant relatives, they are not. God has no cousins, only children.

We are, incredibly, the body of Christ. And though we may not act like our Father, there is no greater truth than this: We are his. Unalterably. He loves us. Undyingly. Nothing can separate us from the love of Christ (see Rom. 8:38–39).

Had God not said those words, I would be a fool to write them. But since he did, I'm a fool not to believe them. Nothing can separate us from the love of Christ . . . but how difficult it is for some to embrace this truth.

You think you've committed an act that places you outside his love. A treason. A betrayal. An aborted promise. You think he would love you more if you hadn't done it, right? You think he would love you more if you did more, right? You think if you were better his love would be deeper, right?

Wrong. Wrong. Wrong.

God's love is not human. His love is not normal. His love sees your sin and loves you still. Does he approve of your error? No. Do you need to repent? Yes. But do you repent for his sake or yours? Yours. His ego needs no apology. His love needs no bolstering.

And he could not love you more than he does right now.

When Jesus said, "I am he," they moved back and fell to the ground.

John 18:6

Lessons from the Garden
The God Who Reclaims the Sacred

MY FATHER TAUGHT me the lesson early: Don't create havoc in the garden. You can play ball in the yard. You can have races in the alley. You can build a fort in the tree. But the garden? Leave it alone.

It was a small garden, about the size of a walk-in closet. We grew nothing exotic, except for some mint. We'd soak the leaves in our summer tea. Though the vegetables were tasty, we didn't need to grow them. We could have bought them at the market. So why did Dad insist on having a garden?

He loved to see life. And a garden is a place of life, a place where buds explode and plants push back the soil. A place of turnips and tulips and tomato plants. A place worthy of love and protection. Flowers are fragile. Plants are precious. So yank the weeds and scatter the varmints. Put up a fence. Grow a hedge. Make a scarecrow.

"Son, whatever you do, don't go trampling around in the garden."

I hate to think I have anything in common with the devil, but I guess I do. Satan learned the same lesson: Don't mess around with a garden—especially a garden that belongs to the Father.

The Bible is the story of two gardens. Eden and Gethsemane. In the first, Adam took a fall. In the second, Jesus took a stand. In the first, God sought Adam. In the second, Jesus sought God. In Eden,

Adam hid from God. In Gethsemane, Jesus emerged from the tomb. In Eden, Satan led Adam to a tree that led to his death. From Gethsemane, Jesus went to a tree that led to our life.

Satan was never invited to the Garden of Eden. He did not belong there. He was not wanted there. He slithered as a snake into God's garden and infected God's children.

That's all he's done since. Hasn't he entered a few of your holy gardens?

We even call it "holy matrimony." The word altar implies the presence of God. Marriage was God's idea. The first wedding occurred in the first garden. But that doesn't make any difference to the devil. He snakes his way into every home with one desire—to destroy.

Sexual intimacy is God's gift. Virginity is a rose plucked from the garden, given by God and intended to be shared with your forever partner. Satan mocks such loyalty. He is the father of incest and abuse. He is the author of immorality. He is the pimp of the garden.

We give sacred oaths and make solemn promises. We vow to be a good parent, a true companion, and a loyal friend. But Satan's head turns when he hears a pledge. "We'll see about that," the father of lies smirks.

In God's eyes, a child is holy. The innocence of youth, the freshness of childhood, the joy of an infant. There was never a moment when Jesus turned away a child. But there has never been a child Satan didn't despise. He was killing babies to kill Moses. He was destroying infants to destroy the Christ. His tactics haven't changed. Millions of babies are still aborted; thousands of children are abused. Jesus said of Satan, "He was a murderer from the beginning" (John 8:44).

Is there a realm untouched by Satan? Is there a place unscarred by his sword? The church? The government? Children? Purity? Promises?

And you! And me! We are called to be holy. We were made to be holy. Set apart for his good work. We are the prized flowers of the garden. But is there one person who has not felt the foot of the intruder?

What Satan did in Eden, he does today. For that reason we need to know that what Jesus did in Gethsemane, he does today. He reclaims the holy. He will not long sit silent while Satan strip-mines the sacred. At the right moment Jesus stands and speaks. And when he stands and speaks, Satan stumbles and is silent.

Exactly what happened in Gethsemane.

John tells us that "Judas came there with a group of soldiers and some guards from the leading priests and Pharisees" (John 18:3). A bit of study reveals that Satan has masterminded a mighty coup. He has enlisted the muscle of each significant force of the drama—the Romans, the Jews, and the apostles.

First he has a "group of soldiers." The Greek word is *speira*. It has three possible meanings. It can signify a Roman cohort of three hundred men. It can refer to a cavalry and infantry totaling nineteen hundred soldiers. Or it can describe a detachment known as a *maniple*, which contained two hundred men.[1]

Amazing. I always had the impression that a handful of soldiers arrested Jesus. I was wrong. At minimum two hundred soldiers were dispatched to deal with a single carpenter and his eleven friends!

Also present were "some guards." This was the temple police. They were assigned to guard the holiest place during the busiest time of the year. They must have been among Israel's finest.

And then there was Judas. One of the inner circle. Not only had Satan recruited the Romans and the Jews, he had infiltrated the cabinet. Hell must have been rejoicing. There was no way Jesus could escape. Satan sealed every exit. His lieutenants anticipated every move, except one.

Jesus had no desire to run. He had no intent of escape. He hadn't come to the garden to retreat. What they found among the trees was no coward; what they found was a conqueror.

Note the dialogue that ensued:

> Knowing everything that would happen to him, Jesus went out and asked, "Who is it you are looking for?"

They answered, "Jesus from Nazareth."

"I am he," Jesus said. (Judas, the one who turned against Jesus, was standing there with them.) When Jesus said, "I am he," they moved back and fell to the ground.

Jesus asked them again, "Who is it you are looking for?"

They said, "Jesus of Nazareth."

"I told you that I am he," Jesus said. "So if you are looking for me, let the others go" (John 18:4–8).

Remarkable. They stand only a few feet from his face and don't recognize him. Not even Judas realizes who stands before them. What a truth. Seeing Jesus is more than a matter of the eyes; it is a matter of the heart. The enemy is next to Jesus and doesn't realize it.

He reveals himself. "I am he." His voice flicks the first domino, and down they tumble. Were the moment not so solemn it would be comic. These are the best soldiers with Satan's finest plan; yet one word from Jesus, and they fall down! The Roman guard becomes the Keystone Cops. Two hundred fighting men collapse into a noisy pile of shields, swords, and lamps. Don't miss the symbolism here: When Jesus speaks, Satan falls.

Doesn't matter who the evil one has recruited. Doesn't matter if he has infiltrated the government. Doesn't matter if he has seduced the temple. Doesn't matter if he has enlisted one of the original, handpicked apostles. The best of Satan melts as wax before the presence of Christ.

Jesus has to ask them again whom they seek. "Who are you after?"

When they answer that they are looking for Jesus of Nazareth, he instructs them, "So if you are looking for me, let the others go."

What is this? Jesus commanding them! A Jew instructing a Roman? A renegade directing the temple guard? We turn to the commander, expecting a reply. We look at Judas, awaiting his retort. We listen, expecting someone to announce, "You're not the one in charge here, Nazarene! We'll take whoever we want."

But not only are they silent, they are obedient. The apostles are set free.

Many players appear on the stage of Gethsemane. Judas and his betrayal. Peter and his sword. The disciples and their fears. The soldiers and their weapons. And though these are crucial, they aren't instrumental. The encounter is not between Jesus and the soldiers; it is between God and Satan. Satan dares to enter yet another garden, but God stands and Satan hasn't a prayer.

Don't miss the message:

> Our fight is not against people on earth but against the rulers and authorities and the powers of this world's darkness, against the spiritual powers of evil in the heavenly world (Eph. 6:12).

> The Son of God came for this purpose: to destroy the devil's work (1 John 3:8).

Don't miss the promises:

Satan falls in the presence of Christ. One word from his lips, and the finest army in the world collapsed.

Satan is silent in the proclamation of Christ. Not once did the enemy speak without Jesus' invitation. Before Christ, Satan has nothing to say.

Satan is powerless against the protection of Christ. "I have not lost any of the ones you gave me" (John 18:9).

When Jesus says he will keep you safe, he means it. Hell will have to get through him to get to you. Jesus is able to protect you. When he says he will get you home, he will get you home.

Let me conclude this chapter with an important question. Has Satan invaded a garden of your life? Has he profaned a holy part of your world? Your marriage? Your purity? Your honesty? Has he taken away from you a rose God gave? If so, let Jesus claim it back. Today. Now. Before you turn the page.

Forgive me for sounding urgent, but I am. Satan has no authority over you. If he has invaded a garden of your life, then invite Jesus to reclaim it. Open the gate to God. He will enter and do what he did at Gethsemane. He will pray, and he will protect.

Why don't you do that?

Don't know how? It's easy. I'll help you. Let's pray. You and me. I'll show you the way; you fill in the blanks.

> Precious Father, I praise your name. You have reclaimed so much in my life. I was lost, and you found me. I was confused, and you guided me. I had nothing to offer, but still you loved me.
>
> I confess that I still need help. I have a part of my life that needs your touch. Satan is battling for a garden in my heart. Don't let him win. Drive him out. He is a liar and has been since the beginning. Please defeat him. I'll give you the glory.
>
> Father, here is the area where I need your strength _____.

(And here is the place where I step out. I'll leave you and God to talk over the details. I'll be waiting for you in the next chapter.)

Don't let your hearts be troubled. Trust in God, and trust in me.

John 14:1

What to Do with Birthdays
The God of Grave Victory

THE COMMENTS BEGAN a couple of months ago.

> "Getting close to the top there, Max? Be careful. You pick up speed going downhill."

> "Almost there, eh, Max? Won't be long before you'll stop combing your hair and start arranging it."

Thirty days out, the word started to spread (so did my waist). Reminders became more frequent.

> "Look at it this way. All your life you've been taught to respect your elders. Now you don't have to respect anyone."

> "Don't worry, Max. Old age isn't bad when you consider the alternative."

This week the phone calls started to arrive.

> "I don't know whether to send condolences or congratulations."

"Able to make it out of bed this morning?" my brother asked today.

Actually I got out of bed earlier than normal this morning. On a typical birthday I might have waved off my morning jog and stayed in bed. But this isn't a typical birthday. And the thought of staying in bed never entered my mind. The thought of jogging an extra mile did, but not the thought of sleeping late.

It's the big one. The fortieth. In defiance of age, I stepped onto the dark streets and ran. I wanted to see what a forty-year-old jogger feels like. Know what I learned? He feels like a thirty-nine-year-old jogger.

But even though I feel the same as I did yesterday, my driver's license reminds me I am forty. They say that life begins at forty. But so do bad eyesight, arthritis, and the habit of telling the same joke three times to the same person.

Lucille Ball said the secret of staying young is to live honestly, eat slowly, and lie about your age. Easier said than done. It's hard to lie about the obvious. When you are young you make a lot of faces in the mirror. When you are old the mirror gets even. But I tell myself that turning forty isn't too bad; next to a Galapagos turtle I'm still a child.

I've gotten several laughs out of the comments that have come my way. Thought you might enjoy a few:

> "You know you are getting older when you try to straighten out the wrinkles in your socks only to find you aren't wearing any."

> "At twenty we don't care what the world thinks of us; at thirty we start to worry about what the world thinks of us; at forty we realize the world isn't thinking of us at all."

> "I've gotten to the age where I need my false teeth and hearing aid before I can ask where I left my glasses."

> "Forty is when you stop patting yourself on the back and start patting yourself under the chin."

I'll leave it to Dave Barry to sum it up:

> As a person starts reaching this milestone (your fortieth birthday) you need to take time to learn about the biological changes that are taking place within your body, so that you will be better able to understand and cope with the inevitable and completely natural elements of the aging process—the minor aches, pains, dental problems, intestinal malfunctions, muscle deterioration, emotional instability, memory lapses, hearing and vision loss, impotence, seizures, growths, prostate problems, greatly reduced limb function, massive coronary failure, death and, of course, painful hemorrhoid swelling—that can make up this exciting adventure we call "middle age."[1]

Growing older. Aging. We laugh about it, and we groan about it. We resist it, but we can't stop it. And with the chuckles and wrinkles come some serious thoughts and questions about what happens when we die. Is death when we go to sleep? Or is death when we finally wake up?

As a minister, I'm often asked to speak at funerals. I no longer have to ask the family what they want me to say; I already know. Oh, I may have to ask a question or two about the deceased, and that I do, but I don't ask them about what they want me to say. I know.

They want to hear what God says about death. They want to hear how God would answer their questions about the life hereafter. They don't want my opinion; nor do they want the thoughts of a philosopher or the research of a scientist. They want to know what God says. If Jesus were here, at the head of this casket, in the middle of this cemetery, what would he say?

And so under the canopy of sorrow, I give God's words. I share the eulogy Jesus gave for himself. The disciples did not know it was his farewell address. No one did, but it was. He knew he had just witnessed his final sunset. He knew death would come with the morning. So he spoke about death. Here is how he began.

> Don't let your hearts be troubled. Trust in God, and trust in me. There are many rooms in my Father's house; I would not tell you this if it were not true. I am going there to prepare a place for you. After I go and prepare a place for you, I will come back and take you to be with me so that you may be where I am (John 14:1–4).

What kind of statement is that? Trust me with your death. When you face the tomb, don't be troubled—trust me! You get the impression that to God the grave is a no-brainer. He speaks as casually as the mechanic who says to a worried client, "Sure, the engine needs an overhaul, but don't worry. I can do it." For us it's an ordeal. For him it's no big deal.

The other night I did something that every parent has done dozens of times. I carried my daughter to bed. Five-year-old Sara fell asleep on the floor, and I picked her up, carried her up the stairs, and put her in bed. Why? I knew it was time for her to rest, and I knew that rest was better up there than down here.

Doesn't God do the same? Doesn't he, knowing more than we, carry us to the place of rest he created? For God, death is no tragedy. In God's economy, the termination of the body is the beginning of life.

Can you imagine if Sara's sisters objected to my decision to carry her upstairs? "Don't take her. We'll miss her. Please keep her here so we will all be together."

How would I answer? "Oh, but she'll rest so much better in the room I have prepared for her. Besides, you'll be coming up yourselves soon."

By calling us home, God is doing what any father would do. He is providing a better place to rest. A place he has "prepared for us." Heaven is not mass-produced; it is tailor-made.

Sometime ago I indulged and ordered two shirts from a tailor. I selected the cloth. The tailor measured my body. And several weeks later, I received two shirts made especially for me. There is a big difference between these two shirts and the other shirts in my closet. The tailored shirts were made with me in mind. The other shirts were made for any hundred thousand or so males my size. But not these two. They were made just for me.

As a result, they fit! They don't bulge. They don't choke. They are just right. Such is the promise of heaven. It was made with us in mind. Elsewhere Jesus invites us to "receive the kingdom God has prepared for you since the world was made" (Matt. 25:34).

The problem with this world is that it doesn't fit. Oh, it will do for now, but it isn't tailor-made. We were made to live with God, but on earth we live by faith. We were made to live forever, but on this earth we live but for a moment. We were made to live holy lives, but this world is stained by sin.

This world wears like a borrowed shirt. Heaven, however, will fit like one tailor-made.

By the way, I've often thought it curious how few people Jesus raised from the dead. He healed hundreds and fed thousands, but as far as we know he only raised three: the daughter of Jairus, the boy near Nain, and Lazarus. Why so few? Could it be because he knew he'd be doing them no favors? Could it be because he couldn't get any volunteers? Could it be that once someone is there, the last place they want to return to is here?

We must trust God. We must trust not only that he does what is best but that he knows what is ahead. Ponder these words of Isaiah 57:1–2: "The good men perish; the godly die before their time and no one seems to care or wonder why. No one seems to realize that God is taking them away from the evil days ahead. For the godly who die shall rest in peace" (TLB).

My, what a thought. God is taking them away from the evil days ahead. Could death be God's grace? Could the funeral wreath be God's safety ring? Why does an eight-year-old die of cancer? Why is a young mother taken from her children? As horrible as the grave may be, could it be God's protection from the future?

Trust in God, Jesus urges, and trust in me.

Several years ago I heard then Vice President George Bush speak at a prayer breakfast. He told of his trip to Russia to represent the United States at the funeral of Leonid Brezhnev. The funeral was as precise and stoic as the communist regime. No tears were seen, and no emotion displayed. With one exception. Mr. Bush told how Brezhnev's widow was the last person to witness the body before the coffin was closed. For several seconds she stood at his side and then reached down and performed the sign of the cross on her husband's chest.

In the hour of her husband's death, she went not to Lenin, not to Karl Marx, not to Khrushchev. In the hour of death she turned to a Nazarene carpenter who had lived two thousand years ago and who dared to claim: "Don't let your hearts be troubled. Trust in God, and trust in me."[2]

So what do we do with birthdays? As much as we'd like to avoid them, we can't. Pretty soon the candles cost as much as the cake. And as much as we'd like to think we are exempt from the grave, we aren't. So rather than avoid them, welcome them! Welcome them as mile-markers that remind you that you aren't home yet, but you're closer than you've ever been.

When I go away, I will send the Helper to you. If I do not go away, the Helper will not come. When the Helper comes, he will prove to the people of the world the truth about sin, about being right with God, and about judgment.

John 16:7–9

Music for the Dance
The God Who Sends the Song

LET'S IMAGINE THAT you want to learn to dance. Being the rational, cerebral person you are, you go to a bookstore and buy a book on dancing. After all, a book helped you learn to program a computer, and a book taught you accounting—surely a book can teach you how to shuffle your feet.

You take the book home and get to work. You do everything it says. The book says sway; you sway. The book says shuffle; you shuffle. The book says spin; you spin. You even cut out paper shoe patterns and place them around the living-room floor so you'll know where to step.

Finally, you think you've got it, and you invite your wife to come in and watch. You hold the book open and follow the instructions step by step. You even read the words aloud so she'll know that you've done your homework. "Lean with your right shoulder," and so you lean. "Now step with your right foot," and so you step. "Turn slowly to the left," and so you do.

You continue to read, then dance, read, then dance, until the dance is completed. You plop exhausted on the couch, look at your wife, and proclaim, "I executed it perfectly."

"You executed it, all right," she sighs. "You killed it."

"What?"

"You forgot the most important part. Where is the music?"

Music?

You never thought about music. You remembered the book. You learned the rules. You laid out the pattern. But you forgot the music.

"Do it again," she says, putting in a CD. "This time don't worry about the steps; just follow the music."

She extends her hand and the music begins. The next thing you know, you are dancing—and you don't even have the book.

We Christians are prone to follow the book while ignoring the music. We master the doctrine, outline the chapters, memorize the dispensations, debate the rules, and stiffly step down the dance floor of life with no music in our hearts. We measure each step, calibrate each turn, and flop into bed each night exhausted from another day of dancing by the book.

Dancing with no music is tough stuff.

Jesus knew that. For that reason, on the night before his death he introduced the disciples to the song maker of the Trinity, the Holy Spirit.

> When I go away I will send the Helper to you. If I do not go away, the Helper will not come. When the Helper comes, he will prove to the people of the world the truth about sin, about being right with God, and about judgment (John 16:7–9).

If I were to ask you to describe your heavenly Father, you'd give me a response. If I were to ask you to tell me what Jesus did for you, you'd likely give a cogent answer. But if I were to ask about the role of the Holy Spirit in your life . . . ? Eyes would duck. Throats would be cleared. And it would soon be obvious that of the three persons of the Godhead, the Holy Spirit is the one we understand the least.

Perhaps the most common mistake made regarding the Spirit is perceiving him as a power but not a person, a force with no identity. Such is not true. The Holy Spirit is a person.

The world cannot accept *him*, because it does not see him or know *him*. But you know *him*, because *he* lives with you and *he* will be in you (John 14:17, emphasis mine).

The Holy Spirit is not an "it." He is a person. He has knowledge (1 Cor. 2:11). He has a will (1 Cor. 12:11). He has a mind (Rom. 8:27). He has affections (Rom. 15:30). You can lie to him (Acts 5:3–4). You can insult him (Heb. 10:29). You can grieve him (Eph. 4:30).

The Holy Spirit is not an impersonal force. He is not Popeye's spinach or the surfer's wave. He is God within you to help you. In fact John calls him the Helper.

Envision a father helping his son learn to ride a bicycle, and you will have a partial picture of the Holy Spirit. The father stays at the son's side. He pushes the bike and steadies it if the boy starts to tumble. The Spirit does that for us; he stays our step and strengthens our stride. Unlike the father, however, he never leaves. He is with us to the end of the age.

What does the Spirit do?

He comforts the saved. "When I go away, I will send the Helper to you" (John 16:7).

He convicts the lost. "When the Helper comes, he will prove to the people of the world the truth about sin, about being right with God, and about judgment" (John 16:8).

He conveys the truth. "I have many more things to say to you, but they are too much for you now. When the Spirit of truth comes, he will lead you into all truth" (John 16:12).

Is John saying we don't need the book in order to dance? Of course not; he helped write it. Emotion without knowledge is as dangerous as knowledge without emotion. God seeks a balance. "God is spirit, and those who worship him must worship in spirit and truth" (John 4:24).

What is essential is that you know the music is in you. "If Christ is in you, then the Spirit gives you life" (Rom. 8:10). You don't need a formula to hear it. I don't have a four-step plan to help you know it. What I do have is his promise that the helper would come to comfort, convict, and convey.

So think about it; have you ever been comforted? Has God ever brought you peace when the world brought you pain? Then you heard the music.

Have you ever been convicted? Have you ever sensed a stab of sorrow for your actions? Then you've been touched by the Holy Spirit.

Or have you ever understood a new truth? Or seen an old principle in a new way? The light comes on. Your eyes pop open. "Aha, now I understand." Ever happen to you? If so, that was the Holy Spirit conveying to you a new truth.

What do you know? He's been working in your life already.

By the way, for those of us who spent years trying to do God's job, that is great news. It's much easier to raise the sail than row the boat. And it's a lot easier getting people to join the dance when God is playing the music.

I am the good shepherd. The good shepherd gives his life for his sheep. The worker who is paid to keep the sheep is different from the shepherd who owns them.

John 10:11–12

I am the good shepherd. I know my sheep as the Father knows me.

John 10:14–15

A Different Kind of Hero

The God Who Knows Your Name

BEHOLD A HERO of the west: the cowboy.

He rears his horse to a stop on the rim of the canyon. He shifts his weight in his saddle, weary from the cattle trail. One finger pushes his hat up on his head. One jerk of the kerchief reveals a sun-leathered face.

A thousand head of cattle pass behind him. A thousand miles of trail lie before him. A thousand women would love to hold him. But none do. None will. He lives to drive cattle, and he drives cattle to live. He is honest in poker and quick with a gun. Hard riding. Slow talking. His best friend is his horse, and his strength is his grit.

He needs no one. He is a cowboy. The American hero.

Behold a hero in the Bible: the shepherd.

On the surface he appears similar to the cowboy. He, too, is rugged. He sleeps where the jackals howl and works where the wolves prowl. Never off duty. Always alert. Like the cowboy, he makes his roof the stars and the pasture his home.

But that is where the similarities end.

The shepherd loves his sheep. It's not that the cowboy doesn't appreciate the cow; it's just that he doesn't know the animal. He doesn't even want to. Have you ever seen a picture of a cowboy caressing a cow? Have you ever seen a shepherd caring for a sheep? Why the difference?

Simple. The cowboy leads the cow to slaughter. The shepherd leads the sheep to be shorn. The cowboy wants the meat of the cow. The shepherd wants the wool of the sheep. And so they treat the animals differently.

The cowboy drives the cattle. The shepherd leads the sheep.

A herd has a dozen cowboys. A flock has one shepherd.

The cowboy wrestles, brands, herds, and ropes. The shepherd leads, guides, feeds, and anoints.

The cowboy knows the name of the trail hands. The shepherd knows the name of the sheep.

The cowboy whoops and hollers at the cows. The shepherd calls each sheep by name.

Aren't we glad Christ didn't call himself the Good Cowboy? But some do perceive God that way. A hard-faced, square-jawed ranchhand from heaven who drives his church against its will to places it doesn't want to go.

But that's a wrong image. Jesus called himself the Good Shepherd. The Shepherd who knows his sheep by name and lays down his life for them. The Shepherd who protects, provides, and possesses his sheep. The Bible is replete with this picture of God.

"The Lord is my shepherd" (Ps. 23:1).

"We are your people, the sheep of your flock" (Ps. 79:13).

"Shepherd of Israel, listen to us. You lead the people of Joseph like a flock" (Ps. 80:1).

"He is our God and we are the people he takes care of and the sheep that he tends" (Ps. 95:7).

"He made us, and we belong to him; we are his people, the sheep he tends" (Ps. 100:3).

The imagery is carried over to the New Testament.

He is the shepherd who will risk his life to save the one straying sheep (see Luke 15:4).

He has pity on people because they are like sheep without a shepherd (see Matt. 9:36).

His disciples are his flock (see Luke 12:32.)

When the shepherd is attacked, the sheep are scattered (see Matt. 26:31).

He is the shepherd of the souls of men (see 1 Peter 2:25).

He is the great shepherd of the sheep (see Heb. 13:20).

Eighty percent of Jesus' listeners made their living off of the land. Many were shepherds. They lived on the mesa with the sheep. No flock ever grazed without a shepherd, and no shepherd was ever off duty. When sheep wandered, the shepherd found them. When they fell, he carried them. When they were hurt, he healed them.

Sheep aren't smart. They tend to wander into running creeks for water, then their wool grows heavy and they drown. They need a shepherd to lead them to "calm water" (Ps. 23:2). They have no natural defense—no claws, no horns, no fangs. They are helpless. Sheep need a shepherd with a "rod and . . . walking stick" (Ps. 23:4) to protect them. They have no sense of direction. They need someone to lead them "on paths that are right" (Ps. 23:3).

So do we. We, too, tend to be swept away by waters we should have avoided. We have no defense against the evil lion who prowls about seeking who he might devour. We, too, get lost. "We all have wandered away like sheep; each of us has gone his own way" (Isa. 53:6).

We need a shepherd. We don't need a cowboy to herd us; we need a shepherd to care for us and to guide us.

And we have one. One who knows us by name.

I don't need to tell you why this is so important, do I? You know. Like me, you've probably been in a situation where someone forgot your name. Perhaps a situation where no one knew who you were—or even cared.

Not long ago my assistant, Karen Hill, underwent surgery. When she awoke in the recovery room, she could hear a fellow patient groaning. She heard a well-meaning nurse comforting him. "Settle down, Tom," she said. "Settle down." But still he moaned. The nurse returned. "It's all right, Tom. Just go with the pain." He was quiet for a few moments but then began groaning again. "It's okay, Tom. You'll be fine." Finally the patient spoke. With a low, painful voice he said, "My name's not Tom."

There was a moment of silence as the nurse picked up his chart. Then she said, "It's all right, Harry; it's all right."

It's never easy to be in a place where no one knows your name, but few of us know this as much as John Doe No. 24. His story, as recorded by the Associated Press, reads like this:

UNKNOWN SINCE '45,
JOHN DOE TAKES HIS
SECRET TO THE GRAVE

JACKSONVILLE, ILL.

The mystery of John Doe No. 24 outlived him. There were few clues when he was found, wandering the streets of Jacksonville in 1945, a deaf, blind teenager.

Since he was unable to speak and his relatives could not be found, he was placed in an institution. He became John Doe No. 24 because he was the twenty-fourth unidentified man in the state's mental health system. Officials believe he was sixty-four when he died of a stroke at the Sharon Oaks nursing home in Peoria.

John Doe's caretakers believe diabetes made him lose his sight, and records indicate he was severely retarded. But workers remember a proud man, more intelligent than the standard tests showed. They remember the tantalizing hints to his identity—the way he would scrawl "Lewis" and his pantomimed wild accounts of foot-stomping jazz bars and circus parades. "It was so obvious from what he panto-mimed that he had quite a life at one time," said Kim Cornwell, a caseworker. "Like my grandfather, he could probably tell funny stories. We just couldn't reach out enough to get them." . . .

He had a straw hat he loved to wear and he took a back-pack with his collection of rings, glasses and silverware with him everywhere. At Christmas parties he danced to vibrations from the music. Last Christmas the staff bought him a harmonica. . . .

At a brief graveside service last Wednesday in Jacksonville, a woman asked if anyone had any words to say. No one did.[1]

Somewhere in the darkness of John Doe No. 24 there was a story. There was a name. There were memories of a mother who held him, a father who carried him. Behind those sightless eyes were eyes that could see the past, and all we can do is wonder, *What did they see? A kid with a cane pole on a muddy river? A wide-eyed youngster eating popcorn at a circus? A jazz band in New Orleans?*

No one will ever know. No one will know because he could never tell. He couldn't even speak his name. And on the day he died no one had words to say. What do you say when you bury a life no one knew?

It's easy to say this, but I wish I'd been there. I would have opened the Bible to the tenth chapter of the Gospel of John and read verse 3, "He calls his own sheep by name and leads them out."

It's not true that no one knew this man's name. God did . . . and God does. And it's wrong to say that this man never heard his name. Who knows how many times God spoke it to him through the years? In the silence. Through the dark. When we thought he couldn't hear, who is to say he wasn't hearing the only voice that matters?

The Good Shepherd knows each sheep by name. He's not a cow-boy, and we aren't cattle. He doesn't brand us, and we're not on the way to the market. He guides, feeds, and anoints. And Word has it that he won't quit until we reach the homeland.

I give them eternal life, and they will never die, and no one can steal them out of my hand.

John 10:28

Held by His Hands

The God Who Won't Let You Fall

I WOULD LIKE to confess a fall. I've kept it secret long enough. I can't deny the stumble; nor can I dismiss the truth. I fell. There were witnesses to my slip. They can tell you. Graciously, they have told no one. Out of concern for my reputation, they kept the event a secret. But it has been a secret long enough. The time has come for my mistake to be shared.

I lost my footing at a family camp.

My daughters and I chose to climb a wall—a simulated rock climb. The wall is made of wood with occasional rock-shaped fingerholds bolted into the surface. For safety, the climber wears a harness around his waist. The harness is attached to a rope that runs up through a pulley and then down into the hands of a guide who secures it as the climber climbs.

I gave it a go. What's a fifty-foot wall for a middle-aged author? I gave the guide the "thumbs-up" and began. The first half of the trip I did well. About midway, however, I began to get tired. These hands and feet are not accustomed to climbing.

With about twenty feet left to go, I honestly began to wonder if I would make it. I gave serious thought to telling the guide just to pull me up the rest of the way. My fingers were sore, and my legs were starting to tremble, and I was regretting every Big Mac I'd ever eaten, but the thought of surrender was lost in the cheers of my daughters who were already on the top.

"Come on, Dad. You can make it!"

So I gave it all I had. But all I had was not enough. My feet slipped, my hands slipped, and down I fell. I fell hard. But I didn't fall far. My guide had a firm hold on the rope. Because he was alert and because he was strong, my tumble lasted only a couple of seconds. I bounced and swung in the harness, suspended in midair. Everyone watching let out a sigh, and I gulped and resumed the climb.

Guess what I did when I made it to the top? Do you think I boasted? Do you think I bragged about conquering the wall? No way. I looked down at the one who kept me from falling. "Thanks, pal," I told him. I didn't pat myself on the back or raise my fist in triumph. I didn't ask everybody if they'd seen what I did. I did the only thing that was right; I said thanks to the one who held me.

Would that all my tumbles were so simple. So brief. So harmless. They haven't been. I've been known to let go of much more than imitation rocks. I've let go of promises and convictions. There have been times when my fingers slipped off the very stones of truth I treasure. And I can't tell you how many times I've expected to hit the bottom only to find myself suspended in midair, secured by a pair of nail-pierced hands.

"Try again," he urges. And so I resume.

You and I are on a great climb. The wall is high, and the stakes are higher. You took your first step the day you confessed Christ as the Son of God. He gave you his harness—the Holy Spirit. In your hands he placed a rope—his Word.

Your first steps were confident and strong, but with the journey came weariness, and with the height came fear. You lost your footing. You lost your focus. You lost your grip, and you fell. For a moment, which seemed like forever, you tumbled wildly. Out of control. Out of self-control. Disoriented. Dislodged. Falling.

But then the rope tightened, and the tumble ceased. You hung in the harness and found it to be strong. You grasped the rope and found it to be true. You looked at your guide and found Jesus securing your soul. With a sheepish confession, you smiled at him and he smiled at you, and the journey resumed.

Now you are wiser. You have learned to go slowly. You are careful. You are cautious, but you are also confident. You trust the rope. You rely on the harness. And though you can't see your guide, you know him. You know he is strong. You know he is able to keep you from falling.

And you know you are only a few more steps from the top. So whatever you do, don't quit. Though your falls are great, his strength is greater. You will make it. You will see the summit. You will stand at the top. And when you get there, the first thing you'll do is join with all the others who have made the climb and sing this verse:

"To him who is able to keep you from falling and to present you before his glorious presence without fault and with great joy—to the only God our Savior be glory, majesty, power and authority, through Jesus Christ our Lord, before all ages, now and forevermore! Amen" (Jude 24 NIV).

Carrying his own cross, Jesus went out to a place called The Place of the Skull. . . . There they crucified Jesus. They also crucified two other men, one on each side, with Jesus in the middle.

John 19:17

A Cinderella Story

The God Who Gave His Beauty Away

GOD BETWEEN TWO thieves. Exactly the place he wants to be.

Three men on three crosses, a well-known scene. Even casual students of Christ are acquainted with the trio on Skull's Hill. We've pondered their sufferings and sketched their faces and analyzed their words.

But let's imagine this scene from another perspective. Rather than stand on ground level and look up, let's stand at the throne of God and look down. What does God see? What is the perspective of heaven? Does God see the timber and nails? Does God witness the torn flesh and spilt blood? Can heaven hear the mallet slam and the voices cry?

Certainly. But God sees much more. He sees his Son surrounded by sin and two thieves covered with sin. A shadow hangs over their spirits. The crowd cringes at the sight of the blood on their skin, but heaven laments over the darkness of their hearts. Earth pities the condition of their bodies. Heaven weeps over the condition of their souls.

I wonder if we can understand the impact our sin has in heaven. We get a clue in Revelation 3:16 when Jesus threatens to spit the lukewarm church out of his mouth. The verb literally means "to vomit." Their sin, excuse the phrase, made God want to puke. Their acts caused him, not just distaste, but disgust.

Haven't you felt the same? Haven't you witnessed the horror of a human act and wanted to throw up? On last night's news broadcast the story was told of a ten-year-old boy who'd been allegedly set afire by his father. The man had stuffed tissue down his son's T-shirt, covered the boy with lighter fluid, and set him aflame. Why? Because the boy had taken some of the father's food stamps.

Doesn't such a story disgust you? Make you angry? And if we, who are also sinners, have such a reaction, how much more should a holy God? After all, it is his law being broken. His children being abused. His word being ignored.

His holiness being insulted.

The question is not, "Couldn't God overlook sin?" The question instead is, "How in the world is forgiveness an option?" The question is not why God finds it difficult to forgive, but how he finds it possible to do so at all.[1]

From God's angle the tragedy of these men was not that they were about to die, but that they were dying with unresolved sin. They were leaving this earth hostile to God, defiant of his truth, and resistant to his call. "When people's thinking is controlled by the sinful self, they are against God" (Rom. 8:7). Sin is not an unfortunate slip or a regrettable act; it is a posture of defiance against a holy God.

Such is what heaven sees.

The figure on the center cross, however, has no such shadow of sin. "When he lived on earth, he was tempted in every way that we are, but he did not sin" (Heb. 4:15). Stainless. Selfless. Even on a sinner's cross Jesus' holiness illuminates heaven.

The first criminal reads the sign that announces Jesus as the king of the Jews. He hears Jesus pray for those who kill him. Something about the presence of the carpenter convinces him he's in the presence of a king.

The other crook has a different opinion. "Aren't you the Christ? Then save yourself and us" (Luke 23:39). You'd think a man near death would use his energy for something other than slander. Not this one. The shadow over his heart is so thick, even in pain he mocks.

Suddenly someone tells him, "You should fear God!" It's the voice of the first criminal. "We are . . . getting what we deserve for what we did. But this man has done nothing wrong" (Luke 23:41).

Finally someone is defending Jesus. Peter fled. The disciples hid. The Jews accused. Pilate washed his hands. Many could have spoken on behalf of Jesus, but none did. Until now. Kind words from the lips of a thief. He makes his request. "Jesus, remember me when you come into your kingdom" (Luke 23:42).

The Savior turns his heavy head toward the prodigal child and promises, "I tell you the truth, today you will be with me in paradise" (Luke 23:43).

To those at the foot of the cross, the dialogue was curious. But to those at the foot of the throne, the dialogue was outrageous. They couldn't imagine it. How could the thief come to paradise? How could a soul speckled by sin go to heaven? How could a sinner be saved? They were about to see.

Did an angel move, did a demon stir as they witnessed the answering of the prayer? The sins of the thief (and all us thieves!) leave him and go to Jesus. Tiny specks at first, then large flakes, and finally layers of filth. Every evil thought. Each vile deed. The thief's ravings. His cursings. His greed. His sin. All now covering Jesus Christ. What nauseates God now covers his son.

At the same instant, the purity of Jesus lifts and covers the dying thief. A sheet of radiance is wrapped around his soul. As the father robed the prodigal, so now Christ robes the thief. Not just with a clean coat but with Jesus himself! "Baptized into union with him, you have all put on Christ as a garment" (Gal. 3:27 NEB).

The One with no sin becomes sin-filled. The one sin-filled becomes sinless.

It is eternity's most bizarre exchange. Paul explained it like this: "Christ took away the curse the law put on us. He changed places with us and put himself under that curse" (Gal. 3:13).

When he sees sin, a just God must either inflict punishment or assume it. God chose the latter. On the cross "God was in Christ, making peace between the world and himself" (2 Cor. 5:19).

I know John says that Jesus was carrying his own cross as he walked up the hill, but he wasn't. He was carrying ours. The only reason he carried the cross was for us thieves and crooks. "Christ had no sin, but God made him become sin so that in Christ we could become right with God" (2 Cor. 5:21). It wasn't his death he died; it was ours. It wasn't his sin he became; it was ours.

A beautiful illustration of this came my way, even as I was writing this chapter. In between the composition of the two paragraphs above, I received a call from a friend named Kenny. He and his family had just returned from Disney World. "I saw a sight I'll never forget," he said. "I want you to know about it."

He and his family were inside Cinderella's castle. It was packed with kids and parents. Suddenly all the children rushed to one side. Had it been a boat, the castle would have tipped over. Cinderella had entered.

Cinderella. The pristine princess. Kenny said she was perfectly typecast. A gorgeous young girl with each hair in place, flawless skin, and a beaming smile. She stood waist-deep in a garden of kids, each wanting to touch and be touched.

For some reason Kenny turned and looked toward the other side of the castle. It was now vacant except for a boy maybe seven or eight years old. His age was hard to determine because of the disfigurement of his body. Dwarfed in height, face deformed, he stood watching quietly and wistfully, holding the hand of an older brother.

Don't you know what he wanted? He wanted to be with the children. He longed to be in the middle of the kids reaching for Cinderella, calling her name. But can't you feel his fear, fear of yet another rejection? Fear of being taunted again, mocked again?

Don't you wish Cinderella would go to him? Guess what? She did!

She noticed the little boy. She immediately began walking in his direction. Politely but firmly inching through the crowd of children, she finally broke free. She walked quickly across the floor, knelt at eye level with the stunned little boy, and placed a kiss on his face.

"I thought you would appreciate the story," Kenny told me. I did. It reminded me of the one you and I have been studying. The names are different, but isn't the story almost the same? Rather than a princess of Disney, we've been considering the Prince of Peace. Rather than a boy in a castle, we've looked at a thief on a cross. In both cases a gift was given. In both cases love was shared. In both cases the lovely one performed a gesture beyond words.

But Jesus did more than Cinderella. Oh, so much more.

Cinderella gave only a kiss. When she stood to leave, she took her beauty with her. The boy was still deformed. What if Cinderella had done what Jesus did? What if she'd assumed his state? What if she had somehow given him her beauty and taken on his disfigurement?

That's what Jesus did.

"He took our suffering on him and felt our pain for us. . . . He was wounded for the wrong we did; he was crushed for the evil we did. The punishment, which made us well, was given to him, and we are healed because of his wounds" (Isa. 53:4–5).

Make no mistake:

Jesus gave more than a kiss—he gave his beauty.

He paid more than a visit—he paid for our mistakes.

He took more than a minute—he took away our sin.

Then Jesus took the loaves of bread, thanked God for them, and gave them to the people who were sitting there. He did the same with the fish, giving as much as the people wanted.

John 6:11

The Bad News Preacher
The God of Stubborn Faith

I DIDN'T LIKE the preacher I sat by on the plane. I know, I know. You're supposed to like everyone, but this fellow . . .

To begin with, he took the seat next to me. I'd hoped it would stay vacant. The plane was crowded. It was a Sunday afternoon, and I was tired from Sunday-morning services. I was speaking that evening in Atlanta and had planned on taking a nap on the flight.

But this fellow had other ideas. Though he had been assigned another seat, he took the one next to me since it was closer to the front. And when he took it, he took every inch of it—and then some. Forgive me, but I get a bit territorial about armrests. This guy staked his claim on the one between us and never relinquished his position.

Knowing I couldn't sleep, I figured I'd review my thoughts for the evening lesson, so I opened my Bible.

"What ya' studying there, buddy?"

I told him, but he never heard.

"The church is lost," he declared. "Hellbound and heartsick."

Turns out he is an evangelist. He speaks in a different church every weekend. "I wake 'em up," he growled. "Christians are asleep. They don't pray. They don't love. They don't care."

With that pronouncement, he took on his preaching tone and cadence and started listing all the woes and weaknesses of the church, "Too lazy-uh, too rich-uh, too spoiled-uh, too fat-uh . . ."

The folks around were beginning to listen, and my face was beginning to redden. I shouldn't have let it bug me, but it did. I'm one of those fellows who never knows what to say at the time but then spends the next week thinking, *I wish I'd thought to say that.*

Well, I've spent the last few days thinking about it, and here is what I wish I'd said to the bad news preacher: God's faithfulness has never depended on the faithfulness of his children. He is faithful even when we aren't. When we lack courage, he doesn't. He has made a history out of using people in spite of people.

Need an example? The feeding of the five thousand. It's the only miracle, aside from those of the final week, recorded in all four Gospels. Why did all four writers think it worth repeating? Maybe they knew some preachers like the one I sat next to. Perhaps they wanted to show how God doesn't give up even when his people do.

The day begins with the news of the death of John the Baptist. It continues with the return of the disciples from a short-term missionary journey. Following the disciples are five thousand men and their families. Jesus tries to get away from the crowd by crossing the sea, only to find the crowd waiting for him on the other side. He wanted to mourn in solitude, but instead he was surrounded by people. He wanted to spend time with just the disciples, but instead he got a crowd. He wanted time to think, but instead he had people to face.[1]

He spends time teaching them, and then he turns to Philip and inquires, "Where can we buy enough bread for all these people to eat?" (John 6:5). Keep in mind that Philip has been forcing out demons and healing the sick (Mark 6:13). We'd expect him to be optimistic. A bit of faith would be appropriate. After all, he's just spent several weeks seeing the impossible happen.

But how does Philip respond? He sounds like the preacher I met on the plane. He knows the problem, but he has no clue as to the solution. "We would all have to work a month to buy enough bread for each person to have only a little piece" (John 6:7).

He can cite the stats, but he can't see how to help. He can crunch the numbers, but he can't construct the answer. And though the answer to prayer is standing next to him, he doesn't even pray.

Equally disturbing is the silence of the other disciples. Are they optimistic? Read their words, and see for yourself. "No one lives in this place and it is already very late. Send the people away so they can go to the countryside and towns around here to buy themselves something to eat" (Mark 6:35–36).

Come on, guys. How about a little faith? "You can feed them, Jesus. No challenge is too great for you. We've seen you heal the sick and raise the dead; we know you can feed the crowd."

But that's not what they said. If faith is a candle, those fellows were in the dark.

It never occurred to the disciples to turn the problem over to Jesus. Only Andrew had such a thought, but even his faith was small. "Here is a boy with five loaves of barley bread and two little fish, but that is not enough for so many people" (John 6:9).

Andrew at least comes to Jesus with an idea. But he doesn't come with much faith. In fact, one would be hard pressed to find much faith on the hill that day.

Philip was cynical.

Andrew was doubtful.

The other disciples were negative.

The preacher I met on the flight would've felt right at home with these guys. Look at them: They aren't praying, they aren't believing, they aren't even seeking a solution. If they are doing anything, they are telling Christ what to do! "Send the people away" (Mark 6:36). A bit bossy, don't you think?

Looks like the disciples are "hellbound and heartsick." Looks like they are "too lazy-uh, too rich-uh, too spoiled-uh, too fat-uh." Let me be clear. I agree with the preacher that the church is weak. When he bemoans the condition of the saints, I could sing the second verse. When he laments the health of many churches, I don't argue.

But when he proclaims that we are going to hell in a handbasket, I do! I simply think God is greater than our weakness. In fact, I think it is our weakness that reveals how great God is. He told another struggler, "When you are weak, my power is made perfect in you" (2 Cor. 12:9). The feeding of the five thousand is an ideal example. The scene answers the question, What does God do when his children are weak?

If God ever needed an excuse to give up on people, he has one here. Surely God is going to banish these followers until they learn to believe.

Is that what he does? You decide. "Then Jesus took the loaves of bread, thanked God for them, and gave them to the people who were sitting there. He did the same with the fish, giving as much as the people wanted" (John 6:11).

When the disciples didn't pray, Jesus prayed. When the disciples didn't see God, Jesus sought God. When the disciples were weak, Jesus was strong. When the disciples had no faith, Jesus had faith. He thanked God.

For what? The crowds? The pandemonium? The weariness? The faithless disciples? No, he thanked God for the basket of bread. He ignored the clouds and found the ray and thanked God for it.

Look what he does next. "Jesus divided the bread and gave it to his followers, who gave it to the people" (Matt. 14:19).

Rather than punish the disciples, he employs them. There they go, passing out the bread they didn't request, enjoying the answer to the prayer they didn't even pray. If Jesus would have acted according to the faith of his disciples, the multitudes would have gone unfed. But he didn't, and he doesn't. God is true to us even when we forget him.

God's blessings are dispensed according to the riches of his grace, not according to the depth of our faith. "If we are not faithful, he will still be faithful, because he cannot be false to himself" (2 Tim. 2:13).

Why is that important to know? So you won't get cynical. Look around you. Aren't there more mouths than bread? Aren't there more wounds than physicians? Aren't there more who need the truth than those who tell it? Aren't there more churches asleep than churches afire?

So what do we do? Throw up our hands and walk away? Tell the world we can't help them? That's what the disciples wanted to do. Should we just give up on the church? That seemed to be the approach of the preacher I met on the plane.

No, we don't give up. We look up. We trust. We believe. And our optimism is not hollow. Christ has proven worthy. He has shown that he never fails, though there is nothing but failure in us.

I'll probably never see that proclaimer of pessimism again, but maybe you will. If you do, will you give him a message for me?

God is faithful even when his children are not.

That's what makes God, God.

Jesus did many other miracles in the presence of his followers that are not written in this book. But these are written so that you may believe that Jesus is the Christ, the Son of God. Then, by believing, you may have life through his name.

John 20:30

The Final Witness
The God Who Proves His Point

JOHN DOESN'T TELL us everything Jesus did. But he tells us those acts that will lead us to faith. John selects seven miracles. He begins softly with the quiet miracle of water to wine and then crescendos to the public resurrection of Lazarus. Seven miracles are offered, and seven witnesses are examined, each one building on the testimony of the previous.

Let's see if we can feel their full impact.

Pretend you are in a courtroom, a nearly empty courtroom. Present are four people: a judge, a lawyer, an orphan, and a would-be guardian. The judge is God, Jesus is the one who seeks to be the guardian, and you are the orphan. You have no name, no inheritance, no home. The lawyer is proposing that you be placed in Jesus' care.

Who is the lawyer? A Galilean fisherman by the name of John.

He has presented the court with six witnesses. It is time for the seventh. But before calling him to the stand, the lawyer reviews the case. "We started this case with the wedding in Cana." He paces as he speaks, measuring each word. "They had no wine, none at all. But when Jesus spoke, water became wine. The best wine. Delicious wine. You heard the testimony of the wedding attendants. They saw it happen."

He pauses, then moves on. "Then we heard the words of the foreign official. His son was nearly dead."

You nod. You remember the man's testimony. Articulate, he had spoken of how he had called every doctor and tried every treatment, but nothing had helped his son. Just when he was about to give up hope, someone told him about a healer in Galilee.

Through his thickened accent the dignitary had explained, "I had no other choice. I went to him out of desperation. Look! Look what the teacher did for my son." The boy had stood, and you had stared. It was hard to believe such a healthy youngster had ever been near death.

You listen intently as John continues, "And, your honor, don't forget the crippled man near the pool. For thirty-eight years he had not walked. But then Jesus came and, well, the court saw him. Remember? We saw him walk into this room. We heard his story.

"And, as if that was not enough, we also heard the testimony of the boy with the lunch. He was part of a crowd of thousands who had followed Jesus in order to hear him teach and to see him heal. Just when the little boy was about to open his lunch basket to eat, he was asked to bring it to Jesus. One minute it held a lunch; the next it held a feast."

John pauses again, letting the silence of the courtroom speak. No one can deny these testimonies. The judge listens. The lawyer listens. And you, the orphan, say nothing.

"Then there was the storm. Peter described it to us. The boat bouncing on the waves. Thunder. Lightning. Storms like that can kill. I know. I used to make a living on a boat! Peter's testimony about what happened was true. I was there. The Master walked on the water. And the moment he stepped into the boat, we were safe."

John pauses again. Sunlight squared by a window makes a box on the floor. John steps into the box. "Then, yesterday, you met a man who had never seen light. His world was dark. Black. He was blind. Blind from birth."

John pauses and dramatically states what the man born blind had said: "Jesus healed my eyes."

Six testimonies have been given. Six miracles have been verified. John gestures toward the table where sit the articles of evidence: The water jugs that held the wine. The signed affidavit of the doctor who'd treated the sick son. The cot of the cripple, the basket of the boy. Peter had brought a broken oar to show the strength of the storm. And the blind man had left his cup and cane. He didn't need to beg anymore.

"And now," John says, turning to the judge, "we have one final witness to call and one more piece of evidence to submit."

He goes to his table and returns with a white linen sheet. You lean forward, unsure of what he is holding. "This is a burial shroud," he explains. Placing the clothing on the table he requests, "Your honor permitting, I call our final witness to the chair, Lazarus of Bethany."

Heavy courtroom doors open, and a tall man enters. He strides down the aisle and pauses before Jesus long enough to place a hand on his shoulder and say, "Thank you." You can hear the tenderness in his voice. Lazarus then turns and takes his seat in the witness chair.

"State your name for the court."

"Lazarus."

"Have you heard of a man called Jesus of Nazareth?"

"Who hasn't?"

"How do you know him?"

"He is my friend. We, my sisters and I, have a house in Bethany. When he comes to Jerusalem, he often stays with us. My sisters, Mary and Martha, have become believers in him as well."

"Believers?"

"Believers that he is the Messiah. The Son of God."

"Why do you believe that?"

Lazarus smiles. "How could I not believe? I was dead. I had been dead for four days. I was in the tomb. I was prayed for and buried. I was dead. But Jesus called me out of the grave."

"Tell us what happened."

"Well, I've always been sickly. That's why I've stayed with my sisters, you know. They care for me. My heart never has been the strongest, so I have to be careful. Martha, the oldest sister, she's, well, she's like a mother to me. It was Martha who called Jesus when my heart failed."

"Is that when you died?"

"No, but almost. I lingered for a few days. But I knew I was near the edge. The doctors would just come in and shake their heads and walk out. I had one sandal in the grave."

"Is that when Jesus came?"

"No, we kept hoping he would. Martha would sit by the bed at night, and she would whisper over and over and over, 'Be strong, Lazarus. Jesus will be here any minute.' We just knew he would come. I mean, he had healed all those strangers; surely he would heal me. I was his friend."

"What delayed him?"

"For the longest time we didn't know. I thought he might be in prison or something. I kept waiting and waiting. Every day I got weaker. My vision faded, and I couldn't see. I drifted in and out. Every time someone entered my room, I thought it might be him. But it never was. He never came."

"Were you angry?"

"More confused than angry. I just didn't understand."

"Then what happened?"

"Well, I woke up one night. My chest was so tight I could hardly breathe. I must have sat up because Martha and Mary came to my bed. They took my hand. I heard them calling my name, but then I began to fall. It was like a dream, I was falling, spinning wildly in midair. Their voices grew fainter and fainter and then nothing. The spinning stopped, the falling stopped. And the hurting stopped. I was at peace."

"At peace?"

"Like I was asleep. Resting. Tranquil. I was dead."

"Then what happened?"

"Well, Martha can tell the details. The funeral was planned. The family came. Friends traveled from Jerusalem. They buried me."

"Did Jesus come to the funeral?"

"No."

"He still wasn't there?"

"No, when he heard I was buried, he waited an extra four days."

"Why?"

Lazarus stopped and looked at Jesus. "To make his point."

John smiled knowingly.

"What happened next?"

"I heard his voice."

"Whose voice?"

"The voice of Jesus."

"But I thought you were dead."

"I was."

"I, uh, thought you were in a grave."

"I was."

"How does a dead man in a grave hear the voice of a man?"

"He doesn't. The dead hear only the voice of God. I heard the voice of God."

"What did he say?"

"He didn't say it; he shouted it."

"What did he shout?"

"'Lazarus, come out!'"

"And you heard him?"

"As if he were in the tomb with me. My eyes opened; my fingers moved. I lifted my head. I was alive again. I heard the stone being rolled away. The light poured in. It took a minute for my eyes to adjust."

"What did you see?"

"A circle of faces looking in at me."

"Then what did you do?"

"I stood up. Jesus gave me his hand and pulled me out. He told the people to get me some real clothes, and they did."

"So you died, were in the tomb four days, then Jesus called you back to life? Were there any witnesses to this?"

Lazarus chuckles. "Only a hundred or so."

"That's all, Lazarus, thank you. You may step down."

John returns to the judge. "You have heard the testimonies. I now leave the decision in your hands." With that he returns to the table and takes his seat. The guardian stands. He doesn't identify himself. He doesn't need to. All recognize him. He is Jesus Christ.

Jesus' voice fills the courtroom. "I represent an orphan who is the sum of all you have seen. Like the party that had no wine, this one has no cause for celebration. Like the dignitary's son, this child is spiritually ill. Like the cripple and the beggar, he can't walk and is blind. He is starving, but earth has no food to fill him. He faces storms as severe as the one on Galilee, but earth has no compass to guide him. And most of all, he is dead. Just like Lazarus. Dead. Spiritually dead."

"I will do for him what I did for them. I'll give him joy, strength, healing, sight, safety, nourishment, new life. All are his. If you will permit."

The judge speaks his answer. "You are my Son, whom I love, and I am very pleased with you" (Luke 3:22). God looks at you. "I will permit it," he says, "on one condition. That the orphan request it."

John has presented the witnesses.

The witnesses have told their stories.

The Master has offered to do for you what he did for them. He will bring wine to your table, sight to your eyes, strength for your step and, most of all, power over your grave. He will do for you what he did for them.

The Judge has given his blessing. The rest is up to you.

Now the choice is yours.

Our Choice

On one side stands the crowd.
  Jeering.
    Baiting.
      Demanding.

On the other stands a peasant.
  Swollen lips.
    Lumpy eye.
      Lofty promise.

One promises acceptance,
  the other a cross.
One offers flesh and flash,
  the other offers faith.

The crowd challenges, "Follow us and fit in."
  Jesus promises, "Follow me and stand out."

They promise to please.
  God promises to save.

A basin of water?
  Or the blood of the Savior?

God looks at you and asks . . .
  Which will be your choice?

I tell you the truth, unless one is born again, he cannot be in God's kingdom.

John 3:3

16

Inside Out

Born Once or Born Twice?

Two sons of the king brought their father a question. "Is a gentleman born or made?"

"What do you think? he replied.

"I think a gentleman is born a gentleman," replied one son.

"I disagree," replied the other. "A man becomes a gentleman by training and discipline."

The king looked at his sons and issued a challenge. "Prove your case by presenting me an example. I give each of you a week to return with proof of your opinions."

And so the two sons departed in different directions. The son who believed a gentleman was made, not born, found his proof in a tavern. He'd ordered a cup of tea and was amazed when he saw that the waiter was a cat. This cat had been trained to stand on his hind legs and carry the tray in his forepaws. He wore a tiny uniform and hat and was proof that a creature could overcome his nature with training and discipline.

The first son had his example. If a cat can be changed, couldn't a man? So the prince purchased the animal and took him to the court.

The other son was not so fortunate. He'd searched the kingdom but was unable to find any support for his theory. He returned home empty-handed. What's worse, word had leaked about his brother's discovery. News of the walking cat made him doubt his convictions. But then, just hours before the two were to appear before the king, he saw something in a store window that made him smile.

He made the purchase but told no one.

The two sons entered the court of the king, each one carrying a box. The first son announced that he could prove that a man could overcome any obstacle and become a gentleman. As the king watched, the son presented the cat, dressed in miniature court dress, who gave the king a tray of chocolates.

The king was stunned, his son was proud, and the court broke into applause. What excellent proof! Who could deny the evidence of the walking cat? Everyone pitied the second son. But he was not discouraged. With a bow to the king, he opened the box he had brought, releasing several mice into the court. Instantly the cat scampered after the mice.[1]

The cat's true nature had been revealed, and the point had been made. A walking cat is still a cat. You can change his clothes. You can teach him tricks. You can give him a hat and train him to walk. And for a while he will appear to be changed. But present him with the one thing he can't resist, and you'll be faced with an undeniable truth—a walking cat is still a cat.

The same is true with people. We can change our clothes. We can change our habits. We can change our vocabulary, our reading level, even our attitude. But according to the Bible, there is one thing we cannot change—our sinful state.

Society would agree with the first son. It says change the outside and the inside will follow. Give a person education, training, the right habits, and the right disciplines, and the person will be changed. Oh, we try. Boy, do we try. We buy clothes. We seek degrees, awards, achievements.

We tell it to our kids. *Make something of your life.*

We tell it to our employees. *Act yourself into a better way of feeling.*

We tell it to the discouraged. *Try, try again.*

We even tell it to our church members. *Come to church, and you'll have a better attitude.*

But peel away the layers, take away the costumes, remove the makeup, and underneath you see our true nature—a selfish, prideful, sinful heart. Just bring out the mice and see what we do.

No one describes it better than Paul. Listen to his confession:

> I realize that I don't have what it takes. I can will it, but I can't do it. I decide to do good, but I don't really do it; I decide not to do bad, but then I do it anyway. My decisions, such as they are, don't result in actions. Something has gone wrong deep within me and gets the better of me every time.
>
> It happens so regularly that it's predictable. The moment I decide to do good, sin is there to trip me up. I truly delight in God's commands, but it's pretty obvious that not all of me joins in that delight. Parts of me covertly rebel, and just when I least expect it, they take charge.
>
> I've tried everything and nothing helps. I'm at the end of my rope. Is there no one who can do anything for me? Isn't that the real question? (Rom. 7:18–24, TM)

Paul is saying that no matter what I do, how hard I try, how much I strive, I still sin against God. Put clothes on me, teach me to walk on my hind legs, take me into the presence of the king himself, but let a few mice cross my trail and *BOOM!* The real me comes out.

I lose my temper,

  I forget my purpose,

    I demand my way,

      I lie,

        I lust,

          I turn,

            I fall . . .

The animal within takes over.

Please remember who wrote those words. The apostle Paul! Paul, the missionary. Paul, the zealot. Paul, the martyr. Paul, the Bible writer.

Paul, the sinner.

The same Paul who asked the question, "Who will save me from this body that brings me death?" and the Paul who answered the dilemma by proclaiming, "I thank God for saving me through Jesus Christ our Lord" (Rom. 7:25).

Changing the clothes doesn't change the man. Outward discipline doesn't alter what is within. New habits don't make a new soul. That's not to say that outward change is not good. That is to say that outward change is not enough. If one would see the kingdom, he must be born again.

That phrase, *born again*, belongs to Jesus. He first used it when he was talking to Nicodemus. Nicodemus was a good man. A very good man. He was a Pharisee, a religious ruler, a member of the Sanhedrin, one of the decision makers in Jerusalem. No doubt he had been taught and had taught that if you change the outside, you change the inside. He, like Paul, revered the law. He, like Paul, wanted to do right.

He thought the right training could make a waiter out of a cat.

But Jesus told him, "I tell you the truth, unless one is born again, he cannot be in God's kingdom" (John 3:3). Nicodemus's response is sincere. He didn't ask *Why?* He asked *How?* Perhaps you are asking the same question. How is a person born again?

To get an idea, think back to your own birth. Put the VCR of your days in reverse, and pause at your first moments. Look at yourself. Brand-new. New hands. New eyes. New mouth. No pre-owned parts. All original material.

Now tell me, who gave you these parts? Who gave you eyes so you could see? Who gave you hands so you could work? Who gave you feet that you could walk? Did you make your own eyes? Your own hands? Your own feet?

No, you made nothing; God made everything. He was the one who made everything new the first time, and he is the one who makes everything new the second. The Creator creates again! "If anyone belongs to Christ, there is a new creation. The old things have gone; everything is made new!" (2 Cor. 5:17)

Here is (dare I say it?) the greatest miracle of God. It is astounding when God heals the body. It is extraordinary when God hears the prayer. It is incredible when God provides the new job, the new car, the new child. But none of these compares to when God creates new life.

At our new birth God remakes our souls and gives us what we need, again. New eyes so we can see by faith. A new mind so we can have the mind of Christ. New strength so we won't grow tired. A new vision so we won't lose heart. A new voice for praise and new hands for service. And most of all, a new heart. A heart that has been cleansed by Christ.

And, oh, how we need it. We have soiled what he gave us the first time. We have used our eyes to see impurity, our hands to give pain, our feet to walk the wrong path, our minds to think evil thoughts. All of us need to be made new again.

The first birth was for earthly life; the second one is for eternal life. The first time we received a physical heart; the second time we receive a spiritual heart. The first birth enabled us to have life on earth. The second birth enables us to have life eternal.

But the analogy contains another truth. May I ask another question about your birth? How active were you in the process? (Don't look at me like that. Of course I'm being serious.) How active were you? Did you place your hands against the top of the womb and shove yourself out? Were you in radio communication with your mother, telling her when to push? Did the doctor ask you to measure the contractions and report on conditions inside the womb?

Hardly. You were passive. You were not born because of what you did. Someone else did all the work. Someone else felt all the pain. Your mom did the pushing and the struggling. Your birth was due to someone else's effort.

The same is true for our spiritual birth. It is through God's pain that we are born. It's not our struggle, but God's. It's not our blood shed, but his.

Jesus illustrates this by reminding Nicodemus of Moses lifting up the serpent in the wilderness. "Just as Moses lifted up the snake in the desert, so the Son of Man must be lifted up" (John 3:14). Israel had been complaining against God, and so God sent snakes that bit the people. Some died, and others were dying. The people confessed that they had sinned and cried to Moses for relief. Moses turned to God, and the Father told him to make a brass snake and fix it on a pole and tell the bitten people to look on it in faith and they would be healed.

Just as the serpent was lifted up . . . so the Christ was lifted up. Just as the serpent was fixed to a pole . . . so on the cross Christ nailed the power of the serpent of Eden to a pole. And just as the snake was a curse . . . so Christ became a curse for us (Gal. 3:13). And just as the people were healed when they looked on the serpent, so we are healed when we look to the cross.

That's all the people were commanded to do.

The poisoned people weren't told to take medicine or to extract the poison by suction. They weren't told to engage in good works to make an offering. They weren't told to examine their wounds, argue their plight, or pray to the serpent. Nor were they told to look at Moses. They were told simply, oh, how simply, to look to Christ.

Sin began when Eve looked at the tree (see Gen. 3:6). Salvation comes when we look to Christ. Astonishing simplicity. Summarized in the great promise of John 3:16: "God loved the world so much that he gave his one and only Son so that whoever believes in him may not be lost, but have eternal life."

God, the Lover. God, the Giver. God, the Savior. And man, the believer. And for those who believe, he has promised a new birth.

But despite the simplicity, there are still those who don't believe. They don't trust the promise. They can't imagine how God would know their name, much less forgive their sins. It's almost too good to be true.

If only they would try. If only they would test it. But God is as polite as he is passionate. He never forces his way in. The choice is theirs.

And for those who do come, he has promised a new birth.

Does that mean you'll never chase mice again? Does that mean the old nature will never rear its ugly head? Does that mean you will instantly be able to resist any temptation?

Go to the delivery room to answer that question. Look at the newborn baby. What can he do? Can he walk? Can he feed himself? Can he sing or read or speak? No, not yet. But someday he will.

It takes time to grow. But is the parent in the delivery room ashamed of the baby? Is the mom embarrassed that the infant can't spell . . . that the baby can't walk . . . that the newborn can't give a speech?

Of course not. The parents aren't ashamed; they are proud. They know that growth will come with time. So does God. "God is being patient with you. He does not want anyone to be lost, but he wants all people to change their hearts and lives" (2 Pet. 3:9).

God is often more patient with us than we are with ourselves. We assume that if we fall, we aren't born again. If we stumble, then we aren't truly converted. If we have the old desires, then we must not be a new creation.

If you are anxious about this, please remember, "God began doing a good work in you, and I am sure he will continue it until it is finished when Jesus Christ comes again" (Phil. 1:6).

In many ways your new birth is like your first: In your new birth God provides what you need; someone else feels the pain, and someone else does the work. And just as parents are patient with their newborn, so God is patient with you. But there is one difference. The first time you had no choice about being born; this time you do. The power is God's. The effort is God's. The pain is God's. But the choice is yours.

I am a man who has told you the truth which I heard from God. . . . But because I speak the truth, you don't believe me.

John 8:40, 45

The Yay-Yuck Man

The Crowds or the Christ

BOB LOVED TO make people happy.

Bob lived to make people happy.

If people weren't happy, Bob wasn't happy. So every day Bob set out to make people happy. Not an easy task, for what makes some people happy makes other people angry.

Bob lived in a land where everyone wore coats. The people never removed their coats. Bob never asked *Why?* He only asked *Which?* "Which coat should I wear?"

Bob's mother loved blue. So to please her he wore a blue coat. When she would see him wearing blue she would say, "Yay, Bob! I love it when you wear blue." So he wore the blue coat all the time. And since he never left his house and since he saw no one but his mother, he was happy, for she was happy and she said "Yay, Bob" over and over.

Bob grew up and got a job. The first day of his first job he got up early and put on his best blue coat and walked down the street.

The crowds on the street, however, didn't like blue. They liked green. Everyone on the street wore green. As he walked past, everyone looked at his blue coat and said, "Yuck!"

Yuck! was a hard word for Bob to hear. He felt guilty that he had caused a "yuck" to come out of a person's mouth. He loved to hear "yay!" He hated to hear "yuck!"

When the people saw his blue coat and said "yuck," Bob dashed into a clothing store and bought a green coat. He put it on over his blue coat and walked back out in the street. "Yay!" the people shouted as he walked past. He felt better because he had made them feel better.

When he arrived at his workplace, he walked into his boss's office wearing a green coat. "Yuck!" said his boss.

"Oh, I'm sorry," said Bob, quickly removing the green coat and revealing the blue. "You must be like my mother."

"Double yuck!" responded the boss. He got up from his chair, walked to the closet, and produced a yellow coat. "We like yellow here," he instructed.

"Whatever you say, sir," Bob answered, relieved to know he wouldn't have to hear his boss say "yuck" anymore. He put the yellow coat over the green coat, which was over the blue coat. And so he went to work.

When it was time for him to go home, he replaced the yellow coat with the green and walked through the streets. Just before he got to his house, he put the blue coat over the green and yellow coats and went inside.

Bob learned that life with three coats was hard. His movements were stiff, and he was always hot. There were also times when the cuff of one coat would peek out and someone would notice, but before the person could say "yuck" Bob would tuck it away.

One day he forgot to change his coat before he went home, and when his mother saw green she turned purple with disgust and started to say, "Yuck." But before she could, Bob ran and put his hand on her mouth and held the word in while he traded coats and then removed his hand so she said, "Yay!"

It was at this moment that Bob realized he had a special gift. He could change his colors with ease. With a little practice, he was able to shed one coat and replace it with another in a matter of seconds.

Even Bob didn't understand his versatility, but he was pleased with it. For now he could be any color anytime and please every person.

His skill at changing coats quickly elevated him to high positions. Everyone liked him because everyone thought he was just like them. With time he was elected mayor over the entire city.

His acceptance speech was brilliant. Those who loved green thought he was wearing green. Those who loved yellow thought he was wearing yellow, and his mother just knew he was wearing blue. Only he knew that he was constantly changing from one to the other.

It wasn't easy, but it was worth it, because at the end everyone said, "Yay!"

Bob's multicolored life continued until one day some yellow-coated people stormed into his office. "We have found a criminal who needs to be executed," they announced, shoving a man toward Bob's desk. Bob was shocked at what he saw. The man wasn't wearing a coat at all, just a T-shirt.

"Leave him with me," Bob instructed, and the yellow coats left.

"Where is your coat?" asked the mayor.

"I don't wear one."

"You don't have one?"

"I don't want one."

"You don't want a coat? But everyone wears a coat. It, it, it's the way things are here."

"I'm not from here."

"What coat do they wear where you are from?"

"No coat."

"None?"

"None."

Bob looked at the man with amazement. "But what if people don't approve?"

"It's not their approval I seek."

Bob had never heard such words. He didn't know what to say. He'd never met a person without a coat. The man with no coat spoke again.

"I am here to show people they don't have to please people. I am here to tell the truth."

If Bob had ever heard of the word *truth*, he'd long since rejected it. "What is truth?" he asked.

But before the man could answer, people outside the mayor's office began to scream, "Kill him! Kill him!"

A mob had gathered outside the window. Bob went to it and saw the crowd was wearing green. Putting on his green coat, he said, "There is nothing wrong with this man."

"Yuck!" they shouted. Bob fell back at the sound.

By then the yellow coats were back in his office. Seeing them, Bob changed his colors and pleaded, "The man is innocent."

"Yuck!" they proclaimed. Bob covered his ears at the word.

He looked at the man and pleaded, "Who are you?"

The man answered simply, "Who are you?"

Bob did not know. But suddenly he wanted to. Just then his mother, who'd heard of the crisis, entered the office. Without realizing it, Bob changed to blue. "He is not one of us," she said.

"But, but, . . ."

"Kill him!"

A torrent of voices came from all directions. Bob again covered his ears and looked at the man with no coat. The man was silent. Bob was tormented. "I can't please them and set you free!" he shouted over their screams.

The man with no coat was silent.

"I can't please you and them!"

Still the man was silent.

"Speak to me!" Bob demanded.

The man with no coat spoke one word. "Choose."

"I can't!" Bob declared. He threw up his hands and screamed, "Take him, I wash my hands of the choice."

But even Bob knew in making no choice he had made one. The man was led away, and Bob was left alone. Alone with his coats.

When all the wine was gone, Jesus' mother said to him, "They have no more wine."

John 2:3

Calamities of the Common Scale

Worry or Trust?

You're at your best friend's wedding reception. The two of you have talked about this day since you were kids, and now it's here. The ceremony was great; the wedding was beautiful. The minister was flawless, and the vows were honest. What a day!

"I'll take care of the reception," you'd volunteered. You planned the best party possible. You hired the band, rented the hall, catered the meal, decorated the room, and asked your Aunt Bertha to bake the cake.

Now the band is playing and the guests are milling, but Aunt Bertha is nowhere to be seen. Everything is here but the cake. You sneak over to the pay phone and dial her number. She's been taking a nap. She thought the wedding was next week.

Oh boy! Now what do you do? Talk about a problem! Everything is here but the cake . . .

Sound familiar?

It might. It's exactly the dilemma Jesus' mother, Mary, was facing. The wedding was moving. The guests were celebrating . . . but the wine was gone. Back then, wine was to a wedding what cake is to a wedding today. Can you imagine a wedding without cake? They couldn't imagine a wedding without wine. To offer wine was to show respect to your guests. Not to offer wine at a wedding was an insult.

What Mary faced was a social problem. A foul-up. A snafu. A calamity on the common scale. No need to call 911, but no way to sweep the embarrassment under the rug, either.

When you think about it, most of the problems we face are of the same caliber. Seldom do we have to deal with dilemmas of national scale or world conflict. Seldom do our crises rock the Richter scale. Usually the waves we ride are made by pebbles, not boulders. We're late for a meeting. We leave something at the office. A coworker forgets a report. Mail gets lost. Traffic gets snarled. The waves rocking our lives are not life threatening yet. But they can be. A poor response to a simple problem can light a fuse. What begins as a snowflake can snowball into an avalanche unless proper care is taken.

For that reason you might want to note how Mary reacted. Her solution poses a practical plan for untangling life's knots. "They have no more wine," she told Jesus (John 2:3). That's it. That's all she said. She didn't go ballistic. She simply assessed the problem and gave it to Christ.

"A problem well stated is a problem half solved," John Dewey said. Mary would have liked that, for that's what she did. She defined the problem.

She could have exploded: "Why didn't you plan better? There's not enough wine! Whose fault is this anyway? You guys never do anything right. If anything is to be done right around here I have to do it myself!"

Or she could have imploded: "This is my fault. I failed. I'm to blame. I deserve it. If only I'd majored in culinary art. I'm a failure in life. Go ahead; do the world a favor. Tie me up and march me to the gallows. I deserve it."

It's so easy to focus on everything but the solution. Mary didn't do that. She simply looked at the knot, assessed it, and took it to the right person. "I've got one here I can't untie, Jesus."

"When all the wine was gone Jesus' mother said to him, 'They have no more wine'" (John 2:3).

Please note, she took the problem to Jesus before she took it to anyone else. A friend told me about a tense deacons' meeting he attended. Apparently there was more agitation than agreement, and after a lengthy discussion, someone suggested, "Why don't we pray about it?" to which another questioned, "Has it come to that?"

What causes us to think of prayer as the last option rather than the first? I can think of two reasons: feelings of independence and feelings of insignificance.

Sometimes we're independent. We begin to think we are big enough to solve our own problems.

At our house we have had a banner year. Our third daughter has learned how to swim. That means that three can walk. Three can swim. And two out of the three have the training wheels off their bikes. With each achievement they have delightedly pointed out, "Look, Dad, I can do it on my own." Denalyn and I have applauded and celebrated each accomplishment our daughters have made. Their maturity and mobility is good and necessary, but I hope they never get to the point where they are too grown up to call their daddy.

God feels the same way about us.

Other times we don't feel independent; we feel insignificant. We think, "Sure, Mary can take her problems to Jesus. She's his mother. He doesn't want to hear my problems. Besides, he's got famine and the Mafia to deal with. I don't want to trouble him with my messes."

If that is your thought, may I share with you a favorite verse of mine? (Of course I can, I'm writing the book!) I like it so much I wrote it on the first page of my Bible.

"Because he delights in me, he saved me" (Ps. 18:19).

And you thought he saved you because of your decency. You thought he saved you because of your good works or good attitude or good looks. Sorry. If that were the case, your salvation would be lost when your voice went south or your works got weak. There are many reasons God saves you: to bring glory to himself, to appease his justice, to demonstrate his sovereignty. But one of the sweetest reasons God saved you is because he is fond of you. He likes having you around. He thinks you are the best thing to come down the pike in quite awhile. "As a man rejoices over his new wife, so your God will rejoice over you" (Isa. 62:5).

If God had a refrigerator, your picture would be on it. If he had a wallet, your photo would be in it. He sends you flowers every spring and a sunrise every morning. Whenever you want to talk, he'll listen. He can live anywhere in the universe, and he chose your heart. And the Christmas gift he sent you in Bethlehem? Face it, friend. He's crazy about you.

The last thing you should worry about is being a nuisance to God. All you need to concentrate on is doing what he tells you to do. Note the sequence of events in the next verse: "Jesus said to the servants, 'Fill the jars with water.' So they filled the jars to the top. Then he said to them, 'Now take some out and give it to the master of the feast.' So they took the water to the master. When he tasted it, the water had become wine" (John 2:7–9).

Did you see the sequence? First the jars were filled with water. Then Jesus instructed the servants to take the water (not the wine) to the master.

Now, if I'm a servant, I don't want to do that. How is that going to solve the problem? And what is the master going to say when I give him a cup of water? But these servants either had enough naivete or trust to do what Jesus said, and so the problem was solved. Note, the water became wine after they had obeyed, not before.

What if the servants had refused? What if they had said, "No way"? Or, to bring the point closer to home, what if *you* refuse? What if you identify the problem, take it to Jesus, and then refuse to do what he says?

That's possible. After all, God is asking you to take some pretty gutsy steps. Money is tight, but he still asks you to give. You've been offended, but he asks you to forgive your offender. Someone else blew the assignment, but he still asks you to be patient. You can't see God's face, but he still asks you to pray.

Not commands for the faint of faith. But then again, he wouldn't ask you to do it if he thought you couldn't. So go ahead. Next time you face a common calamity, follow the example of Mary at the wineless wedding:

Identify the problem. (You'll half-solve it.)

Present it to Jesus. (He's happy to help.)

Do what he says. (No matter how crazy.)

And buy your Aunt Bertha a new calendar.

They had a dinner for Jesus. Martha served the food, and Lazarus was one of the people eating with Jesus. Mary brought in a pint of very expensive perfume made from pure nard. She poured the perfume on his feet, and then she wiped his feet with her hair. And the sweet smell from the perfume filled the whole house.

John 12:2–3

Your Place in God's Band

At Work or at Odds?

TWO OF MY teenage years were spent carrying a tuba in my high school marching band. My mom wanted me to learn to read music, and the choir was full while the band was a tuba-tooter short, so I signed up. Not necessarily what you would describe as a call from God, but it wasn't a wasted experience either.

I had a date with a twirler.

I learned to paint white shoe polish on school buses.

I learned that when you don't know your music, you need to put your lips to the horn and pretend you do rather than play and remove all doubt.

And I learned some facts about harmony that I'll pass on to you.

I marched next to the bass-drum player. What a great sound. *Boom. Boom. Boom.* Deep, cavernous, thundering. At the right measure in the right music, there is nothing better than the sound of a bass drum. *Boom. Boom. Boom.*

And at the end of my flank marched the flute section. Oh, how their music soared. Whispering, lifting, rising into the clouds.

Ahead of me, at the front of my line, was our first-chair trumpet. A band member through and through. While some guys shot hoops and others drove hot rods, he played the trumpet. And it showed.

Put him on the fifty yard line and let him blow. He could raise the spirit. He could raise the flag. He could have raised the roof on the stadium if we'd had one.

Flute and trumpets sound very different. (See? I told you I learned a lot in band.) The flute whispers. The trumpet shouts. The flute comforts. The trumpet bugles. There's nothing like a trumpet—in limited dosages. A person can only be blasted at for so long. After a while you need to hear something softer. Something sweeter. You need to hear a little flute. But even the sound of the flute can go flat if there is no rhythm or cadence. That's why you also need the drum.

But who wants the drum all by itself? Ever seen a band made up of bass drums? Would you attend a concert of a hundred drums? Probably not. But what band would want to be without a bass drum or flute or trumpet?

The soft flute
    needs
        the brash trumpet
        needs
            the steady drum
            needs
                the soft flute
                needs
                    the brash trumpet.

Get the idea? The operative word is *need*. They need each other. By themselves they make music. But together, they make magic.

Now, what I saw two decades ago in the band, I see today in the church. We need each other. Not all of us play the same instrument. Some believers are lofty, and others are solid. Some keep the pace while others lead the band. Not all of us make the same sound. Some are soft, and others are loud. And not all of us have the same ability. Some need to be on the fifty yard line raising the flag. Others need to be in the background playing backup. But each of us has a place.

Some play the drums (like Martha).

Some play the flute (like Mary).

And others sound the trumpet (like Lazarus).

Mary, Martha, and Lazarus were like family to Jesus. After the Lord raised Lazarus from the dead, they decided to give a dinner for Jesus. They decided to honor him by having a party on his behalf (see John 12:2).

They didn't argue over the best seat. They didn't resent each other's abilities. They didn't try to outdo each other. All three worked together with one purpose. But each one fulfilled that purpose in his or her unique manner. Martha served; she always kept everyone in step. Mary worshiped; she anointed her Lord with an extravagant gift, and its aroma filled the air. Lazarus had a story to tell, and he was ready to tell it.

Three people, each one with a different skill, a different ability. But each one of equal value. Think about it. Could their family have done without one of the three?

Could we do without one of the three today?

Every church needs a Martha. Change that. Every church needs a hundred Marthas. Sleeves rolled and ready, they keep the pace for the church. Because of Marthas, the church budget gets balanced, the church babies get bounced, and the church building gets built. You don't appreciate Marthas until a Martha is missing, and then all the Marys and Lazaruses are scrambling around looking for the keys and the thermostats and the overhead projectors.

Marthas are the Energizer bunnies of the church. They keep going and going and going. They store strength like a camel stores water. Since they don't seek the spotlight, they don't live off the applause. That's not to say they don't need it. They just aren't addicted to it.

Marthas have a mission. In fact, if Marthas have a weakness, it is their tendency to elevate the mission over the Master. Remember when Martha did that? A younger Martha invites a younger Jesus to come for dinner. Jesus accepts and brings his disciples.

The scene Luke describes has Mary seated and Martha fuming. Martha is angry because Mary is, horror of horrors, sitting at the feet of Jesus. How impractical! How irrelevant! How unnecessary! I mean, who has time to sit and listen when there is bread to be baked, tables to be set, and souls to be saved? So Martha complained, "Lord, don't you care that my sister has left me alone to do all the work? Tell her to help me" (Luke 10:40).

My, my! Aren't we testy? All of a sudden Martha has gone from serving Jesus to making demands of Jesus. The room falls silent. The disciples duck their eyes. Mary flushes red. And Jesus speaks. He speaks not only to Martha of Bethany, but to all Marthas who tend to think that a bass drum is the only instrument in the band.

"Martha, Martha, you are worried and upset about many things. Only one thing is important. Mary has chosen the better thing, and it will never be taken away from her" (Luke 10:41–42).

Apparently Martha got the point, for later we find her serving again.

"Here a dinner was given in Jesus' honor. Martha served, while Lazarus was among those reclining at the table with him. Then Mary took about a pint of pure nard, an expensive perfume; she poured it on Jesus' feet and wiped his feet with her hair. And the house was filled with the fragrance of the perfume" (John 12:2–3 NIV).

Is Mary in the kitchen? No, she is playing her flute for Jesus. She is worshiping, for that is what she loves to do. But this time Martha doesn't object. She has learned that there is a place for praise and worship, and that is what Mary is doing. And what is Mary's part in the dinner? She brings a pint of very expensive perfume and pours it on Jesus' feet, then wipes his feet with her hair. The smell of the perfume fills the house, just like the sound of praise can fill a church.

An earlier Martha would have objected. Such an act was too lavish, too extravagant, too generous. But this mature Martha has learned that just as there is a place in the kingdom of God for sacrificial service, there is also a place for extravagant praise.

Marys are gifted with praise. They don't just sing; they worship. They don't simply attend church; they go to offer praise. They don't just talk about Christ; they radiate Christ.

Marys have one foot in heaven and the other on a cloud. It's not easy for them to come to earth, but sometimes they need to. Sometimes they need to be reminded that there are bills to be paid and classes to be taught. But don't remind them too harshly. Flutes are fragile. Marys are precious souls with tender hearts. If they have found a place at the foot of Jesus, don't ask them to leave. Much better to ask them to pray for you.

That's what I do. When I find a Mary (or a Michael), I'm quick to ask, "How do I get on your prayer list?"

Every church desperately needs some Marys.

We need them to pray for our children.

We need them to put passion in our worship.

We need them to write songs of praise and sing songs of glory.

We need them to kneel and weep and lift their hands and pray.

We need them because we tend to forget how much God loves worship. Marys don't forget. They know that God wants to be known as a father. They know that a father likes nothing more than to have his children sit as his feet and spend time with him.

Marys are good at that.

They, too, must be careful. They must meditate often on Luke 6:46. "Why do you call me 'Lord, Lord,' but do not do what I say?"

Marys need to remember that service is worship.

Marthas need to remember that worship is service.

And Lazarus? He needs to remember that not everyone can play the trumpet.

You see, as far as we know, Lazarus did nothing at the dinner. He saved his actions for outside the house. Read carefully John 12:9:

"A large crowd of Jews heard that Jesus was in Bethany. So they went there to see not only Jesus, but Lazarus, whom Jesus raised from the dead. So the leading priests made plans to kill Lazarus, too. Because of Lazarus many Jews were leaving them and believing in Jesus."

Wow! Because of Lazarus many Jews were "believing in Jesus."

Lazarus has been given a trumpet. He has a testimony to give—and what a testimony he has!

"I was always a good fellow," he would say. "I paid my bills. I loved my sisters. I even enjoyed being around Jesus. But I wasn't one of the followers. I didn't get as close as Peter and James and those guys. I kept my distance. Nothing personal. I just didn't want to get carried away.

"But then I got sick. And then I died. I mean, I died dead.

"Nothing left. Stone-cold. No life. No breath. Nothing. I died to everything. I saw life from the tomb. And then Jesus called me from the grave. When he spoke, my heart beat and my soul stirred, and I was alive again. And I want you to know he can do the same for you."

God gave Martha a bass drum of service. God gave Mary a flute for praise. And God gave Lazarus a trumpet. And he stood on center stage and played it.

God still gives trumpets. God still calls people from the pits. God still gives pinch-me-I'm-dreaming, too-good-to-be-true testimonies. But not everyone has a dramatic testimony. Who wants a band full of trumpets?

Some convert the lost. Some encourage the saved. And some keep the movement in step. All are needed.

If God has called you to be a Martha, then serve! Remind the rest of us that there is evangelism in feeding the poor and there is worship in nursing the sick.

If God has called you to be a Mary, then worship! Remind the rest of us that we don't have to be busy to be holy. Urge us with your example to put down our clipboards and megaphones and be quiet in worship.

If God has called you to be a Lazarus, then testify. Remind the rest of us that we, too, have a story to tell. We, too, have neighbors who are lost. We, too, have died and been resurrected.

Each of us has our place at the table.

Except one. There was one at Martha's house who didn't find his place. Though he had been near Jesus longer than any of the others, he was furthest in his faith. His name was Judas. He was a thief. When Mary poured the perfume he feigned spirituality. "The perfume could have been sold and given to the poor," he said. But Jesus knew Judas's heart, and Jesus defended Mary's worship. Years later, John, too, knew Judas's heart, and John explained that Judas was a thief (John 12:6). And all these years he had been dipping his hand in the treasury. The reason he wanted the perfume to be sold and the money put in the treasury was so that he could get his hands on it.

What a sad ending to a beautiful story. But what an appropriate ending. For in every church there are those like Martha who take time to serve. There are those like Mary who take time to worship. There are those like Lazarus who take time to testify.

And there are those like Judas who take, take, take, and never give in return. Are you a Judas? I ask the question carefully, yet honestly. Are you near Christ but far from his heart? Are you at the dinner with a sour soul? Are you always criticizing the gifts of others yet seldom, if ever, giving your own? Are you benefiting from the church while never giving to it? Do others give sacrificially while you give miserly? Are you a Judas?

Do you take, take, take, and never give? If so, you are the Judas in this story.

If you are a Martha, be strengthened. God sees your service.

If you are a Mary, be encouraged. God receives your worship.

If you are a Lazarus, be strong. God honors your conviction.

But if you are a Judas, be warned. God sees your selfishness.

The work God wants you to do is this: Believe in the One he sent.

John 6:29

Extravagant Love

Earn It or Receive It?

Disbelief has peculiar children:

There was the woman who was afraid to fly. After her flight she was asked if she had been nervous. "No," she responded. "I never sat down on the seat."

* * *

There was a king who left his servant in charge of the castle while he went on a journey. The king had a falcon. The servant had never seen a falcon and so when he saw the king's falcon, he thought it was a deformed pigeon. Out of compassion for the bird, he clipped its claws and filed its beak so it would look more like a pigeon.

* * *

There was a handsome prince who fell in love with a simple maiden. She wasn't attractive. She didn't trust his love. "How could you love me?" She would ask. "I'm not beautiful. I'm not rich. I'm not royalty."

"I just love you," he would answer.

He asked her to marry him. She still didn't trust his love, but she agreed. "I will marry you. I will clean your house and prepare your meals and bear your children."

"But I don't want to marry you for what you will do for me. I want to marry you because I love you."

And so they married. And so she cleaned his house and fixed his meals and bore his children. And he loved her. But she left him. She told a friend she didn't think he loved her anymore.

* * *

And so we have three people. Three people who couldn't believe. A woman who never enjoyed the flight because she couldn't trust the plane. A man who maimed a falcon because he'd never seen one. And a woman who lost the love of her life because she tried to earn what he wanted to give.

Disbelief has peculiar children. Children who are miserable on the journey, blind to the beauty, and oblivious to once-in-a-lifetime romance with God. Children who never fully relax in the palm of his grace. Children who forever trim and file at the splendor of his love. And children who hear his proposal but are always looking for the fine print and the hidden agenda.

The feelings of these children are captured in John 6:27–29. Jesus begins by saying: "Don't work for the food that spoils. Work for the food that stays good always and gives eternal life. The Son of Man will give you this food, because on him God the Father has put his power."

Jesus reduces the number of life's struggles to two. We either strive for food that rots or food that lasts. Food that rots is anything that is temporal: achievements, awards, applause . . . Any object that stays in the grave is a food that spoils.

Food that lasts, on the other hand, is anything that is eternal. And how do we get this food? Underline the promise, "The Son of Man will give you this food." You don't buy it, barter for it, or earn it. It is a gift. Just board the plane and sit down. Just unleash the falcon and watch it fly. Just accept his love and enjoy it . . .

Just believe.

But his listeners didn't get it. Look at their question: "What are the things God wants us to do?" (John 6:28). That, my friends, is the question of disbelief. "I know he said he would give it, but honestly now, how do we pay for this bread? How do we earn this meal? How long do we have to stand in the cafeteria line to get the eternal food?"

They missed the point. Didn't Jesus say, "The Son of Man will give you this food"?

Suppose I missed the point with you. Suppose you gave me a gift. Let's say you presented me with a new tie. I take it out of the box and examine it. I say thank you and then reach for my wallet. "Now how much do I owe you?" I ask.

You think I am kidding. "It's a gift," you say. "You don't need to pay me."

"Oh, I understand," I respond, but then show I don't by asking, "Could I write you a check?"

You're stunned. "I don't want you to pay me. I want you to accept the gift."

"Oh, I see," I respond. "Perhaps I could do some work around your house in exchange for the tie?"

"You just don't get it, do you?" you state firmly. "I want to give this to you. It is a present. You can't buy a present."

"Oh, forgive me," I hasten. "Perhaps if I promised to purchase you a tie in return."

By this time you're insulted. In trying to buy your gift I have degraded your grace. I have robbed you of the joy of giving.

How often we rob God.

Have you ever considered what an insult it is to God when we try to pay him for his goodness? God loves a cheerful giver because he is a cheerful giver. If we, who are evil, enjoy giving gifts, how much more does he? If we, who are human, are offended when people want to turn our gift into a bribe, how much more is God?

Spend some moments slowly reading the response of Jesus to their question, "What are the things God wants us to do?" (John 6:28).

Jesus replied: "The work God wants you to do is this . . ."

Can't you see the people lean closer, their minds racing? "What is the work he wants us to do? Pray more? Give more? Study? Travel? Memorize the Torah? What is the work he wants?" Sly is this scheme of Satan. Rather than lead us away from grace, he causes us to question grace or to earn it . . . and in the end we never even know it.

What is it, then, that God wants us to do? What is the work he seeks? Just believe. Believe the One he sent. "The work God wants you to do is this: Believe the One he sent."

Someone is reading this and shaking his or her head and asking, "Are you saying it is possible to go to heaven with no good works?" The answer is no. Good works are a requirement. Someone else is reading and asking, "Are you saying it is possible to go to heaven without good character?" My answer again is no. Good character is also required. In order to enter heaven one must have good works and good character.

But, alas, there is the problem. You have neither.

Oh, you've done some nice things in your life. But you do not have enough good works to go to heaven regardless of your sacrifice. No matter how noble your gifts, they are not enough to get you into heaven.

Nor do you have enough character to go to heaven. Please don't be offended. (Then, again, be offended, if necessary.) You're probably a very decent person. But decency isn't enough. Those who see God are not the decent; they are the holy. "Anyone whose life is not holy will never see the Lord" (Heb. 12:14).

You may be decent. You may pay taxes and kiss your kids and sleep with a clean conscience. But apart from Christ you aren't holy. So how can you go to heaven?

Only believe.

Accept the work already done, the work of Jesus on the cross. Only believe.

Accept the goodness of Jesus Christ. Abandon your own works and accept his. Abandon your own decency and accept his. Stand before God in his name, not yours. "Anyone who believes and is baptized will be saved, but anyone who does not believe will be punished" (Mark 16:16).

It's that simple? It's that simple. It's that easy? There was nothing easy at all about it. The cross was heavy, the blood was real, and the price was extravagant. It would have bankrupted you or me, so he paid it for us. Call it simple. Call it a gift. But don't call it easy. Call it what it is. Call it grace.

I have other sheep which are not of this flock and I must bring them also. They will listen to my voice, and there will be one flock and one shepherd.

John 10:16

Father, I pray that they can be one. . . . Then the world will know that you sent me and that you loved them as much as you loved me.

John 17:21, 23

God's Fondest Dream

Division or Unity

SOME TIME AGO I came upon a fellow on a trip who was carrying a Bible.

"Are you a believer?" I asked him.

"Yes," he said excitedly.

I've learned you can't be too careful.

"Virgin birth?" I asked.

"I accept it."

"Deity of Jesus?"

"No doubt."

"Death of Christ on the cross?"

"He died for all people."

Could it be that I was face to face with a Christian? Perhaps. Nonetheless, I continued my checklist.

"Status of man."

"Sinner in need of grace."

"Definition of grace."

"God doing for man what man can't do."

"Return of Christ?"

"Imminent."

"Bible?"

"Inspired."

"The church?"

"The body of Christ."

I started getting excited. "Conservative or liberal?"

He was getting interested too. "Conservative."

My heart began to beat faster.

"Heritage?"

"Southern Congregationalist Holy Son of God Dispensationalist Triune Convention."

That was mine!

"Branch?"

"Pre-millennial, post-trib, noncharismatic, King James, one-cup communion."

My eyes misted. I had only one other question.

"Is your pulpit wooden or fiberglass?"

"Fiberglass," he responded.

I withdrew my hand and stiffened my neck. "Heretic!" I said and walked away.

* * *

Far-fetched? If so, only a little. Suspicion and distrust often lurk at God's table. The Baptists distrust the Methodists. The Church of Christ avoids the Presbyterians. The Calvinists scoff at the Armenians. Charismatics. Immersionists. Patternists. Around the table the siblings squabble, and the Father sighs.

The Father sighs because he has a dream. "I have other sheep that are not in this flock, and I must bring them also. They will listen to my voice, and there will be one flock and one shepherd" (John 10:16).

God has only one flock. Somehow we missed that. Religious division is not his idea. Franchises and sectarianism are not in God's plan. God has one flock. The flock has one shepherd. And though we may think there are many, we are wrong. There is only one.

Never in the Bible are we told to create unity. We are simply told to maintain the unity that exists. Paul exhorts us to preserve "the unity which the Spirit gives" (Eph. 4:3, NEB). Our task is not to invent unity, but to acknowledge it.

I have two sisters and a brother. We are siblings because we came from the same family. We have the same father and mother. I'm sure there have been times when they didn't want to call me their brother, but they don't have that choice.

Nor do we. When I see someone calling God Father and Jesus Savior, I meet a brother or a sister—regardless of the name of their church or denomination.

By the way, the church names we banter about? They do not exist in heaven. The Book of Life does not list your denomination next to your name. Why? Because it is not the denomination that saves you. And I wonder, if there are no denominations in heaven, why do we have denominations on earth?

What would happen (I know this is a crazy thought), but what would happen if all the churches agreed, on a given day, to change their names to simply "church"? What if any reference to any denomination were removed and we were all just Christians? And then when people chose which church to attend, they wouldn't do so by the sign outside . . . they'd do so by the hearts of the people inside. And then when people were asked what church they attended, their answer wouldn't be a label but just a location.

And then we Christians wouldn't be known for what divides us; instead we'd be known for what unites us—our common Father.

Crazy idea? Perhaps.

But I think God would like it. It was his to begin with.

I am the true vine; my Father is the gardener. He cuts off every branch of mine that does not produce fruit. And he trims and cleans every branch that produces fruit so that it will produce even more fruit.

John 15:1–3

God's Been Known to Niggle

Do You Trust Him or Cuss Him?

EVERYONE LOVES WHAT Deborah Ricketts does. But nobody loves it while she's doing it. Everyone loves the product, but no one enjoys the process.

She is an independent researcher for the film industry. Do you want your movie to be accurate? Want your facts to be reliable? Send a script and a check to this former librarian and watch the facts begin to fly.

A film set in the thirties needs everything to look like the thirties. You can't have a person reading from a newspaper that didn't exist back then or a band playing a song that wasn't yet written. Such mistakes occur.

In *Raiders of the Lost Ark* the map that charted Indiana Jones's flight routed him over Thailand. Problem: The movie was set in 1936. Thailand was called Siam until 1939.

In *Die Hard II* Bruce Willis makes a phone call from what is supposed to be a Dulles Airport pay phone in Washington, D.C. No one noticed that the phone booth read Pacific Bell.

Deborah Ricketts lives to find these errors. She is on a scavenger hunt for flubs. She winds her way into props and sets and examines everything. Other people's oversights are her undertakings.[1]

She niggles for the scriptwriter's own good. The process is not pleasant, but the result is rewarding.

God has been known to niggle a few times, too. It's not that God loves to find fault. It's just that God loves to find anything that impedes our growth. Jesus portrays him as the Good Gardener who cuts and trims the vine. "I am the true vine; my Father is the gardener. He cuts off every branch of mine that does not produce fruit. And he trims and cleans every branch that produces fruit so that it will produce even more fruit" (John 15:1–3).

Jesus likely spoke these words while walking from the upper room to the Garden of Gethsemane. Perhaps he saw a vine hanging over a fence or draped along the wall. He lifted up a section of the plant and explained the chain of command in the universe. God is the Gardener. Jesus is the vine. We are the grapes.

Vines grew abundantly in Palestine. Carefully pruned, they produced sweet grapes. But left unkept, they crept everywhere and into everything. The gardener trimmed the vines. Why? So they could bear more fruit. God trims us. Why? For the same reason.

"I gave you this work," he explained, "to go and produce fruit, fruit that will last" (John 15:16).

A good gardener will do what it takes to help a vine bear fruit. What fruit does God want? Love, joy, peace, patience, kindness, goodness, faithfulness, gentleness, and self-control (see Gal. 5:22–23). These are the fruits of the Spirit. And this is what God longs to see in us. And like a careful gardener, he will clip and cut away anything that interferes.

A good track coach looks into the face of the runner and says, "We can break the record, but this is what it will take." And then the coach lists a regimen of practice and discipline.

A good editor reads the manuscript and says, "This work has potential, but here is what we need to cut." And the writer groans as the red ink flows.

A good piano instructor says, "I think you can master this piece for the competition, but to do so here is our rehearsal schedule." And the pianist sighs as she sees the hours required.

Deborah Rickets studies a script and offers: "It's good, but here are some ways to make it better."

God lifts up a branch of his vine and says, "You can be fruitful, but I'm going to have to clip some diseased leaves." And though the process is painful, we can see on the soil below us the spotted greenery he has clipped. Arrogance. Vain ambitions. Bad relationships. Dangerous opportunities. Revenge.

Does God take this process lightly? I don't think so. Listen to this serious statement. "He cuts off every branch of mine that does not produce fruit" (John 15:2). The verb "to cut off" is from the Greek word *airo*. It has at least two meanings; one is to "cut off," and the other is to "pick up" or "lift up." I believe both are implied.

Before God cuts a fruitless branch, he lifts it up. A gardener does this. He repositions the fruitless branch so it can get more sun or more space. Grapes are not like squash or pumpkins. They don't develop while lying on the ground. They grow better hanging free. A good vine dresser will stretch the vine on the arbor to afford it more air and sun.

You've seen gardeners realign a plant, and you've probably seen God realign a life. The family uprooted and transferred to another city—was it so they could learn to trust God? The person so healthy, suddenly sick—was it to remind him to rely on the Gardener? The income stream dried up—was it God's way of lifting you out of the soil of self and drawing you closer to himself? Leaders with questionable motives and morals are elected. Is it God's way of stirring people to revival?

God "does everything just right and on time, but people can never completely understand what he is doing" (Eccles. 3:11). (Did I just hear someone say "Amen"?) God is up to something. He is the busy, active Gardener who clears the field and removes the stones. He constructs the trellises and plants the seeds. He inspects the plants and pulls the weeds. And, most of all, he is good. He is the Good Gardener who cares for his vine.

So what are we to do? We branches on the vine, what is our response? How do we react? An answer commonly given at this point is the imperative, "Bear fruit!"

But is that the right response? Answer the question in a garden. If a branch is fruitless does it help if the gardener demands fruit? Or, if you are a branch, will you bear fruit by resolving to do so? You close your knobby eyes and grit your wooden teeth and strain until your bark turns red. Can you will a grape into existence? No. Please note, the branch cannot make fruit.

You cannot either. You've tried. With resolve in your eyes and grit in your jaw, you've tried. "Today I will be happy," you growl between clinched teeth.

Or, "I'm going to be patient, and I am going to be patient right now."

Or, "Okay, I'll be a cheerful giver. Give me that stupid collection plate."

Or, "I'm going to forgive that jerk if it kills me."

See what I mean? You can't force fruit. That's why nowhere in this text does Jesus tell you to go out and bear fruit.

What?

That's right. Nowhere does he command you to bear fruit. Go ahead, look. I did. It ain't there. Then what does he command us to do? Read John 15 for yourself:

"Remain in me . . ." (v. 4).

"Remain in the vine . . ." (v. 4).

"If any remain in me and I remain in them, they produce much fruit" (v. 5).

"Remain in me . . ." (v. 6).

"Remain in me . . ." (v. 7).

"Remain in my love . . ." (v. 9).

"Remain in my love . . ." (v. 10).

Our task? It's clear. Stay close to the vine. As long as we do, we'll be fruitful. Life comes through the vine. Apart from the vine, the branch does nothing. Jesus said it: "Apart from me you can do nothing" (John 15:5 NIV).

I doubt if it's easy for a scriptwriter to turn his manuscript over to someone like Deborah Rickets. He knows she's on the hunt for errors. But he also knows the end result will be a better story.

It's certainly not easy for us to turn our lives over to the gardener. Even now, some of you are hearing the snip-snip-snip of his shears. It hurts. But take heart. You'll be better as a result.

Besides, aren't you glad he thinks you are worth the effort?

I am the voice of the one calling out in the desert:
"Make the road straight for the Lord."

John 1:23

The Parable of the Sandwich Sign

Your Way or His?

THE FACES OF the three men were solemn as the mayor informed them of the catastrophe. "The rains have washed away the bridge. During the night many cars drove over the edge and into the river."

"What can we do?" asked one.

"You must stand on the side of the road and warn the drivers not to make the left turn. Tell them to take the one-lane road that follows the side of the river."

"But they drive so fast! How can we warn them?"

"By wearing these sandwich signs," the mayor explained, producing three wooden double-signs, hinged together to hang from one's shoulders. "Stand at the crossroads so drivers can see these signs until I can get someone out there to fix the bridge."

And so the men hurried out to the dangerous curve and put the signs over their shoulders.

"The drivers should see me first," spoke one. The others agreed. His sign warned, "Bridge Out!" He walked several hundred yards before the turn and took his post.

"Perhaps I should be second, so the drivers will slow down," spoke the one whose sign declared, "Reduce Speed."

"Good idea," agreed the third. "I'll stand here at the curve so people will get off the wide road and onto the narrow." His sign read simply "Take Right Road" and had a finger pointing toward the safe route.

And so the three men stood with their three signs ready to warn the travelers of the washed-out bridge. As the cars approached, the first man would stand up straight so the drivers could read, "Bridge Out."

Then the next would gesture to his sign, telling the cars to "Reduce Speed."

And as the motorists complied, they would then see the third sign, "Right Road Only." And though the road was narrow, the cars complied and were safe. Hundreds of lives were saved by the three sign holders. Because they did their job, many people were kept from peril.

But after a few hours they grew lax in their task.

The first man got sleepy. "I'll sit where people can read my sign as I sleep," he decided. So he took his sign off his shoulders and propped it up against a boulder. He leaned against it and fell asleep. As he slept his arm slid over the sign, blocking one of the two words. So rather than read "Bridge Out," his sign simply stated "Bridge."

The second didn't grow tired, but he did grow conceited. The longer he stood warning the people the more important he felt. A few even pulled off to the side of the road to thank him for the job well done.

"We might have died had you not told us to slow down," they applauded.

"You're so right," he thought to himself. "How many people would be lost were it not for me?"

Presently he came to think that he was just as important as his sign. So he took it off, set it up on the ground, and stood beside it. As he did, he was unaware that he, too, was blocking one word of his warning. He was standing in front of the word "Speed." All the drivers could read was the word "Reduce." Most thought he was advertising a diet plan.

The third man was not tired like the first, nor self-consumed like the second. But he was concerned about the message of his sign. "Right Road Only," it read.

It troubled him that his message was so narrow, so dogmatic. "People should be given a choice in the matter. Who am I to tell them which is the right road and which is the wrong road?"

So he decided to alter the wording of the sign. He marked out the word "Only" and changed it to "Preferred."

"Hmm," he thought, "that's still too strident. One is best not to moralize. So he marked out the word "Preferred" and wrote "Suggested."

That still didn't seem right, "Might offend people if they think I'm suggesting I know something they don't."

So he thought and thought and finally marked through the word "Suggested" and replaced it with a more neutral phrase.

"Ahh, just right," he said to himself as he backed off and read the words:

"Right Road—One of Two Equally Valid Alternatives."

And so as the first man slept and the second stood and the third altered the message, one car after another plunged into the river.

He is the One who comes after me. I am not good enough to tie the strings of his sandals.

John 1:27

The Winsomeness of Holiness

Leading or Misleading?

JOHN THE BAPTIST would never get hired today. No church would touch him. He was a public relations disaster. He "wore clothes made from camel's hair, had a leather belt around his waist, and ate locusts and wild honey" (Mark 1:6). Who would want to look at a guy like that every Sunday?

His message was as rough as his dress: a no-nonsense, bare-fisted challenge to repent because God was on his way.

Didn't matter to John if you were a Jew, a priest, a Baptist, or all three. What mattered was that you get off your duff and get right with God because he's coming and he don't mean maybe.

No, John would never get hired today. His tactics lacked tact. His style wasn't smooth. He made few friends and lots of enemies, but what do you know? He made hundreds of converts. "All the people from Judea and Jerusalem were going out to him. They confessed their sins and were baptized by him in the Jordan River" (Mark 1:5).

Look at that. "All the people of Judea and Jerusalem. . . . " How do we explain such a response? It certainly wasn't his charisma or clothing. Nor was it his money or position, for he had neither. Then what did he have?

One word. *Holiness.*

John the Baptist set himself apart for one task, to be a voice of Christ. Everything about John centered on his purpose. His dress. His diet. His actions. His demands.

He reminded his hearers of Elijah. And he reminds us of this truth: "There is winsomeness in holiness." You don't have to be like the world to have an impact on the world. You don't have to be like the crowd to change the crowd. You don't have to lower yourself down to their level to lift them up to your level.

Nor do you have to be weird. You don't need to wear camel's-hair clothing or eat insects. Holiness doesn't seek to be odd. Holiness seeks to be like God.

You want to make a difference in your world? Live a holy life:

Be faithful to your spouse.

Be the one at the office who refuses to cheat.

Be the neighbor who acts neighborly.

Be the employee who does the work and doesn't complain.

Pay your bills.

Do your part and enjoy life.

Don't speak one message and live another.

Note the last line of Paul's words in 1 Thessalonians 4:11–12.

> Do all you can to lead a peaceful life. Take care of your own business, and do your own work as we have already told you. If you do, then people who are not believers will respect you.

A peaceful life leads nonbelievers to respect believers. What if John's life had not matched his words? What if he'd preached repentance and lived in immorality? What if he'd called for holiness and yet had a reputation for dishonesty? If John's life had not matched his words, his message would have fallen on deaf ears.

So will ours.

People are watching the way we act more than they are listening to what we say.

Saint Francis of Assisi once invited a young monk to accompany him to town to preach. The novice was honored at the opportunity.

The two set out for the city, then walked up and down the main street, then several side streets. They chatted with peddlers and greeted the citizens. After some time they returned by another route to the abbey.

The younger man reminded Francis of his original intent. "You have forgotten, Father, that we went to town to preach."

"My son," he replied, "we have preached. We have been seen by many. Our behavior was closely watched. Our attitudes were closely measured. Our words have been overheard. It was by thus that we preached our morning sermon."[1]

John was a voice for Christ with more than his voice. His life matched his words. When a person's ways and words are the same, the fusion is explosive. But when a person says one thing and lives another, the result is destructive. People will know we are Christians, not because we bear the name, but because we live the life.

It's the life that earns the name, not the name that creates the life. Here's a story that illustrates this point.

A Jewish couple were arguing over the name to give their firstborn. They finally asked the rabbi to come and intercede.

"What is the problem?" the rabbi asked.

The wife spoke first. "He wants to name the boy after his father, and I want to name the boy after my father."

"What is your father's name?" he asked the man.

"Joseph."

"And what is your father's name?" he asked the woman.

"Joseph."

The rabbi was stunned. "So, what is the problem?"

It was the wife who spoke again. "His father was a horse thief, and mine was a righteous man. How can I know my son is named after my father and not his?"

The rabbi thought and then replied, "Call the boy Joseph. Then see if he is a horse thief or a righteous man. You will know which father's name he wears."

To call yourself a child of God is one thing. To be called a child of God by those who watch your life is another thing altogether.

As Jesus was walking along, he saw a man who had been born blind. His followers asked him, "Teacher, whose sin caused this man to be born blind— his own sin or his parents' sin?"

John 9:1–2

25

Look Before You Label

Caring or Condemning?

RECENTLY WE TOOK our kids on a vacation to a historical city. While going on a tour through an old house, we followed a family from New York City. They didn't tell me they were from New York. They didn't have to. I could tell. They wore New York City clothes. Their teenager had one half of his head shaved and on the other half of his head, his hair hung past his shoulders. The daughter wore layered clothes and long beads. The mother looked like she'd raided her daughter's closet, and the dad's hair was down the back of his neck.

I had them all figured out. The kid was probably on drugs. The parents were going through a midlife crisis. They were rich and miserable and in need of counseling. Good thing I was nearby in case they wanted spiritual counsel.

After a few moments they introduced themselves. I was right; they were from New York City. But that is all I got right. When I told them my name, they were flabbergasted. "We can't believe it!" they said. "We've read your books. We use them in our Sunday school class in church. I tried to get over to hear you when you spoke in our area, but that was our family night and . . ."

Sunday school? Church? Family night? Oh, boy. I'd made a mistake. A big mistake. I'd applied the label before examining the contents.

We've all used labels. We stick them on jars and manila folders so we'll know what's inside. We also stick them on people for the same reason.

John tells of a time the disciples applied a label. Jesus and his followers came upon a man who had been blind from birth. Here is the question the disciples asked Jesus: "Teacher, whose sin caused this man to be born blind—his own sin or his parents' sin?" (John 9:2).

Never mind that the man is a beggar in need of help. Never mind that the man has spent his life in a dark cave. Never mind that the man seated in front of them is in earshot of their voices. Let's talk about his sin.

How could they be so harsh? So insensitive? So . . . blind.

The answer? (You may not like it.) It's easier to talk about a person than to help a person. It's easier to debate homosexuality than to be a friend to a gay person. It's easier to discuss divorce than to help the divorced. It's easier to argue abortion than to support an orphanage. It's easier to complain about the welfare system than to help the poor.

It's easier to label than to love.

It's especially easy to talk theology. Such discussions make us feel righteous. Self-righteous.

As long as I'm confessing sins, I might as well confess another. We had such a theological discussion in Brazil. We missionaries debated whether we should offer Communion to people who are not members of our church. Our reasoning? What if they aren't faithful? What if they aren't truly converted? What if their hearts aren't right? If we offer them Communion, we could be leading them to eat the bread or drink of the cup in an unworthy manner, thereby leading them to sin (see 1 Cor. 11:27). So we decided that first-time visitors could not partake.

We meant well. It sounded right. But I learned a lesson.

Guess what happened. That very week a friend told me he would like to visit the church. The same friend we had been inviting for weeks. The same friend who had shown no interest was suddenly interested. At first I was elated; then my heart sank. I told him he could come, but he couldn't partake of Communion.

As long as I live, I'll never forget the look on his face as he passed the Communion plate to the person next to him. He never returned. Who could blame him? We'd applied the label before we looked inside.

Is that to say religious discussion is wrong? Of course not. Is that to say we should be unconcerned for doctrine or lax in a desire for holiness? Absolutely not. That is to say there is something wrong with applying the label before examining the contents. Do you like it when people label you before they know you?

"So, you're unemployed?" (Translation: *Must be a bum.*)

"Hmm, you're an accountant?" (Translation: *Must be dull.*)

"She's an Episcopalian." (Translation: *Must be liberal.*)

"She's an Episcopalian who voted for the democrats." (Translation: *Must be liberal beyond help.*)

"Oh, I'm sorry; I didn't know you were a divorcee." (Translation: *Must be immoral.*)

"He's a fundamentalist." (Translation: *Narrow-minded half-wit.*)

Labels. A fellow gave me one the other day. We got into a lively discussion about some ethical issues. Somewhere in our conversation he asked me what kind of work I was in. I told him I was minister, and he said, "Oh, I see," and grew silent.

I wanted to say, "No, you don't. Don't you put me in that box. I'm not a minister. I am Max-who-ministers. Don't you put me in that box with all those hucksters and hypocrites you may know. That's not fair."

Labels. So convenient. Stick them on a person, and you know what pantry to use.

What if God did that with us? What if God judged us by our outward appearance? What if he judged us based on where we grew up? Or what we do for a living? Or the mistakes we made when we were young? He wouldn't do that, would he?

"Don't judge other people, or you will be judged. You will be judged in the same way you judge others, and the amount you give to others will be given to you" (Matt. 7:1–2).

Be careful when you judge. That doesn't mean we shouldn't discern. That does mean we shouldn't pass the verdict. The amount of grace you give is the amount you get.

Jesus had another view of the man born blind. Rather than see him as an opportunity for discussion, he saw him as an opportunity for God. Why was he blind? "So God's power could be shown in him" (John 9:3).

What a perspective! The man wasn't a victim of fate; he was a miracle waiting to happen. Jesus didn't label him. He helped him. Jesus was more concerned about the future than the past.

Who do you best relate to in this story? Some of you relate to the man born blind. You have been the topic of conversation. You have been left on the outside looking in. You've been labeled.

If so, learn what this man learned: When everyone else rejects you, Christ accepts you. When everyone else leaves you, Christ finds you. When no one else wants you, Christ claims you. When no one else will give you the time of day, Jesus will give you the words of eternity.

Others of you will relate to the observers. You've judged. You've labeled. You've slammed the gavel and proclaimed the guilt before knowing the facts. If that is you, go back to John 9:4 and understand what the work of God is: "While it is daytime we must continue doing the work of the One who sent me."

What is the work of God? Accepting people. Loving before judging. Caring before condemning.

Look before you label.

Then some of the people who lived in Jerusalem said, . . . "We know where this man is from. And when the real Christ comes, no one will know where he comes from."

John 7:25–27

26

Looking for the Messiah

How Do You See Him?

SUPPOSE JESUS CAME to your church. I don't mean symbolically. I mean visibly. Physically. Actually. Suppose he came to your
church.

Would you recognize him? It might be difficult. Jesus didn't wear
religious clothes in his day. Doubtful that he would wear them in ours.
If he came today to your church, he'd wear regular clothes. Nothing
fancy, just a jacket and shoes and a tie. Maybe a tie . . . maybe not.

He would have a common name. "Jesus" was common. I suppose he might go by Joe or Bob or Terry or Elliot.

Elliot . . . I like that. Suppose Elliot, the Son of God, came to
your church.

Of course, he wouldn't be from Nazareth or Israel. He'd hail
from some small spot down the road like Hollow Point or Chester
City or Mt. Pleasant.

And he'd be a laborer. He was a carpenter in his day. No reason
to think he'd change, but let's say he did. Let's say that this time
around he was a plumber. Elliot, the plumber from Mt. Pleasant.

God, a plumber?

Rumor has it that he fed a football field full of people near the
lake. Others say he healed a senator's son from Biloxi. Some say

he's the Son of God. Others say he's the joke of the year. You don't know what to think.

And then, one Sunday, he shows up.

About midway through the service he appears in the back of the auditorium and takes a seat. After a few songs he moves closer to the front. After yet another song he steps up on the platform and announces, "You are singing about me. I am the Son of God." He holds a Communion tray. "This bread is my body. This wine is my blood. When you celebrate this, you celebrate me!"

What would you think?

Would you be offended? *The audacity of it all. How irreverent, a guy named Elliot as the Son of God!*

Would you be interested? *Wait a minute, how could he be the Son of God? He never went to seminary, never studied at a college. But there is something about him . . .*

Would you believe? *I can't deny it's crazy. But I can't deny what he has done.*

It's easy to criticize contemporaries of Jesus for not believing in him. But when you realize how he came, you can understand their skepticism.

Jesus didn't fit their concept of a Messiah. Wrong background. Wrong pedigree. Wrong hometown. No Messiah would come from Nazareth. Small, hick, one-stoplight town. He didn't fit the Jews' notion of a Messiah, and so, rather than change their notion, they dismissed him.

He came as one of them. He was Jesus from Nazareth. Elliot from Mt. Pleasant. He fed the masses with calloused hands. He raised the dead wearing bib overalls and a John Deere Tractor cap.

They expected lights and kings and chariots from heaven. What they got was sandals and sermons and a Galilean accent.

And so, some missed him.

And so, some miss him still.

We have our own preconceptions, don't we? We still think we know which phone God uses and which car he drives. We still think we know what he looks like. But he's been known to surprise us.

We expect God to speak through peace, but sometimes he speaks through pain.

We think God talks through the church, but he also talks through the lost.

We look for the answer among the Protestants, but he's been known to speak through the Catholics.

We listen for him among the Catholics but find him among the Quakers.

We think we hear him in the sunrise, but he is also heard in the darkness.

We listen for him in triumph, but he speaks even more distinctly through tragedy.

We must let God define himself.

We must put away our preconceptions; otherwise we'll make the same mistake a lady in Baltimore made recently. Our radio ministry was hosting a radio rally. After my talk, I stayed around to meet the folks who listen to my program. These people had never seen me, but they had heard my voice. Presently a small, elderly woman stepped up.

"You don't look like you," was her first statement.

"Excuse me?"

"You don't look like you. Max Lucado is older, and his hair is grayer."

I hated to disappoint the lady, but she was wrong. I looked just like me. My face would match the picture on my driver's license, but that didn't matter to her. She wanted a face to match her preconception.

She had an image in her mind that didn't match the image she saw. She had to make a choice. She had to accept the true me or live with the wrong impression. We must do the same with God.

When we do, when we let God define himself, a whole new world opens before us. How, you ask? Let me explain with a story.

Once there was a man whose life was one of misery. The days were cloudy, and the nights were long. Henry didn't want to be unhappy, but he was. With the passing of the years, his life had changed. His children were grown. The neighborhood was different. The city seemed harsher.

He was unhappy. He decided to ask his minister what was wrong.

"Am I unhappy for some sin I have committed?"

"Yes," the wise pastor replied. "You have sinned."

"And what might that sin be?"

"Ignorance," came the reply. "The sin of ignorance. One of your neighbors is the Messiah in disguise, and you have not seen him."

The old man left the office stunned. "The Messiah is one of my neighbors?" He began to think who it might be.

Tom the butcher? No, he's too lazy. Mary, my cousin down the street? No, too much pride. Aaron the paperboy? No, too indulgent. The man was confounded. Every person he knew had defects. But one was the Messiah. He began to look for Him.

He began to notice things he hadn't seen. The grocer often carried sacks to the cars of older ladies. *Maybe he is the Messiah.* The officer at the corner always had a smile for the kids. *Could it be?* And the young couple who'd moved next door. *How kind they are to their cat. Maybe one of them . . .*

With time he saw things in people he'd never seen. And with time his outlook began to change. The bounce returned to his step. His eyes took on a friendly sparkle. When others spoke he listened. After all, he might be listening to the Messiah. When anyone asked for help, he responded; after all this might be the Messiah needing assistance.

The change of attitude was so significant that someone asked him why he was so happy. "I don't know," he answered. "All I know is that things changed when I started looking for God."

Now, that's curious. The old man saw Jesus because he didn't know what he looked like. The people in Jesus' day missed him because they thought they did.

How are things looking in your neighborhood?

As Simon Peter was standing and warming himself, they said to him, "Aren't you one of that man's followers?" Peter said it was not true; he said, "No, I am not."

One of the servants of the high priest was there. This servant was a relative of the man whose ear Peter had cut off. The servant said, "Didn't I see you with him in the garden?"

Again Peter said it wasn't true. At once the rooster crowed.

John 18:25–27

Peter, Me, and Wile E. Coyote

Guilt or Grace?

WILE E. COYOTE furiously chases Roadrunner. The bird suddenly stops. The coyote tries to but can't, and he skids past the roadrunner out to the edge of a cliff. The ground gives way and for just a moment we see his saucer eyes. Then down Wile E. plummets. *Poof!*

I love to watch old *Roadrunner* cartoons. Wile E. Coyote and I share a common plight. I, too, have ventured too close to the edge. I've found myself on shaky ground and taken a fall. I've stared that "oh-boy-this-is-gonna-hurt" stare. I've looked up from the bottom of the pit, dazed and stunned.

But Wile E. has something I don't. He's invincible. He never gets hurt. The falls don't faze him. In the next scene of the cartoon he's stacking Acme dynamite or painting a wall to make it appear like a tunnel. Within moments, he's out of the pit, back on the trail.

You and I don't recover so easily. Like Wile E., we fall. But unlike Wile E., we wander in the canyon for a while. Stunned, hurt . . . and wondering if this ravine has a way out.

Few of us have been in a pit deeper than Peter's. Which is ironic, for just an hour or two before, he was high on the pinnacle and far from the pit. "Simon Peter, who had a sword, pulled it out and struck the servant of the high priest, cutting off his right ear" (John 18:10).

Smugly, Peter stands next to Jesus, flashing his sword. "Step aside, Jesus, I'll take care of this one for you." My hunch is Peter expected a fight. My hunch is Peter was stunned when Jesus told him to put away his sword. Next thing Peter knows, the Savior and the soldiers are headed down the hill and Peter's alone with his decision. Does he stick close to Jesus or duck in the shadows? He opts to do neither.

Luke tells us that Peter followed Jesus and his captors from a distance (see Luke 22:54). Not too close, yet not too far. Near enough to see him, but not near enough to be seen with him. Love made Peter ashamed to run; fear made him ashamed to draw near. The disciples chose the left side of the road and ran. Jesus chose the right side of the road and obeyed. But Peter chose the yellow stripe down the middle. BIG mistake.

He would have been better off in the shadows with the disciples. He would have been better off in the courtyard with his master. But instead Peter is warming his hands on the devil's hearth. A young girl recognizes him and asks, "Aren't you one of that man's followers?"

"No, I am not!" he defies.

Moments later he is asked the question again: "Aren't you one of the man's followers?" And a second time he denies his Lord. The third question comes from a relative of Malchus: "Didn't I see you with him in the garden?" This time Peter curses the very thought of it (Matt. 26:74).

With each denial Peter inches closer to the edge of the canyon . . . until the ground gives way and he falls.

Have you been there? Have you felt the ground of conviction give way beneath your feet? The ledge crumbles, your eyes widen, and down you go. *Poof!*

Now what do you do? You could stay in the canyon. Many do. Many live their lives in the shadows. Many never return. Some dismiss their deeds. "Well, everybody has a little slip now and then."

Some deny their deeds. "Fall? Me? Are you kidding? These aren't bruises. These aren't cuts. I'm as healthy as I've ever been. Me and Jesus? We are tight." Some distort their deeds. "I'm not to blame. It's his fault. It's society's responsibility. If the people hadn't asked me, I wouldn't have answered. Don't point the finger at me."

When we fall, we can dismiss it. We can deny it. We can distort it. Or we can deal with it.

Luke adds a chilling phrase to his account of Peter's denial of Christ. When the cock crowed, "the Lord turned and looked straight at Peter" (Luke 22:61).

The rooster reminds Peter of Jesus' warning. Peter lifts his eyes and looks across the courtyard, only to find Jesus looking at him. Jesus is being assailed by accusations, but he doesn't hear them. He hears only the denial of his friend.

If Peter ever thought he could keep his fall a secret, he now knows he can't. "Nothing in all the world can be hidden from God. Everything is clear and lies open before him, and to him we must explain the way we have lived" (Heb. 4:13).

We keep no secrets from God. Confession is not telling God what we did. He already knows. Confession is simply agreeing with God that our acts were wrong. Did Peter do this? Again let Luke speak: "And Peter remembered what the Lord had said: 'Before the rooster crows this day you will say three times that you don't know me.' Then Peter went outside and cried painfully" (Luke 22:61–62).

Each tear a confession, each sob an admission, Peter remembers the words of Jesus and weeps.

There is an old story about the time Emperor Frederick the Great visited Potsdam Prison. He spoke with the prisoners, and each man claimed to be innocent, a victim of the system. One man, however, sat silently in the corner.

The ruler asked him, "And you, sir, who do you blame for your sentence?"

His response was, "Your majesty, I am guilty and richly deserve my punishment." Surprised, the emperor shouted for the prison warden: "Come and get this man out of here before he corrupts all these innocent people."[1]

The ruler can set us free once we admit we are wrong.

We do ourselves no favors in justifying our deeds or glossing over our sins. Some time ago my daughter Andrea got a splinter in her finger. I took her to the restroom and set out some tweezers, ointment, and a Band-Aid.

She didn't like what she saw. "I just want the Band-Aid, Daddy."

Sometimes we are just like Andrea. We come to Christ with our sin, but all we want is a covering. We want to skip the treatment. We want to hide our sin. And one wonders if God, even in his great mercy, will heal what we conceal. "If we say we have no sin, we are fooling ourselves, and the truth is not in us. But if we confess our sins, he will forgive our sins, because we can trust God to do what is right" (1 John 1:8–9).

Going to God is not going to Santa Claus. A child sits on the chubby lap of Ol' Saint Nick and Santa pinches the youngster's cheek and asks, "Have you been a good little girl?"

"Yes," she giggles. Then she tells him what she wants and down she bounds. It's a game. It's childish. No one takes Santa's question seriously. That may work in a department store, but it won't work with God.

How can God heal what we deny? How can God touch what we cover up? How can we have communion while we keep secrets? How can God grant us pardon when we won't admit our guilt?

Ahh, there's that word: *guilt*. Isn't that what we avoid? Guilt. Isn't that what we detest? But is guilt so bad? What does guilt imply if not that we know right from wrong, that we aspire to be better than we are, that we know there is a high country and we are in the low country. That's what guilt is: a healthy regret for telling God one thing and doing another.

Guilt is the nerve-ending of the heart. It yanks us back when we are too near the fire. Godly sorrow "makes people change their hearts and lives. This leads to salvation, and you cannot be sorry for that" (2 Cor. 7:10).

To feel guilt is no tragedy; to feel no guilt is.

When Peter saw Jesus looking at him from across the courtyard, he was flooded with guilt.

What if Peter hadn't dealt with his feelings of guilt? What if Peter had dismissed, denied, or distorted his sin? What if he had never exited the canyon? How many sermons would have gone unpreached? How many lives would have gone untouched or epistles gone unwritten?

Had Peter not felt the guilt in the courtyard, he never would have proclaimed the grace on Pentecost. Had Peter not left the canyon, he never would have shared the Christ.

Which leads us to wonder how many untold stories walk the canyon floor today . . . How many lives have been neutralized by guilt? How many Peters are in the shadows, wanting to come out, if only they knew the way.

Peter shows the way.

Please note, there are two fires in Peter's story. The first is the fire of denial, but the second is the fire of discovery. The first fire was built by men; the second was built by Christ. At the first fire, Peter denied Jesus. At the second, Peter confessed him.

What took Peter from one fire to the next? How did he journey from the fire of denial to the fire of discovery? In between the fires are two events: the tears of Peter and the cross of Jesus. Both are essential. If Peter had shed tears but not seen the cross, he would have known only despair. Had he seen the cross but shed no tears, he would have known only arrogance. But since he saw both, he knew redemption.

Mingle the tears of the sinner with the cross of the Savior and the result is a joyful escort out of the canyon of guilt.

There are many rooms in my Father's house; I would not tell you this if it were not true. I am going there to prepare a place for you.

John 14:2

Ready for Home
Ready or Not

HAD YOU BEEN on the British Coast in 1845 you might have seen two ships boarded by 138 of England's finest sailors setting sail for the Arctic. Their task? To chart the Northwest Passage around the Canadian Arctic to the Pacific Ocean.

The captain, Sir John Franklin, hoped this effort would be the turning point in Arctic exploration. History shows that it was. Not because of its success, but because of its failure. The ships never returned. Every crew member perished. And those who followed in the expedition's path to the pole learned this lesson: Prepare for the journey.

Apparently Franklin didn't. Though the voyage was projected to last two or three years, he only carried a twelve-day supply of coal for the auxiliary steam engines. But what he lacked in fuel, he made up for in entertainment. Each ship carried a "1,200 volume library, a hand-organ, china place settings for officers and men, cut-glass wine goblets and sterling silver flatware."[1]

Was the crew planning for an Arctic expedition or a Caribbean cruise? Judging from the supplies, one would have thought the latter. The sailors carried no special clothing to protect them against the cold. Only the uniforms of Her Majesty's fleet. Noble and respectful, but thin and inadequate.

The silver knives, forks, and spoons were as ornate as those found in the dining rooms of the Royal Navy officers clubs: heavy at the handles, intricately designed. Years later, some of these place settings would be found near a clump of frozen, cannibalized bodies. The inevitable had occurred. The two ships had sailed ill-prepared into the frigid waters. Ice coated the deck, the spars, and the rigging. The sea froze around the rudder and trapped the ship.

The sailors set out to search for help, wearing their uniforms and carrying their belongings. Inuit Indians reported seeing a group dragging a wooden boat across the ice. For the next twenty years, remains of the expedition were found all over the frozen sea. The boat, or a similar one, was later discovered containing the bodies of thirty-five men. Other Indians discovered a tent on the ice and in it, thirty bodies.

Franklin died on the boat. Search parties would later find a piece of the backgammon board Lady Jane Franklin had given her husband as a farewell present.

Many miles from the vessel, the skeleton of a frozen officer was discovered, still wearing trousers and jacket of "fine blue cloth . . . edged with silk braid, with sleeves slashed and bearing five buttons each. Over his uniform the dead man had worn a blue greatcoat, with a black silk neckerchief."[2]

Strange how men could embark on such a journey ill-prepared, more equipped for afternoon tea than for the open sea.

Stranger still how we do the same. Don't Franklin's men remind you of us? We sometimes act as if the Christian life is a retirement cruise. We have little fuel but lots of entertainment. We are more concerned with looking snappy than with being prepared. We give more thought to table settings than to surviving the journey. We give little thought to the destination, but we make sure there's plenty of silver to go around.

And so when the freeze comes, we step out on the ice with forks, games, and skimpy clothing and pass our final days walking against the wind, often blaming God for getting us into this mess.

But God is not to blame. If we sail unprepared it's in spite of—not because of—God. He left detailed instructions about this voyage. His Word is our map; the Holy Spirit is our compass.

He outlined the route and described the landmarks we should seek.

He even told us what to pack for the trip: love, joy, peace, patience, kindness, goodness, faithfulness, gentleness, self-control (see Gal. 5:22–23).

And most remarkably, he's gone before us and goes with us. He's both a pioneer and a co-traveler! And when we grow weary, all we need to do is listen to his voice. He's got special promises to keep us on the journey.

Here is one of the best.

"There are many rooms in my father's house."

What a tender phrase. A house implies rest, safety, warmth, a table, a bed, a place to be at home. But this isn't just any house. It is our Father's house.

All of us know what it is like to be in a house that is not our own. Perhaps you've spent time in a dorm room or army barrack. Maybe you've slept in your share of hotels or bunked in a few hostels. They have beds. They have tables. They may have food and they may be warm, but they are a far cry from being "your father's house."

Your father's house is where your father is.

Perhaps you can remember the voice of your father? Coming home from work filling the hallways? Sounding through the rooms? Some of you can. And for many, the memory is fond.

Others of you don't have that memory, but you will. "If my father and mother leave me, the LORD will take me in" (Ps. 27:10).

Your Father is preparing a place for you. A place with *many* rooms. An ample place. A place with space for you. There is a special room for you. You will be welcome.

We don't always feel welcome here on earth. We wonder if there is a place here for us. People can make us feel unwanted. Tragedy leaves us feeling like intruders. Strangers. Interlopers in a land not ours. We don't always feel welcome here.

We shouldn't. This isn't our home. To feel unwelcome is no tragedy. Indeed it is healthy. We are not home here. This language we speak, it's not ours. This body we wear, it isn't us. And the world we live in, this isn't home.

Ours isn't finished yet.

But when it is, our brother will come and take us home. "I would not tell you this if it were not true. . . . I will come back," he said before he left, "and take you to be with me so that you may be where I am" (John 14:2–3).

That first sentence is a curious one. "*I would not tell you this if it were not true.*" Why did he say that? Did he see doubt in the heart of the disciples? Did he read confusion on their faces? I don't know what he saw in their eyes. But I know what he sees in ours.

He sees what the airline attendant sees when she gives her pre-flight warnings.

He sees what physicians often see when they tell patients to stop smoking.

He sees what ministers see when they tell a Sunday morning audience that each one of them could die today.

"*Yeah, sure. But probably not.*"

We don't say the words. But we think them. Sure, this plane could crash, but then again it probably won't. *So rather than listen I'll read my magazine. Sure I could die of cancer, but then again, maybe I won't. So rather than stop smoking today I'll wait awhile. Sure I could die today, but then again . . .*

General William Nelson was a Union general in the Civil War. Though he faced death every day, he never prepared for his own. Who knows what he was thinking as he rode into battle after battle? Maybe he was too busy staying alive to prepare for death.

All that changed, however, one day as he was relaxing in a house with his men. A brawl broke out, and he was shot in the chest. Knowing he was dying, he had only one request: "Send for a clergyman."

What had happened? Why the urgency? Did the general suddenly learn something about God that he had never known? No.

But he did learn something about himself. He realized death was near. Suddenly only one thing mattered.[3]

Why hadn't it mattered before? Couldn't he have said yes to God the week before or that very morning? Absolutely. Why didn't he? Why was the salvation of his soul so urgent after the shot and so optional before it? Why had he postponed his decision to accept Christ until his deathbed?

Because he assumed he had time.

A dangerous assumption. "Teach us how short our lives really are," prayed Moses, "so that we may be wise" (Ps. 90:12).

What fear strikes a man when the end is near and he's not prepared.

What fear must have struck the crew of Sir John Franklin when they became stuck in the ice. What anxiety to search for food and find silver, to dig in the closets for coats and find uniforms, to explore the ship for picks and axes and find backgammon games and novels.

Don't you know they would have swapped it all in a heartbeat for what they needed to get home safely?

By the way, what supplies are you taking? Are you carrying your share of silver and games? Don't be fooled; they may matter here, but they matter not when you reach your Father's house. What matters is if you are known by the Father.

It's not what you have; it's who you know. Be prepared. You don't want to be left out in the cold.

He came to the world that was his own, but his own people did not accept him.

John 1:11

The Cave People
Will You Share the Light?

LONG AGO, OR maybe not so long ago, there was a tribe in a dark, cold cavern.

The cave dwellers would huddle together and cry against the chill. Loud and long they wailed. It was all they did. It was all they knew to do. The sounds in the cave were mournful, but the people didn't know it, for they had never known joy. The spirit in the cave was death, but the people didn't know it, for they had never known life.

But then, one day, they heard a different voice. "I have heard your cries," it announced. "I have felt your chill and seen your darkness. I have come to help."

The cave people grew quiet. They had never heard this voice. Hope sounded strange to their ears. "How can we know you have come to help?"

"Trust me," he answered. "I have what you need."

The cave people peered through the darkness at the figure of the stranger. He was stacking something, then stooping and stacking more.

"What are you doing?" one cried, nervous.

The stranger didn't answer.

"What are you making?" one shouted even louder.

Still no response.

"Tell us!" demanded a third.

The visitor stood and spoke in the direction of the voices. "I have what you need." With that he turned to the pile at his feet and lit it. Wood ignited, flames erupted, and light filled the cavern.

The cave people turned away in fear. "Put it out!" they cried. "It hurts to see it."

"Light always hurts before it helps," he answered. "Step closer. The pain will soon pass."

"Not I," declared a voice.

"Nor I," agreed a second.

"Only a fool would risk exposing his eyes to such light."

The stranger stood next to the fire. "Would you prefer the darkness? Would you prefer the cold? Don't consult your fears. Take a step of faith."

For a long time no one spoke. The people hovered in groups covering their eyes. The fire builder stood next to the fire. "It's warm here," he invited.

"He's right," one from behind him announced. "It's warmer." The stranger turned and saw a figure slowly stepping toward the fire. "I can open my eyes now," she proclaimed. "I can see."

"Come closer," invited the fire builder.

She did. She stepped into the ring of light. "It's so warm!" She extended her hands and sighed as her chill began to pass.

"Come, everyone! Feel the warmth," she invited.

"Silence, woman!" cried one of the cave dwellers. "Dare you lead us into your folly? Leave us. Leave us and take your light with you."

She turned to the stranger. "Why won't they come?"

"They choose the chill, for though it's cold, it's what they know. They'd rather be cold than change."

"And live in the dark?"

"And live in the dark."

The now-warm woman stood silent. Looking first at the dark, then at the man.

"Will you leave the fire?" he asked.

She paused, then answered, "I cannot. I cannot bear the cold." Then she spoke again. "But nor can I bear the thought of my people in darkness."

"You don't have to," he responded, reaching into the fire and removing a stick. "Carry this to your people. Tell them the light is here, and the light is warm. Tell them the light is for all who desire it."

And so she took the small flame and stepped into the shadows.

I have good plans for you, not plans to hurt you. I will give you hope and a good future.

Jeremiah 29:11

30

If Only You Knew

WHAT I INTENDED as good was interpreted as bad . . . by a hummingbird.

Dozens of the little fellows linger around our house. It's a cordial relationship. We provide the nectar, and they provide the amusement.

Yesterday one of them got into trouble. He flew into the garage and got lost. Though the door was open for him to exit, he didn't see it. He insisted, instead, on bashing his head against a closed window. He was determined to get out, but his determination would not break the glass.

Soon our whole family was in the garage, empathizing with his confusion. "Help him out, Daddy," came the chorus from my kids.

So I tried. I raised the window, hoping he'd fly out—he didn't. He rode the frame as it rose. I nudged him with a broom handle, hoping he'd fly though the open window below. He didn't. I bumped him harder. He wouldn't budge. Finally, after several firm pokes he made a move . . . the wrong way. Instead of flying forward, he fluttered backward inside the two window panes. Now he was trapped.

What a pitiful sight. A little bird bouncing inside the glass. I had no choice. I stuck my fingers in the opening, grabbed a few feathers, and jerked him out. I'm sure he didn't appreciate the yank, but at least he was free. And when he got back to his nest, did he ever have a story to tell.

"I had a horrible day, Martha. I got stuck in this huge room with a fake exit. They made it look like a hole, but it wasn't. Then they tried to crush me with this moving ledge. But it stopped just before it reached the top. The big, ugly one came after me with a stick. Just when he was about to spear me I made a move for it. I dodged him but fell into their trap—a narrow room with invisible walls. How cruel. I could see them pointing at me. I'm sure they were hungry. Then the ugly one came after me again, this time with his fingers. He was going for my neck. I outfoxed him, though. Just when he pulled me out, I kicked loose and put it in turbocharge and escaped. It's a good thing I did or they would have had hummingburgers for dinner."

I was being kind. The bird thought I was cruel. If only the little bird had known that I had come to help. If only the little fellow had known that I was on his side. If only he had understood that the moving ledge and stick were for his protection.

If only he knew . . .

Now, I may be overdoing it with the hummingbird, but I'm not overdoing it with the point. Daily, God's extended aid is misinterpreted as intended hurt. We complain of closed windows, not noticing the huge open doors. We panic as the ledge rises, oblivious to the exit below. We dodge the stick that guides and avoid the fingers that liberate.

"If only you knew . . ." were my words to the bird.

"If only you knew . . ." are God's words to us.[1]

No lectures. No speeches. No homilies on how far he has come to help. No finger-pointing at our past. None of that. Just an appeal. An appeal for trust. "If only you knew . . ."

"If only you knew that I came to help and not condemn. If only you knew that tomorrow will be better than today. If only you knew the gift I have brought: eternal life. If only you knew I want you safely home."

If only you knew.

What wistful words to come from the lips of God. How kind that he would let us hear them. How crucial that we pause to hear them. If only we knew to trust. Trust that God is in our corner. Trust that God wants what is best. Trust that he really means it when he says, "I have good plans for you, not plans to hurt you. I will give you hope and a good future" (Jer. 29:11).

If only we could learn to trust him.

But how hard it is. We quiver like the bird on the ledge, ducking the hand that comes to help. We forget that he is the pilot and we are his passenger.

We accuse, falsely. We reject, naively.

If only we knew.

When he washed the disciples' feet, he was washing ours; when he calmed their storms, he was calming yours; when he forgave Peter, he was forgiving all the penitent. If only we knew.

He still sends pigeons to convince the lost and music to inspire the dance.

He still makes our storms his path, our graves his proof, and our souls his passion.

He hasn't changed.

He trims branches so we can bear fruit;

    he calls the sheep that we might be safe;

        he hears the prayers of crooks so we might go home.

His thunder is still gentle.

And his gentleness still thunders.

If only you knew "the free gift of God and who it is that is asking you . . ."

The gift and the Giver. If you know them, you know all you need.

Notes

Chapter 2   The Hound of Heaven

1. Francis Thompson, *Poetical Works of Francis Thompson* (New York: Oxford University Press, 1969), 89–94.

2. Ibid.

3. Fred Craddock, *Overhearing the Gospel* (Nashville: Abingdon, 1978), 105–8.

4. Ibid.

5. Frederick Buechner, *The Alphabet of Grace* (New York: HarperCollins, 1970), 43–44.

Chapter 4   Miracle at Midnight

1. They entered the boat at early evening (John 6:16); this probably means around 6:00 P.M. Jesus came to them between 3:00 and 6:00 A.M. (Matt. 14:25).

2. See Deuteronomy 1:2.

Chapter 8   Lessons from the Garden

1. William Barclay, *The Gospel of John*, vol. 2 (Philadelphia: Westminster Press, 1975), 222.

Chapter 9   What to Do with Birthdays

1. This comment and many of the other quips shared here are excerpted from *A Spread of Over 40s Jokes*, edited by Helen Exley and published by Exley Publications, Ltd., Mount Kisco, New York 1992.

2. This story was also told by Gary Thomas in "Wise Christians Clip Obituaries," *Christianity Today*, 3 Oct. 1994, 24–27.

Chapter 11   A Different Kind of Hero

1. This Associated Press story appeared in the insert accompanying the audio tape, "Stones in the Road" by Mary Chapin Carpenter, 1994, Sony Music Entertainment, Inc., New York. Mary Chapin Carpenter wrote a song, "John Doe No. 24," after she read this story in the newspaper.

Chapter 13   A Cinderella Story

1. John R. W. Stott, *The Cross of Christ* (Downers Grove, Ill.: InterVarsity Press, 1986), 88.

Chapter 14   The Bad News Preacher

1. This day is outlined and developed in Max Lucado, *In the Eye of the Storm: A Day in the Life of Jesus* (Dallas: Word, 1991).

Chapter 16   Inside Out

1. Adapted from John Phillips, *Exploring the Gospels: John* (Neptune, N.J.: Loizeaux Brother, 1989), 64–65.

Chapter 22   God's Been Known to Niggle

1. Beth Arnold, "The Need to Niggle," *American Way*, 1 June 1991, 44.

Chapter 24   The Winsomeness of Holiness

1. A. Gordon Nasby, ed., *1041 Sermon Illustrations, Ideas and Expositions* (Grand Rapids: Baker, 1976), 186.

Chapter 27   Peter, Me, and Wile E. Coyote
1. James F. Colianni, *The Book of Pulpit Humor* (Ventnor, N.J.: Voicings Publications, 1992), 128.

Chapter 28   Ready for Home
1. Annie Dillard, *Teaching a Stone to Talk* (New York: HarperCollins, 1988), 43.
2. Ibid.
3. Gary Thomas, "Wise Christians Clip Obituaries," *Christianity Today*, 3 October 1994, 24–27.

Chapter 30   If Only You Knew
1. See John 4:10.

Discussion Guide

Prepared by Steve Halliday

How to Use This Discussion Guide

Each of these short studies is designed not only to help you digest and apply the ideas developed in *A Gentle Thunder*, but also to point you back to Scripture as the wellspring of those ideas.

The first section of each study, "Echoes of Thunder," excerpts portions of each chapter and supplies questions for group discussion. The second section, "Flashes of Lightning," helps you dig a little deeper into Scripture's perspective on the topic under discussion.

His Voice, Our Choice

Echoes of Thunder

1. "How far do you want God to go in getting your attention? If God has to choose between your eternal safety and your earthly comfort, which do you hope he chooses?"
    A. Answer Max's two questions above.
    B. How far have you seen God go in getting others' attention?

2. "For all its peculiarities and unevenness, the Bible has a simple story. God made man. Man rejected God. God won't give up until he wins him back."
    A. What does Max mean by the Bible's "peculiarities and unevenness"?
    B. Name several biblical examples of what Max is describing here.

3. "God is as creative as he is relentless. The same hand that sent manna to Israel sent Uzzah to his death. The same hand that set the children free from Egypt also sent them captive to Babylon. Both kind and stern. Tender and tough."
    A. How could God be both kind and stern?
    B. In what ways has God been "creative" in your own life? How have you seen both his kindness and his toughness?

4. "God will whisper. He will shout. He will touch and tug. He will take away our burdens; he'll even take away our blessings. If there are a thousand steps between us and him, he will take all but one. But he will leave the final one for us. The choice is ours."
    A. How does it make you feel to know that God will go to such extremes to retrieve us? Explain.
    B. What is this "final choice" Max writes about? What choice have you made? Explain.

Flashes of Lightning

1. Read Psalm 81:6–16.
    A. How does this passage demonstrate both the kindness and the toughness of God? What events does this psalm describe?
    B. What is the Lord's chief desire for us, according to this psalm (see especially verses 10,13–14,16)?

2. Read Romans 11:22.
   A. What two traits is Paul contrasting in this verse?
   B. What example does Paul use to illustrate what he says in this verse?

3. Read John 5:6; 9:35; 11:25–26.
   A. What is Jesus doing in each of these texts? Why is he doing this?
   B. What choice would Jesus ask you to make if he were to speak to you today, face-to-face?

Chapter 1   The Author of Life

Echoes of Thunder

1. "The Author starts each life story, but each life will write his or her own ending."
   A. What does Max mean in his statement above?
   B. What kind of "ending" are you writing for your own story?

2. "Love is only love if chosen."
   A. Do you agree with this statement? Why or why not?
   B. Is love merely a choice, or is it more than that? Explain.

3. "Emmanuel would stand at the crossroads of life and death and make a choice."
   A. What choice did Emmanuel have to make? How did this affect you personally?
   B. How did Emmanuel make the choice he made? What gave him the strength to do so?

Flashes of Lightning

1. Read Deuteronomy 30:15–20.
   A. What choice was set before the nation of Israel? How is this choice similar to the one before us? How is it different?
   B. What choice did the nation finally make? What were the results? Can this be an example for us? Explain.

2. Read 1 John 4:7–21.
   A. What do you learn about love in this passage? Is it chosen? How can you tell?
   B. What is the primary example of love described in this passage (v. 10)? Was this love chosen? Explain.

3. Read Matthew 4:1–11; Luke 22:39–44.
   A. What choice did Emmanuel have to make in the Matthew passage? How did he make this choice?
   B. What choice did Emmanuel have to make in the Luke passage? How did he make this choice?
   C. How can we follow Emmanuel's example in the choices we make?

Chapter 2   The Hound of Heaven

Echoes of Thunder

1. "The rest of the world is occupied with Germany and Hitler. Every headline is reporting the actions of Roosevelt and Churchill. The globe is locked in a battle for freedom . . . and the Father is in the Pacific sending a missionary pigeon to save a soul."
   A. What does this incident teach us about God? How wide is his field of view?
   B. What kinds of "missionary pigeons" has God sent into your own life or into the lives of loved ones? Describe them.

2. "If anyone is in Christ, it is because Christ has called him."
   A. Do you agree with this statement? Why or why not?
   B. How did Christ call you?

3. "It isn't the circumstance that matters; it is God in the circumstance. It isn't the words; it is God speaking them."
   A. What do you think Max means by this statement? What point is he trying to make?
   B. Give an example from your own life of the difference between circumstances and God in those circumstances.

4. "The cradle and the cross were as common as grass. What made them holy was the One laid upon them."
   A. In what way were the cradle and the cross made "holy"? What does it mean that they were made holy?
   B. What makes common things holy today? What is being made holy in your own experience?

Flashes of Lightning

1. Read John 4:4.
   A. How is the story of the Samaritan woman like the one about the American flyers in World War II? What similarities do you see?

B. Why do you think Jesus "had" to go through Samaria?

2. Read John 6:37–40, 44–45.
   A. According to these verses, how do people come to Christ?
   B. What promise does Jesus make in verses 39–40? Is this a promise you can claim? Explain.

3. Read Ephesians 4:22–24.
   A. What are we commanded to do in this passage? Why?
   B. How does "holiness" work its way out into everyday living? Name several examples.

Chapter 3   Come and See

Echoes of Thunder

1. "Is the life of the young Nazarene carpenter really worth considering?"
   A. Answer Max's question above, then give a reason for your answer.
   B. What about the "life of the young Nazarene carpenter" is most worth considering, in your opinion? Why?

2. "Come and see the pierced hand of God touch the most common heart, wipe the tear from the wrinkled face, and forgive the ugliest sin."
   A. Does the "pierced hand of God" continue to do these things today? If so, how?
   B. Give examples from your own life of how Christ has done the three things listed in Max's statement above.

3. "Come and see. He avoids no seeker. He ignores no probe. He fears no search. Come and see."
   A. Why would Jesus "avoid no seeker, ignore no probe, or fear no search"? What enabled him to live this way?
   B. Do you invite people to "come and see" Jesus today? Explain.

Flashes of Lightning

1. Read Hebrews 12:3.
   A. Who are we asked to "consider" in this verse? What reason is given?
   B. In what way do you "consider" him? How does this help your everyday life?

2. Read Isaiah 42:1–4.
   A. List the activities of the coming Messiah as described in this passage.
   B. How do Jesus' activities compare to this list?

3. Read John 1:43–46.
   A. What happens in this passage? Describe it.
   B. What "evangelistic method" does Philip use in this passage? Can you use this method? Why or why not?

Chapter 4   Miracle at Midnight

Echoes of Thunder

1. "They did exactly what Jesus said, and look what it got them! A night on a storm-tossed sea with their Master somewhere on the shore."
   A. How do you think the disciples were feeling at this point? Why?
   B. Have you ever felt like this? If so, describe the circumstances.

2. "It's one thing to suffer for doing wrong. Something else entirely to suffer for doing right. But it happens."
   A. How does suffering for doing something wrong differ from suffering from doing right? They're both suffering, aren't they?
   B. If you have ever suffered for doing right, describe the circumstances.

3. "God was more concerned that they arrive *prepared* than that they arrive *soon*."
   A. What did it mean in this case that the disciples arrive "prepared"?
   B. In what way is this a good summary of God's work in our own lives?

4. "There are certain passions learned only by pain. And there are times when God, knowing that, allows us to endure the pain for the sake of the song."
   A. What kind of "passions" are learned only by pain? Why is pain the best teacher?
   B. Describe an instance in your own life when God allowed you to endure pain "for the sake of the song."

5. "We have our share of feasts, but we also have our share of baloney sandwiches. And to have the first we must endure the second."

A. Do you agree with this statement? Why or why not?

B. What kind of "feasts" have you enjoyed? Did they usually follow "baloney sandwiches"? Explain.

Flashes of Lightning

1. Read John 6:16–21.

    A. How was this experience like those we sometimes have?

    B. How did the disciples react when they saw Jesus? Did they know it was Jesus right away? What did they do when they made the discovery?

2. Read 1 Peter 4:15–16.

    A. What kinds of suffering does this passage describe?

    B. What kind of suffering should not make us ashamed? Why?

3. Read Acts 14:21–22.

    A. What did Paul and Barnabas do in Lystra, Iconium and Antioch? How did they do this?

    B. What did they tell the disciples in verse 22? How could this actually be an encouragement?

Chapter 5   The Secret of Forgiveness

Echoes of Thunder

1. "Logic says: 'She doesn't deserve it.' Jesus says: 'You're right, but you don't either.'"

    A. Why does logic say, "She doesn't deserve it"? Have you ever thought this way? If so, explain.

    B. Does Jesus refute this logic? How does he respond to it? Why is this important?

2. "We cannot cleanse our own filth. We cannot remove our own sin. Our feet must be in his hands."

    A. Why cannot we cleanse our own filth?

    B. In what sense today must our "feet . . . be in his hands"?

3. "Jesus is assuming the role of the servant. He will wash the grimiest part of your life. If you let him."

    A. Do you think Jesus will still assume the role of the servant today? Explain.

    B. How does Jesus "wash the grimiest" part of our life? What is necessary for this to happen?

4. "We will never be cleansed until we confess we are dirty."
   A. Why is it necessary to confess we are "dirty"? What does this entail?
   B. Have you made such a confession? Explain.

5. "God will never call you to do what he hasn't already done."
   A. Do you agree with this statement? Why or why not?
   B. What is the hardest thing God has called you to do? How do you know he called you to do it? How can you accomplish it?

Flashes of Lightning

1. Read John 13:3–5,12–17.
   A. What reason is given in verse 3 for what Jesus did? How is this significant?
   B. What lesson did Jesus want his disciples to learn in verses 12–17? What lesson is here for us?

2. Read 1 John 1:8–10.
   A. How does this text say we sometimes deceive ourselves?
   B. How can we be forgiven for our sins?
   C. In what way do some people call God a liar?

3. Read 2 Thessalonians 2:13–17.
   A. According to verse 13, how are we saved?
   B. What is the result of this in verse 14?
   C. What is Paul's prayer in verses 16–17? How is this connected to verses 13–15?

Chapter 6   The Bread of Life

Echoes of Thunder

1. "What bread is to hunger, Jesus claims to be for the soul."
   A. What does bread do for hunger?
   B. What does Jesus claim to do for our soul? In what way does Jesus want us to see him like bread?

2. "Jesus adapts himself to meet our need."
   A. How does Jesus adapt himself to meet our need?
   B. In what ways has Jesus adapted himself to meet your need?

3. "Jesus experienced each part of the process of making bread: the growing, the pounding, the firing."
   A. Describe the "growing, the pounding, and the firing" that Jesus went through.
   B. Why was it important for Jesus to go through all these steps? Why not bypass some or all of them?

4. "We can't force people to eat the bread, but we can make sure they have it. Yet, for some reason we are reluctant to do so. It's much easier to stay in the bakery than get into the truck."
   A. How can we make sure people have this "bread"? Have you made sure they had it? Explain.
   B. Why do we find it easier to stay in the bakery? How can we motivate ourselves to get into the truck?

5. "I don't know what is more incredible: that God packages the bread of life in the wrapper of a country carpenter or that he gives us the keys to the delivery truck."
   A. Which of these two facts is more incredible to you? Why?
   B. What are you doing with the keys to the delivery truck? Explain.

Flashes of Lightning

1. Read John 6:35–36.
   A. What claim did Jesus make in verse 35?
   B. What is one possible reaction to Jesus' claim (verse 36)?

2. Read Isaiah 55:1–3.
   A. What invitation is given here? How is it similar to what Jesus said in John 6?
   B. How would you answer the question in verse 2?
   C. What is promised in verses 2b–3?

3. Read Luke 24:25–26.
   A. To whom was Jesus speaking in this verse? Why do you think he took this tone with them?
   B. What did Jesus explain in verse 26? How does this help to explain what happened at Calvary?

Chapter 7   For Longer Than Forever

Echoes of Thunder

1. "We are a gnat on the tail of one elephant in a galaxy of Africas, and yet we demand that God finds us a parking place when we ask."
   A. What point is Max driving at in the statement above?
   B. Have you ever found yourself making such a demand? If so, describe the circumstances. How do you feel about it now?

2. "Our evil cannot diminish God's love. Our goodness cannot increase it. Our faith does not earn it any more than our stupidity jeopardizes it."
   A. Why can't our evil diminish God's love? Why can't our goodness increase it?
   B. If our faith doesn't "earn" God's love, how can we receive it? Why can't our stupidity jeopardize that love?

3. "God has no cousins, only children."
   A. Explain the statement above. What does it mean?
   B. Why doesn't God have any cousins, only children? What kind of people might be tempted to think they're God's cousins?

4. "Nothing can separate us from the love of Christ . . . but how difficult it is for some to embrace this truth."
   A. Why is it sometimes difficult for us to embrace the fact that nothing can separate us from the love of Christ?
   B. How do you respond to this truth personally? How do you remind yourself of it? Does it affect the way you live? Explain.

Flashes of Lightning

1. Read John 13:1
   A. What time was it, according to this verse? How did Jesus know this?
   B. What was Jesus about to show his disciples? How would he show them this?

2. Read Psalm 136.
   A. What refrain is repeated multiple times in this psalm?
   B. Why is this so important? What lesson is being taught?

3. Read Romans 8:38–39.
   A. What promise is given in this passage?
   B. How does God love us, according to this passage? Why is this crucial?

Chapter 8   Lessons from the Garden

Echoes of Thunder

1. "Were the moment not so solemn it would be comic. These are the best soldiers with Satan's finest plan, yet one word from Jesus and they fall down!"
   A. In what way is this moment solemn? In what way might it be comic?
   B. What do you think might have been running through Satan's mind at this time? What might Judas have been thinking?

2. "Don't miss the symbolism here: When Jesus speaks, Satan falls."
   A. In what way is this statement a spiritual principle?
   B. Have you ever seen this principle at work in the life of your family or church? If so, explain.

3. "When Jesus says he will keep you safe, he means it. Hell will have to get through him to get to you."
   A. How does this statement make you feel? Why?
   B. In what ways has Jesus kept you safe thus far?

4. "I'll show you the way; you fill in the blanks:
   "Precious Father, I praise your name. You have reclaimed so much in my life. I was lost, and you found me. I was confused, and you guided me. I had nothing to offer but still you loved me.
   "I confess that I still need help. I have a part of my life that needs your touch. Satan is battling for a garden in my heart. Don't let him win. Drive him out. He is a liar and has been since the beginning. Please defeat him. I'll give you the glory.
   "Here is the area where I need your strength _____."

Flashes of Lightning

1. Read John 18:1–9.
   A. Who appears to be in charge of this event? Why do you say this?
   B. In what way were the events of the garden a fulfillment of prophecy (see especially verse 9)?

2. Read Ephesians 6:10–13.
   A. What are we instructed to do in verses 10 and 11? What is the reason for this command?
   B. What kind of struggle are we involved in (verse 12)? How should this change our strategies?

3. Read 2 Timothy 4:16–18.
   A. What had happened to Paul?
   B. Who alone stood with Paul? Why did he stand with him?
   C. What promise is made in verse 18?

Chapter 9   What to Do with Birthdays

Echoes of Thunder

1. "When you are young you make a lot of faces in the mirror. When you are old the mirror gets even."
   A. Is your own mirror getting even with you?
   B. How do you think most people feel about getting older? When does it finally start to dawn on them that one day they'll have to face death?

2. "Is death when we go to sleep? Or is death when we finally wake up?"
   A. How would you answer Max's question above?
   B. How do you think most of your friends view death?

3. "For God, death is no tragedy. In God's economy the termination of the body is the beginning of life."
   A. Why does God view death differently than we do?
   B. In what way is the termination of the body the beginning of life? What biblical support can you cite for this view?

4. "By calling us home, God is doing what any father would do. He is providing a better place to rest."
   A. Why would heaven be a better place to rest than where we are now?
   B. Where do you expect to be resting after your time on earth is finished? Explain.

5. "I've often thought it curious how few people Jesus raised from the dead. Could it be that once someone is there, the last place they want to return to is here?"

   A. What do you think about Max's question? How would you respond?

   B. Suppose you were to die tonight. Would you want to be called back to live on earth in four days? Explain.

Flashes of Lightning

1. Read John 14:1–3.

   A. What command does Jesus give in verse 1? What reason does he give for following the command?

   B. What promise does Jesus give us in verses 2–3?

2. Read Luke 12:37–38.

   A. To what does Jesus liken his return in this passage?

   B. What does he promise us?

3. Read Isaiah 57:1–2 and Psalm 116:15.

   A. Why does God sometimes take good people home "early," according to Isaiah? What benefit do they receive?

   B. How does God view the death of his children, according to the psalmist? How can he view it this way?

Chapter 10   Music for the Dance

Echoes of Thunder

1. "We Christians are prone to follow the book while ignoring the music."

   A. What does Max mean by this statement?

   B. Is this an error you are prone to make? Why or why not?

2. "Of the three persons of the Godhead, the Holy Spirit is the one we understand the least."

   A. Would you agree with this statement? Why or why not?

   B. How well do you think you understand the Holy Spirit? Where do you get your information?

3. "Emotion without knowledge is as dangerous as knowledge without emotion. God seeks a balance."

   A. Why is emotion without knowledge dangerous? Why is knowledge without emotion dangerous?

B. How can you practically balance emotion with knowledge?

Flashes of Lightning

1. Read John 16:7–15; 14:17; 4:24.
   A. What do you learn about the Spirit in John 16:7–15?
   B. What do you learn about the Spirit in John 14:17?
   C. What do you learn about the Spirit's work in John 4:24?

2. Read Romans 8:10–12.
   A. What work of the Spirit is described in verse 11?
   B. Because this is true, to what are we obligated (verse 12)?

3. Read Acts 5:3–4; Ephesians 4:30; Hebrews 10:29.
   A. How does the Acts passage demonstrate that the Holy Spirit is a person?
   B. How does the Ephesians passage demonstrate that the Holy Spirit is a person?
   C. How does Hebrews 10:29 demonstrate that the Holy Spirit is a person?

Chapter 11   A Different Kind of Hero

Echoes of Thunder

1. "Aren't we glad Christ didn't call himself the Good Cowboy?"
   A. What's the main difference between a shepherd and a cowboy?
   B. Are you glad Christ didn't call himself the Good Cowboy? Explain.

2. "We don't need a cowboy to herd us; we need a shepherd to care for us and to guide us."
   A. Do you know of anyone who sees God as a cowboy rather than a shepherd? If so, describe him or her.
   B. Have you ever felt like you were being "herded" rather than "shepherded" by someone in authority? If so, what was the difference? How did you feel about it?

3. "He guides, feeds, and anoints. And Word has it that he won't quit until we reach the homeland."
   A. How does Jesus guide us today? How does he feed us? How does he anoint us?
   B. How do you know "he won't quit until we reach the homeland"? What is this homeland?

Flashes of Lightning

1. Read John 10:1–16.
   A. What lessons was Jesus trying to give his disciples in verses 1–5? Did they understand?
   B. How did Jesus make clear the lesson in verses 7–16?

2. Read Psalm 23:1–4; 79:13; 80:1; 95:7; 100:3.
   A. How did Jesus build on all these passages in his speech of John 10?
   B. What implication was Jesus making?

3. Read 1 Peter 2:25; Hebrews 13:20.
   A. How does Peter picture the Lord?
   B. How does the writer of Hebrews picture the Lord?

Chapter 12   Held by His Hands

Echoes of Thunder

1. "I can't tell you how many times I've expected to hit the bottom only to find myself suspended in midair, secured by a pair of pierced hands."
   A. If you have ever had an experience such as the one Max mentions above, describe it.
   B. How does it give us confidence to know that we have such a God?

2. "Though you can't see your guide, you know him. You know he is strong. You know he is able to keep you from falling."
   A. How can you know your guide if you can't see him?
   B. How do you know God is able to keep you from falling?

3. "You are only a few more steps from the top. So whatever you do, don't quit. Though your falls are great, his strength is greater. You *will* make it."
   A. If you have ever known someone who was tempted to quit just a few steps from the top, describe what happened.
   B. What would tempt you to quit just a few steps from the top? How would you overcome these temptations?

Flashes of Lightning

1. Read John 10:28–30.
   A. What does Jesus say he does in verse 28? What does he say no one can do?

B. How does what Jesus says in verses 29-30 back up what he said in verse 28?

2. Read Jude 24–25.
   A. What is promised in verse 24?
   B. What should be our response (verse 25)?

3. Read Philippians 1:6.
   A. Who began "a good work" in you?
   B. What else will he do? When will this job be finished?

Chapter 13   A Cinderella Story

Echoes of Thunder

1. "God between two thieves. Exactly the place he wants to be."
   A. Why would God want to be between two thieves?
   B. In what way does God still want to be between two thieves?

2. "Sin is not an unfortunate slip or a regrettable act; it is a posture of defiance against a holy God."
   A. How would the people you work with define sin? How would your neighbors define it?
   B. In what way is every sin an act of defiance against a holy God?

3. "The one with no sin becomes sin-filled. The one sin-filled becomes sinless. It's eternity's most bizarre exchange."
   A. Why would Max call this "eternity's most bizarre exchange"? When did this exchange take place?
   B. Can we completely understand this exchange? Explain. What mystery might still remain?

4. "Jesus gave more than a kiss—he gave his beauty. He paid more than a visit—he paid for our mistakes. He took more than a minute—he took away our sin."
   A. In what ways was Jesus' act similar to that of the woman who played Cinderella? In what ways was it different?
   B. How did Jesus pay for our mistakes? How did he take away our sin? Why could only he do this?

Flashes of Lightning

1. Read Luke 23:39–43.
   A. How were the two criminals' responses different from one another?

   B. What request did one of the criminals make? How was it answered?

2. Read Psalm 51:1–4.
   A. What request did David make in verses 1–2?
   B. What confession did David make in verses 3–4? Why is verse 4 especially important?

3. Read 2 Corinthians 5:19, 21.
   A. What is "the message of reconciliation"? Who bears it?
   B. What exchange is detailed in verse 21? In what way is this the gospel in brief?

4. Read Isaiah 53:4–6.
   A. Who is being described in verses 4-5? What did he do?
   B. How are we described in verse 6? How is this connected to verses 4-5?

Chapter 14   The Bad News Preacher

Echoes of Thunder

1. "God's faithfulness has never depended on the faithfulness of his children. He is faithful even when we aren't."
   A. Why doesn't God's faithfulness depend on our own faithfulness?
   B. Describe a time in your life when this truth was highlighted.

2. "Though the answer to prayer is standing next to him, he doesn't even pray."
   A. Why do you think the disciples failed to ask Jesus to do something about their situation?
   B. In what way are we often like the disciples?

3. "I simply think God is greater than our weakness. In fact, I think it is our weakness that reveals how great God is."
   A. How does our weakness reveal how great God is?
   B. How has God shown his greatness through your own weakness?

4. "If Jesus would have acted according to the faith of his disciples, the multitudes would have gone unfed. But he didn't, and he doesn't. God is true to us even when we forget him."
   A. Why do you think God sometimes chooses to act according to our faith and sometimes not?

   B. Describe some times in your own life when God was true to you even when you perhaps forgot him.

Flashes of Lightning

   1. Read John 6:5–13.
      A. What question did Jesus ask in verse 5? Why did he ask this according to verse 6?
      B. What was the main lesson of verses 7–13?

   2. Read 2 Corinthians 12:9–10.
      A. What claim did God make in verse 9?
      B. How did Paul respond to this claim in verse 10?

   3. Read 2 Timothy 2:13.
      A. What happens when we are "faithless," according to this verse?
      B. Why does this happen? What does this mean?

Chapter 15   The Final Witness

Echoes of Thunder

   1. "'The dead hear only the voice of God . . . ,' said Lazarus . . . 'I heard the voice of God.'"
      A. If a man is dead, how can he hear anything?
      B. How did Lazarus know it was the voice of God he heard?
      C. In what way do "dead men" still hear the voice of God today?

   2. "Jesus said, 'I will do for him what I did for them. I'll give him joy, strength, healing, sight, safety, nourishment, new life.'"
      A. Does Jesus still give us joy, strength, healing, sight, safety, nourishment, and new life today? If so, how?
      B. Which of the gifts listed above means the most to you? Explain your choice.

   3. "The Master has offered to do for you what he did for them. He will bring wine to your table, sight to your eyes, strength for your step and, most of all, power over your grave. He will do for you what he did for them. The Judge has given his blessing. The rest is up to you."
      A. Name some Scripture verses where God offers you the things listed above.
      B. What is the choice you must make? What choice have you made? Why did you make this choice?

Flashes of Lightning

1. Read John 20:29–31.
   A. Who is especially blessed, according to verse 29? Why?
   B. What was the purpose of writing down Jesus' miracles? Have they had this intended effect on you? Why or why not?

2. Read Luke 3:21–22.
   A. What happened as described in this text?
   B. Why is this so crucial to everything that happens later?

3. Read Ephesians 2:1–5.
   A. How could we be described in our pre-Christian days, according to verses 1–3?
   B. How was our status changed as described in verses 4–5? What prompted this change in status?

Chapter 16   Inside Out

Echoes of Thunder

1. "A walking cat is still a cat. The same is true with people."
   A. What does Max mean by the statement above?
   B. Does this mean that not even God can change our basic natures? Explain.

2. "According to the Bible, there is one thing we cannot change—our sinful state."
   A. Why can't we change our sinful state on our own?
   B. Does this mean we are left to deal with this sinful state throughout our lives? Explain.

3. "It is through God's pain that we are born. It's not our struggle, but God's. It's not our blood shed, but his."
   A. How is God "pained" through our spiritual birth?
   B. In what way is our salvation God's struggle? Whose blood was shed to gain our salvation? How does this "work"?

4. "God is as polite as he is passionate. He never forces his way in. The choice is theirs."
   A. Do you agree with this statement? Why or why not?
   B. Does God ever intrude into our lives without asking? What about in the life of Saul (who became the apostle Paul) described in Acts 9:1–17?

5. "The first time you had no choice about being born; this time you do."
    A. What choice have you made about being born a second time?
    B. What prompted you to make this choice?

Flashes of Lightning

1. Read John 3:3–8,14–18.
    A. What is the only way to enter the kingdom of God, according to this passage? What does this mean?
    B. What illustration does Jesus give in verses 14–18? How does this illustration help explain what he was to do?

2. Read 2 Corinthians 6:1–2.
    A. What does it mean to "receive God's grace in vain"? How is this possible?
    B. When is the best time to be saved, according to verse 2?

3. Read Galatians 3:13-14.
    A. How did Christ redeem us from the curse? What does it mean to be redeemed from the curse?
    B. Why did he redeem us, according to verse 14?

Chapter 17 The Yay-Yuck Man

Echoes of Thunder

1. "Now Bob could be any color, any time, and please every person."
    A. If you were asked to pick one word to describe Bob, what would it be? Why would you pick this word?
    B. Why are we sometimes tempted to act like Bob?

2. "Everyone liked him because everyone thought he was just like them."
    A. Why do we like others who seem just like us?
    B. What is the huge trap concealed in this kind of attitude?

3. "'It's not their approval I seek,' said the man."
    A. Who does this man represent? Why do you think so?
    B. Whose approval do you seek? Why?

4. "'I am here to show people they don't have to please people,' the man said. 'I am here to tell the truth.'"
    A. Have you ever felt as if you had to please people? If so, why did you feel this way?

    B. What is the best way of reminding ourselves we don't have to please people?

Flashes of Lightning

  1. Read John 8:39–47.
    A. What truth did Jesus tell the Pharisees? How did they respond?
    B. Why couldn't the Pharisees believe Jesus, according to verse 47?

  2. Read Galatians 4:16–18.
    A. What question did Paul ask in verse 16? How might this be possible?
    B. Why did Paul tell them the truth, according to verses 17–18?

  3. Read Galatians 1:10.
    A. What question did Paul ask here?
    B. What answer does he give to his own question? What does this imply for us?

Chapter 18   Calamities of the Common Scale

Echoes of Thunder

  1. "She simply assessed the problem and gave it to Christ."
    A. Why is it important to assess a problem? How do you assess problems in your own life?
    B. What does it mean to "give a problem to Christ"? How do you do this in a practical sense?

  2. "What causes us to think of prayer as the last option rather than the first?"
    A. How would you answer Max's question?
    B. How quickly do you normally think of prayer when a problem arises? Are you satisfied with this? Why or why not?

  3. "My daughters' maturity and mobility are good and necessary, but I hope they never get to the point where they are too grown up to call their daddy."
    A. In what way might this statement be a reflection of God's thoughts about us?
    B. Have you ever known anyone who thought they were "too grown up" for God? If so, explain.

4. "Note, the water became wine *after* they had they obeyed, not before."
   A. Why is it significant that the water became wine after the men had obeyed?
   B. How is this applicable to us today?

Flashes of Lightning

1. Read John 2:1–11.
   A. What instruction did Mary give in verse 5? Why do you think she did this?
   B. What was the purpose of this demonstration, according to verse 11? What was the result?

2. Read Psalm 50:15–21.
   A. What are we instructed to do in verse 15? What does God promise to do? How are we to respond?
   B. To whom is this promise directed? How do verses 16–21 make this clear?

3. Read 1 Samuel 15:22–23a.
   A. What question is asked in verse 22a? What response is given in 22b?
   B. To what is disobedience compared in verse 23? How is this significant?

Chapter 19 Your Place in God's Band

Echoes of Thunder

1. "Marthas are the Energizer bunnies of the church. They keep going and going and going."
   A. Are you more like a Martha, a Mary, or a Lazarus? Explain.
   B. Describe some of the Marthas in your church.

2. "Marys are gifted with praise. They don't just sing; they worship. They don't simply attend church; they go to offer praise. They don't just talk about Christ; they radiate Christ."
   A. What's the difference between mere singing and worship? Between attending church and offering praise? Between talking about Christ and radiating Christ?
   B. Describe some of the Marys in your church.

3. "Marys need to remember that service is worship. Marthas need to remember that worship is service. And Lazarus? He needs to remember that not everyone can play the trumpet."
   A. How can service be worship? How can worship be service?
   B. Can you "play the trumpet"? Why or why not? If you can't, who in your acquaintance can? Explain.

4. "Are you near Christ, but far from his heart? Are you at the dinner with a sour soul? Are you always criticizing the gifts of others, yet seldom, if ever, giving your own? Are you benefiting from the church while never giving to it? Do others give sacrificially while you give miserly? Are you a Judas?"
   A. How would you answer each of the six questions listed above?
   B. Are you satisfied with how you're fitting in with God's band? Why or why not?

Flashes of Lightning

1. Read John 12:1–6.
   A. What did Mary do in this passage? Why did she do it?
   B. How did Judas respond? Why did he respond like this?
   C. What lesson is intended for us?

2. Read Luke 10:38–42.
   A. What's was Martha's complaint? What prompted it?
   B. How did Jesus respond? What principle did he lay down?

3. Read Romans 12:4–8.
   A. What does this passage teach us about unity? What does it teach us about diversity?
   B. What does it teach us about the relationship of the two?

Chapter 20   Extravagant Love

Echoes of Thunder

1. "Jesus reduces the number of life's struggles to two. We either strive for food that rots or food that lasts."
   A. How do you strive for food that rots? What kind of food is this?
   B. How do you strive for food that lasts? What kind of food is this?

2. "I know he said he would give it but, honestly now, how do we pay for this bread? How do we earn this meal? How long do we have to stand in the cafeteria line to get the eternal food?"

   A. Do you ever find yourself thinking along the lines described above? If so, explain.

   B. Why are we so often tempted to try to pay back grace? Why is this impossible?

3. "Have you ever considered what an insult it is to God when we try to pay him for his goodness?"

   A. Answer Max's question above.

   B. Why is this such an insult?

4. "Apart from Christ you aren't holy. So how may we go to heaven? Only believe."

   A. Why aren't we holy apart from Christ?

   B. How does Christ make us holy? Has he made you holy? Explain.

Flashes of Lightning

1. Read John 6:26–29.

   A. What command does Jesus give in verse 27?

   B. How do his hearers respond in verse 28?

   C. What reply does Jesus give in verse 29? What is unusual about this response?

2. Read Hebrews 12:14–17.

   A. What command are we given in verse 14? What warning is given?

   B. What practical outworking of this command is described in verses 15–17? How are these verses related to verse 14?

3. Read Acts 17:24–31.

   A. What does Paul tell his hearers about God in verse 25? Why is this significant?

   B. What is God's desire as expressed in verse 27?

   C. What does God demand in verse 30?

   D. What does he warn in verse 31?

Chapter 21   God's Fondest Dream

Echoes of Thunder

1. "Suspicion and distrust often lurk at God's table. Around the table the siblings squabble and the Father sighs."
   A. Why do suspicion and distrust often lurk at God's table?
   B. How have you seen "the siblings squabble"? Why does the Father sigh?

2. "Never in the Bible are we told to create unity. We are simply told to maintain the unity that exists."
   A. Why does the Bible not ask us to create unity?
   B. How are we to maintain unity with one another?

3. "We Christians wouldn't be known for what divides us, but instead we'd be known for what unites us—our common Father."
   A. Do you think we Christians are known for what divides us? Explain your answer.
   B. How could we become known for what unites us? What would we have to do? What would we have to change?

Flashes of Lightning

1. Read John 17:20–23.
   A. What is Jesus' primary request in this passage?
   B. Why does he make this request, according to verse 23?

2. Read Ephesians 4:2–13.
   A. What commands are given in verses 2–3?
   B. What basis for these commands is given in verses 4–11?
   C. What is the purpose of these commands as detailed in verses 12–13?

3. Read 1 John 3:11–18.
   A. What command is given in verse 11?
   B. What negative example is given in verse 12? How is this significant?
   C. How does John make unity a practical matter in verses 13–18?

Chapter 22   God's Been Known to Niggle

Echoes of Thunder

1. "God loves to find anything that impedes our growth. Jesus portrays him as the Good Gardener who cuts and trims the vine."
   A. What things most often impede your growth?
   B. How does God cut and trim the vines in your own life?

2. "You've seen gardeners realign a plant, and you've probably seen God realign a life."
   A. How do gardeners realign a plant? What do they do?
   B. How is God's work like this? What similarities do you see?

3. "You can't force fruit. That's why nowhere in this text does Jesus tell you to go out and bear fruit."
   A. Do you know people who feel as if they must force fruit to appear in their life? Why do you think they feel this way? What could you tell them?
   B. If Jesus doesn't tell us to bear fruit, what does he tell us to do? How do we do this?

4. "Our task? It's clear. Stay close to the vine. As long as we do, we'll be fruitful."
   A. What do you do in order to stay close to the vine? What moves you away from the vine?
   B. When you are close to the vine, what kind of fruit do you produce? What happens when you move away from the vine?

5. "Even now, some of you are hearing the snip-snip-snip of his shears. It hurts. But take heart. You'll be better as a result."
   A. What kind of pruning is needed most in your life right now? Why do you say this?
   B. Does realizing what God is doing in your life help you bear the pain of the pruning? Explain.

Flashes of Lightning

1. Read John 15:1–8.
   A. In what ways is God like a gardener?
   B. In what ways is Jesus like a vine?
   C. In what ways are we like branches?

2. Read Galatians 5:22–23.
   A. What kind of fruit is God most interested in?
   B. Does this fruit characterize you? Why or why not?

3. Read Hebrews 12:11.
   A. What does this verse admit about discipline?
   B. What encouragement does it give us to continue on?

Chapter 23   The Parable of the Sandwich Sign

Echoes of Thunder

1. "You must stand on the side of the road and warn the drivers not to make the left turn."
   A. Who do these men represent in this parable?
   B. What are they required to do? Why?

2. "Hundreds of lives were saved by the three sign holders. Because they did their job, many people were kept from peril."
   A. With which of the three sign holders can you most readily identify? Why?
   B. How do we keep people from peril in our own world?

3. "The first man got sleepy. The second didn't grow tired, but he did grow conceited. The third man was concerned about the message of his sign. It troubled him that his message was so narrow, so dogmatic."
   A. Which of the men's three different problems would be most likely to trouble you? Why?
   B. How would you help someone overcome each of the three problems listed here?

4. "As the first man slept and the second stood and the third altered the message, one car after another plunged into the river."
   A. What was the result of these men's failure to do their job?
   B. What lesson does this parable teach us? Is this a lesson you especially need to hear? Explain.

Flashes of Lightning

1. Read John 1:23.
   A. What was John the Baptist's sole purpose, according to this verse?
   B. How did he fulfill this verse?

2. Read Ezekiel 33:7–9.
   A. What does it mean to be a "watchman"?
   B. What instruction is given in verses 8–9? What warning? Does this apply in any way to us? Why or why not?

3. Read 2 Corinthians 5:19b–20.
   A. To whom is the "message of reconciliation" committed?
   B. How did Paul see his responsibilities to the unsaved? How is this connected to us today?

Chapter 24   The Winsomeness of Holiness

Echoes of Thunder

1. "What mattered was that you get off your duff and get right with God because he's coming and he don't mean maybe."
   A. How do you "get off your duff and get right with God"?
   B. What is a huge incentive for doing this?

2. "You don't have to be like the world to have an impact on the world."
   A. Do you agree with this statement? Why or why not?
   B. What kind of an impact on the world do Christians who look just like the world normally enjoy? Why?

3. "Holiness seeks to be like God."
   A. What does the word "holiness" mean to you?
   B. Why does holiness seek to be like God? What kind of attitudes does this produce in us?

4. "When a person's ways and words are the same, the fusion is explosive. But when a person says one thing and lives another, the result is destructive."
   A. Why is the fusion explosive when a person's ways and words are the same?
   B. Why is the result destructive when a person says one thing and lives another?

5. "To call yourself a child of God is one thing. To be called a child of God by those who watch your life is another thing altogether."
   A. Do you call yourself a child of God? Would others who watch your life agree with you? Explain.
   B. How would non-Christians most likely describe you?

Flashes of Lightning

1. Read Luke 1:76–80.
   A. What role was prophesied for John?
   B. What purpose was he to serve?

2. Read Mark 1:4–8.
   A. What did John do in verse 4? What did he look like (verse 6)?
   B. How did the crowds react in verse 5?
   C. What was his particular message (verse 7–8)?

3. Read 1 Thessalonians 4:11–12 and 1 Peter 2:11–12.
   A. What advice does Paul give to the Thessalonians? Why does he give this advice?
   B. What advice does Peter give in verse 11? What reason does he give in verse 12?

Chapter 25   Look Before You Label

Echoes of Thunder

1. "It's easier to talk about a person than to help a person."
   A. Why is it such a big temptation to talk about others in a negative way?
   B. How can we encourage ourselves to refrain from this sinful habit?

2. "Is that to say religious discussion is wrong? Of course not. Is that to say we should be unconcerned for doctrine or lax in a desire for holiness? Absolutely not."
   A. What kind of religious discussion pleases God? What kind displeases him?
   B. What kind of concern for doctrine and desire for holiness pleases God? What kind displeases him?

3. "The man wasn't a victim of fate; he was a miracle waiting to happen."
   A. How was this man "a miracle waiting to happen"?
   B. Do we ever know ahead of time who is a miracle waiting to happen? What does this fact suggest to you?

4. "What is the work of God? Accepting people. Loving before judging. Caring before condemning."
   A. How can we learn to accept people if this has not been our practice?

B. Would anyone disagree with Max's words above? How could they be just nice-sounding words? How can we put them into practice? What can you do *today*?

Flashes of Lightning

1. Read John 9:1–7.
   A. What reason does Jesus give for the man's blindness in verse 3? Why might this sound cruel to some people? Is it? Explain.
   B. How does this episode demonstrate that Jesus is the light of the world?

2. Read Ephesians 4:15, 25–32.
   A. What does it mean to "speak the truth in love"? How do you do this in practice?
   B. How are verses 25–32 an illustration of verse 15?

3. Read Matthew 7:1–5.
   A. What command does Jesus give us in verse 1? What is the reason for this command in verse 2?
   B. How are verses 3–5 an illustration of Jesus' command in verse 1?

Chapter 26   Looking for the Messiah

Echoes of Thunder

1. "Suppose Jesus came to your church. I don't mean symbolically. I mean visibly. Physically. Actually."
   A. Try to imagine the above scene. What would Jesus look like? What would he do?
   B. How do you think your church would react? Why?

2. "It's easy to criticize contemporaries of Jesus for not believing in him. But when you realize how he came, you can understand their skepticism."
   A. What is it about Jesus' coming that would make skepticism understandable, if not excusable?
   B. Try to put yourself back in first-century Israel. How do you think you would have seen Jesus? Explain.

3. "We still think we know which phone God uses and which car he drives. We still think we know what he looks like. But he's been known to surprise us."
   A. What does Max mean in his first two sentences above?

B. How has God been known to surprise you?

4. "When we let God define himself, a whole new world opens before us."
   A. How do we let God define himself?
   B. Why does a new world open before us when we let God define himself?

5. "The old man saw Jesus because he didn't know what he looked like. The people in Jesus' day missed him because they thought they did."
   A. How can we find God if we don't know what his appearances will look like?
   B. What lessons can we learn from Max's insight above?

Flashes of Lightning

1. Read John 7:25–29.
   A. What did the people start to suspect in verse 25? Why did they change their minds in verse 27?
   B. How does Jesus use their questions to make a claim about himself? What claim does he make?

2. Read Luke 7:33–35.
   A. What was the people's objection to John the Baptist (verse 33)?
   B. What was the people's objection to Jesus (verse 34)?
   C. What conclusion does Jesus make (verse 35)?

3. Read Matthew 25:34–45.
   A. How does this passage teach us it is possible to be in contact with Jesus today and yet not recognize him?
   B. How can this result in both good and bad consequences?

Chapter 27   Peter, Me, and Wile E. Coyote

Echoes of Thunder

1. "Like Wile E. we fall. But unlike Wile E., we wander in the canyon for a while. Stunned, hurt . . . and wondering if this ravine has a way out."
   A. What kind of "canyons" have you wandered in? What pulled you out?
   B. In what ways are you and Wile E. Coyote alike? In what ways are you different?

2. "When we fall, we can dismiss it. We can deny it. We can distort it. Or we can deal with it."
   A. How do we dismiss our falls? How do we deny them? How do we distort them?
   B. What is the best way to deal with our falls? Is this easy? Explain.

3. "We keep no secrets from God. Confession is not telling God what we did. He already knows. Confession is simply agreeing with God that our acts were wrong."
   A. Do you think this is a good definition of confession? Explain.
   B. Why does God insist that we confess our sins?

4. "Mingle the tears of the sinner with the cross of the Savior and the result is a joyful escort out of the canyon of guilt."
   A. How do the tears of a sinner and the cross of the Savior combine to bring joy?
   B. Have you known this joy that Max talks about? Explain.

Flashes of Lightning

1. Read John 18:25–27.
   A. What kind of stumbling is described here?
   B. Could it have been prevented? If so, how?

2. Read Luke 22:61.
   A. What kind of look do you think the Lord gave to Peter? Explain.
   B. What effect did this look have on Peter? Why do you think it had this effect?

3. Read 2 Corinthians 7:8–11.
   A. What did Paul do as described in verse 8? How did he feel about this?
   B. What was the result of Paul's action? How did this make him feel?
   C. What principle is laid out in verse 10?
   D. How is this principle "fleshed out" in verse 11?

Chapter 28   Ready for Home

Echoes of Thunder

1. "We sometimes act as if the Christian life is a retirement cruise."

A. What does Max mean by his statement above?

B. Have you ever seen Christians acting out this statement? Have you ever been tempted to do so? Explain.

2. "When the freeze comes, we step out on the ice with forks, games, and skimpy clothing, and pass our final days walking against the wind, often blaming God for getting us into this mess."

A. What times of "freezing" have you experienced in your own life?

B. Why does it seem so easy for us to blame God for things that are not his doing?

3. "Why was the salvation of his soul so urgent after the shot and so optional before it? Why had he postponed his decision to accept Christ until his deathbed? Because he assumed he had time."

A. How often do you think we make the same mistake the general did? Why do we make this mistake?

B. What are some effective ways to demonstrate the danger of this kind of mistake? If you were working with someone who also assumed he had time, what would you do?

4. "What supplies are you taking? Are you carrying your share of silver and games? Don't be fooled; they may matter here, but they matter not when you reach your Father's house. What matters is if you are known by the Father."

A. What supplies are you taking?

B. Are you known by the Father? How do you know for sure?

Flashes of Lightning

1. Read Psalm 27:7–14.
   A. What requests does the psalmist make in verses 7–9 and 11–12?
   B. What expectation does he have in verse 10?
   C. What hope does he have in verse 13?
   D. What advice does he give in verse 14?

2. Read James 1:13–16.
   A. What are some of us prone to do when we get into trouble (verse 13)?
   B. How does James respond to this?
   C. What warning does he give in verse 16? Why put this here?

3. Read James 4:13–16.
   A. Why is it foolish to plan ahead without taking God into consideration?
   B. What instead should be our attitude?

Chapter 29   The Cave People

Echoes of Thunder

1. "The sounds in the cave were mournful, but the people didn't know it, for they had never known joy. The spirit in the cave was death, but the people didn't know it, for they had never known life."
   A. How can someone not know their true condition?
   B. What people do you know who are unaware of their true condition?

2. "Light always hurts before it helps," he answered. "Step closer. The pain will soon pass."
   A. Why does "light" always hurt before it helps? What does the light represent in this parable?
   B. How does light finally help? How important is the pain? Explain.

3. "Carry this to your people. Tell them the light is here and the light is warm. Tell them the light is for all who desire it."
   A. What is the point of this passage?
   B. What light have you been asked to carry to your own people? Who are your own people? Are they seeing light in your hands? Explain.

Flashes of Lightning

1. Read John 1:3–13.
   A. In what way is Jesus our light?
   B. How are men prone to respond to this light (verses 10–11)?
   C. What promise is given in verses 12–13?

2. Read Romans 1:13–17.
   A. What was Paul's goal in verse 13?
   B. What was Paul's attitude in verses 14–15?

   C. What was Paul's confidence in verses 16–17?

3. Read 1 Corinthians 9:19–23.

    A. What was Paul's commitment in verse 19?
    B. What was Paul's method in verses 20–22?
    C. What was Paul's goal in verse 23?

Chapter 30   If Only You Knew

Echoes of Thunder

1. "I was being kind. The bird thought I was cruel."
    A. What was the bird probably thinking?
    B. How are we often like the bird when God is trying to deal with us?

2. "If only we could learn to trust him. But how hard it is."
    A. Why is trusting God hard for many of us?
    B. How can we learn to trust God more?

3. "His thunder is still gentle. And his gentleness still thunders."
    A. In what way is God's "thunder" gentle?
    B. In what way does God's gentleness "thunder"?

4. "The gift and the Giver. If you know them, you know all you need."
    A. What is the gift Max mentions? Who is the Giver? What is crucial about both of them?
    B. Do you know this gift and this Giver? How do you know for sure?

Flashes of Lightning

1. Read John 4:10–15, 23–26.
    A. What kind of water did the woman want? What kind of water did Jesus offer her?
    B. What is the Father seeking, according to verse 23?
    C. What claim did Jesus make for himself in verse 26?

2. Read Jeremiah 29:11.
    A. What kind of plans does the Lord have for us?
    B. How does this make you feel? Why?

3. Read Psalm 9:10.
    A. Who will trust the Lord? What does this mean?
    B. Whom does the Lord never forsake? Does this include you? Why or why not?

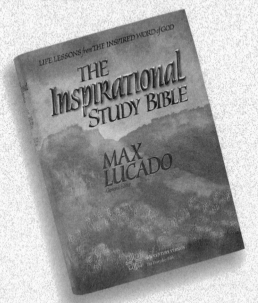

JOHN

*H*e's an old man, this one who sits on the stool and leans against the wall. Eyes closed and face soft, were it not for his hand stroking his beard, you'd think he was asleep.

Some in the room assume he is. He does this often during worship. As the people sing, his eyes will close and his chin will fall until it rests on his chest, and there he will remain motionless. Silent.

Those who know him well know better. They know he is not resting. He is traveling. Atop the music he journeys back, back, back until he is young again. Strong again. There again. There on the seashore with James and the apostles. There on the trail with the disciples and the women. There in the Temple with Caiaphas and the accusers.

It's been sixty years, but John sees him still. The decades took John's strength, but they didn't take his memory. The years dulled his sight, but they didn't dull his vision. The seasons may have wrinkled his face, but they didn't soften his love.

He had been with God. God had been with him. How could he forget?

❀ The wine that moments before had been water—John could still taste it.

❀ The mud placed on the eyes of the blind man in Jerusalem—John could still remember it.

❀ The aroma of Mary's perfume as it filled the room—John could still smell it.

And the voice. Oh, the voice. His voice. John could still hear it.

I am the light of the world, it rang ... I am the door ... I am the way, the truth, the life.

I will come back, it promised, and take you to be with me.

Those who believe in me, it assured, will have life even if they die.

John could hear him. John could see him. Scenes branded on his heart. Words seared into his soul. John would never forget. How could he? He had been there.

He opens his eyes and blinks. The singing has stopped. The teaching has begun. John looks at the listeners and listens to the teacher.

If only you could have been there, he thinks.

But he wasn't. Most weren't. Most weren't even born. And most who were there are dead. Peter is. So is James. Nathanael, Martha, Philip. They are all gone. Even Paul, the apostle who came late, is dead.

Only John remains.

He looks again at the church. Small but earnest. They lean forward to hear the teacher. John listens to him. What a task. Speaking of one he never saw. Explaining words he never heard. John is there if the teacher needs him.

But what will happen when John is gone? What will the teacher do then? When John's voice is silent and his tongue stilled? Who will tell them how Jesus silenced the waves? Will they hear how he fed the thousands? Will they remember how he prayed for unity?

How will they know? If only they could have been there.

Suddenly, in his heart he knows what to do.

Later, under the light of a sunlit shaft, the old fisherman unfolds the scroll and begins to write the story of his life ...

In the beginning there was the Word ...

LIFE LESSON
John 1:1-51

SITUATION ✍ The Greeks and the Jews were familiar with the concept of the *word*. For the Jews it was an expression of God's wisdom, and for the Greeks it meant reason and intellect.

OBSERVATION ✍ Leaving his heavenly home, Jesus put on human flesh to bring us God's Good News.

INSPIRATION ✍ It all happened in a moment, a most remarkable moment. . . . that was like none other. For through that segment of time a spectacular thing occurred. God became a man. While the creatures of earth walked unaware, Divinity arrived. Heaven opened herself and placed her most precious one in a human womb. . . .

God as a fetus. Holiness sleeping in a womb. The creator of life being created.

God was given eyebrows, elbows, two kidneys, and a spleen. He stretched against the walls and floated in the amniotic fluids of his mother.

God had come near. . . .

The hands that first held him were unmanicured, calloused, and dirty.

No silk. No ivory. No hype. No party. No hoopla.

Were it not for the shepherds, there would have been no reception. And were it not for a group of star-gazers, there would have been no gifts. . . .

Christ Comes to the World

*I*n the beginning there was the Word." The Word was with God, and the Word was God. [2]He was with God in the beginning. [3]All things were made by him, and nothing was made without him. [4]In him there was life, and that life was the light of all people. [5]The Light shines in the darkness, and the darkness has not overpowered it.

[6]There was a man named John" who was sent by God. [7]He came to tell people the truth about the Light so that through him all people could hear about the Light and believe. [8]John was not the Light, but he came to tell people the truth about the Light. [9]The true Light that gives light to all was coming into the world!

[10]The Word was in the world, and the world was made by him, but the world did not know him. [11]He came to the world that was his own, but his own people did not accept him. [12]But to all who did accept him and believe in him he gave the right to become children of God. [13]They did not become his children in any human way—by any human parents or human desire. They were born of God.

[14]The Word became a human and lived among us. We saw his glory— the glory that belongs to the only Son of the Father—and he was full of grace and truth. [15]John tells the truth about him and cries out, saying, "This is the One I told you about: 'The One who comes after me is greater than I am, because he was living before me.'"

[16]Because he was full of grace and truth, from him we all received one gift after another. [17]The law was given through Moses, but grace and truth came through Jesus Christ. [18]No one has ever seen God. But God the only Son is very close to the Father," and he has shown us what God is like.

John Tells People About Jesus

[19]Here is the truth John" told when the Jews in Jerusalem sent priests and Levites to ask him, "Who are you?"

[20]John spoke freely and did not refuse to answer. He said, "I am not the Christ."

[21]So they asked him, "Then who are you? Are you Elijah?"

He answered, "No, I am not."

"Are you the Prophet?"" they asked.

He answered, "No."

[22]Then they said, "Who are you? Give us an answer to tell those who sent us. What do you say about yourself?"

[23]John told them in the words of the prophet Isaiah:

"I am the voice of one
    calling out in the desert:
'Make the road straight for the Lord.'"   *Isaiah 40:3*

Word   The Greek word is "logos," meaning any kind of communication; it could be translated "message." Here, it means Christ, because Christ was the way God told people about himself.

John   John the Baptist, who preached to people about Christ's coming (Matthew 3, Luke 3).

But . . . Father   This could be translated, "But the only God is very close to the Father." Also, some Greek copies say, "But the only Son is very close to the Father."

John   John the Baptist, who preached to people about Christ's coming (Matthew 3, Luke 3).

Elijah   A man who spoke for God. He lived hundreds of years before Christ and was expected to return before Christ (Malachi 4:5-6).

Prophet   They probably meant the prophet that God told Moses he would send (Deuteronomy 18:15-19).

²⁴Some Pharisees who had been sent asked John: ²⁵"If you are not the Christ or Elijah or the Prophet, why do you baptize people?"

²⁶John answered, "I baptize with water, but there is one here with you that you don't know about. ²⁷He is the One who comes after me. I am not good enough to untie the strings of his sandals."

²⁸This all happened at Bethany on the other side of the Jordan River, where John was baptizing people.

²⁹The next day John saw Jesus coming toward him. John said, "Look, the Lamb of God," who takes away the sin of the world! ³⁰This is the One I was talking about when I said, 'A man will come after me, but he is greater than I am, because he was living before me.' ³¹Even I did not know who he was, although I came baptizing with water so that the people of Israel would know who he is."

³²⁻³³Then John said, "I saw the Spirit come down from heaven in the form of a dove and rest on him. Until then I did not know who the Christ was. But the God who sent me to baptize with water told me, 'You will see the Spirit come down and rest on a man; he is the One who will baptize with the Holy Spirit.' ³⁴I have seen this happen, and I tell you the truth: This man is the Son of God."

The First Followers of Jesus

³⁵The next day John" was there again with two of his followers. ³⁶When he saw Jesus walking by, he said, "Look, the Lamb of God!"

³⁷The two followers heard John say this, so they followed Jesus. ³⁸When Jesus turned and saw them following him, he asked, "What are you looking for?"

They said, "Rabbi, where are you staying?" ("Rabbi" means "Teacher.")

³⁹He answered, "Come and see." So the two men went with Jesus and saw where he was staying and stayed there with him that day. It was about four o'clock in the afternoon.

⁴⁰One of the two men who followed Jesus after they heard John speak about him was Andrew, Simon Peter's brother. ⁴¹The first thing Andrew did was to find his brother Simon and say to him, "We have found the Messiah." ("Messiah" means "Christ.")

⁴²Then Andrew took Simon to Jesus. Jesus looked at him and said, "You are Simon son of John. You will be called Cephas." ("Cephas" means "Peter.")

⁴³The next day Jesus decided to go to Galilee. He found Philip and said to him, "Follow me."

⁴⁴Philip was from the town of Bethsaida, where Andrew and Peter lived. ⁴⁵Philip found Nathanael and told him, "We have found the man that Moses wrote about in the law, and the prophets also wrote about him. He is Jesus, the son of Joseph, from Nazareth."

⁴⁶But Nathanael said to Philip, "Can anything good come from Nazareth?"

Philip answered, "Come and see."

⁴⁷As Jesus saw Nathanael coming toward him, he said, "Here is truly an Israelite. There is nothing false in him."

For thirty-three years he would feel everything you and I have ever felt. He felt weak. He grew weary. He was afraid of failure. He was susceptible to wooing women. He got colds, burped, and had body odor. His feelings got hurt. His feet got tired. And his head ached.

To think of Jesus in such a light is—well, it seems almost irreverent, doesn't it? It's not something we like to do; it's uncomfortable. It is much easier to keep the humanity out of the incarnation. He's easier to stomach that way....

But don't do it. For heaven's sake, don't. Let him be as human as he intended to be. Let him into the mire and muck of our world. For only if we let him in can he pull us out.

(From *God Came Near* by Max Lucado)

APPLICATION If people want to know what God is like, they can look at Jesus. If they want to know what Jesus is like, they should be able to look at his followers. Can people see Christ in you?

EXPLORATION The Word is Born—John 14:6-7; 1 Corinthians 8:5-6; Galatians 4:4; Philippians 2:7, 8; 1 Timothy 3:16; Hebrews 2:14; 13:8; 1 John 1:1-2; 4:2.

Lamb of God Name for Jesus. Jesus is like the lambs that were offered for a sacrifice to God.
Peter The Greek name "Peter," like the Aramaic name "Cephas," means "rock."